CAMBRIDGE LIBRAR

Books of enduring scho

Classics

From the Renaissance to the nineteenth century, Latin and Greek were
compulsory subjects in almost all European universities, and most early
modern scholars published their research and conducted international
correspondence in Latin. Latin had continued in use in Western Europe long
after the fall of the Roman empire as the lingua franca of the educated classes
and of law, diplomacy, religion and university teaching. The flight of Greek
scholars to the West after the fall of Constantinople in 1453 gave impetus
to the study of ancient Greek literature and the Greek New Testament.
Eventually, just as nineteenth-century reforms of university curricula were
beginning to erode this ascendancy, developments in textual criticism and
linguistic analysis, and new ways of studying ancient societies, especially
archaeology, led to renewed enthusiasm for the Classics. This collection
offers works of criticism, interpretation and synthesis by the outstanding
scholars of the nineteenth century.

The Golden Bough: The Third Edition

This work by Sir James Frazer (1854–1941) is widely considered to be one of
the most important early texts in the fields of psychology and anthropology.
At the same time, by applying modern methods of comparative ethnography
to the classical world, and revealing the superstition and irrationality beneath
the surface of the classical culture which had for so long been a model for
Western civilisation, it was extremely controversial. Frazer was greatly
influenced by E.B. Tylor's *Primitive Culture* (also reissued in this series), and
by the work of the biblical scholar William Robertson Smith, to whom the
first edition is dedicated. The twelve-volume third edition, reissued here, was
greatly revised and enlarged, and published between 1911 and 1915; the two-
volume first edition (1890) is also available in this series. Volume 4 (1911),
'The Dying God', discusses the tradition by which the priest/king must be
killed by his successor.

Cambridge University Press has long been a pioneer in the reissuing of out-of-print titles from its own backlist, producing digital reprints of books that are still sought after by scholars and students but could not be reprinted economically using traditional technology. The Cambridge Library Collection extends this activity to a wider range of books which are still of importance to researchers and professionals, either for the source material they contain, or as landmarks in the history of their academic discipline.

Drawing from the world-renowned collections in the Cambridge University Library and other partner libraries, and guided by the advice of experts in each subject area, Cambridge University Press is using state-of-the-art scanning machines in its own Printing House to capture the content of each book selected for inclusion. The files are processed to give a consistently clear, crisp image, and the books finished to the high quality standard for which the Press is recognised around the world. The latest print-on-demand technology ensures that the books will remain available indefinitely, and that orders for single or multiple copies can quickly be supplied.

The Cambridge Library Collection brings back to life books of enduring scholarly value (including out-of-copyright works originally issued by other publishers) across a wide range of disciplines in the humanities and social sciences and in science and technology.

The Golden Bough
The Third Edition

VOLUME 4:
THE DYING GOD

J.G. FRAZER

CAMBRIDGE
UNIVERSITY PRESS

CAMBRIDGE UNIVERSITY PRESS

Cambridge, New York, Melbourne, Madrid, Cape Town,
Singapore, São Paolo, Delhi, Mexico City

Published in the United States of America by Cambridge University Press, New York

www.cambridge.org
Information on this title: www.cambridge.org/9781108047333

© in this compilation Cambridge University Press 2012

This edition first published 1911
This digitally printed version 2012

ISBN 978-1-108-04733-3 Paperback

THE GOLDEN BOUGH

A STUDY IN MAGIC AND RELIGION

THIRD EDITION

PART III

THE DYING GOD

MACMILLAN AND CO., Limited
LONDON · BOMBAY · CALCUTTA
MELBOURNE

THE MACMILLAN COMPANY
NEW YORK · BOSTON · CHICAGO
ATLANTA · SAN FRANCISCO

THE MACMILLAN CO. OF CANADA, Ltd.
TORONTO

THE DYING GOD

BY

J. G. FRAZER, D.C.L., LL.D., Litt.D.

FELLOW OF TRINITY COLLEGE, CAMBRIDGE

PROFESSOR OF SOCIAL ANTHROPOLOGY IN THE UNIVERSITY OF LIVERPOOL

MACMILLAN AND CO., LIMITED
ST. MARTIN'S STREET, LONDON

1911

PREFACE

WITH this third part of *The Golden Bough* we take up the question, Why had the King of the Wood at Nemi regularly to perish by the hand of his successor? In the first part of the work I gave some reasons for thinking that the priest of Diana, who bore the title of King of the Wood beside the still lake among the Alban Hills, personated the great god Jupiter or his duplicate Dianus, the deity of the oak, the thunder, and the sky. On this theory, accordingly, we are at once confronted with the wider and deeper question, Why put a man-god or human representative of deity to a violent death? Why extinguish the divine light in its earthly vessel instead of husbanding it to its natural close? My general answer to that question is contained in the present volume. If I am right, the motive for slaying a man-god is a fear lest with the enfeeblement of his body in sickness or old age his sacred spirit should suffer a corresponding decay, which might imperil the general course of nature and with it the existence of his worshippers, who believe the cosmic energies to be mysteriously knit up with those of their human divinity. Hence, if there is any measure of truth in this theory, the practice of putting divine men and particularly divine kings to death, which seems to have been common at a particular stage in the evolution of society and religion, was a crude but pathetic attempt to disengage an immortal spirit from its mortal envelope, to arrest the forces of decomposition in nature by retrenching

v

with ruthless hand the first ominous symptoms of decay. We may smile if we please at the vanity of these and the like efforts to stay the inevitable decline, to bring the relentless revolution of the great wheel to a stand, to keep youth's fleeting roses for ever fresh and fair ; but perhaps in spite of every disillusionment, when we contemplate the seemingly endless vistas of knowledge which have been opened up even within our own generation, many of us may cherish in our heart of hearts a fancy, if not a hope, that some loophole of escape may after all be discovered from the iron walls of the prison-house which threaten to close on and crush us ; that, groping about in the darkness, mankind may yet chance to lay hands on " that golden key that opes the palace of eternity," and so to pass from this world of shadows and sorrow to a world of untroubled light and joy. If this is a dream, it is surely a happy and innocent one, and to those who would wake us from it we may murmur with Michael Angelo,

"*Però non mi destar, deh ! parla basso.*"

J. G. FRAZER.

CAMBRIDGE,
11*th June* 1911.

CONTENTS

Chapter VI.—Sacrifice of the King's
Son   .   .   .   .   .   . Pp. 160-195

Temporary kings sometimes related by blood to the royal family, 161 ; Aun,
King of Sweden, and the sacrifice of his nine sons, 160 *sq.* ; tradition of
King Athamas and his children, 161-163 ; family of royal descent liable
to be sacrificed at Orchomenus, 163 *sq.* ; Thessalian and Boeotian kings
seem to have sacrificed their sons instead of themselves, 164-166 ; sacrifice of king's sons among the Semites, 166 ; sacrifice of children to Baal
among the Semites, 166-168 ; Canaanite and Hebrew custom of burning
firstborn children in honour of Baal or Moloch, 168-174 ; tradition of
the origin of the Passover, 174-178 ; custom of sacrificing all the firstborn, whether animals or men, probably a very ancient Semitic institution,
178 *sq.* ; sacrifice of firstborn children among many peoples, 179-186 ;
the "Sacred Spring" in ancient Italy, 186 *sq.* ; different motives may
have led to the killing of the firstborn, 187 *sq.* ; the doctrine of rebirth
may have furnished one motive for the infanticide of the firstborn, 188 *sq.* ;
the same belief may explain the rule of infant succession in Polynesia and
may partly account for the prevalence of infanticide in that region, 190 *sq.* ;
abdication or deposition of the father when his son attains to manhood,
191 *sq.* ; traces of such customs in Greek myth and legend, 192-194 ;
on the whole the sacrifice of a king's son as a substitute for his father
would not be surprising, at least in Semitic lands, 194 *sq.*

Chapter VII. — Succession to the
Soul   .   .   .   .   .   . Pp. 196-204

Tendency of a custom of regicide to extinguish a royal family no bar to the
observance of such a custom among peoples who set little value on human
life, 196-198 ; transmission of the soul of the slain divinity to his successor, 198 ; transmission of the souls of chiefs and others in Nias,
America, and elsewhere, 198-200 ; inspired representatives of dead kings
in Africa, 200-202 ; right of succession to the kingdom conferred by the
possession of corporeal relics of dead kings, such as their skulls, their
teeth, or their hair, 202 *sq.* ; souls of slain Shilluk kings transmitted to
their successors, 204.

Chapter VIII.—The Killing of the
Tree-Spirit   .   .   .   .   . Pp. 205-271

§ 1. *The Whitsuntide Mummers*, pp. 205-214.—The single combat of the King
of the Wood at Nemi probably a mitigation of an older custom of putting
him to death at the end of a fixed period, 205 *sq.* ; the theory confirmed

CHAPTER I

THE MORTALITY OF THE GODS

AT an early stage of his intellectual development man deems himself naturally immortal, and imagines that were it not for the baleful arts of sorcerers, who cut the vital thread prematurely short, he would live for ever. The illusion, so flattering to human wishes and hopes, is still current among many savage tribes at the present day,[1] and

---

[1] For examples see M. Dobrizhoffer, *Historia de Abiponibus* (Vienna, 1784), ii. 92 *sq.*, 240 *sqq.* ; C. Gay, " Fragment d'un voyage dans le Chili et au Cusco," *Bulletin de la Société de Géographie* (Paris), Deuxième Série, xix. (1843) p. 25 ; H. Delaporte, "Une Visite chez les Araucaniens," *Bulletin de la Société de Géographie* (Paris), Quatrième Série, x. (1855) p. 30 ; K. von den Steinen, *Unter den Naturvölker Zentral-Brasiliens* (Berlin, 1894), pp. 344, 348 ; E. F. im Thurn, *Among the Indians of Guiana* (London, 1883), pp. 330 *sq.* ; A. G. Morice, "The Canadian Dénés," *Annual Archaeological Report, 1905* (Toronto, 1906), p. 207 ; (Sir) George Grey, *Journals of Two Expeditions of Discovery into North-West and Western Australia* (London, 1841), ii. 238 ; A. Oldfield, "The Aborigines of Australia," *Transactions of the Ethnological Society of London*, N.S. iii. (1865) p. 236 ; J. Dawson, *Australian Aborigines* (Melbourne, Sydney, and Adelaide, 1881), p. 63 ; Rev. G. Taplin, "The Narrinyeri," *Native Tribes of South Australia* (Adelaide, 1879), p. 25 ; C. W. Schürmann,

"The Aboriginal Tribes of Port Lincoln," *Native Tribes of South Australia*, p. 237 ; H. E. A. Meyer, in *Native Tribes of South Australia*, p. 195 ; R. Brough Smyth, *The Aborigines of Victoria* (Melbourne, 1878), i. 110, ii. 289 *sq.* ; W. Stanbridge, in *Transactions of the Ethnological Society of London*, New Series, i. (1861) p. 299 ; L. Fison and A. W. Howitt, *Kamilaroi and Kurnai*, pp. 250 *sq.* ; A. L. P. Cameron, "Notes on some Tribes of New South Wales," *Journal of the Anthropological Institute*, xiv. (1885) pp. 361, 362 *sq.* ; W. Ridley, *Kamilaroi*, Second Edition (Sydney, 1875), p. 159 ; Baldwin Spencer and F. J. Gillen, *Native Tribes of Central Australia* (London, 1899), pp. 46-48 ; *Cambridge Anthropological Expedition to Torres Straits*, v. (Cambridge, 1904) pp. 248, 323 ; E. Beardmore, "The Natives of Mowat, British New Guinea," *Journal of the Anthropological Institute*, xix. (1890) p. 461 ; R. E. Guise, "On the Tribes inhabiting the Mouth of the Wanigela River, New Guinea," *Journal of the Anthropological Institute*, xxviii. (1899) p. 216 ; C. G. Seligmann, *The Melanit may be supposed to have prevailed universally in that Age of Magic which appears to have everywhere preceded the Age of Religion.   But in time the sad truth of human mortality was borne in upon our primitive philosopher with a force of demonstration which no prejudice could resist and no sophistry dissemble.   Among the manifold influences which combined to wring from him a reluctant assent to the necessity of death must be numbered the growing influence of religion, which by exposing the vanity of magic and of all the extravagant pretensions built on it gradually lowered man's proud and defiant attitude towards nature, and taught him to believe that there are mysteries in the universe which his feeble intellect can never fathom, and forces which his puny hands can never control.   Thus more and more he learned to bow to the inevitable and to console himself for the brevity and the sorrows of life on earth by the hope of a blissful eternity hereafter.   But if he reluctantly acknowledged the existence of beings at once superhuman and supernatural, he was as yet far from suspecting the width and the depth of the gulf which divided him from them. The gods with whom his imagination now peopled the darkness of the unknown were indeed admitted by him to be his superiors in knowledge and in power, in the joyous splendour of their life and in the length of its duration.   But, though he knew it not, these glorious and awful beings were merely, like the spectre of the Brocken, the

esians of British New Guinea (Cambridge, 1910), p. 279; K. Vetter, Komm herüber und hilf uns! oder die Arbeit der Neuen-Dettelsauer Mission, iii. (Barmen, 1898) pp. 10 sq.; id., in Nachrichten über Kaiser-Wilhelmsland und den Bismarck-Archipel, 1897, pp. 94, 98; A. Deniau, "Croyances religieuses et mœurs des indigènes de l'île Malo," Missions Catholiques, xxxiii. (1901) pp. 315 sq.; C. Ribbe, Zwei Jahre unter den Kannibalen der Salomo-Inseln (Dresden-Blasewitz, 1903), p. 268; P. A. Kleintitschen, Die Küstenbewohner der Gazellehalbinsel (Hiltrup bei Münster, N.D.), p. 344; P. Rascher, "Die Sulka," Archiv für Anthropologie, xxix. (1904) pp. 221 sq.; R. Parkinson, Dreissig

Jahre in der Südsee (Stuttgart, 1907), pp. 199-201; G. Brown, D.D., Melanesians and Polynesians (London, 1910), p. 176; Father Abinal, "Astrologie Malgache," Missions Catholiques, xi. (1879) p. 506; A. Grandidier, "Madagascar," Bulletin de la Société de Géographie (Paris), Sixième Série, iii. (1872) p. 399; Father Campana, "Congo, Mission Catholique de Landana," Missions Catholiques, xxvii. (1895) pp. 102 sq.; Th. Masui, Guide de la Section de l'État Indépendant du Congo à l'Exposition de Bruxelles-Tervueren en 1897 (Brussels, 1897), p. 82. The discussion of this and similar evidence must be reserved for another work.

reflections of his own diminutive personality exaggerated into gigantic proportions by distance and by the mists and clouds upon which they were cast. Man in fact created gods in his own likeness and being himself mortal he naturally supposed his creatures to be in the same sad predicament. Thus the Greenlanders believed that a wind could kill their most powerful god, and that he would certainly die if he touched a dog. When they heard of the Christian God, they kept asking if he never died, and being informed that he did not, they were much surprised, and said that he must be a very great god indeed.[1] In answer to the enquiries of Colonel Dodge, a North American Indian stated that the world was made by the Great Spirit. Being asked which Great Spirit he meant, the good one or the bad one, " Oh, neither of *them*," replied he, " the Great Spirit that made the world is dead long ago. He could not possibly have lived as long as this."[2] A tribe in the Philippine Islands told the Spanish conquerors that the grave of the Creator was upon the top of Mount Cabunian.[3] Heitsi-eibib, a god or divine hero of the Hottentots, died several times and came to life again. His graves are generally to be met with in narrow defiles between mountains. When the Hottentots pass one of them, they throw a stone on it for good luck, sometimes muttering " Give us plenty of cattle."[4] The grave of Zeus, the great god of Greece, was shewn to visitors in Crete as late as about the beginning of our era.[5] The body of Dionysus was buried at Delphi beside the golden statue of Apollo, and his tomb bore the inscription, " Here lies Dionysus dead, the son of Semele."[6]

Mortality of Greek gods.

---

[1] C. Meiners, *Geschichte der Religionen* (Hanover, 1806-1807), i. 48.

[2] R. I. Dodge, *Our Wild Indians*, p. 112.

[3] F. Blumentritt, "Der Ahnencultus und die religiösen Anschauungen der Malaien des Philippinen-Archipels," *Mittheilungen d. Wiener geogr. Gesellschaft*, 1882, p. 198.

[4] Sir James E. Alexander, *Expedition of Discovery into the Interior of Africa*, i. 166 ; H. Lichtenstein, *Reisen im Südlichen Africa* (Berlin, 1811-1812), i. 349 *sq.* ; W. H. I. Bleek, *Reynard the Fox in South*

Africa (London, 1864), pp. 75 *sq.* ; Theophilus Hahn, *Tsuni-][Goam, the Supreme Being of the Khoi-Khoi* (London, 1881), pp. 56, 69.

[5] Callimachus, *Hymn to Zeus*, 9 *sq.*; Diodorus Siculus, iii. 61 ; Lucian, *Philopseudes*, 3 ; *id., Jupiter Tragoedus*, 45 ; *id., Philopatris*, 10 ; Porphyry, *Vita Pythagorae*, 17 ; Cicero, *De natura deorum*, iii. 21. 53 ; Pomponius Mela, ii. 7. 112 ; Minucius Felix, *Octavius*, 21 ; Lactantius, *Divin. instit.* i. 11.

[6] Plutarch, *Isis et Osiris*, 35 ; Philochorus, *Fragm.* 22, in C. Müller's *Fragmenta historicorum Graecorum*,

According to one account, Apollo himself was buried at Delphi; for Pythagoras is said to have carved an inscription on his tomb, setting forth how the god had been killed by the python and buried under the tripod.[1] The ancient god Cronus was buried in Sicily,[2] and the graves of Hermes, Aphrodite, and Ares were shewn in Hermopolis, Cyprus, and Thrace.[3]

Mortality of Egyptian gods. The great gods of Egypt themselves were not exempt from the common lot. They too grew old and died. For like men they were composed of body and soul, and like men were subject to all the passions and infirmities of the flesh. Their bodies, it is true, were fashioned of more ethereal mould, and lasted longer than ours, but they could not hold out for ever against the siege of time. Age converted their bones into silver, their flesh into gold, and their azure locks into lapis-lazuli. When their time came, they passed away from the cheerful world of the living to reign as dead gods over dead men in the melancholy world beyond the grave. Even their souls, like those of mankind, could only endure after death so long as their bodies held together; and hence it was as needful to preserve the corpses of the gods as the corpses of common folk, lest with the divine body the divine spirit should also come to an untimely end. At first their remains were laid to rest under the desert sands of the mountains, that the dryness of the soil and the purity of the air might protect them from putrefaction and decay. Hence one of the oldest titles of the Egyptian gods is " they who are under the sands." But when at a later time the discovery of the art of embalming gave a new lease of life to the souls of the dead by preserving their bodies for an indefinite time from corruption, the deities were permitted to share the benefit of an invention which held out to gods as well as to men a reasonable hope of immortality. Every province then had the tomb and mummy of its dead god. The mummy of Osiris was to be seen at Mendes; Thinis boasted of the

i. p. 378; Tatian, *Oratio ad Graecos*, 8, ed. Otto; J. Tzetzes, *Schol. on Lycophron*, 208. Compare Ch. Petersen, " Das Grab und die Todtenfeier des Dionysos," *Philologus*, xv. (1860) pp. 77-91. The grave of Dionysus is also said to have been at Thebes (Clemens Romanus, *Recognitiones*,

x. 24; Migne's *Patrologia Graeca*, i. col. 1434).

[1] Porphyry, *Vit. Pythag.* 16.

[2] Philochorus, *Fr.* 184, in C. Müller's *Fragmenta historicorum Graecorum*, ii. p. 414.

[3] Ch. Lobeck, *Aglaophamus* (Königsberg, 1829), pp. 574 *sq.*

mummy of Anhouri; and Heliopolis rejoiced in the possession of that of Toumou.[1] But while their bodies lay swathed and bandaged here on earth in the tomb, their souls, if we may trust the Egyptian priests, shone as bright stars in the firmament. The soul of Isis sparkled in Sirius, the soul of Horus in Orion, and the soul of Typhon in the Great Bear.[2] But the death of the god did not involve the extinction of his sacred stock; for he commonly had by his wife a son and heir, who on the demise of his divine parent succeeded to the full rank, power, and honours of the godhead.[3] The high gods

---

[1] G. Maspero, *Histoire ancienne des peuples de l'Orient classique: les origines*, pp. 108-111, 116-118. On the mortality of the Egyptian gods see further A. Moret, *Le Rituel du culte divin journalier en Égypte* (Paris, 1902), pp. 219 *sqq.*

[2] Plutarch, *Isis et Osiris*, 21, 22, 38, 61; Diodorus Siculus, i. 27. 4; Dittenberger, *Orientis Graeci inscriptiones selectae*, i. No. 56, p. 102.

[3] A. Wiedemann, *Die Religion der alten Aegypter*, pp. 59 *sq.*; G. Maspero, *Histoire ancienne des peuples de l'Orient classique: les origines*, pp. 104-108, 150. Indeed it was an article of the Egyptian creed that every god must die after he had begotten a son in his own likeness (A. Wiedemann, *Herodots zweites Buch*, p. 204). Hence the Egyptian deities were commonly arranged in trinities of a simple and natural type, each comprising a father, a mother, and a son. "Speaking generally, two members of such a triad were gods, one old and one young, and the third was a goddess, who was, naturally, the wife, or female counterpart, of the older god. The younger god was the son of the older god and goddess, and he was supposed to possess all the attributes and powers which belonged to his father. . . . The feminine counterpart or wife of the chief god was usually a local goddess of little or no importance; on the other hand, her son by the chief god was nearly as important as his father, because it was assumed that he would succeed to his rank and throne when the elder god had passed away. The conception of the triad or trinity is, in

Egypt, probably as old as the belief in gods, and it seems to be based on the anthropomorphic views which were current in the earliest times about them" (E. A. Wallis Budge, *The Gods of the Egyptians*, London, 1904, i. 113 *sq.*). If the Christian doctrine of the Trinity took shape under Egyptian influence, the function originally assigned to the Holy Spirit may have been that of the divine mother. In the apocryphal *Gospel to the Hebrews*, as Mr. F. C. Conybeare was kind enough to point out to me, Christ spoke of the Holy Ghost as his mother. The passage is quoted by Origen (*Comment. in Joan. II.* vol. iv. col. 132, ed. Migne), and runs as follows: "My mother the Holy Spirit took me a moment ago by one of my hairs and carried me away to the great Mount Tabor." Compare Origen, *In Jeremiam Hom. XV. 4*, vol. iii. col. 433, ed. Migne. In the reign of Trajan a certain Alcibiades, from Apamea in Syria, appeared at Rome with a volume in which the Holy Ghost was described as a stalwart female about ninety-six miles high and broad in proportion. See Hippolytus, *Refut. omnium haeresium*, ix. 13, p. 462, ed. Duncker and Schneidewin. The Ophites represented the Holy Spirit as "the first woman," "mother of all living," who was beloved by "the first man" and likewise by "the second man," and who conceived by one or both of them "the light, which they call Christ." See H. Usener, *Das Weihnachtsfest*, pp. 116 *sq.*, quoting Irenaeus, i. 28. As to a female member of the Trinity, see further *id., Dreiheit, ein Versuch mytho-*

of Babylon also, though they appeared to their worshippers only in dreams and visions, were conceived to be human in their bodily shape, human in their passions, and human in their fate ; for like men they were born into the world, and like men they loved and fought and died.[1]

The death of the Great Pan. One of the most famous stories of the death of a god is told by Plutarch. It runs thus. In the reign of the emperor Tiberius a certain schoolmaster named Epitherses was sailing from Greece to Italy. The ship in which he had taken his passage was a merchantman and there were many other passengers on board. At evening, when they were off the Echinadian Islands, the wind died away, and the vessel drifted close in to the island of Paxos. Most of the passengers were awake and many were still drinking wine after dinner, when suddenly a voice hailed the ship from the island, calling upon Thamus. The crew and passengers were taken by surprise, for though there was an Egyptian pilot named Thamus on board, few knew him even by name. Twice the cry was repeated, but Thamus kept silence. However, at the third call he answered, and the voice from the shore, now louder than ever, said, "When you are come to Palodes, announce that the Great Pan is dead." Astonishment fell upon all, and they consulted whether it would be better to do the bidding of the voice or not. At last Thamus resolved that, if the wind held, he would pass the place in silence, but if it dropped when they were off Palodes he would give the message. Well, when they were come to Palodes, there was a great calm ; so Thamus standing in the stern and looking towards the land cried out, as he had been bidden, "The Great Pan is dead." The words had hardly passed his lips when a loud sound of lamentation broke on their ears, as if a multitude were

logischer Zahlenlehre (Bonn, 1903), pp. 41 *sqq.* ; Gibbon, *Decline and Fall of the Roman Empire*, ch. l. vol. ix. p. 261, note g (Edinburgh, 1811). Mr. Conybeare tells me that Philo Judaeus, who lived in the first half of the first century of our era, constantly defines God as a Trinity in Unity, or a Unity in Trinity, and that the speculations of this Alexandrian Jew deeply influenced the course of Christian thought on the mystical nature of the deity. Thus it seems not impossible that the ancient Egyptian doctrine of the divine Trinity may have been distilled through Philo into Christianity. On the other hand it has been suggested that the Christian Trinity is of Babylonian origin. See H. Zimmern, in E. Schrader's *Die Keilinschriften und das Alte Testament,*[3] pp. 418 *sq.,* 440.

[1] L. W. King, *Babylonian Religion and Mythology* (London, 1899), p. 8.

mourning. This strange story, vouched for by many on board, soon got wind at Rome, and Thamus was sent for and questioned by the emperor Tiberius himself, who caused enquiries to be made about the dead god.[1] In modern times, also, the annunciation of the death of the Great Pan has been much discussed and various explanations of it have been suggested. On the whole the simplest and most natural would seem to be that the deity whose sad end was thus mysteriously proclaimed and lamented was the Syrian god Tammuz or Adonis, whose death is known to have been annually bewailed by his followers both in Greece and in his native Syria. At Athens the solemnity fell at midsummer, and there is no improbability in the view that in a Greek island a band of worshippers of Tammuz should have been celebrating the death of their god with the customary passionate demonstrations of sorrow at the very time when a ship lay becalmed off the shore, and that in the stillness of the summer night the voices of lamentation should have been wafted with startling distinctness across the water and should have made on the minds of the listening passengers a deep and lasting impression.[2]   However that may be,

---

[1] Plutarch, *De defectu oraculorum*, 17.

[2] This is in substance the explanation briefly suggested by F. Liebrecht, and developed more fully and with certain variations of detail by S. Reinach. See F. Liebrecht, *Des Gervasius von Tilbury Otia Imperialia* (Hanover, 1856), p. 180; S. Reinach, *Cultes, mythes et religions*, iii. (Paris, 1908), pp. 1 *sqq.* As to the worship of Tammuz or Adonis in Syria and Greece see my *Adonis, Attis, Osiris*, Second Edition (London, 1907). In Plutarch's narrative confusion seems to have arisen through the native name (Tammuz) of the deity, which either accidentally coincided with that of the pilot (as S. Reinach thinks) or was erroneously transferred to him by a narrator (as F. Liebrecht supposed). An entirely different explanation of the story has been proposed by Dr. W. H. Roscher. He holds that the god whose death was lamented was the great ram-god of Mendes in Egypt, whom Greek writers constantly mistook for a goat-god and identified with Pan. A living ram was always revered as an incarnation of the god, and when it died there was a great mourning throughout all the land of Mendes. Some stone coffins of the sacred animal have been found in the ruins of the city. See Herodotus, ii. 46, with A. Wiedemann's commentary; W. H. Roscher, "Die Legende vom Tode des groszen Pan," *Fleckeisen's Jahrbücher für classische Philologie*, xxxviii. (1892) pp. 465-477. Dr. Roscher shews that Thamus was an Egyptian name, comparing Plato, *Phaedrus*, p. 274 D E; Polyaenus, iii. 2. 5; Philostratus, *Vit. Apollon. Tyan.* vi. 5. 108. As to the worshipful goat, or rather ram, of Mendes, see also Diodorus Siculus, i. 84; Strabo, xvii. 1. 19, p. 802; Clement of Alexandria, *Protrept.* ii. 39, p. 34, ed. Potter; Suidas, *s.v.* Μένδην.

stories of the same kind found currency in western Asia down
to the Middle Ages. An Arab writer relates that in the year
1063 or 1064 A.D., in the reign of the caliph Caiem,
a rumour went abroad through Bagdad, which soon spread
all over the province of Irac, that some Turks out hunting in
the desert had seen a black tent, where many men and
women were beating their faces and uttering loud cries, as it
is the custom to do in the East when some one is dead.
And among the cries they distinguished these words, " The
great King of the Jinn is dead, woe to this country ! " In
consequence of this a mysterious threat was circulated from
Armenia to Chuzistan that every town which did not lament
the dead King of the Jinn should utterly perish. Again, in
the year 1203 or 1204 A.D. a fatal disease, which attacked
the throat, raged in parts of Mosul and Irac, and it was
divulged that a woman of the Jinn called Umm 'Uncūd or
" Mother of the Grape-cluster " had lost her son, and that all
who did not lament for him would fall victims to the epidemic.
So men and women sought to save themselves from death by
assembling and beating their faces, while they cried out in a
lamentable voice, "O mother of the Grape-cluster, excuse us ;
the Grape-cluster is dead ; we knew it not." [1]

---

[1] F. Liebrecht, *op. cit.* pp. 180 *sq.* ;
W. Robertson Smith, *Religion of the
Semites*,[2] pp. 412, 414. The latter
writer observes with justice that "the
wailing for 'Uncūd, the divine Grape-
cluster, seems to be the last survival of
an old vintage piaculum." "The
dread of the worshippers," he adds,
"that the neglect of the usual ritual
would be followed by disaster, is particularly intelligible if they regarded
the necessary operations of agriculture
as involving the violent extinction of a
particle of divine life." On the mortality of the gods in general and of the
Teutonic gods in particular, see J.
Grimm, *Deutsche Mythologie*,[4] i. 263
sqq.; compare E. H. Meyer, *Mythologie
der Germanen* (Strasburg, 1903), p.
288. As to the mortality of the Irish
gods, see Douglas Hyde, *Literary
History of Ireland* (London, 1899),
pp. 80 *sq.*

CHAPTER II

THE KILLING OF THE DIVINE KING

§ 1. *Preference for a Violent Death*

IF the high gods, who dwell remote from the fret and fever of this earthly life, are yet believed to die at last, it is not to be expected that a god who lodges in a frail tabernacle of flesh should escape the same fate, though we hear of African kings who have imagined themselves immortal by virtue of their sorceries.[1] Now primitive peoples, as we have seen,[2] sometimes believe that their safety and even that of the world is bound up with the life of one of these god-men or human incarnations of the divinity. Naturally, therefore, they take the utmost care of his life, out of a regard for their own. But no amount of care and precaution will prevent the man-god from growing old and feeble and at last dying. His worshippers have to lay their account with this sad necessity and to meet it as best they can. The danger is a formidable one ; for if the course of nature is dependent on the man-god's life, what catastrophes may not be expected from the gradual enfeeblement of his powers and their final extinction in death ? There is only one way of averting these dangers. The man-god must be killed as soon as he shews symptoms that his powers are beginning to fail, and his soul must be transferred to a vigorous successor before it has been seriously impaired by the threatened decay. The advantages of thus

Human gods are killed to prevent them from growing old and feeble.

---

[1] "Der Muata .Cazembe und die Völkerstämme der Maravis, Chevas, Muembas, Lundas und andere von Süd-Afrika," *Zeitschrift für allgemeine Erdkunde*, vi. (1856) p. 395 ; F. T. Valdez, *Six Years of a Traveller's Life in Western Africa* (London, 1861), ii. 241 *sq.*

[2] See *Taboo and the Perils of the Soul*, pp. 6, 7 *sq.*

putting the man-god to death instead of allowing him to die of old age and disease are, to the savage, obvious enough. For if the man-god dies what we call a natural death, it means, according to the savage, that his soul has either voluntarily departed from his body and refuses to return, or more commonly that it has been extracted, or at least detained in its wanderings, by a demon or sorcerer.[1]   In any of these cases the soul of the man-god is lost to his worshippers ; and with it their prosperity is gone and their very existence endangered.   Even if they could arrange to catch the soul of the dying god as it left his lips or his nostrils and so transfer it to a successor, this would not effect their purpose ; for, dying of disease, his soul would necessarily leave his body in the last stage of weakness and exhaustion, and so enfeebled it would continue to drag out a languid, inert existence in any body to which it might be transferred.   Whereas by slaying him his worshippers could, in the first place, make sure of catching his soul as it escaped and transferring it to a suitable successor ; and, in the second place, by putting him to death before his natural force was abated, they would secure that the world should not fall into decay with the decay of the man-god.   Every purpose, therefore, was answered, and all dangers averted by thus killing the man-god and transferring his soul, while yet at its prime, to a vigorous successor.

Preference for a violent death : the sick and old killed.   Some of the reasons for preferring a violent death to the slow death of old age or disease are obviously as applicable to common men as to the man-god.   Thus the Mangaians think that " the spirits of those who die a natural death are excessively feeble and weak, as their bodies were at dissolution ; whereas the spirits of those who are slain in battle are strong and vigorous, their bodies not having been reduced by disease." [2]   The Barongo believe that in the world beyond the grave the spirits of their dead ancestors appear with the exact form and lineaments which their bodies exhibited at the moment of death ; the spirits are young or old according as their bodies were young or old when they died ; there

[1] See *Taboo and the Perils of the Soul*, pp. 26 *sqq.*

[2] W. W. Gill, *Myths and Songs of the South Pacific* (London, 1876), p. 163.

are baby spirits who crawl about on all fours.[1]   The Lengua
Indians of the Gran Chaco are persuaded that the souls of
the departed correspond exactly in form and characteristics
to the bodies which they quitted at death ; thus a tall man
is tall, a short man is short, and a deformed man is deformed
in the spirit-land, and the disembodied soul of a child remains
a child, it never develops into an adult.   Hence they burn
the body of a murderer and scatter the ashes to the winds,
thinking that this treatment will prevent his spirit from
assuming human shape in the other world.[2]   So, too, the
Naga tribes of Manipur hold that the ghost of a dead man
is an exact image of the deceased as he was at the moment
of death, with his scars, tattoo marks, mutilations, and all
the rest.[3]   The Baganda think that the ghosts of men who
were mutilated in life are mutilated in like manner after
death ; so to avoid that shame they will rather die with all
their limbs than lose one by amputation and live.[4]   Hence,
men sometimes prefer to kill themselves or to be killed before
they grow feeble, in order that in the future life their souls
may start fresh and vigorous as they left their bodies, instead
of decrepit and worn out with age and disease.   Thus in Fiji,
" self-immolation is by no means rare, and they believe that
as they leave this life, so they will remain ever after.   This
forms a powerful motive to escape from decrepitude, or from a
crippled condition, by a voluntary death." [5]   Or, as another
observer of the Fijians puts it more fully, " the custom of
voluntary suicide on the part of the old men, which is among
their most extraordinary usages, is also connected with their
superstitions respecting a future life.   They believe that
persons enter upon the delights of their elysium with the
same faculties, mental and physical, that they possess at the
hour of death, in short, that the spiritual life commences
where the corporeal existence terminates.   With these views,
it is natural that they should desire to pass through this
change before their mental and bodily powers are so enfeebled

---

[1] H. A. Junod, *Les Ba - Ronga*
(Neuchatel, 1898), pp. 381 *sq.*

[2] W. Barbrooke Grubb, *An Unknown People in an Unknown Land*
(London, 1911), p. 120.

[3] T. C. Hodson, *The Naga Tribes*

of Manipur (London, 1911), p. 159.

[4] Rev. J. Roscoe, *The Baganda*
(London, 1911), p. 281.

[5] Ch. Wilkes, *Narrative of the U.S.
Exploring Expedition* (London, 1845),
iii. 96.

by age as to deprive them of their capacity for enjoyment. To this motive must be added the contempt which attaches to physical weakness among a nation of warriors, and the wrongs and insults which await those who are no longer able to protect themselves. When therefore a man finds his strength declining with the advance of age, and feels that he will soon be unequal to discharge the duties of this life, and to partake in the pleasures of that which is to come, he calls together his relations, and tells them that he is now worn out and useless, that he sees they are all ashamed of him, and that he has determined to be buried." So on a day appointed they used to meet and bury him alive.[1] In Vaté, one of the New Hebrides, the aged were buried alive at their own request. It was considered a disgrace to the family of an old chief if he was not buried alive.[2] Of the Kamants, a Jewish tribe in Abyssinia, it is reported that "they never let a person die a natural death, but that if any of their relatives is nearly expiring, the priest of the village is called to cut his throat ; if this be omitted, they believe that the departed soul has not entered the mansions of the blessed."[3] The old Greek philosopher Heraclitus thought that the souls of those who die in battle are purer than the souls of those who die of disease.[4]

Preference for a violent death : the sick and aged killed. Among the Chiriguanos, a tribe of South American Indians on the river Pilcomayo, when a man was at the point of death his nearest relative used to break his spine by a blow of an axe, for they thought that to die a natural death was the greatest misfortune that could befall a man.[5] Whenever a Payagua Indian of Paraguay, or a Guayana of south-eastern Brazil, grew weary of life, a feast was made, and amid the revelry and dancing the man was gummed and feathered with the plumage of many-coloured birds. A huge jar had been previously fixed in the ground to be

---

[1] *U.S. Exploring Expedition, Ethnology and Philology*, by H. Hale (Philadelphia, 1846), p. 65. Compare Th. Williams, *Fiji and the Fijians*,[2] i. 183 ; J. E. Erskine, *Journal of a Cruise among the Islands of the Western Pacific* (London, 1853), p. 248.

[2] G. Turner, *Samoa*, p. 335.

[3] Martin Flad, *A Short Description of the Falasha and Kamants in Abyssinia*, p. 19.

[4] H. Diels, *Die Fragmente der Vorsokratiker*,[2] i. (Berlin, 1906) p. 81 ; *id.*, *Herakleitos von Ephesos*[2] (Berlin, 1909), p. 50, Frag. 136, ψυχαὶ ἀρηίφατοι καθαρώτεραι ἢ ἐνὶ νούσοις.

[5] F. de Castelnau, *Expédition dans les parties centrales de l'Amérique du Sud*, iv. (Paris, 1851) p. 380. Compare *id.* ii. 49 *sq.* as to the practice of the Chavantes, a tribe of Indians on the Tocantins river.

ready for him ; in this he was placed, the mouth of the jar was covered with a heavy lid of baked clay, the earth was heaped over it, and thus " he went to his doom more joyful and gladsome than to his first nuptials."[1] Among the Koryaks of north-eastern Asia, when a man felt that his last hour was come, superstition formerly required that he should either kill himself or be killed by a friend, in order that he might escape the Evil One and deliver himself up to the Good God.[2] Similarly among the Chukchees of the same region, when a man's strength fails and he is tired of life, he requests his son or other near relation to despatch him, indicating the manner of death he prefers to die. So, on a day appointed, his friends and neighbours assemble, and in their presence he is stabbed, strangled, or otherwise disposed of according to his directions.[3] The turbulent Angamis are the most warlike and bloodthirsty of the wild head-hunting tribes in the valley of the Brahmapootra. Among them, when a warrior dies a natural death, his nearest male relative takes a spear and wounds the corpse by a blow on the head, in order that the man may be received with honour in the other world as one who has died in battle.[4] The heathen Norsemen believed that only those who fell fighting were received by Odin in Valhalla ; hence it appears

[1] R. Southey, *History of Brazil*, iii. (London, 1819) p. 619 ; R. F. Burton, in *The Captivity of Hans Stade of Hesse* (Hakluyt Society, London, 1874), p. 122.

[2] C. von Dittmar, " Über die Koräken und die ihnen sehr nahe verwandten Tschuktschen," *Bulletin de la Classe philologique de l'Académie Impériale des Sciences de St-Pétersbourg*, xiii. (1856) coll. 122, 124 *sq.* The custom has now been completely abandoned. See W. Jochelson, "The Koryak, Religion and Myths " (Leyden and New York, 1905), p. 103 (*Memoir of the American Museum of Natural History, The Jesup North Pacific Expedition*, vol. vi. part i.).

[3] C. von Dittmar, *op. cit.* col. 132 ; De Wrangell, *Le Nord de la Sibérie* (Paris, 1843), i. 263 *sq.* ; " Die Ethnographie Russlands nach A. F. Rittich," *Petermann's Mittheilungen, Ergänzungsheft, No.* 54 (Gotha, 1878), pp. 14 *sq.* ; " Der Anadyr-Bezirk nach A. W. Olssufjew," *Petermann's Mittheilungen*, xlv. (1899) p. 230 ; V. Priklonski, " Todtengebräuche der Jakuten," *Globus*, lix. (1891) p. 82 ; R. von Seidlitz, " Der Selbstmord bei den Tschuktschen," *ib.* p. 111 ; Cremat, " Der Anadyrbezirk Sibiriens und seine Bevölkerung," *Globus*, lxvi. (1894) p. 287 ; H. de Windt, *Through the Gold-fields of Alaska to Bering Straits* (London, 1898), pp. 223-225 ; W. Bogaras, " The Chukchee " (Leyden and New York, 1904-1909), pp. 560 *sqq.* (*Memoir of the American Museum of Natural History, The Jesup North Pacific Expedition*, vol. vii.).

[4] L. A. Waddell, " The Tribes of the Brahmaputra Valley," *Journal of the Asiatic Society of Bengal*, lxix. part iii. (1901) pp. 20, 24 ; T. C. Hodson, *The Naga Tribes of Manipur* (London, 1911), p. 151.

to have been customary to wound the dying with a spear, in order to secure their admission to the happy land. The custom may have been a mitigation of a still older practice of slaughtering the sick.[1] We know from Procopius that among the Heruli, a Teutonic tribe, the sick and old were regularly slain at their own request and then burned on a pyre.[2] The Wends used to kill their aged parents and other kinsfolk, and having killed them they boiled and ate their bodies; and the old folks preferred to die thus rather than to drag out a weary life of weakness and decrepitude.[3]

§ 2. Kings killed when their Strength fails

Divine kings put to death. The Chitomé of Congo.

But it is with the death of the god-man—the divine king or priest—that we are here especially concerned. The mystic kings of Fire and Water in Cambodia are not allowed to die a natural death. Hence when one of them is seriously ill and the elders think that he cannot recover, they stab him to death.[4] The people of Congo believed, as we have seen,[5] that if their pontiff the Chitomé were to die a natural death, the world would perish, and the earth, which he alone sustained by his power and merit, would immediately be annihilated. Accordingly when he fell ill and seemed likely to die, the man who was destined to be his successor entered the pontiff's house with a rope or a club and strangled or clubbed him to death.[6] A fuller account of this custom is given by an old Italian writer as follows: "Let us pass to the death of the magicians, who often die a violent death, and that for the most part voluntarily. I shall speak only of the head of this crew, from whom his followers take example. He is called Ganga Chitome, being reputed god of the earth. The first-fruits

---

[1] K. Simrock, *Handbuch der deutschen Mythologie*,[5] pp. 177 *sq.*, 507; H. M. Chadwick, *The Cult of Othin* (London, 1899), pp. 13 *sq.*, 34 *sq.*

[2] Procopius, *De bello Gothico*, ii. 14.

[3] J. Grimm, *Deutsche Rechtsalterthümer*,[3] p. 488. A custom of putting the sick and aged to death seems to have prevailed in several branches of the Aryan family; it may at one time have been common to the whole stock.

See J. Grimm, *op. cit.* pp. 486 *sqq.*; O. Schrader, *Reallexikon der indogermanischen Altertumskunde*, pp. 36-39.

[4] See *The Magic Art and the Evolution of Kings*, ii. 4 *sq.*

[5] *Taboo and the Perils of the Soul*, pp. 5 *sq.*

[6] J. B. Labat, *Relation historique de l'Éthiopie occidentale* (Paris, 1732), i. 260 *sq.*; W. Winwood Reade, *Savage Africa* (London, 1863), p. 362.

of all the crops are offered to him as his due, because they are thought to be produced by his power, and not by nature at the bidding of the Most High God. This power he boasts he can impart to others, when and to whom he pleases. He asserts that his body cannot die a natural death, and therefore when he knows he is near the end of his days, whether it is brought about by sickness or age, or whether he is deluded by the demon, he calls one of his disciples to whom he wishes to communicate his power, in order that he may succeed him. And having made him tie a noose to his neck he commands him to strangle him, or to knock him on the head with a great cudgel and kill him. His disciple obeys and sends him a martyr to the devil, to suffer torments with Lucifer in the flames for ever. This tragedy is enacted in public, in order that his successor may be manifested, who hath the power of fertilising the earth, the power having been imparted to him by the deceased ; otherwise, so they say, the earth would remain barren, and the world would perish. Oh too great foolishness and palpable blindness of the gentiles, to enlighten the eye of whose mind there would be needed the very hand of Christ whereby he opened the bodily eyes of him that had been born blind ! I know that in my time one of these magicians was cast into the sea, another into a river, a mother put to death with her son, and many more seized by our orders and banished." [1]   The Ethiopian kings of Meroe were worshipped as gods; but whenever the priests chose, they sent a messenger to the king, ordering him to die, and alleging an oracle of the gods as their authority for the command. This command the kings always obeyed down to the reign of Ergamenes, a contemporary of Ptolemy II., King of Egypt. Having received a Greek education which emancipated him from the superstitions of his countrymen, Ergamenes ventured to disregard the command of the priests, and, entering the Golden Temple with a body of soldiers, put the priests to the sword. [2]

Ethiopian kings of Meroe.

[1] G. Merolla, *Relazione del viaggio nel regno di Congo* (Naples, 1726), p. 76. The English version of this passage (Pinkerton's *Voyages and Travels*, xvi. 228) has already been quoted by Sir John Lubbock (Lord Avebury) in his *Origin of Civilisation*,[4] pp. 358 *sq.* In that version the native title of the pontiff is misspelt.

[2] Diodorus Siculus, iii. 6 ; Strabo, xvii. 2. 3, p. 822.

Customs of the same sort appear to have prevailed in this region down to modern times. Thus we are told that in Fazoql, a district in the valley of the Blue Nile, to the west of Abyssinia, it was customary, as late as the middle of the nineteenth century, to hang a king who was no longer beloved. His relatives and ministers assembled round him, and announced that as he no longer pleased the men, the women, the asses, the oxen, and the fowls of the country, it was better he should die. Once on a time, when a king was unwilling to take the hint, his own wife and mother urged him so strongly not to disgrace himself by disregarding the custom, that he submitted to his fate and was strung up in the usual way. In some tribes of Fazoql the king had to administer justice daily under a certain tree. If from sickness or any other cause he was unable to discharge this duty for three whole days, he was hanged on the tree in a noose, which contained two razors so arranged that when the noose was drawn tight by the weight of the king's body they cut his throat.[1] At Fazolglou an annual festival, which partook of the nature of a Saturnalia, was preceded by a formal trial of the king in front of his house. The judges were the chief men of the country. The king sat on his royal stool during the trial, surrounded by armed men, who were ready to carry out a sentence of death. A little way off a jackal and a dog were tied to a post. The conduct of the king during his year of office was discussed, complaints were heard, and if the verdict was unfavourable, the king was executed and his successor chosen from among the members of his family. But if the monarch was acquitted, the people at once paid their homage to him afresh, and the dog or the jackal was killed in his stead. This custom lasted down to the year 1837 or 1838, when king Yassin was thus condemned and executed.[2] His nephew Assusa was

---

[1] R. Lepsius, *Letters from Egypt, Ethiopia, and the peninsula of Sinai* (London, 1853), pp. 202, 204. I have to thank Dr. E. Westermarck for pointing out these passages to me. Fazoql lies in the fork between the Blue Nile and its tributary the Tumat. See J. Russeger, *Reisen in Europa, Asien und Afrika*, ii. 2 (Stuttgart, 1844), p. 552 note.

[2] Brun-Rollet, *Le Nil Blanc et le Soudan* (Paris, 1855), pp. 248 *sq.* For the orgiastic character of these annual festivals, see *id.* p. 245. Fazolglou is probably the same as Fazoql. The people who practise the custom are called Bertat by E. Marno (*Reisen im Gebiete des blauen und weissen Nil* (Vienna, 1874), p. 68).

compelled under threats of death to succeed him in the office.[1] Afterwards it would seem that the death of the dog was regularly accepted as a substitute for the death of the king. At least this may be inferred from a later account of the Fazoql practice, which runs thus : "The meaning of another of their customs is quite obscure. At a certain time of the year they have a kind of carnival, where every one does what he likes best. Four ministers of the king then bear him on an anqareb out of his house to an open space of ground ; a dog is fastened by a long cord to one of the feet of the anqareb. The whole population collects round the place, streaming in on every side. They then throw darts and stones at the dog, till he is killed, after which the king is again borne into his house." [2]

A custom of putting their divine kings to death at the first symptoms of infirmity or old age prevailed until lately, if indeed it is even now extinct and not merely dormant, among the Shilluk of the White Nile, and in recent years it has been carefully investigated by Dr. C. G. Seligmann, to whose researches I am indebted for the following detailed information on the subject.[3] The Shilluk are a tribe or nation who inhabit a long narrow fringe of territory on the western bank of the White Nile from Kaka in the north to Lake No in the south, as well as a strip on the eastern bank of the river, which stretches from Fashoda to Taufikia and for some thirty-five miles up the Sobat River. The country of the Shilluk is almost entirely in grass, hence the principal wealth of the people consists in their flocks and herds, but they also grow a considerable quantity of the species of millet which is known as durra. But though the Shilluk

[side note: Shilluk custom of putting divine kings to death.]

---

[1] J. Russegger, *Reisen in Europa, Asien und Afrika*, ii. 2, p. 553. Russegger met Assusa in January 1838, and says that the king had then been a year in office. He does not mention the name of the king's uncle who had, he tells us, been strangled by the chiefs ; but I assume that he was the Yassin who is mentioned by Brun-Rollet. Russegger adds that the strangling of the king was performed publicly, and in the most solemn manner, and was said to happen often in Fazoql and the neighbouring countries.

[2] R. Lepsius, *Letters from Egypt, Ethiopia, and the peninsula of Sinai* (London, 1853), p. 204. Lepsius's letter is dated "The Pyramids of Meroë, 22nd April 1844." His informant was Osman Bey, who had lived for sixteen years in these regions. An *anqareb* or *angareb* is a kind of bed made by stretching string or leather thongs over an oblong wooden framework.

[3] I have to thank Dr. Seligmann for his kindness and courtesy in transmitting to me his unpublished account and allowing me to draw on it at my discretion.

are mainly a pastoral people, they are not nomadic, but live in many settled villages. The tribe at present numbers about forty thousand souls, and is governed by a single king (*ret*), whose residence is at Fashoda. His subjects take great care of him, and hold him in much honour. In the old days his word was law and he was not suffered to go forth to battle. At the present day he still keeps up considerable state and exercises much authority ; his decisions on all matters brought before him are readily obeyed ; and he never moves without a bodyguard of from twelve to twenty men. The reverence which the Shilluk pay to their king appears to arise chiefly from the conviction that he is a reincarnation of the spirit of Nyakang, the semi-divine hero who founded the dynasty and settled the tribe in their present territory, to which he is variously said to have conducted them either from the west or from the south. Tradition has preserved the pedigree of the kings from Nyakang to the present day. The number of kings recorded between Nyakang and the father of the reigning monarch is twenty, distributed over twelve generations ; but Dr. Seligmann is of opinion that many more must have reigned, and that the genealogy of the first six or seven kings, as given to him, has been much abbreviated. There seems to be no reason to doubt the historical character of all of them, though myths have gathered like clouds round the persons of Nyakang and his immediate successors. The Shilluk about Kodok (Fashoda) think of Nyakang as having been a man in appearance and physical qualities, though unlike his royal descendants of more recent times he did not die but simply disappeared. His holiness is manifested especially by his relation to Jŭok, the great god of the Shilluk, who created man and is responsible for the order of nature. Jŭok is formless and invisible and like the air he is everywhere at once. He is far above Nyakang and men alike, but he is not worshipped directly, and it is only through the intercession of Nyakang, whose favour the Shilluk secure by means of sacrifices, that Jŭok can be induced to send the needed rain for the cattle and the crops.[1]   In his character

The Shilluk kings supposed to be reincarnations of Nyakang, the semi-divine founder of the dynasty.

---

[1] As to Jŭok (Čuok), the supreme being of the Shilluk, see P. W. Hofmayr, "Religion der Schilluk," *Anthropos*, vi. (1911) pp. 120-122, whose account

of rain-giver Nyakang is the great benefactor of the Shilluk. Their country, baked by the burning heat of the tropical sun, depends entirely for its fertility on the waters of heaven, for the people do not resort to artificial irrigation. When the rain falls, then the grass sprouts, the millet grows, the cattle thrive, and the people have food to eat. Drought brings famine and death in its train.[1] Nyakang is said not only to have brought the Shilluk into their present land, but to have made them into a nation of warriors, divided the country among them, regulated marriage, and made the laws.[2] The religion of the Shilluk at the present time consists mainly of the worship paid to this semi-divine hero, the traditionary ancestor of their kings. There seems to be no reason to doubt that the traditions concerning him are substantially correct ; in all probability he was simply a man whom the superstition of his fellows in his own and subsequent ages has raised to the rank of a deity.[3] No less than ten shrines are dedicated to his worship ; the three most famous are at Fashoda, Akurwa, and Fenikang. They consist of one or more huts enclosed by a fence ; generally there are several huts within the enclosure, one or more of them being occupied by the guardians of the shrine. These guardians are old men, who not only keep the hallowed spot scrupulously clean, but also act as priests, killing the sacrificial victims which are brought to the shrine, sharing their flesh, and taking the skins for themselves. All the shrines of Nyakang are called graves of Nyakang (*kengo Nyakang*), though it is well known that nobody is buried there.[4] Sacred spears are kept in all of them and are used to slaughter the victims offered in sacrifice at the shrines. The originals of these spears are said to have belonged to Nyakang and his companions, but they have disappeared and been replaced by others.

The shrines of Nyakang.

agrees with the briefer one given by Dr. C. G. Seligmann. Otiose supreme beings (*dieux fainéants*) of this type, who having made the world do not meddle with it and to whom little or no worship is paid, are common in Africa.

[1] P. W. Hofmayr, "Religion der Schilluk," *Anthropos*, vi. (1911) pp. 123, 125. This writer gives Nykang

as the name of the first Shilluk king.

[2] P. W. Hofmayr, *op. cit.* p. 123.

[3] This is the view both of Dr. C. G. Seligmann and of Father P. W. Hofmayr (*op. cit.* p. 123).

[4] The word *kengo* is applied only to the shrines of Nyakang and the graves of the kings. Graves of commoners are called *roro*.

Annual
rain-
making
ceremony
performed
at the
shrines of
Nyakang.
Two great ceremonies are annually performed at the shrines of Nyakang: one of them is intended to ensure the fall of rain, the other is celebrated at harvest. At the rain-making ceremony, which is held before the rains at the beginning of the month *alabor*, a bullock is slain with a sacred spear before the door of the shrine, while the king stands by praying in a loud voice to Nyakang to send down the refreshing showers on the thirsty land. As much of the blood of the victim as possible is collected in a gourd and thrown into the river, perhaps as a rain-charm. This intention of the sacrifice comes out more plainly in a form of the ritual which is said to be observed at Ashop. There the sacrificial bullock is speared high up in the flank, so that the wound is not immediately fatal. Then the wounded animal is allowed and indeed encouraged to walk to and from the river before it sinks down and dies. In the blood that streams from its side on the ground the people may see a symbol of the looked-for rain.[1] Care is taken not to break the bones of the animal, and they, like the blood, are thrown into the river. At the annual rain-making ceremony a cow is also dedicated to Nyakang: it is not killed but added to the sacred herd of the shrine. The other great annual ceremony observed at the shrines of Nyakang falls at harvest.

When the millet has been reaped, every one brings a portion of the grain to a shrine of Nyakang, where it is ground into flour, which is made into porridge with water fetched from the river. Then some of the porridge is poured out on the threshold of the hut which the spirit of Nyakang is supposed to inhabit; some of it is smeared on the outer walls of the building; and some of it is emptied out on the ground outside. Even before harvest it is customary to bring some of the ripening grain from the fields and to thrust it into the thatch of the huts in the shrines, no doubt in order to secure the blessing of Nyakang on the crops. Sacrifices are also offered at these shrines for the benefit of sick people. A sufferer will bring or send a sheep to the nearest sanctuary, where the guardians will slaughter the animal with a sacred spear and pray for the patient's recovery.

---

[1] On the use of flowing blood in rain-making ceremonies see *The Magic*   *Art and the Evolution of Kings*, i. 256, 257 *sq.*

It is a fundamental article of the Shilluk creed that the spirit of the divine or semi-divine Nyakang is incarnate in the reigning king, who is accordingly himself invested to some extent with the character of a divinity. But while the Shilluk hold their kings in high, indeed religious reverence and take every precaution against their accidental death, nevertheless they cherish "the conviction that the king must not be allowed to become ill or senile, lest with his diminishing vigour the cattle should sicken and fail to bear their increase, the crops should rot in the fields, and man, stricken with disease, should die in ever increasing numbers." [1] To prevent these calamities it used to be the regular custom with the Shilluk to put the king to death whenever he shewed signs of ill-health or failing strength. One of the fatal symptoms of decay was taken to be an incapacity to satisfy the sexual passions of his wives, of whom he has very many, distributed in a large number of houses at Fashoda. When this ominous weakness manifested itself, the wives reported it to the chiefs, who are popularly said to have intimated to the king his doom by spreading a white cloth over his face and knees as he lay slumbering in the heat of the sultry afternoon. Execution soon followed the sentence of death. A hut was specially built for the occasion : the king was led into it and lay down with his head resting on the lap of a nubile virgin : the door of the hut was then walled up ; and the couple were left without food, water, or fire to die of hunger and suffocation. This was the old custom, but it was abolished some five generations ago on account of the excessive sufferings of one of the kings who perished in this way. He survived his companion for some days, and in the interval was so distressed by the stench of her putrefying body that he shouted to the people, whom he could hear moving outside, never again to let a king die in this prolonged and exquisite agony. After a time his cries died away into silence ; death had released him from his sufferings ; but since then the Shilluk have adopted a quicker and more merciful mode of executing their kings. What the exact form of execution has been in later times Dr. Seligmann found it very difficult to ascertain,

[1] Dr. C. G. Seligmann, *The Shilluk Divine Kings* (in manuscript).

though with regard to the fact of the execution he tells us that there is not the least doubt. It is said that the chiefs announce his fate to the king, and that afterwards he is strangled in a hut which has been specially built for the occasion.

Shilluk kings formerly liable to be attacked and killed at any time by rival claimants to the throne.

From Dr. Seligmann's enquiries it appears that not only was the Shilluk king liable to be killed with due ceremony at the first symptoms of incipient decay, but even while he was yet in the prime of health and strength he might be attacked at any time by a rival and have to defend his crown in a combat to the death. According to the common Shilluk tradition any son of a king had the right thus to fight the king in possession and, if he succeeded in killing him, to reign in his stead. As every king had a large harem and many sons, the number of possible candidates for the throne at any time may well have been not inconsiderable, and the reigning monarch must have carried his life in his hand. But the attack on him could only take place with any prospect of success at night; for during the day the king surrounded himself with his friends and bodyguards, and an aspirant to the throne could hardly hope to cut his way through them and strike home. It was otherwise at night. For then the guards were dismissed and the king was alone in his enclosure with his favourite wives, and there was no man near to defend him except a few herdsmen, whose huts stood a little way off. The hours of darkness were therefore the season of peril for the king. It is said that he used to pass them in constant watchfulness, prowling round his huts fully armed, peering into the blackest shadows, or himself standing silent and alert, like a sentinel on duty, in some dark corner. When at last his rival appeared, the fight would take place in grim silence, broken only by the clash of spears and shields, for it was a point of honour with the king not to call the herdsmen to his assistance.[1]

When the king did not perish in single combat, but was

---

[1] On this subject Dr. Seligmann writes to me (March 9th, 1911) as follows: "The assumption of the throne as the result of victory in single combat doubtless occurred once; at the present day and perhaps for the whole of the historic period it has been superseded by the ceremonial killing of the king, but I regard these stories as folk-lore indicating what once really happened."

put to death on the approach of sickness or old age, it became necessary to find a successor for him. Apparently the successor was chosen by the most powerful chiefs from among the princes (*niǎret*), the sons either of the late king or of one of his predecessors. Details as to the mode of election are lacking. So far as Dr. Seligmann could ascertain, the kings elect shewed no reluctance to accept the fatal sovereignty ; indeed he was told a story of a man who clamoured to be made king for only one day, saying that he was perfectly ready to be killed after that. The age at which the king was killed would seem to have commonly been between forty and fifty.[1] To the improvident and unimaginative savage the prospect of being put to death at the end of a set time, whether long or short, has probably few terrors ; and if it has any, we may suspect that they are altogether outweighed in his mind by the opportunities for immediate enjoyment of all kinds which a kingdom affords to his unbridled appetites and passions.

An important part of the solemnities attending the accession of a Shilluk king appears to be intended to convey to the new monarch the divine spirit of Nyakang, which has been transmitted from the founder of the dynasty to all his successors on the throne. For this purpose a sacred four-legged stool and a mysterious object which bears the name of Nyakang himself are brought with much solemnity from the shrine of Nyakang at Akurwa to the small village of Kwom near Fashoda, where the king elect and the chiefs await their arrival. The thing called Nyakang is said to be of cylindrical shape, some two or three feet long by six inches broad. The chief of Akurwa informed Dr. Seligmann that the object in question is a rude wooden figure of a man, which was fashioned long ago at the command of Nyakang in person. We may suppose that it represents the divine king himself and that it is, or was formerly, supposed to house his spirit, though the chief of Akurwa denied to Dr. Seligmann that it does so now. Be that as it may, the object plays a prominent part at the installation of a new

Ceremonies at the accession of a Shilluk king.

---

[1] These particulars I take from letters of Dr. C. G. Seligmann's to me (dated 8th February and 9th March 1911). They are not mentioned in the writer's paper on the subject.

king. When the men of Akurwa arrive at Kwom with the sacred stool and the image of Nyakang, as we may call it, they engage in a sham fight with the men who are waiting for them with the king elect. The weapons used on both sides are simply stalks of millet. Being victorious in the mock combat, the men of Akurwa escort the king to Fashoda, and some of them enter the shrine of Nyakang with the stool. After a short time they bring the stool forth again and set it on the ground outside of the sacred enclosure. Then the image of Nyakang is placed on the stool; the king elect holds one leg of the stool and an important chief holds another. The king is surrounded by a crowd of princes and nobles, and near him stand two of his paternal aunts and two of his sisters. After that a bullock is killed and its flesh eaten by the men of certain families called *ororo*, who are said to be descended from the third of the Shilluk kings. Then the Akurwa men carry the image of Nyakang into the shrine, and the *ororo* men place the king elect on the sacred stool, where he remains seated for some time, apparently till sunset. When he rises, the Akurwa men carry the stool back into the shrine, and the king is escorted to three new huts, where he stays in seclusion for three days. On the fourth night he is conducted quietly, almost stealthily, to his royal residence at Fashoda, and next day he shews himself publicly to his subjects. The three new huts in which he spent the days of his seclusion are then broken up and their fragments cast into the river. The installation of a new king generally takes place about the middle of the dry season; and it is said that the men of Akurwa tarry at Fashoda with the image of Nyakang till about the beginning of the rains. Before they leave Fashoda they sacrifice a bullock, and at every waddy or bed of a stream that they cross they kill a sheep.

Worship of the dead Shilluk kings. Like Nyakang himself, their founder, each of the Shilluk kings after death is worshipped at a shrine, which is erected over his grave, and the grave of a king is always in the village where he was born.[1] The tomb-shrine of a king

---

[1] When one of the king's wives is with child, she remains at Fashoda till the fourth or fifth month of her pregnancy; she is then sent away to a village, not necessarily her own, where she remains under the charge of the village chief until she has finished nursing the child. Afterwards she returns to Fashoda, but the child invariably remains in the village of his

resembles the shrine of Nyakang, consisting of a few huts
enclosed by a fence; one of the huts is built over the
king's grave, the others are occupied by the guardians of
the shrine. Indeed the shrines of Nyakang and the shrines
of the kings are scarcely to be distinguished from each
other, and the religious rituals observed at all of them
are identical in form and vary only in matters of detail,
the variations being due apparently to the far greater
sanctity attributed to the shrines of Nyakang. The grave-
shrines of the kings are tended by certain old men or women,
who correspond to the guardians of the shrines of Nyakang.
They are usually widows or old men-servants of the deceased
king, and when they die they are succeeded in their office
by their descendants. Moreover, cattle are dedicated to the
grave-shrines of the kings and sacrifices are offered at them
just as at the shrines of Nyakang. Thus when the millet
crop threatens to fail or a murrain to break out among the
cattle, either Nyakang himself or one of his successors on
the throne will appear to somebody in a dream and demand
a sacrifice. The dream is reported to the king, who thereupon at once sends a cow and a bullock to one or more of
the shrines of Nyakang, if it was he who appeared in the
vision, or to the grave-shrine of the particular king whom
the dreamer saw in his dream. The bullock is then sacrificed
and the cow added to the sacred herd belonging to the
shrine. Further, the harvest ceremony which is performed
at the shrines of Nyakang is usually, though not necessarily,
performed also at the grave-shrines of the kings; and, lastly,
sick folk send animals to be sacrificed as offerings on their
behalf at the shrines of the kings just as they send them to
the shrines of Nyakang.

Sick people have, indeed, a special reason for sacrificing
to the spirits of the dead kings in the hope of recovery,
inasmuch as one of the commonest causes of sickness,
according to the Shilluk, is the entrance of one of these
royal spirits into the body of the sufferer, whose first care,
therefore, is to rid himself as quickly as possible of his

Sick people and others supposed to be possessed by the spirits of dead Shilluk kings.

or her birth and is brought up there.
All royal children of either sex, in
whatever part of the Shilluk territory
they may happen to die, are buried in
the village where they were born.

august but unwelcome guest.   Apparently, however, it is
only the souls of the early kings who manifest themselves in
this disagreeable fashion.   Dr. Seligmann met with a woman,
for example, who had been ill and who attributed her illness
to the spirit of Dag, the second of the Shilluk kings, which
had taken possession of her body.   But a sacrifice of two
sheep had induced the spirit to quit her, and she wore anklets
of beads, with pieces of the ears of the sheep strung on them,
which she thought would effectually guard her against the
danger of being again possessed by the soul of the dead
king.   Nor is it only in sickness that the souls of dead kings
are thought to take possession of the bodies of the living.
Certain men and women, who bear the name of *ajuago*,
are believed to be permanently possessed by the spirit of
one or other of the early kings, and in virtue of this
inspiration they profess to heal the sick and do a brisk
trade in amulets.   The first symptom of possession may
take the form of illness or of a dream from which the sleeper
awakes trembling and agitated.   A long and complicated
ceremony follows to abate the extreme force of the spiritual
manifestations in the new medium, for were these to continue
in their first intensity he would not dare to approach his
women.   But whichever of the dead kings may manifest
himself to the living, whether in dreams or in the form of
bodily possession, his spirit is deemed, at least by many of
the Shilluk, to be identical with that of Nyakang ; they do
not clearly distinguish, if indeed they distinguish at all,
between the divine spirit of the founder of the dynasty and
its later manifestations in all his royal successors.

The
principal
element
in the
religion
of the
Shilluk is
the worship
of their
kings.
In general the principal element in the religion of the
Shilluk would seem to be the worship which they pay to
their sacred or divine kings, whether dead or alive.   These
are believed to be animated by a single divine spirit, which
has been transmitted from the semi-mythical, but probably
in substance historical, founder of the dynasty through all
his successors to the present day.   Yet the divine spirit, as
Dr. Seligmann justly observes, is clearly not thought of as
congenital in the members of the royal house ; it is only con-
veyed to each king on his accession by means of the mysterious
object called Nyakang, in which, as Dr. Seligmann with great

probability conjectures, the holy spirit of Nyakang may be supposed to reside. Hence, regarding their kings as incarnate divinities on whom the welfare of men, of cattle, and of the corn implicitly depends, the Shilluk naturally pay them the greatest respect and take every care of them ; and however strange it may seem to us, their custom of putting the divine king to death as soon as he shews signs of ill-health or failing strength springs directly from their profound venera- tion for him and from their anxiety to preserve him, or rather the divine spirit by which he is animated, in the most perfect state of efficiency : nay, we may go further and say that their practice of regicide is the best proof they can give of the high regard in which they hold their kings. For they believe, as we have seen, that the king's life or spirit is so sympathetically bound up with the prosperity of the whole country, that if he fell ill or grew senile the cattle would sicken and cease to multiply, the crops would rot in the fields, and men would perish of widespread disease. Hence, in their opinion, the only way of averting these calamities is to put the king to death while he is still hale and hearty, in order that the divine spirit which he has inherited from his predecessors may be transmitted in turn by him to his successor while it is still in full vigour and has not yet been impaired by the weakness of disease and old age. In this connexion the particular symptom which is commonly said to seal the king's death-warrant is highly significant ; when he can no longer satisfy the passions of his numerous wives, in other words, when he has ceased, whether partially or wholly, to be able to reproduce his kind, it is time for him to die and to make room for a more vigorous successor. Taken along with the other reasons which are alleged for putting the king to death, this one suggests that the fertility of men, of cattle, and of the crops is believed to depend sympathetic- ally on the generative power of the king, so that the complete failure of that power in him would involve a corresponding failure in men, animals, and plants, and would thereby entail at no distant date the entire extinction of all life, whether human, animal, or vegetable. No wonder, that with such a danger before their eyes the Shilluk should be most careful not to let the king die what we should call a

The kings put to death in order to preserve their divine spirit from natural de- cay, which would sympa- thetically affect the crops, the cattle, and mankind.

natural death of sickness or old age. It is characteristic of their attitude towards the death of the kings that they refrain from speaking of it as death : they do not say that a king has died but simply that he has " gone away " like his divine ancestors Nyakang and Dag, the two first kings of the dynasty, both of whom are reported not to have died but to have disappeared. The similar legends of the mysterious disappearance of early kings in other lands, for example at Rome and in Uganda,[1] may well point to a similar custom of putting them to death for the purpose of preserving their life.

Parallel between the Shilluk kings and the King of the Wood at Nemi.

On the whole the theory and practice of the divine kings of the Shilluk correspond very nearly to the theory and practice of the priests of Nemi, the Kings of the Wood, if my view of the latter is correct.[2] In both we see a series of divine kings on whose life the fertility of men, of cattle, and of vegetation is believed to depend, and who are put to death, whether in single combat or otherwise, in order that their divine spirit may be transmitted to their successors in full vigour, uncontaminated by the weakness and decay of sickness or old age, because any such degeneration on the part of the king would, in the opinion of his worshippers, entail a corresponding degeneration on mankind, on cattle, and on the crops. Some points in this explanation of the custom of putting divine kings to death, particularly the method of transmitting their divine souls to their successors, will be dealt with more fully in the sequel. Meantime we pass to other examples of the general practice.

The Dinka of the Upper Nile.

The Dinka are a congeries of independent tribes in the valley of the White Nile, whose territory, lying mostly on the eastern bank of the river and stretching from the sixth to the twelfth degree of North Latitude, has been estimated to comprise between sixty and seventy thousand square miles. They are a tall long-legged people rather slender than fat, with curly hair and a complexion of the deepest black. Though ill-fed, they are strong and healthy and in general reach a great age. The nation embraces a number of independent

---

[1] As to the disappearance of the early Roman kings see *The Magic Art and the Evolution of Kings*, vol. ii. pp. 312 *sqq.* ; as to the disappearance of the early kings of Uganda, see the Rev.

J. Roscoe, *The Baganda* (London, 1911), p. 214.

[2] See *The Magic Art and the Evolution of Kings*, i. 1 *sqq.*, ii. 376 *sqq.*

tribes, and each tribe is mainly composed of the owners of
cattle ; for the Dinka are essentially a pastoral people,
passionately devoted to the care of their numerous herds
of oxen, though they also keep sheep and goats, and the
women cultivate small quantities of millet (durra) and
sesame.   The tribes have no political union.   Each village
forms a separate community, pasturing its herds together in
the same grass-land.   With the change of the seasons the
people migrate with their flocks and herds to and from the
banks of the Nile.   In summer, when the plains near the great
river are converted into swamps and covered with clouds of
mosquitoes, the herdsmen and their families drive their beasts
to the higher land of the interior, where the animals find firm
ground, abundant fodder, and pools of water at which to slake
their thirst in the fervour of the noonday heat.   Here in the
clearings of the forest the community takes up its abode, each
family dwelling by itself in one or more conical huts enclosed
by a strong fence of stakes and thorn-bushes.   It is in the
patches of open ground about these dwellings that the women
grow their scanty crops of millet and sesame.   The mode of
tillage is rude.   The stumps of the trees which have been
felled are left standing to a height of several feet ; the ground
is hacked by the help of a tool between a hoe and a spade,
and the weeds are uprooted with the hand.   Such as it is,
the crop is exposed to the ravages of apes and elephants by
night and of birds by day.   The hungry blacks do not
always wait till the corn is ripe, but eat much of it while
the ears are still green.   The cattle are kept in separate
parks (*murahs*) away from the villages.   It is in the season.
of the summer rains that the Dinka are most happy and
prosperous.   Then the cattle find sweet grass, plentiful
water, coolness and shade in the forest ; then the people
subsist in comfort on the milk of their flocks and herds,
supplementing it with the millet which they reap and the
wild fruits which they gather in the forest ; then they brew
the native beer, then they marry and dance by night under
the bright moon of the serene tropical sky.   But in autumn
a great change passes over the life of the community.
When October has come, the rains are over, the grass of
the pastures is eaten down or withered, the pools are dry ;

thirst compels the whole village, with its lowing herds and bleating flocks, to migrate to the neighbourhood of the river. Now begins a time of privation and suffering.   There is no grass for the cattle save in some marshy spots, where the herdsman must fight his rivals in order to win a meagre supply of fodder for his starveling beasts.   There is no milk for the people, no fruits on the trees, except a bitter sort of acorns, from which a miserable flour is ground to stay the pangs of hunger.   The lean and famished natives are driven to fish in the river for the tubers of water-lilies, to grub in the earth for roots, to boil the leaves of trees, and as a last resource to drink the blood drawn from the necks of their wretched cattle. The gaunt appearance of the people at this season fills the beholder with horror.   The herds are decimated by famine, but even more beasts perish by dysentery and other diseases when the first rains cause the fresh grass to sprout.[1]

Dengdit, the Supreme Being of the Dinka.

It is no wonder that the rain, on which the Dinka are so manifestly dependent for their subsistence, should play a great part in their religion and superstition.   They worship a supreme being whose name of Dengdit means literally Great Rain.[2]   It was he who created the world and established the present order of things, and it is he who sends down the rain from the "rain-place," his home in the upper regions of the air.   But according to the Niel Dinka this

Totemism of the Dinka.

great being was once incarnate in human form.   Born of a woman, who descended from the sky, he became the ancestor of a clan which has the rain for its totem ; for the recent researches of Dr. C. G. Seligmann have proved that every Dinka tribe is divided into a number of clans, each of which

[1] "E. de Pruyssenaere's Reisen und Forschungen im Gebiete des Weissen und Blauen Nil," *Petermann's Mittheilungen, Ergänzungsheft*, No. 50 (Gotha, 1877), pp. 18-23.   Compare G. Schweinfurth, *The Heart of Africa*, Third Edition (London, 1878), i. 48 *sqq.*   In the text I have followed de Pruyssenaere's description of the privations endured by the Dinka in the dry season.   But that description is perhaps only applicable in seasons of unusual drought, for Dr. C. G. Seligmann, writing from personal observation, informs me that he regards the description

as much overdrawn ; in an average year, he tells me, the cattle do not die of famine and the natives are not starving. According to his information the drinking of the blood of their cattle is a luxury in which the Dinka indulge themselves at any time of the year.

[2] For this and the following information as to the religion, totemism, and rain-makers of the Dinka I am indebted to the kindness of Dr. C. G. Seligmann, who investigated the Shilluk and Dinka in 1909-1910 and has most obligingly placed his manuscript materials at my disposal.

reveres as its totem a species of animals or plants or other
natural objects, such as rain or fire. Animal totems seem
to be the commonest ; amongst them are the lion, the
elephant, the crocodile, the hippopotamus, the fox, the
hyaena, and a species of small birds called *amur*, clouds of
which infest the cornfields and do great damage to the
crops. Each clan speaks of its totemic animal or plant
as its ancestor and refrains from injuring and eating it.
Men of the Crocodile clan, for example, call themselves
" Brothers of the Crocodile," and will neither kill nor eat the
animal ; indeed they will not even eat out of any vessel
which has held crocodile flesh. And as they do not injure
crocodiles, so they imagine that their crocodile kinsfolk will
not injure them ; hence men of this clan swim freely in the
river, even by night, without fear of being attacked by the
dangerous reptiles. And when the totem is a carnivorous
animal, members of the clan may propitiate it by killing sheep
and throwing out the flesh to be devoured by their animal
brethren either on the outskirts of the village or in the river.
Members of the Small Bird (*amur*) clan perform ceremonies
to prevent the birds from injuring the crops. The relationship between a clan and its animal ancestor or totem is
commonly explained by a legend that in the beginning an
ancestress gave birth to twins, one of whom was the totemic
animal and the other the human ancestor. Like most totemic
clans, the clans of the Dinka are exogamous, that is, no man
may marry a woman of his own clan. The descent of the
clans is in the paternal line ; in other words, every man and
woman belongs to his or her father's clan, not to that of his
or her mother. But the Rain clan of the Niel Dinka has for
its ancestor, as we have seen, the supreme god himself, who
deigned to be born of a woman and to live for a long time
among men, ruling over them, till at last he grew very old and
disappeared appropriately, like Romulus, in a great storm of
rain. Shrines erected in his honour appear to be scattered
all over the Dinka country and offerings are made at them.

Perhaps without being unduly rash we may conjecture
that the great god of the Dinka, who gives them the rain,
was indeed, what tradition represents him as having been, a
man among men, in fact a human rain-maker, whom at his
Rain-
makers
among the
Dinka.

Rain
makers
among the
Dinka.
death the superstition of his fellows promoted to the rank of a deity above the clouds. Be that as it may, the human rain-maker (*bain*) is a very important personage among the Dinka to this day; indeed the men in authority whom travellers dub chiefs or sheikhs are in fact the actual or potential rain-makers of the tribe or community.[1] Each of them is believed to be animated by the spirit of a great rain-maker, which has come down to him through a succession of rain-makers; and in virtue of this inspiration a successful rain-maker enjoys very great power and is consulted on all important matters. For example, in the Bor tribe of Dinka at the present time there is an old but active rain-maker named Biyordit, who is reputed to have immanent in him a great and powerful spirit called Lerpiu, and by reason of this reputation he exercises immense influence over all the Dinka of the Bor and Tain tribes. While the mighty spirit Lerpiu is supposed to be embodied in the rain-maker, it is also thought to inhabit a certain hut which serves as a shrine. In front of the hut stands a post to which are fastened the horns of many bullocks that have been sacrificed to Lerpiu; and in the hut is kept a very sacred spear which bears the name of Lerpiu and is said to have fallen from heaven six generations ago. As fallen stars are also called Lerpiu, we may suspect that an intimate connexion is supposed to exist between meteorites and the spirit which animates the rain-maker; nor would such a connexion seem unnatural to the savage, who observes that meteorites and rain alike descend from the sky. In spring, about the month of April, when the new moon is a few days old, a sacrifice of bullocks is offered to Lerpiu for the purpose of inducing him to move Dengdit, the great heavenly rain-maker, to send down rain on the parched and thirsty earth. Two bullocks are led twice round the shrine and afterwards tied by the rain-maker to the post in front of it. Then the drums beat and the people, old and young, men and women, dance round the shrine and sing, while the beasts are being sacrificed, " Lerpiu, our ancestor, we have brought you a sacrifice. Be

---

[1] On the importance of the rain-makers among the Dinka and other tribes of the Upper Nile, see *The* *Magic Art and the Evolution of Kings*, i. 345 *sqq.*

pleased to cause rain to fall." The blood of the bullocks is collected in a gourd, boiled in a pot on the fire, and eaten by the old and important people of the clan. The horns of the animals are attached to the post in front of the shrine.

In spite, or rather in virtue, of the high honour in which he is held, no Dinka rain-maker is allowed to die a natural death of sickness or old age ; for the Dinka believe that if such an untoward event were to happen, the tribe would suffer from disease and famine, and the herds would not yield their increase. So when a rain-maker feels that he is growing old and infirm, he tells his children that he wishes to die. Among the Agar Dinka a large grave is dug and the rain-maker lies down in it on his right side with his head resting on a skin. He is surrounded by his friends and relatives, including his younger children ; but his elder children are not allowed to approach the grave lest in their grief and despair they should do themselves a bodily injury. For many hours, generally for more than a day, the rain-maker lies without eating or drinking. From time to time he speaks to the people, recalling the past history of the tribe, reminding them how he has ruled and advised them, and instructing them how they are to act in the future. Then, when he has concluded his admonition, he tells them that it is finished and bids them cover him up. So the earth is thrown down on him as he lies in the grave, and he soon dies of suffocation. Such, with minor variations, appears to be the regular end of the honourable career of a rain-maker in all the Dinka tribes. The Khor-Adar Dinka told Dr. Seligmann that when they have dug the grave for their rain-maker they strangle him in his house. The father and paternal uncle of one of Dr. Seligmann's informants had both been rain-makers and both had been killed in the most regular and orthodox fashion. Even if a rain-maker is quite young he will be put to death should he seem likely to perish of disease. Further, every precaution is taken to prevent a rain-maker from dying an accidental death, for such an end, though not nearly so serious a matter as death from illness or old age, would be sure to entail sickness on the tribe. As soon as a rain-maker is killed, his valuable spirit is supposed to pass to a suitable successor, whether a son or other near blood relation.

Dinka rain-makers not allowed to die a natural death.

Kings
put to
death in
Unyoro
and other
parts of
Africa.

In the Central African kingdom of Unyoro down to
recent years custom required that as soon as the king fell
seriously ill or began to break up from age, he should die by
his own hand ; for, according to an old prophecy, the
throne would pass away from the dynasty if ever the king
were to die a natural death. He killed himself by
draining a poisoned cup. If he faltered or were too ill to
ask for the cup, it was his wife's duty to administer the
poison.[1] When the king of Kibanga, on the Upper
Congo, seems near his end, the sorcerers put a rope round
his neck, which they draw gradually tighter till he dies.[2]
If the king of Gingero happens to be wounded in war, he is
put to death by his comrades, or, if they fail to kill him, by
his kinsfolk, however hard he may beg for mercy. They
say they do it that he may not die by the hands of his
enemies.[3] The Jukos are a heathen tribe of the Benue
river, a great tributary of the Niger. In their country " the
town of Gatri is ruled by a king who is elected by the
big men of the town as follows. When in the opinion of
the big men the king has reigned long enough, they give
out that ' the king is sick '—a formula understood by all to
mean that they are going to kill him, though the intention
is never put more plainly. They then decide who is to be
the next king. How long he is to reign is settled by the
influential men at a meeting ; the question is put and
answered by each man throwing on the ground a little piece
of stick for each year he thinks the new king should rule.
The king is then told, and a great feast prepared, at which
the king gets drunk on guinea-corn beer. After that he is
speared, and the man who was chosen becomes king. Thus
each Juko king knows that he cannot have very many more
years to live, and that he is certain of his predecessor's fate.
This, however, does not seem to frighten candidates. The

[1] *Emin Pasha in Central Africa,
being a Collection of his Letters and
Journals* (London, 1888), p. 91 ; J. G.
Frazer, *Totemism and Exogamy*, ii.
529 *sq.* (from information given by the
Rev. John Roscoe).

[2] Father Guillemé, in *Annales de la
Propagation de la Foi*, lx. (1888) p. 258 ;
id., " Credenze religiose dei Negri di

Kibanga nell' Alto Congo," *Archivio
per lo studio delle tradizioni popolari*,
vii. (1888) p. 231.

[3] *The Travels of the Jesuits in
Ethiopia*, collected and historically
digested by F. Balthazar Tellez, of the
Society of Jesus (London, 1710), p.
197. We may compare the death of
Saul (1 Samuel, xxxi. 3-6).

same custom of king-killing is said to prevail at Quonde and Wukari as well as at Gatri."[1] In the three Hausa kingdoms of Gobir, Katsina, and Daura, in Northern Nigeria, as soon as a king shewed signs of failing health or growing infirmity, an official who bore the title of Killer of the Elephant (*kariagiwa*) appeared and throttled him by holding his windpipe. The king elect was afterwards conducted to the centre of the town, called Head of the Elephant (*kan giwa*), where he was made to lie down on a bed. Then a black ox was slaughtered and its blood allowed to pour all over his body. Next the ox was flayed, and the remains of the dead king, which had been disembowelled and smoked for seven days over a slow fire, were wrapt up in the hide and dragged along the ground to the place of burial, where they were interred in a circular pit. After his bath of ox blood the new king had to remain for seven days in his mother's house, undergoing ablutions daily. On the eighth day he was conducted in state to his palace. In the kingdom of Daura the new monarch had moreover to step over the corpse of his predecessor.[2]

The Matiamvo is a great king or emperor in the interior of Angola. One of the inferior kings of the country, by name Challa, gave to a Portuguese expedition the following account of the manner in which the Matiamvo comes by his end. " It has been customary," he said, " for our Matiamvos to die either in war or by a violent death, and the present Matiamvo must meet this last fate, as, in consequence of his great exactions, he has lived long enough. When we come to this understanding, and decide that he should be killed, we invite him to make war with our enemies, on which occasion we all accompany him and his family to the war, when we lose some of our people. If he escapes unhurt, we return to the war again and fight for three or four days. We then suddenly abandon him and his family to their fate, leaving him in the enemy's hands. Seeing himself thus deserted, he causes his throne to be erected, and, sitting down, calls his family around him.

The Matiamvo of Angola.

---

[1] Lieut. H. Pope-Hennessy, "Notes on the Jukos and other Tribes of the Middle Benue," *Journal of the Anthropological Institute*, xxx. (1900) p. (29).

[2] J. G. Frazer, *Totemism and Exogamy*, ii. 608, on the authority of Mr. H. R. Palmer, Resident in Charge of Katsina.

He then orders his mother to approach ; she kneels at his feet ; he first cuts off her head, then decapitates his sons in succession, next his wives and relatives, and, last of all, his most beloved wife, called Anacullo. This slaughter being accomplished, the Matiamvo, dressed in all his pomp, awaits his own death, which immediately follows, by an officer sent by the powerful neighbouring chiefs, Caniquinha and Canica. This officer first cuts off his legs and arms at the joints, and lastly he cuts off his head ; after which the head of the officer is struck off. All the potentates retire from the encamp⌐ ment, in order not to witness his death. It is my duty to remain and witness his death, and to mark the place where the head and arms have been deposited by the two great chiefs, the enemies of the Matiamvo. They also take possession of all the property belonging to the deceased monarch and his family, which they convey to their own residence. I then provide for the funeral of the mutilated remains of the late Matiamvo, after which I retire to his capital and proclaim the new government. I then return to where the head, legs, and arms have been deposited, and, for forty slaves, I ransom them, together with the merchandise and other property belonging to the deceased, which I give up to the new Matiamvo, who has been proclaimed. This is what has happened to many Matiamvos, and what must happen to the present one." [1]

Zulu kings put to death on the approach of old age.

It appears to have been a Zulu custom to put the king to death as soon as he began to have wrinkles or grey hairs. At least this seems implied in the following passage written by one who resided for some time at the court of the notorious Zulu tyrant Chaka, in the early part of the nineteenth century : " The extraordinary violence of the king's rage with me was mainly occasioned by that absurd nostrum, the hair oil, with the notion of which Mr. Farewell had impressed him as being a specific for removing all indications of age. From the first moment of his having heard that such a preparation was attainable, he evinced a solicitude to procure it, and on every occasion never forgot to remind us of his anxiety respecting it ; more especially on our departure on the mission his injunctions were particularly directed to

---

[1] F. T. Valdez, *Six Years of a Traveller's Life in Western Africa* (London, 1861), ii. 194 *sq.*

this object. It will be seen that it is one of the barbarous customs of the Zoolas in their choice or election of their kings that he must neither have wrinkles nor grey hairs, as they are both distinguishing marks of disqualification for becoming a monarch of a warlike people. It is also equally indispensable that their king should never exhibit those proofs of having become unfit and incompetent to reign ; it is therefore important that they should conceal these indications so long as they possibly can. Chaka had become greatly apprehensive of the approach of grey hairs ; which would at once be the signal for him to prepare to make his exit from this sublunary world, it being always followed by the death of the monarch."[1] The writer to whom we are indebted for this instructive anecdote of the hair-oil omits to specify the mode in which a grey-haired and wrinkled Zulu chief used " to make his exit from this sublunary world " ; but on analogy we may conjecture that he did so by the simple and perfectly sufficient process of being knocked on the head.

The custom of putting kings to death as soon as they suffered from any personal defect prevailed two centuries ago in the Caffre kingdom of Sofala, to the north of the present Zululand. We have seen that these kings of Sofala, each of whom bore the official name of Quiteve, were regarded as gods by their people, being entreated to give rain or sunshine, according as each might be wanted.[2] Nevertheless a slight bodily blemish, such as the loss of a tooth, was considered a sufficient cause for putting one of these god-men to death, as we learn from the following passage of an old Portuguese historian : " It was formerly the custom of the kings of this land to commit suicide by taking poison when any disaster or natural physical defect fell upon them, such as impotence, infectious disease, the loss of their front teeth, by which they were disfigured, or any other deformity or affliction. To put an end to such defects they killed themselves, saying that the king should be free from any blemish, and if not, it was better for his honour that he should die and seek another life where he would be made whole, for there

Kings of Sofala put to death on account of bodily blemishes.

---

[1] Nathaniel Isaacs, *Travels and Adventures in Eastern Africa* (London, 1836), i. 295 *sq.*, compare pp. 232, 290 *sq.*
[2] *The Magic Art and the Evolution of Kings*, i. 392.

everything was perfect. But the Quiteve who reigned when
I was in those parts would not imitate his predecessors in
this, being discreet and dreaded as he was ; for having lost
a front tooth he caused it to be proclaimed throughout the
kingdom that all should be aware that he had lost a tooth
and should recognise him when they saw him without it, and
if his predecessors killed themselves for such things they
were very foolish, and he would not do so ; on the contrary,
he would be very sorry when the time came for him to die a
natural death, for his life was very necessary to preserve his
kingdom and defend it from his enemies ; and he recommended his successors to follow his example."[1] The same
historian tells us that "near the kingdom of Quiteve is
another of which Sedanda is king, the laws and customs of
which are very similar to those of Quiteve, all these Kaffirs
being of the same nation, and these two kingdoms having
formerly been one, as I shall relate hereafter. When I was
in Sofala it happened that King Sedanda was seized with a
severe and contagious leprosy, and seeing that his complaint
was incurable, having named the prince who was to succeed
him, he took poison and died, according to the custom of those
kings when they are afflicted with any physical deformity."[2]

Kings
required
to be un-
blemished.

The king of Sofala who dared to survive the loss of his
front tooth was thus a bold reformer like Ergamenes, king
of Ethiopia. We may conjecture that the ground for putting
the Ethiopian kings to death was, as in the case of the Zulu
and Sofala kings, the appearance on their person of any
bodily defect or sign of decay; and that the oracle which
the priests alleged as the authority for the royal execution
was to the effect that great calamities would result from the
reign of a king who had any blemish on his body ; just as
an oracle warned Sparta against a "lame reign," that is, the
reign of a lame king.[3] It is some confirmation of this conjecture that the kings of Ethiopia were chosen for their size,

[1] J. dos Santos, "Eastern Ethiopia,"
in G. McCall Theal's *Records of South-
eastern Africa*, vii. (1901) pp. 194 *sq.*
A more highly - flavoured and full-
bodied, though less slavishly accurate,
translation of this passage is given in
Pinkerton's *Voyages and Travels*, xvi.
684, where the English translator has

enriched the unadorned simplicity of
the Portuguese historian's style with
"the scythe of time" and other
flowers of rhetoric.

[2] J. dos Santos, *op. cit.* p. 193.

[3] Xenophon, *Hellenica*, iii. 3. 3;
Plutarch, *Agesilaus*, 3 ; *id.*, *Lysander*,
22 ; Pausanias, iii. 8. 9.

strength, and beauty long before the custom of killing them was abolished.[1] To this day the Sultan of Wadai must have no obvious bodily defect, and the king of Angoy cannot be crowned if he has a single blemish, such as a broken or a filed tooth or the scar of an old wound.[2] According to the Book of Acaill and many other authorities no king who was afflicted with a personal blemish might reign over Ireland at Tara. Hence, when the great King Cormac Mac Art lost one eye by an accident, he at once abdicated.[3] It is only natural, therefore, to suppose, especially with the other African examples before us, that any bodily defect or symptom of old age appearing on the person of the Ethiopian monarch was the signal for his execution. At a later time it is recorded that if the king of Ethiopia became maimed in any part of his body all his courtiers had to suffer the same mutilation.[4] But this rule may perhaps have been instituted at the time when the custom of killing the king for any personal defect was abolished ; instead of compelling the king to die because, for example, he had lost a tooth, all his subjects would be obliged to lose a tooth, and thus the invidious superiority of the subjects over the king would be cancelled. A rule of this sort is still observed in the same region at the court of the Sultans of Darfur. When the Sultan coughs, every one makes the sound *ts ts* by striking the tongue against the root of the upper teeth ; when he sneezes, the whole assembly utters a sound like the cry of the jeko ; when he falls off his horse, all his followers must fall off likewise ; if any one of them remains in the saddle, no matter how high his rank, he is laid on the ground and beaten.[5] At the court of the king of Uganda in central

Courtiers required to imitate their sovereign.

[1] Herodotus, iii. 20 ; Aristotle, *Politics*, iv. 4. 4. ; Athenaeus, xiii. 20, p. 566. According to Nicolaus Damascenus (*Fr.* 142, in *Fragmenta historicorum Graecorum*, ed. C. Müller, iii. p. 463), the handsomest and bravest man was only raised to the throne when the king had no heirs, the heirs being the sons of his sisters. But this limitation is not mentioned by the other authorities.

[2] G. Nachtigal, *Saharâ und Sûdân*, iii. (Leipsic, 1889) p. 225 ; A. Bastian, *Die deutsche Expedition an der Loango-Küste* (Jena, 1874-75), i. 220.

[3] P. W. Joyce, *Social History of Ancient Ireland* (London, 1903), i. 311.

[4] Strabo, xvii. 2. 3, p. 823 ; Diodorus Siculus, iii. 7.

[5] Mohammed Ebn-Omar El-Tounsy, *Voyage au Darfour* (Paris, 1845), pp. 162 *sq.*; *Travels of an Arab Merchant in Soudan*, abridged from the French by Bayle St. John (London, 1854), p. 78 ; *Bulletin de la Société de Géographie* (Paris), IVme Série, iv. (1852) pp. 539 *sq.*

Africa, when the king laughs, every one laughs ; when he sneezes, every one sneezes ; when he has a cold, every one pretends to have a cold ; when he has his hair cut, so has everybody.[1]   At the court of Boni in Celebes it is a rule that whatever the king does all the courtiers must do.   If he stands, they stand ; if he sits, they sit ; if he falls off his horse, they fall off their horses ; if he bathes, they bathe, and passers-by must go into the water in the dress, good or bad, which they happen to have on.[2]   When the emperor of China laughs, the mandarins in attendance laugh also ; when he stops laughing, they stop ; when he is sad, their countenances are chopfallen ; "you would say that their faces are on springs, and that the emperor can touch the springs and set them in motion at pleasure."[3]   But to return to the death of the divine king.

Many days' journey to the north-east of Abomey, the old capital of Dahomey, lies the kingdom of Eyeo.   "The Eyeos are governed by a king, no less absolute than the king of Dahomy, yet subject to a regulation of state, at once humiliating and extraordinary.   When the people have conceived an opinion of his ill-government, which is sometimes insidiously infused into them by the artifice of his discontented ministers, they send a deputation to him with a present of parrots' eggs, as a mark of its authenticity, to represent to him that the burden of government must have so far fatigued him that they consider it full time for him to repose from his cares and indulge himself with a little sleep.   He thanks his subjects for their attention to his ease, retires to his own apartment as if to sleep, and there gives directions to his women to strangle him.   This is immediately executed, and his son quietly

Kings of Eyeo put to death.

<hr/>

[1] R. W. Felkin, "Notes on the Waganda Tribe of Central Africa," in *Proceedings of the Royal Society of Edinburgh*, xiii. (1884-1886) p. 711 ; J. Roscoe, "Further Notes on the Manners and Customs of the Baganda," *Journal of the Anthropological Institute*, xxxii. (1902) p. 77 (as to sneezing).

[2] *Narrative of Events in Borneo and Celebes, from the Journal of James Brooke, Esq., Rajah of Sarawak*, by Captain R. Mundy, i. 134.   My friend the late Mr. Lorimer Fison, in a letter of August 26th, 1898, told me that the custom of falling down whenever a chief fell was observed also in Fiji, where it had a special name, *bale muri*, " fall-follow."

[3] Mgr. Bruguière, in *Annales de l'Association de la Propagation de la Foi*, v. (1831) pp. 174 *sq.*

ascends the throne upon the usual terms of holding the reins of government no longer than whilst he merits the approbation of the people." About the year 1774, a king of Eyeo, whom his ministers attempted to remove in the customary manner, positively refused to accept the proffered parrots' eggs at their hands, telling them that he had no mind to take a nap, but on the contrary was resolved to watch for the benefit of his subjects. The ministers, surprised and indignant at his recalcitrancy, raised a rebellion, but were defeated with great slaughter, and thus by his spirited conduct the king freed himself from the tyranny of his councillors and established a new precedent for the guidance of his successors.[1] However, the old custom seems to have revived and persisted until late in the nineteenth century, for a Catholic missionary, writing in 1884, speaks of the practice as if it were still in vogue.[2] Another missionary, writing in 1881, thus describes the usage of the Egbas and the Yorubas of west Africa: "Among the customs of the country one of the most curious is unquestionably that of judging and punishing the king. Should he have earned the hatred of his people by exceeding his rights, one of his councillors, on whom the heavy duty is laid, requires of the prince that he shall 'go to sleep,' which means simply 'take poison and die.' If his courage fails him at the supreme moment, a friend renders him this last service, and quietly, without betraying the secret, they prepare the people for the news of the king's death. In Yoruba the thing is managed a little differently. When a son is born to the king of Oyo, they make a model of the infant's right foot in clay and keep it in the house of the elders (*ogboni*). If the king fails to observe the customs of the country, a messenger, without speaking a word, shews him his child's foot. The king knows what that means. He takes poison and goes to sleep."[3] The old Prussians acknowledged as their supreme lord a ruler who governed them in the name of the gods, and was known as God's Mouth (*Kirwaido*).

Voluntary death by fire of the old Prussian Kirwaido.

---

[1] A. Dalzel, *History of Dahomy* (London, 1793), pp. 12 *sq.*, 156 *sq.*

[2] Father Baudin, "Le Fétichisme ou la religion des Nègres de la Guinée," *Missions Catholiques*, xvi. (1884) p. 215.

[3] Missionary Holley, "Étude sur les Egbas," *Missions Catholiques*, xiii. (1881) pp. 351 *sq.* Here Oyo is probably the same as Eyeo mentioned above.

When he felt himself weak and ill, if he wished to leave a good name behind him, he had a great heap made of thornbushes and straw, on which he mounted and delivered a long sermon to the people, exhorting them to serve the gods and promising to go to the gods and speak for the people. Then he took some of the perpetual fire which burned in front of the holy oak-tree, and lighting the pile with it burned himself to death.[1]

Voluntary deaths by fire.

We need not doubt the truth of this last tradition. Fanaticism or the mere love of notoriety has led men in other ages and other lands to court death in the flames. In antiquity the mountebank Peregrinus, after bidding for fame in the various characters of a Christian martyr, a shameless cynic, and a rebel against Rome, ended his disreputable and vainglorious career by publicly burning himself at the Olympic festival in the presence of a crowd of admirers and scoffers, among whom was the satirist Lucian.[2] Buddhist monks in China sometimes seek to attain Nirvana by the same method, the flame of their religious zeal being fanned by a belief that the merit of their death redounds to the good of the whole community, while the praises which are showered upon them in their lives, and the prospect of the honours and worship which await them after death, serve as additional incentives to suicide. The beautiful mountains of Tien-tai, in the district of Tai-chow, are, or were till lately, the scene of many such voluntary martyrdoms. The victims are monks who, weary of the vanities of earth, have withdrawn even from their monasteries and spent years alone in one or other of the hermitages which are scattered among the ravines and precipices of this wild and secluded region. Their fancy having been wrought and their resolution strung to the necessary pitch by a life of solitude and brooding contemplation, they announce their intention and fix the day of their departure from this world of shadows, always choosing for that purpose a festival which draws a crowd of worshippers and pilgrims to one of the many monasteries of

Peregrinus at Olympia.

Buddhist monks in China.

---

[1] Simon Grunau, *Preussische Chronik*, herausgegeben von Dr. M. Perlbach (Leipsic, 1876), i. p. 97.

[2] Lucian, *De morte Peregrini*. That Lucian's account of the mountebank's death is not a fancy picture is proved by the evidence of Tertullian, *Ad martyres*, 4, " *Peregrinus qui non olim se rogo immisit.*"

the district.   Advertisements of the approaching solemnity
are posted throughout the country, and believers are invited
to attend and assist the martyrs with their prayers.   From
three to five monks are said thus to commit themselves to
the flames every year at Tien-tai.   They prepare by fasting
and ablution for the last fiery trial of their faith.   An
upright chest containing a seat is placed in a brick furnace,
and the space between the chest and the walls of the furnace
is filled with fuel.   The doomed man takes his seat in the
chest ; the door is shut on him and barred ; fire is applied
to the combustibles, and consumes the candidate for heaven.
When all is over, the charred remains are raked together,
worshipped, and reverently buried in a dagoba or shrine
destined for the preservation and worship of the relics of
saints.   The victims, it is said, are not always voluntary.
In remote districts unscrupulous priests have been known to
stupefy a clerical brother with drugs and then burn him
publicly, an unwilling martyr, as a means of spreading the
renown of the monastery and thereby attracting the alms of
the faithful.   On the twenty-eighth of January 1888 the
Spiritual-hill monastery, distant about a day's journey from
the city of Wen-chow, witnessed the voluntary death by fire
of two monks who bore the euphonious names of Perceptive-
intelligence and Effulgent-glamour.   Before they entered the
furnaces, the spectators prayed them to become after death
the spiritual guardians of the neighbourhood, to protect it from
all evil influences, and to grant luck in trade, fine seasons,
plentiful harvests, and every other blessing.   The martyrs com-
plaisantly promised to comply with these requests, and were
thereupon worshipped as living Buddhas, while a stream of
gifts poured into the coffers of the monastery.[1]   Among the
Esquimaux of Bering Strait a shaman has been known to
burn himself alive in the expectation of returning to life with
much stronger powers than he had possessed before.[2]

But the suicides by fire of Chinese Buddhists and
Esquimaux sorcerers have been far surpassed by the frenzies

Religious suicides in Russia.

---

[1] D. S. Macgowan, M.D., "Self-
immolation by Fire in China," *The
Chinese Recorder and Missionary
Journal*, xix. (1888) pp. 445-451,
508-521.

[2] E. W. Nelson, "The Eskimo
about Bering Strait," *Eighteenth
Annual Report of the Bureau of
American Ethnology*, Part I. (Washington, 1899), pp. 320, 433 *sq.*

of Christian fanaticism. In the seventeenth century the internal troubles of their unhappy country, viewed in the

Belief in the approach-ing end of the world.

dim light of prophecy, created a widespread belief among the Russian people that the end of the world was at hand, and that the reign of Antichrist was about to begin. We know from Scripture that the old serpent, which is the devil, has been or will be shut up under lock and key for a thousand years,[1] and that the number of the Beast is six hundred and sixty-six.[2] A simple mathematical calculation, based on these irrefragable data, pointed to the year one thousand six hundred and sixty-six as the date when the final consummation of all things and the arrival of the Beast in question might be confidently anticipated. When the year came and went and still, to the general surprise, the animal failed to put in an appearance, the calculations were revised, it was discovered that an error had crept into them, and the world was respited for another thirty-three years. But though opinions differed as to the precise date of the catastrophe, the pious were unanimous in their conviction of its proximity. Accordingly some of them ceased to till their fields, abandoned their houses, and on certain nights of the year expected the sound of the last trump in coffins which they took the precaution of closing, lest their senses, or what remained of them, should be overpowered by the awful vision of the Judgment Day.

Epidemic of suicide.

It would have been well if the delusion of their dis-ordered intellects had stopped there. Unhappily in many cases it went much further, and suicide, universal suicide, was preached by fervent missionaries as the only means to escape the snares of Antichrist and to pass from the sins and sorrows of this fleeting world to the eternal joys of heaven. Whole communities hailed with enthusiasm the gospel of death, and hastened to put its precepts in practice. An epidemic of suicide raged throughout northern and north-

Suicide by starvation.

eastern Russia. At first the favourite mode of death was by starvation. In the forest of Vetlouga, for example, an old man founded an establishment for the use of religious suicides. It was a building without doors and windows. The aspirants to heaven were lowered into it through a hole in the roof,

---

[1] Revelation xx. 1-3.   [2] Revelation xiii. 18.

the hatch was battened down on them, and men armed
with clubs patrolled the outer walls to prevent the prisoners
from escaping.   Hundreds of persons thus died a lingering
death.   At first the sounds of devotion issued from the walls ;
but as time went on these were replaced by entreaties for
food, prayers for mercy, and finally imprecations on the mis-
creant who had lured these misguided beings to destruction
and on the parents who had brought them into the world to
suffer such exquisite torments.   Thus death by famine was
attended by some obvious disadvantages.   It was slow : it
opened the door to repentance : it occasionally admitted of
rescue.   Accordingly death by fire was preferred as surer and Suicide
more expeditious.   Priests, monks, and laymen scoured the by fire.
villages and hamlets preaching salvation by the flames, some
of them decked in the spoils of their victims ; for the motives
of the preachers were often of the basest sort.   They did
not spare even the children, but seduced them by promises
of the gay clothes, the apples, the nuts, the honey they
would enjoy in heaven.   Sometimes when the people
hesitated, these infamous wretches decided the wavering
minds of their dupes by a false report that the troops were
coming to deliver them up to Antichrist, and so to rob them
of a blissful eternity.   Then men, women, and children
rushed into the flames.   Sometimes hundreds, and even
thousands, thus perished together.   An area was enclosed by
barricades, fuel was heaped up in it, the victims huddled
together, fire set to the whole, and the sacrifice consummated.
Any who in their agony sought to escape were driven or
thrown back into the flames, sometimes by their own relations.
These sinister fires generally blazed at night, reddening the
sky till daybreak.   In the morning nothing remained but
charred bodies gnawed by prowling dogs ; but the stench of
burnt human flesh poisoned the air for days afterwards.[1]

---

[1] Ivan Stchoukine, *Le Suicide col-
lectif dans le Raskol russe* (Paris,
1903), pp. 45-53, 61-78, 84-87,
96-99, 102-112.   The mania in its
most extreme form died away towards
the end of the seventeenth century, but
during the eighteenth and nineteenth
centuries cases of collective suicide
from religious motives occurred from
time to time, people burning themselves in families or in batches of
thirty or forty.   The last of these
suicides by fire took place in 1860,
when fifteen persons thus perished in
the Government of Olonetz.   Twenty-
four others buried themselves alive near
Tiraspol in the winter of 1896-97.   See
I. Stchoukine, *op. cit.* pp. 114-126.

As the Christians expected the arrival of Antichrist in the year 1666, so the Jews cheerfully anticipated the long-delayed advent of their Messiah in the same fateful year. A Jew of Smyrna, by name Sabatei-Sevi, availed himself of this general expectation to pose as the Messiah in person. He was greeted with enthusiasm. Jews from many parts of Europe hastened to pay their homage and, what was still better, their money to the future deliverer of his country, who in return parcelled out among them, with the greatest liberality, estates in the Holy Land which did not belong to him. But the alternative of death by impalement or conversion to Mohammedanism, which the Sultan submitted to his consideration, induced him to revise his theological opinions, and on looking into the matter more closely he discovered that his true mission in life was to preach the total abolition of the Jewish religion and the substitution for it of Islam.[1]

§ 3. *Kings killed at the End of a Fixed Term*

In the cases hitherto described, the divine king or priest is suffered by his people to retain office until some outward defect, some visible symptom of failing health or advancing age, warns them that he is no longer equal to the discharge of his divine duties ; but not until such symptoms have made their appearance is he put to death. Some peoples, however, appear to have thought it unsafe to wait for even the slightest symptom of decay and have preferred to kill the king while he was still in the full vigour of life. Accordingly, they have fixed a term beyond which he might not reign, and at the close of which he must die, the term fixed upon being short enough to exclude the probability of his degenerating physically in the interval. In some parts of Suicide of
the kings of
Quilacare
at the end
of a reign
of twelve
years. southern India the period fixed was twelve years. Thus, according to an old traveller, in the province of Quilacare, about twenty leagues to the north-east of Cape Comorin, "there is a Gentile house of prayer, in which there is an idol which they hold in great account, and every twelve

---

[1] Voltaire, *Essai sur les Mœurs*, iii. 142-145 (*Œuvres complètes de Voltaire*, xiii. Paris, 1878).

years they celebrate a great feast to it, whither all the Gentiles go as to a jubilee.   This temple possesses many lands and much revenue: it is a very great affair.   This province has a king over it, who has not more than twelve years to reign from jubilee to jubilee.   His manner of living is in .this wise, that is to say : when the twelve years are completed, on the day of this feast there assemble together innumerable people, and much money is spent in giving food to Bramans.   The king has a wooden scaffolding made, spread over with silken hangings : and on that day he goes to bathe at a tank with great ceremonies and sound of music, after that he comes to the idol and prays to it, and mounts on to the scaffolding, and there before all the people he takes some very sharp knives, and begins to cut off his nose, and then his ears, and his lips, and all his members, and as much flesh off himself as he can ; and he throws it away very hurriedly until so much of his blood is spilled that he begins to faint, and then he cuts his throat himself.   And he performs this sacrifice to the idol, and whoever desires to reign other twelve years and undertake this martyrdom for love of the idol, has to be present looking on at this : and from that place they raise him up as king."[1]

The king of Calicut, on the Malabar coast, bears the title of Samorin or Samory, which in the native language is said to mean " God on earth."[2]   He "pretends to be of a higher rank than the Brahmans, and to be inferior only to the invisible gods ; a pretention that was acknowledged by his subjects, but which is held as absurd and abominable by the Brahmans, by whom he is only treated as a Sudra."[3] Formerly the Samorin had to cut his throat in public at the end of a twelve years' reign.   But towards the end of the seventeenth century the rule had been modified as follows : " Many strange customs were observed in this country in

Custom of the kings of Calicut.

[1] Duarte Barbosa, *A Description of the Coasts of East Africa and Malabar in the Beginning of the Sixteenth Century* (Hakluyt Society, London, 1866), pp. 172 *sq.*
[2] L. di Varthema, *Travels*, translated by J. W. Jones and edited by G. P. Badger (Hakluyt Society, London, 1863), p. 134.   In a note the Editor says that the name Zamorin (Samorin) according to some " is a corruption of *Tamuri*, the name of the most exalted family of the Nair caste."
[3] Francis Buchanan, " Journey from Madras through the Countries of Mysore, Canara, and Malabar," in Pinkerton's *Voyages and Travels*, viii. 735.

Custom of
the kings
of Calicut. former times, and some very odd ones are still continued. It was an ancient custom for the Samorin to reign but twelve years, and no longer.   If he died before his term was expired, it saved him a troublesome ceremony of cutting his own throat, on a publick scaffold erected for the purpose. He first made a feast for all his nobility and gentry, who are very numerous.   After the feast he saluted his guests, and went on the scaffold, and very decently cut his own throat in the view of the assembly, and his body was, a little while after, burned with great pomp and ceremony, and the grandees elected a new Samorin.   Whether that custom was a religious or a civil ceremony, I know not, but it is now laid aside.   And a new custom is followed by the modern Samorins, that jubilee is proclaimed throughout his dominions, at the end of twelve years, and a tent is pitched for him in a spacious plain, and a great feast is celebrated for ten or twelve days, with mirth and jollity, guns firing night and day, so at the end of the feast any four of the guests that have a mind to gain a crown by a desperate action, in fighting their way through 30 or 40,000 of his guards, and kill the Samorin in his tent, he that kills him succeeds him in his empire. In anno 1695, one of those jubilees happened, and the tent pitched near Pennany, a seaport of his, about fifteen leagues to the southward of Calicut.   There were but three men that would venture on that desperate action, who fell in, with sword and target, among the guard, and, after they had killed and wounded many, were themselves killed.   One of the desperados had a nephew of fifteen or sixteen years of age, that kept close by his uncle in the attack on the guards, and, when he saw him fall, the youth got through the guards into the tent, and made a stroke at his Majesty's head, and had certainly despatched him if a large brass lamp which was burning over his head had not marred the blow ; but, before he could make another, he was killed by the guards ; and, I believe, the same Samorin reigns yet.   I chanced to come that time along the coast and heard the guns for two or three days and nights successively." [1]

The English traveller, whose account I have quoted, did

---

[1] Alex. Hamilton, " A New Account of the East Indies," in Pinkerton's
Voyages and Travels, viii. 374.

not himself witness the festival he describes, though he heard Fuller
the sound of the firing in the distance.   Fortunately, exact account of the Calicut
records of these festivals and of the number of men who custom.
perished at them have been preserved in the archives of the
royal family at Calicut.   In the latter part of the nineteenth
century they were examined by Mr. W. Logan, with the personal assistance of the reigning king, and from his work it
is possible to gain an accurate conception both of the tragedy
and of the scene where it was periodically enacted down to
1743, when the ceremony took place for the last time.

The festival at which the king of Calicut staked his The *Maha*
crown and his life on the issue of battle was known as the *Makham*
or Great
Maha Makham or Great Sacrifice.   It fell every twelfth Sacrifice at
year, when the planet Jupiter was in retrograde motion in Calicut.
the sign of the Crab, and it lasted twenty-eight days,
culminating at the time of the eighth lunar asterism in the
month of Makaram.   As the date of the festival was determined by the position of Jupiter in the sky, and the interval
between two festivals was twelve years, which is roughly
Jupiter's period of revolution round the sun,[1] we may conjecture that the splendid planet was supposed to be in a
special sense the king's star and to rule his destiny, the
period of its revolution in heaven corresponding to the
period of his reign on earth.   However that may be, the
ceremony was observed with great pomp at the Tirunavayi
temple, on the north bank of the Ponnani River.   The spot
is close to the present railway line.   As the train rushes by,
you can just catch a glimpse of the temple, almost hidden
behind a clump of trees on the river bank.   From the
western gateway of the temple a perfectly straight road,
hardly raised above the level of the surrounding rice-fields
and shaded by a fine avenue, runs for half a mile to a high
ridge with a precipitous bank, on which the outlines of three
or four terraces can still be traced.   On the topmost of
these terraces the king took his stand on the eventful day.
The view which it commands is a fine one.   Across the flat

---

[1] The sidereal revolution of Jupiter is completed in 11 years 314.92 days (*Encyclopaedia Britannica*, Ninth Edition, *s.v.* "Astronomy," ii. 808).   The twelve-years revolution of Jupiter was known to the Greek astronomers, from whom the knowledge may perhaps have penetrated into India.   See Geminus, *Eisagoge*, I, p. 10, ed. Halma.

expanse of the rice-fields, with the broad placid river winding through them, the eye ranges eastward to high tablelands, their lower slopes embowered in woods, while afar off looms the great chain of the western Ghauts, and in the furthest distance the Neilgherries or Blue Mountains, hardly distinguishable from the azure of the sky above.

The attack on the king.   But it was not to the distant prospect that the king's eyes naturally turned at this crisis of his fate. His attention was arrested by a spectacle nearer at hand. For all the plain below was alive with troops, their banners waving gaily in the sun, the white tents of their many camps standing sharply out against the green and gold of the rice-fields. Forty thousand fighting men or more were gathered there to defend the king. But if the plain swarmed with soldiers, the road that cuts across it from the temple to the king's stand was clear of them. Not a soul was stirring on it. Each side of the way was barred by palisades, and from the palisades on either hand a long hedge of spears, held by strong arms, projected into the empty road, their blades meeting in the middle and forming a glittering arch of steel. All was now ready. The king waved his sword. At the same moment a great chain of massy gold, enriched with bosses, was placed on an elephant at his side. That was the signal. On the instant a stir might be seen half a mile away at the gate of the temple. A group of swordsmen, decked with flowers and smeared with ashes, has stepped out from the crowd. They have just partaken of their last meal on earth, and they now receive the last blessings and farewells of their friends. A moment more and they are coming down the lane of spears, hewing and stabbing right and left at the spearmen, winding and turning and writhing among the blades as if they had no bones in their bodies. It is all in vain. One after the other they fall, some nearer the king, some further off, content to die, not for the shadow of a crown, but for the mere sake of approving their dauntless valour and swordsmanship to the world. On the last days of the festival the same magnificent display of gallantry, the same useless sacrifice of life was repeated again and again. Yet perhaps no sacrifice is wholly

useless which proves that there are men who prefer honour
to life.[1]

" It is a singular custom in Bengal," says an old native Custom of
kings in
Bengal.
historian of India, " that there is little of hereditary descent
in succession to the sovereignty.   There is a throne allotted
for the king ; there is, in like manner, a seat or station
assigned for each of the *amirs, wazirs*, and *mansabdars*.   It
is that throne and these stations alone which engage the
reverence of the people of Bengal.   A set of dependents,
servants, and attendants are annexed to each of these situa-
tions.   When the king wishes to dismiss or appoint any
person, whosoever is placed in the seat of the one dismissed
is immediately attended and obeyed by the whole establishment of dependents, servants, and retainers annexed to the
seat which he occupies.   Nay, this rule obtains even as to the
royal throne itself.   Whoever kills the king, and succeeds in
placing himself on that throne, is immediately acknowledged
as king ; all the *amirs, wazirs*, soldiers, and peasants instantly
obey and submit to him, and consider him as being as much
their sovereign as they did their former prince, and obey his
orders implicitly.   The people of Bengal say, ' We are faithful
to the throne ; whoever fills the throne we are obedient and
true to it.' " [2]   A custom of the same sort formerly prevailed Custom of
the kings
of Passier.
in the little kingdom of Passier, on the northern coast of
Sumatra.   The old Portuguese historian De Barros, who informs us of it, remarks with surprise that no wise man would
wish to be king of Passier, since the monarch was not allowed
by his subjects to live long.   From time to time a sort of fury
seized the people, and they marched through the streets of
the city chanting with loud voices the fatal words, " The
king must die ! "   When the king heard that song of death
he knew that his hour had come.   The man who struck
the fatal blow was of the royal lineage, and as soon as
he had done the deed of blood and seated himself on
the throne he was regarded as the legitimate king, provided

---

[1] W. Logan, *Malabar* (Madras,
1887), i. 162 - 169. The writer
describes in particular the festival of
1683, when fifty-five men perished in
the manner described.

[2] Sir H. M. Elliot, *The History of*
India as told by its own Historians, iv.
260. I have to thank Mr. R. S.
Whiteway, of Brownscombe, Shotter-
mill, Surrey, for kindly calling my
attention to this and the following
instance of the custom of regicide.

that he contrived to maintain his seat peaceably for a single day. This, however, the regicide did not always succeed in doing. When Fernão Peres d'Andrade, on a voyage to China, put in at Passier for a cargo of spices, two kings were massacred, and that in the most peaceable and orderly manner, without the smallest sign of tumult or sedition in the city, where everything went on in its usual course, as if the murder or execution of a king were a matter of everyday occurrence. Indeed, on one occasion three kings were raised to the dangerous elevation and followed each other on the dusty road of death in a single day. The people defended the custom, which they esteemed very laudable and even of divine institution, by saying that God would never allow so high and mighty a being as a king, who reigned as his vicegerent on earth, to perish by violence

Custom of Slavonic kings. unless for his sins he thoroughly deserved it.[1] Far away from the tropical island of Sumatra a rule of the same sort appears to have obtained among the old Slavs. When the captives Gunn and Jarmerik contrived to slay the king and queen of the Slavs and made their escape, they were pursued by the barbarians, who shouted after them that if they would only come back they would reign instead of the murdered monarch, since by a public statute of the ancients the succession to the throne fell to the king's assassin. But the flying regicides turned a deaf ear to promises which they regarded as mere baits to lure them back to destruction; they continued their flight, and the shouts and clamour of the barbarians gradually died away in the distance.[2]

Custom of *Thalavetti-parothiam* in Malabar. When kings were bound to suffer death, whether at their own hands or at the hands of others, on the expiration of a fixed term of years, it was natural that they should seek to delegate the painful duty, along with some of the privileges of sovereignty, to a substitute who should suffer vicariously in their stead. This expedient appears to have been resorted to by some of the princes of Malabar. Thus we are informed by a native authority on that country that "in some places

---

[1] De Barros, *Da Asia, dos feitos, que os Portuguezes fizeram no descubrimento e conquista dos mares e terras do Oriente*, Decada Terceira, Liv. V. cap. i. pp. 512 *sq.* (Lisbon, 1777).

[2] Saxo Grammaticus, *Historia Danica*, viii. pp. 410 *sq.*, ed. P. E. Müller (p. 334 of Mr. Oliver Elton's English translation).

all powers both executive and judicial were delegated for a
fixed period to natives by the sovereign.   This institution
was styled *Thalavettiparothiam* or authority obtained by
decapitation. *Parothiam* is the name of a supreme authority
of those days.   The name of the office is still preserved in
the Cochin state, where the village headman is called a
Parathiakaran.   This *Thalavettiparothiam* was a terrible
but interesting institution.   It was an office tenable for
five years during which its bearer was invested with supreme
despotic powers within his jurisdiction.   On the expiry of
the five years the man's head was cut off and thrown up in
the air amongst a large concourse of villagers, each of whom
vied with the other in trying to catch it in its course down.
He who succeeded was nominated to the post for the next
five years." [1]   A similar delegation of the duty of dying for Custom of
his country was perhaps practised by the Sultans of Java. the Sultans
At least such a custom would explain a strange scene which of Java.
was witnessed at the court of one of these sultans by the
famous traveller Ibn Batuta, a native of Tangier, who visited
the East Indies in the first half of the fourteenth century.
He says : " During my audience with the Sultan I saw a man
who held in his hand a knife like that used by a grape-gleaner.
He placed it on his own neck and spoke for a long time in a
language which I did not understand.   After that he seized
the knife with both hands at once and cut his throat.   His
head fell to the ground, so sharp was the blade and so great
the force with which he used it.   I remained dumbfoundered
at his behaviour, but the Sultan said to me, ' Does any one
do like that in your country ? '   I answered, ' Never did I
see such a thing.'   He smiled and replied, ' These people
are our slaves, and they kill themselves for love of us.'   Then
he commanded that they should take away him who had
slain himself and should burn him.   The Sultan's officers,
the grandees, the troops, and the common people attended
the cremation.   The sovereign assigned a liberal pension to
the children of the deceased, to his wife, and to his brothers ;

---

[1] T. K. Gopal Panikkar (of the
Madras Registration Department),
Malabar and its Folk (Madras, N.D.,
preface dated Chowghaut, 8th October
1900), pp. 120 *sq.*   I have to thank
my friend Mr. W. Crooke for calling
my attention to this account.

and they were highly honoured because of his conduct.   A
person, who was present at the audience when the event I
have described took place, informed me that the speech made
by the man who sacrificed himself set forth his devotion to
the monarch.   He said that he wished to immolate himself
out of affection for the sovereign, as his father had done for
love of the prince's father, and as his grandfather had done
out of regard for the prince's grandfather."[1]   We may
conjecture that formerly the sultans of Java, like the kings of
Quilacare and Calicut, were bound to cut their own throats
at the end of a fixed term of years, but that at a later time
they deputed the painful, though glorious, duty of dying for
their country to the members of a certain family, who received
by way of recompense ample provision during their life and
a handsome funeral at death.

Religious
suicides in
India.

A similar mode of religious suicide seems to have been
often adopted in India, especially in Malabar, during the
Middle Ages.   Thus we are told by Friar Jordanus that
in the Greater India, by which he seems to mean Malabar
and the neighbouring regions, many sacrifice themselves to
the idols.   When they are sick or involved in misfortune,
they vow themselves to the idol in case they are delivered.
Then, when they have recovered, they fatten themselves
for one or two years ; and when another festival comes
round, they cover themselves with flowers, crown themselves with white garlands, and go singing and playing
before the idol, when it is carried through the land.   There,
after they have shown off a great deal, they take a sword
with two handles, like those used in currying leather, put
it to the back of their neck, and cutting strongly with
both hands sever their heads from their bodies before the
idol.[2]   Again, Nicolo Conti, who travelled in the East in
the early part of the fifteenth century, informs us that in
the city of Cambaita " many present themselves who have
determined upon self immolation, having on their neck a
broad circular piece of iron, the fore part of which is round

[1] *Voyage d'Ibn Batoutah,* texte arabe,
accompagné d'une traduction par C.
Deffrémery et B. R. Sanguinetti (Paris,
1853-58), iv. 246 *sq.*

[2] *The Wonders of the East, by Friar
Jordanus,* translated by Col. Henry
Yule (London, 1863, Hakluyt Society),
pp. 32 *sq.*

and the hinder part extremely sharp. A chain attached to the fore part hangs suspended upon the breast, into which the victims, sitting down with their legs drawn up and their neck bent, insert their feet. Then, on the speaker pronouncing certain words, they suddenly stretch out their legs, and at the same time drawing up their neck, cut off their own head, yielding up their lives as a sacrifice to their idols. These men are regarded as saints." [1] Among the Jaintias or Syntengs, a Khasi tribe of Assam, human sacrifices used to be annually offered on the *Sandhi* day in the month of Ashwin. Persons often came forward voluntarily and presented themselves as victims. This they generally did by appearing before the Rajah on the last day of Shravan and declaring that the goddess had called them to herself. After due enquiry, if the would-be victim were found suitable, it was customary for the Rajah to present him with a golden anklet and to give him permission to live as he chose and to do what he liked, the royal treasury undertaking to pay compensation for any damage he might do in the exercise of his remarkable privileges. But the enjoyment of these privileges was very short. On the day appointed the voluntary victim, after bathing and purifying himself, was dressed in new attire, daubed with red sandal-wood and vermilion, and bedecked with garlands. Thus arrayed, he sat for a time in meditation and prayer on a dais in front of the goddess ; then he made a sign with his finger, and the executioner, after uttering the usual formulas, cut off his head, which was thereafter laid before the goddess on a golden plate. The lungs were cooked and eaten by such *Kandra Yogis* as were present, and it is said that the royal family partook of a small quantity of rice cooked in the blood of the victim. The ceremony was usually witnessed by crowds of spectators who assembled from all parts of the

[1] *India in the Fifteenth Century, being a Collection of Voyages to India in the century preceding the Portuguese discovery of the Cape of Good Hope*, edited by R. H. Major (Hakluyt Society, London, 1857), "The Travels of Nicolo Conti in the East," pp. 27 *sq.* An instrument of the sort described in the text (a crescent-shaped knife with chains and stirrups attached to it for the convenience of the suicide) used to be preserved at Kshira, a village of Bengal near Nadiya : it was called a *karavat.* See *The Book of Ser Marco Polo*, newly translated and edited by Colonel Henry Yule, Second Edition (London, 1875), ii. 334.

neighbouring hills. When the supply of voluntary victims fell short, emissaries were sent out to kidnap strangers from other territories, and it was the practice of such man-hunts that led to the annexation of the Jaintia country by the British.[1]

Pretence of putting the king's proxy to death.

When once kings, who had hitherto been bound to die a violent death at the end of a term of years, conceived the happy thought of dying by deputy in the persons of others, they would very naturally put it in practice; and accordingly we need not wonder at finding so popular an expedient, or traces of it, in many lands. Thus, for example, the Bhuiyas are an aboriginal race of north-eastern India, and one of their chief seats is Keonjhur. At the installation of a Rajah of Keonjhur a ceremony is observed which has been described as follows by an English officer who witnessed it: " Then the sword, a very rusty old weapon, is placed in the Raja's hands, and one of the Bhuiyas, named Anand Kopat, comes before him, and kneel-ing sideways, the Raja touches him on the neck as if about to strike off his head, and it is said that in former days there was no fiction in this part of the ceremony. The family of the Kopat hold their lands on the condition that the victim when required shall be produced. Anand, however, hurriedly arose after the accolade and disappeared. He must not be seen for three days; then he presents himself again to the Raja as miraculously restored to life." [2] Here the custom of putting the king's proxy to death has dwindled, probably under English influence, to a mere pretence; but elsewhere it survives, or survived till recent times, in full force.

Man killed at the in-stallation of a king of Cassange.

Cassange, a native state in the interior of Angola, is ruled by a king, who bears the title of Jaga. When a king is about to be installed in office, some of the chiefs are despatched to find a human victim, who may not be related by blood or marriage to the new monarch. When he comes to the king's camp, the victim is provided with everything he requires, and all his orders are obeyed as promptly as those of the sovereign. On the day of the ceremony the king takes

[1] Major P. R. T. Gurdon, *The Khasis* (London, 1907), pp. 102 *sq.*, quoting Mr. Gait in the *Journal of the Asiatic Society of Bengal* for 1898.

[2] E. T. Dalton, *Descriptive Ethnology of Bengal* (Calcutta, 1872), p. 146.

his seat on a perforated iron stool, his chiefs, councillors, and the rest of the people forming a great circle round about him. Behind the king sits his principal wife, together with all his concubines. An iron gong, with two small bells attached to it, is then struck by an official, who continues to ring the bells during the ceremony. The victim is then introduced and placed in front of the king, but with his back towards him. Armed with a scimitar the king then cuts open the man's back, extracts his heart, and having taken a bite out of it, spits it out and gives it to be burned. The councillors meantime hold the victim's body so that the blood from the wound spouts against the king's breast and belly, and, pouring through the hole in the iron stool, is collected by the chiefs in their hands, who rub their breasts and beards with it, while they shout, "Great is the king and the rites of the state!" After that the corpse is skinned, cut up, and cooked with the flesh of an ox, a dog, a hen, and some other animals. The meal thus prepared is served first to the king, then to the chiefs and councillors, and lastly to all the people assembled. Any man who refused to partake of it would be sold into slavery together with his family.[1] The distinction with which the human victim is here treated before his execution suggests that he is a substitute for the king.

Scandinavian traditions contain some hints that of old the Swedish kings reigned only for periods of nine years, after which they were put to death or had to find a substitute to die in their stead. Thus Aun or On, king of Sweden, is said to have sacrificed to Odin for length of days and to have been answered by the god that he should live so long as he sacrificed one of his sons every ninth year. He sacrificed nine of them in this manner, and would have sacrificed the tenth and last, but the Swedes would not allow him. So he died and was buried in a mound at Upsala.[2]

Sacrifice of the king's sons in Sweden: evidence of a nine years' tenure of the throne.

---

[1] F. T. Valdez, *Six Years of a Traveller's Life in Western Africa* (London, 1861), ii. 158-160. I have translated the title *Maquita* by "chief"; the writer does not explain it.

[2] *Ynglinga Saga*, 29 (*The Heimskringla*, translated by S. Laing, i. 239 sq.). Compare H. M. Chadwick, *The Cult of Othin* (London, 1899), p. 4. According to Messrs. Laing and Chadwick the sacrifice took place every *tenth* year. But I follow Prof. K. Weinhold who translates " *hit tiunda hvert ár* " by " *alle neun Jahre* " (" Die mystische Neunzahl bei den Deutschen," *Abhandlungen der könig. Akademie der Wissen-*

Another indication of a similar tenure of the crown occurs in a curious legend of the disposition and banishment of Odin. Offended at his misdeeds, the other gods outlawed and exiled him, but set up in his place a substitute, Oller by name, a cunning wizard, to whom they accorded the symbols both of royalty and of godhead. The deputy bore the name of Odin, and reigned for nearly ten years, when he was driven from the throne, while the real Odin came to his own again. His discomfited rival retired to Sweden and was afterwards slain in an attempt to repair his shattered fortunes.[1] As gods are often merely men who loom large through the mists of tradition, we may conjecture that this Norse legend preserves a confused reminiscence of ancient Swedish kings who reigned for nine or ten years together, then abdicated, delegating to others the privilege of dying for their country. The great festival which was held at Upsala every nine years may have been the occasion on which the king or his deputy was put to death. We know that human sacrifices formed part of the rites.[2]

§ 4. *Octennial Tenure of the Kingship*

Limited tenure of the kingship in ancient Greece.

There are some grounds for believing that the reign of many ancient Greek kings was limited to eight years, or at least that at the end of every period of eight years a new consecration, a fresh outpouring of the divine grace, was regarded as necessary in order to enable them to discharge their civil and religious duties. Thus it was a rule of the Spartan constitution that every eighth year the ephors should choose a clear and moonless night and sitting down observe the sky in silence. If during their vigil they saw a meteor or shooting star, they inferred that the king had sinned against the deity, and they suspended him from his functions until the Delphic or Olympic oracle should reinstate him in them. This custom, which has all the air of great antiquity, was not

The Spartan kings appear formerly to have held office for periods of eight years only.

---

schaften *zu Berlin*, 1897, p. 6). So in Latin *decimo quoque anno* should be translated "every ninth year."

[1] Saxo Grammaticus, *Historia Danica*, iii. pp. 129-131, ed. P. E. Müller (pp. 98 *sq.* of Oliver Elton's

English translation).

[2] Adam of Bremen, *Descriptio insularum Aquilonis*, 27 (Migne's *Patrologia Latina*, cxlvi. col. 644). See *The Magic Art and the Evolution of Kings*, vol. ii. pp. 364 *sq.*

suffered to remain a dead letter even in the last period of the Spartan monarchy; for in the third century before our era a king, who had rendered himself obnoxious to the reforming party, was actually deposed on various trumped-up charges, among which the allegation that the ominous sign had been seen in the sky took a prominent place.[1]   When we compare this custom with the evidence to be presently adduced of an eight years' tenure of the kingship in Greece, we shall probably agree with K. O. Müller[2] that the quaint Spartan practice was much more than a mere antiquarian curiosity; it was the attenuated survival of an institution which may once have had great significance, and it throws an important light on the restrictions and limitations anciently imposed by religion on the Dorian kingship.   What exactly was the import of a meteor in the opinion of the old Dorians we can hardly hope to determine; one thing only is clear, they regarded it as a portent of so ominous and threatening a kind that its appearance under certain circumstances justified and even required the deposition of their king.   This exaggerated dread of so simple a natural phenomenon is shared by many savages at the present day; and we shall hardly err in supposing that the Spartans inherited it from their barbarous ancestors, who may have watched with consternation, on many a starry night among the woods of Germany, the flashing of a meteor

The dread of meteors shared by savages.

---

[1] Plutarch, *Agis*, 11. Plutarch says that the custom was observed "at intervals of nine years" (δι' ἐτῶν ἐννέα), but the expression is equivalent to our "at intervals of eight years." In reckoning intervals of time numerically the Greeks included both the terms which are separated by the interval, whereas we include only one of them. For example, our phrase "every second day" would be rendered in Greek διὰ τρίτης ἡμέρας, literally "every third day." Again, a cycle of two years is in Greek *trieteris*, literally "a period of three years"; a cycle of eight years is *ennaeteris*, literally "a period of nine years"; and so forth. See Censorinus, *De die natali*, 18. The Latin use of the ordinal numbers is similar, *e.g.* our "every second year" would be *tertio quoque anno* in Latin. However, the Greeks and Romans were not always consistent in this matter, for they occasionally reckoned in our fashion. The resulting ambiguity is not only puzzling to moderns; it sometimes confused the ancients themselves. For example, it led to a derangement of the newly instituted Julian calendar, which escaped detection for more than thirty years. See Macrobius, *Saturn.* i. 14. 13 *sq.* ; Solinus, i. 45-47. On the ancient modes of counting in such cases see A. Schmidt, *Handbuch der griechischen Chronologie* (Jena, 1888), pp. 95 *sqq.* According to Schmidt, the practice of adding both terms to the sum of the intervening units was not extended by the Greeks to numbers above nine.

[2] *Die Dorier*,[2] ii. 96.

through the sky.   It may be well, even at the cost of
a digression, to illustrate this primitive superstition by
examples.

Supersti-
tions of the
Australian
aborigines
as to
shooting
stars. Thus, shooting stars and meteors are viewed with apprehension by the natives of the Andaman Islands, who suppose
them to be lighted faggots hurled into the air by the malignant
spirit of the woods in order to ascertain the whereabouts of
any unhappy wight in his vicinity.   Hence if they happen to
be away from their camp when the meteor is seen, they hide
themselves and remain silent for a little before they venture
to resume the work they were at ; for example, if they are
out fishing they will crouch at the bottom of the boat.[1]
The natives of the Tully River in Queensland believe
falling stars to be the fire-sticks carried about by the spirits
of dead enemies.   When they see one shooting through the
air they take it as a sign that an enemy is near, and accordingly they shout and make as much noise as they can ; next
morning they all go out in the direction in which the star
fell and look for the tracks of their foe.[2]   The Turrbal tribe of
Queensland thought that a falling star was a medicine-man
flying through the air and dropping his fire-stick to kill somebody ; if there was a sick man in the camp, they regarded him
as doomed.[3]   The Ngarigo of New South Wales believed
the fall of a meteor to betoken the place where their foes were
mustering for war.[4]   The Kaitish tribe of central Australia
imagine that the fall of a star marks the whereabouts of a
man who has killed another by means of a magical pointing-
stick or bone.   If a member of any group has been killed
in this way, his friends watch for the descent of a meteor,
march in that direction, slay an enemy there, and leave his
body lying on the ground.   The friends of the murdered
man understand what has happened, and bury his body
where the star fell ; for they recognise the spot by the soft-
ness of the earth.[5]   The Mara tribe of northern Australia

[1] E. Man, *Aboriginal Inhabitants
of the Andaman Islands*, pp. 84 *sq.*
    [2] W. E. Roth, *North Queensland
Bulletin, No.* 5, *Superstition, Magic,
and Medicine* (Brisbane, 1903), p. 8.
    [3] A. W. Howitt, *The Native Tribes
of South-East Australia*, p. 429.
    [4] A. W. Howitt, *op. cit.* p. 430.

One of the earliest writers on New
South Wales reports that the natives
attributed great importance to the falling of a star (D. Collins, *Account of
the English Colony in New South Wales*
(London, 1804), p. 383).
    [5] Spencer and Gillen, *Northern
Tribes of Central Australia*, p. 627.

suppose a falling star to be one of two hostile spirits, father and son, who live up in the sky and come down occasionally to do harm to men. In this tribe the profession of medicine-man is strictly hereditary in the stock which has the falling star for its totem;[1] if these wizards had ever developed into kings, the descent of a meteor at certain times might have had the same fatal significance for them as for the kings of Sparta. The Taui Islanders, to the west of the Bismarck Archipelago, make war in the direction in which they have observed a star to fall,[2] probably for a reason like that which induces the Kaitish to do the same.

When the Baronga of south Africa see a shooting star they spit on the ground to avert the evil omen, and cry, " Go away! go away all alone!" By this they mean that the light, which is so soon to disappear, is not to take them with it, but to go and die by itself.[3] So when a Masai perceives the flash of a meteor he spits several times and says, " Be lost! go in the direction of the enemy!" after which he adds, " Stay away from me."[4] The Namaquas " are greatly afraid of the meteor which is vulgarly called a falling star, for they consider it a sign that sickness is coming upon the cattle, and to escape it they will immediately drive them to some other parts of the country. They call out to the star how many cattle they have, and beg of it not to send sickness."[5] The Bechuanas are also much alarmed at the appearance of a meteor. If they happen to be dancing in the open air at the time, they will instantly desist and retire hastily to their huts.[6] The Ewe negroes of Guinea regard a falling star as a powerful divinity, and worship it as one of their national gods, by the name of Nyikpla or Nyigbla. In their opinion the falling star is especially a war-god who marches at the head of the host and leads it to victory, riding like Castor and Pollux on horseback. But he is also a rain-god, and the showers are sent by

Supersti-tions of the negroes and other African races as to shooting stars.

[1] Spencer and Gillen, *op. cit.* pp. 488, 627 *sq.*

[2] G. Thilenius, *Ethnographische Ergebnisse aus Melanesien,* ii. (Halle, 1903) p. 129.

[3] H. A. Junod, *Les Ba-ronga* (Neuchatel, 1898), p. 470.

[4] A. C. Hollis, *The Masai* (Oxford, 1905), p. 316.

[5] J. Campbell, *Travels in South Africa* (London, 1815), pp. 428 *sq.*

[6] *Id., Travels in South Africa, Second Journey* (London, 1822), ii. 204.

him from the sky. Special priests are devoted to his worship, with a chief priest at their head, who resides in the capital. They are known by the red staves which they carry and by the high-pointed caps, woven of threads and palm-leaves, which they wear on their heads. In times of drought they call upon their god by night with wild howls. Once a year an ox is sacrificed to him at the capital, and the priests consume the flesh. On this occasion the people smear themselves with the pollen of a certain plant and go in procession through the towns and villages, singing, dancing, and beating drums.[1]

Superstitions of the American Indians as to shooting stars.

By some Indians of California meteors were called "children of the moon," and whenever young women saw one of them they fell to the ground and covered their heads, fearing that, if the meteor saw them, their faces would become ugly and diseased.[2] The Tarahumares of Mexico fancy that a shooting star is a dead sorcerer coming to harm a man who harmed him in life. Hence when they see one they huddle together and scream for terror.[3] When a German traveller was living with the Bororos of central Brazil, a splendid meteor fell, spreading dismay through the Indian village. It was believed to be the soul of a dead medicine-man, who suddenly appeared in this form to announce that he wanted meat, and that, as a preliminary measure, he proposed to visit somebody with an attack of dysentery. Its appearance was greeted with yells from a hundred throats: men, women, and children swarmed out of their huts like ants whose nest has been disturbed; and soon watch-fires blazed, round which at a little distance groups of dusky figures gathered, while in the middle, thrown into strong relief by the flickering light of the fire, two red-painted sorcerers reeled and staggered in a state of frantic excitement, snorting and spitting towards the quarter of the sky where the meteor had run its brief but brilliant course. Pressing his right

[1] G. Zündel, "Land und Volk der Eweer auf der Sclavenküste in Westafrika," *Zeitschrift der Gesellschaft für Erdkunde zu Berlin*, xii. (1877) pp. 415 *sq.*; C. Spiess, "Religionsbegriffe der Evheer in Westafrika," *Mittheilungen des Seminars für Orientalische Sprachen zu Berlin*, vi. (1903) Dritte Abtheilung, p. 112.

[2] Boscana, "Chinigchinich, a Historical Account of the Origin, etc., of the Indians of St. Juan Capistrano," in A. Robinson's *Life in California* (New York, 1846), p. 299.

[3] C. Lumholtz, *Unknown Mexico* (London, 1903), i. 324 *sq.*

hand to his yelling mouth, each of them held aloft in his extended left, by way of propitiating the angry star, a bundle of cigarettes. " There ! " they seemed to say, " all that tobacco will we give to ward off the impending visitation. Woe to you, if you do not leave us in peace." [1]   The Lengua Indians of the Gran Chaco also stand in great fear of meteors, imagining them to be stones hurled from heaven at the wicked sorcerers who have done people to death by their charms.[2]   When the Abipones beheld a meteor flashing or heard thunder rolling in the sky, they imagined that one of their medicine-men had died, and that the flash of light and the peal of thunder were part of his funeral honours.[3]

When the Laughlan Islanders see a shooting star they make a great noise, for they think it is the old woman who lives in the moon coming down to earth to catch somebody, who may relieve her of her duties in the moon while she goes away to the happy spirit-land.[4]   In Vedic India a meteor was believed to be the embodiment of a demon, and on its appearance certain hymns or incantations, supposed to possess the power of killing demons, were recited for the purpose of expiating the prodigy.[5]   To this day in India, when women see a falling star, they spit thrice to scare the demon.[6]   Some of the Esthonians at the present time regard shooting stars as evil spirits.[7]   It is a Mohammedan belief that falling stars are demons or jinn who have attempted to scale the sky, and, being repulsed by the angels with stones, are hurled headlong, flaming, from the celestial vault.   Hence every true believer at sight of a

Shooting stars regarded as demons.

[1] K. von den Steinen, *Unter den Naturvölkern Zentral-Brasiliens* (Berlin, 1894), pp. 514 *sq.* The Peruvian Indians also made a prodigious noise when they saw a shooting star. See P. de Cieza de Leon, *Travels* (Hakluyt Society, London, 1864), p. 232.

[2] G. Kurze, " Sitten und Gebräuche der Lengua-Indianer," *Mitteilungen der Geographischen Gesellschaft zu Jena*, xxiii. (1905) p. 17 ; W. Barbrooke Grubb, *An Unknown People in an Unknown Land* (London, 1911), p. 163.

[3] M. Dobrizhoffer, *Historia de Abi-*

ponibus (Vienna, 1784), ii. 86.

[4] W. Tetzlaff, "Notes on the Laughlan Islands," *Annual Report on British New Guinea, 1890-91* (Brisbane, 1892), p. 105.

[5] H. Oldenberg, *Die Religion des Veda*, p. 267.

[6] W. Crooke, *Popular Religion and Folklore of Northern India* (Westminster, 1906), ii. 22.

[7] Holzmayer, "Osiliana," *Verhandlungen der gelehrten Estnischen Gesellschaft zu Dorpat*, vii. (1872) p. 48.

meteor should say, " I take refuge with God from the stoned devil." [1]

Shooting stars associated with the souls of the dead. A widespread superstition, of which some examples have already been given, associates meteors or falling stars with the souls of the dead. Often they are believed to be the spirits of the departed on their way to the other world. The Maoris imagine that at death the soul leaves the body and goes to the nether world in the form of a falling star.[2] The Kingsmill Islanders deemed a shooting star an omen of death to some member of the family which occupied the part of the council-house nearest to the point of the sky whence the meteor took its flight. If the star was followed by a train of light, it foretold the death of a woman ; if not, the death of a man.[3] When the Wotjobaluk tribe of Victoria see a shooting star, they think it is falling with the heart of a man who has been caught by a sorcerer and deprived of his fat.[4] One evening when Mr. Howitt was talking with an Australian black, a bright meteor was seen shooting through the sky. The native watched it and remarked, " An old blackfellow has fallen down there." [5] Among the Yerrunthally tribe of Queensland the ideas on this subject were even more definite. They thought that after death they went to a place away among the stars, and that to reach it they had to climb up a rope ; when they had clambered up they let go the rope, which, as it fell from heaven, appeared to people on earth as a falling star.[6] The natives of the Prince of Wales Islands, off Queensland, are

[1] Guillain, *Documents sur l'histoire, la géographie, et le commerce de l'Afrique Orientale*, ii. (Paris, N.D.) p. 97 ; C. Velten, *Sitten und Gebräuche der Suaheli* (Göttingen, 1903), pp. 339 sq. ; C. B. Klunzinger, *Upper Egypt* (London, 1878), p. 405 ; Budgett Meakin, *The Moors* (London, 1902), p. 353.

[2] E. Dieffenbach, *Travels in New Zealand* (London, 1843), ii. 66. According to another account, meteors are regarded by the Maoris as betokening the presence of a god (R. Taylor, *Te Ika a Maui, or New Zealand and its Inhabitants*,[2] p. 147).

[3] Ch. Wilkes, *Narrative of the United States Exploring Expedition*, v. 88.

[4] A. W. Howitt, *Native Tribes of South-East Australia*, p. 369.

[5] A. W. Howitt, in Brough Smyth's *Aborigines of Victoria*, ii. 309.

[6] E. Palmer, "Notes on some Australian Tribes," *Journal of the Anthropological Institute*, xiii. (1884) p. 292. Sometimes apparently the Australian natives regard crystals or broken glass as fallen stars, and treasure them as powerful instruments of magic. See E. M. Curr, *The Australian Race*, iii. 29 ; W. E. Roth, *North Queensland Ethnography, Bulletin No. 5*, p. 8.

much afraid of shooting stars, for they believe them to be ghosts which, in breaking up, produce young ones of their own kind.[1]   The natives of the Gazelle Peninsula in New Britain think that meteors are the souls of people who have been murdered or eaten ; so at the sight of a meteor flashing they cry out, " The ghost of a murdered man ! "[2] According to the Sulka of New Britain meteors are souls which have been flung into the air in order to plunge into the sea ; and the train of light which they leave behind them is a burning tail of dry coco-nut leaves which has been tied to them by other souls, in order to help them to wing their way through the air.[3]   The Caffres of South Africa often say that a shooting star is the sign of the death of some chief, and at sight of it they will spit on the ground as a mark of friendly feeling towards the dead man.[4] Similarly the Ababua of the Congo valley think that a chief will die in the village into which a star appears to fall, unless the danger of death be averted by a particular dance.[5]   In the opinion of the Masai, the fall of a meteor signifies the death of some one ; at sight of it they pray that the victim may be one of their enemies.[6]   The Wambugwe of eastern Africa fancy that the stars are men, of whom one dies whenever a star is seen to fall.[7]   The Tinneh Indians and the Tchiglit Esquimaux of north-western America believe that human life on earth is influenced by the stars, and they take a shooting star to be a sign that some one has died.[8]   The Lolos, an aboriginal tribe of western China, hold that for each person on earth there is a corresponding star in the sky.   Hence when a man is ill, they sacrifice wine to his star and light four and twenty lamps outside of his room.   On the day after the funeral they dig a hole in the chamber of death

The Supposed relation of the stars to men.

[1] J. Macgillivray, *Narrative of the Voyage of H.M.S. Rattlesnake* (London, 1852), ii. 30.

[2] P. A. Kleintitschen, *Die Küstenbewohner der Gazellehalbinsel* (Hiltrup bei Münster, N.D.), p. 227.

[3] P. Rascher, " Die Sulka," *Archiv für Anthropologie*, xxix. (1904) p. 216.

[4] Dudley Kidd, *Savage Childhood* (London, 1906), p. 149.

[5] J. Halkin, *Quelques Peuplades du district de l'Uelé* (Liège, 1907), p. 102.

[6] O. Baumann, *Durch Massailand zur Nilquelle* (Berlin, 1894), p. 163.

[7] O. Baumann, *Durch Massailand zur Nilquelle* (Berlin, 1894), p. 188.

[8] E. Petitot, *Monographie des Dènè-Dindjé* (Paris, 1876), p. 60 ; *id.*, *Monographie des Esquimaux Tchiglit* (Paris, 1876), p. 24.

and pray the dead man's star to descend and be buried in it. If this precaution were not taken, the star might fall and hit somebody and hurt him very much.[1] In classical antiquity there was a popular notion that every human being had his own star in the sky, which shone bright or dim according to his good or evil fortune, and fell in the form of a meteor when he died.[2]

Modern European beliefs as to meteors.

Superstitions of the same sort are still commonly to be met with in Europe. Thus in some parts of Germany they say that at the birth of a man a new star is set in the sky, and that as it burns brilliantly or faintly he grows rich or poor ; finally when he dies it drops from the sky in the likeness of a shooting star.[3] Similarly in Brittany, Transylvania, Bohemia, the Abruzzi, the Romagna, and the Esthonian island of Oesel it is thought by some that every man has his own particular star in the sky, and that when it falls in the shape of a meteor he expires.[4] A like belief is entertained by Polish Jews.[5] In Styria they say that when a shooting star is seen a man has just died, or a poor soul been released from purgatory.[6] The Esthonians believe that if any one sees a falling star on New Year's night he will die or be visited by a serious illness that

[1] A. Henry, "The Lolos and other Tribes of Western China," *Journal of the Anthropological Institute*, xxxiii. (1903) p. 103.

[2] Pliny, *Nat. Hist.* ii. 28.

[3] F. Panzer, *Beitrag zur deutschen Mythologie*, ii. 293 ; A. Kuhn und W. Schwartz, *Norddeutsche Sagen, Märchen und Gebräuche*, p. 457, § 422; E. Meier, *Deutsche Sagen, Sitten und Gebräuche aus Schwaben*, p. 506, §§ 379, 380.

[4] P. Sébillot, *Traditions et superstitions de la Haute - Bretagne*, ii. 353 ; J. Haltrich, *Zur Volkskunde der Siebenbürger Sachsen* (Vienna, 1885), p. 300 ; W. Schmidt, *Das Jahr und seine Tage in Meinung und Brauch der Romänen Siebenbürgens*, p. 38 ; E. Gerard, *The Land beyond the Forest*, i. 311; J. V. Grohmann, *Aberglauben und Gebräuche aus Böhmen und Mähren*, p. 31, § 164; Br. Jelínek, " Materialien zur Vorgeschichte und Volkskunde Böhmens," *Mittheilungen der anthropo-logischen Gesellschaft in Wien*, xxi. (1891) p. 25 ; G. Finamore, *Credenze, usi e costumi Abruzzesi*, pp. 47 *sq.*; M. Placucci, *Usi e pregiudizj dei contadini della Romagna* (Palermo, 1885), p. 141; Holzmayer, " Osiliana," *Verhandl. der gelehrten Estnischen Gesellschaft zu Dorpat*, vii. (1872) p. 48. The same belief is said to prevail in Armenia. See Minas Tchéraz, " Notes sur la mythologie arménienne," *Transactions of the Ninth International Congress of Orientalists* (London, 1893), ii. 824. Bret Harte has employed the idea in his little poem, " Relieving Guard."

[5] H. Lew, " Der Tod und die Beerdigungs - gebräuche bei den polnischen Juden," *Mittheilungen der anthropologischen Gesellschaft in Wien*, xxxii. (1902) p. 402.

[6] A. Schlossar, " Volksmeinung und Volksaberglaube aus der deutschen Steiermark," *Germania*, N.R., xxiv. (1891) p. 389.

year.[1] In Belgium and many parts of France the people suppose that a meteor is a soul which has just quitted the body, sometimes that it is specially the soul of an unbaptized infant or of some one who has died without absolution. At sight of it they say that you should cross yourself and pray, or that if you wish for something while the star is falling you will be sure to get it.[2] Among the Vosges Mountains in the warm nights of July it is not uncommon to see whole showers of shooting stars. It is generally agreed that these stars are souls, but some difference of opinion exists as to whether they are souls just taking leave of earth, or tortured by the fires of purgatory, or on their passage from purgatory to heaven.[3] The last and most cheering of these views is held by the French peasantry of Beauce and Perche and by the Italian peasantry of the Abruzzi, and charitable people pray for the deliverance of a soul at the sight of a falling star.[4] The downward direction of its flight might naturally suggest a different goal ; and accordingly other people have seen in the transient flame of a meteor the descent of a soul from heaven to be born on earth. In the Punjaub, for example, Hindoos believe that the length of a soul's residence in the realms of bliss is exactly proportioned to the sums which the man distributed in charity during his life ; and that when these are exhausted his time in heaven is up, and down he comes.[5] In Polynesia a shooting star was held to be the flight of a spirit, and to presage the birth of a great prince.[6] The Mandans of north America fancied that the stars were dead people, and that when a woman was brought to bed a star fell from heaven, and entering into her was born as a

Various beliefs as to stars and meteors.

[1] Boecler-Kreutzwald, *Der Ehsten abergläubische Gebräuche, Weisen und Gewohnheiten* (St. Petersburg, 1854), p. 73.
[2] E. Monseur, *Le Folklore wallon*, p. 61 ; A. de Nore, *Coutumes, mythes et traditions des provinces de France*, pp. 101, 160, 223, 267, 284 ; B. Souché, *Croyances, présages et traditions diverses*, p. 23 ; P. Sébillot, *Traditions et superstitions de la Haute-Bretagne*, ii. 352 ; J. Lecœur, *Esquisses du bocage normand*, ii. 13 ; L. Pineau, *Folk-lore du Poitou* (Paris, 1892), pp. 525 *sq.*
[3] L. F. Sauvé, *Le Folk-lore des Hautes-Vosges* (Paris, 1889), pp. 196 *sq.*
[4] F. Chapiseau, *Le Folk-lore de la Beauce et du Perche* (Paris, 1902), i. 290 ; G. Finamore, *Credenze, usi e costumi Abruzzesi* (Palermo, 1890), p. 48.
[5] *North Indian Notes and Queries*, i. p. 102, § 673. Compare *id.* p. 47, § 356 ; *Indian Notes and Queries*, iv. p. 184, § 674 ; W. Crooke, *Popular Religion and Folklore of Northern India* (Westminster, 1896), i. 82.
[6] W. Ellis, *Polynesian Researches*,[2] iii. 171.

child.[1]   On the Biloch frontier of the Punjaub each man is held to have his star, and he may not journey in particular directions when his star is in certain positions.   If duty compels him to travel in the forbidden direction, he takes care before setting out to bury his star, or rather a figure of it cut out of cloth, so that it may not see what he is doing.[2]

The fall of the king's star.   Which, if any, of these superstitions moved the barbarous Dorians of old to depose their kings whenever at a certain season a meteor flamed in the sky, we cannot say.   Perhaps they had a vague general notion that its appearance signified the dissatisfaction of the higher powers with the state of the commonwealth ; and since in primitive society the king is commonly held responsible for all untoward events, whatever their origin, the natural course was to relieve him of duties which he had proved himself incapable of discharging. But it may be that the idea in the minds of these rude barbarians was more definite.   Possibly, like some people in Europe at the present day, they thought that every man had his star in the sky, and that he must die when it fell.   The king would be no exception to the rule, and on a certain night of a certain year, at the end of a cycle, it might be customary to watch the sky in order to mark whether the king's star was still in the ascendant or near its setting. The appearance of a meteor on such a night—of a star precipitated from the celestial vault—might prove for the king not merely a symbol but a sentence of death.   It might be the warrant for his execution.

Reasons for limiting a king's reign to eight years.   If the tenure of the regal office was formerly limited among the Spartans to eight years, we may naturally ask, why was that precise period selected as the measure of a king's reign ?   The reason is probably to be found in those astronomical considerations which determined the early Greek calendar.   The difficulty of reconciling lunar with solar time is one of the standing puzzles which has taxed the ingenuity of men who are emerging from barbarism.   Now an octennial

---

[1] Maximilian Prinz zu Wied, *Reise in das Innere Nord-America* (Coblenz, 1839-1841), ii. 152.   It does not, however, appear from the writer's statement whether the descent of the soul was identified with the flight of a meteor or not.

[2] D. C. J. Ibbetson, *Outlines of Panjab Ethnography* (Calcutta, 1883), p. 118, § 231.

cycle is the shortest period at the end of which sun and The
moon really mark time together after overlapping, so to say,
throughout the whole of the interval. Thus, for example, it
is only once in every eight years that the full moon coincides
with the longest or shortest day ; and as this coincidence
can be observed with the aid of a simple dial, the observation is naturally one of the first to furnish a base for a
calendar which shall bring lunar and solar times into toler-
able, though not exact, harmony.[1] But in early days the
proper adjustment of the calendar is a matter of religious
concern, since on it depends a knowledge of the right seasons
for propitiating the deities whose favour is indispensable to
the welfare of the community.[2] No wonder, therefore, that
the king, as the chief priest of the state, or as himself a god,
should be liable to deposition or death at the end of an
astronomical period. When the great luminaries had run
their course on high, and were about to renew the heavenly
race, it might well be thought that the king should renew
his divine energies, or prove them unabated, under pain of
making room for a more vigorous successor. In southern
India, as we have seen, the king's reign and life terminated
with the revolution of the planet Jupiter round the sun. In
Greece, on the other hand, the king's fate seems to have
hung in the balance at the end of every eight years, ready
to fly up and kick the beam as soon as the opposite scale
was loaded with a falling star.

The same train of thought may explain an ancient Greek The
custom which appears to have required that a homicide should
be banished his country, and do penance for a period of

The octennial cycle based on an attempt to reconcile solar and lunar time.

The octennial cycle in relation to

---

[1] L. Ideler, *Handbuch der mathe-matischen und technischen Chronologie*, ii. 605 *sqq.* Ninety-nine lunar months nearly coincide with eight solar years, as the ancients well knew (Sozomenus, *Historia ecclesiastica*, vii. 18). On the religious and political import of the eight years' cycle in ancient Greece see especially K. O. Müller, *Orcho-menus und die Minyer*,[2] pp. 213-218 ; *id.*, *Die Dorier*,[2] i. 254 *sq.*, 333 *sq.*, 440, ii. 96, 483 ; *id.*, *Prolegomena zu einer wissenschaftlichen Mythologie* (Göttingen, 1825), pp. 422-424.

[2] "Ancient opinion even assigned

the regulation of the calendar by the solstices and equinoxes to the will of the gods that sacrifices should be rendered at similar times in each year, rather than to the strict requirements of agriculture ; and as religion un-doubtedly makes larger demands on the cultivator as agriculture advances, the obligations of sacrifice may probably be reckoned as of equal importance with agricultural necessities in urging the formation of reckonings in the nature of a calendar " (E. J. Payne, *History of the New World called America*, ii. 280).

the Greek doctrine of rebirth.

eight or nine years.[1] With the beginning of a new cycle or great year, as it was called, it might be thought that all nature was regenerate, all old scores wiped out. According to Pindar, the dead whose guilt had been purged away by an abode of eight years in the nether world were born again on earth in the ninth year as glorious kings, athletes, and sages.[2] The doctrine may well be an old popular belief rather than a mere poetical fancy. If so, it would supply a fresh reason for the banishment of a homicide during the years that the angry ghost of his victim might at any moment issue from its prison-house and pounce on him. Once the perturbed spirit had been happily reborn, he might be supposed to forgive, if not to forget, the man who had done him an injury in a former life.

The octennial cycle at Cnossus in Crete.

King Minos and Zeus.

Whatever its origin may have been, the cycle of eight years appears to have coincided with the normal length of the king's reign in other parts of Greece besides Sparta. Thus Minos, king of Cnossus in Crete, whose great palace has been unearthed in recent years, is said to have held office for periods of eight years together. At the end of each period he retired for a season to the oracular cave on Mount Ida, and there communed with his divine father Zeus, giving him an account of his kingship in the years that were past, and receiving from him instructions for his guidance in those which were to come.[3] The tradition plainly implies

---

[1] As to the eight years' servitude of Apollo and Cadmus for the slaughter of dragons, see below, p. 78. For the nine years' penance of the man who had tasted human flesh at the festival of Zeus on Mount Lycaeus, see Pliny, *Nat. hist.* viii. 81 *sq.*; Augustine, *De civitate Dei*, xviii. 17; Pausanias, viii. 2. 6; compare Plato, *Republic*, viii. p. 565 D E. Any god who forswore himself by the water of Styx was exiled for nine years from the society of his fellow-gods (Hesiod, *Theogony*, 793-804). On this subject see further, E. Rohde, *Psyche*,[3] ii. 211 *sq.*; W. H. Roscher, "Die enneadischen und hebdomadischen Fristen und Wochen der ältesten Griechen," *Abhandlungen der philolog. - histor. Klasse der Königl. Sächsischen Gesellschaft der Wissen-*

schaften, xxi. No. 4 (1903), pp. 24 *sqq.*

[2] Plato, *Meno*, p. 81 A-C; Pindar, ed. Boeckh, vol. iii. pp. 623 *sq.*, Frag. 98.

[3] Homer, *Odyssey*, xix. 178 *sq.*,

τῇσι δ' ἐνὶ Κνωσός, μεγάλη πόλις,
ἔνθα τε Μίνως
ἐννέωρος βασίλευε Διὸς μεγάλου
ὀαριστής,

with the Scholia; Plato, *Laws*, i. 1. p. 624 A, B; [*id.*] *Minos*, 13 *sq.*, pp. 319 *sq.*; Strabo, ix. 4. 8, p. 476; Maximus Tyrius, *Dissert.* xxxviii. 2; *Etymologicum magnum*, *s.v.* ἐννέωροι, p. 343, 23 *sqq.*; Valerius Maximus, i. 2, ext. 1; compare Diodorus Siculus, v. 78. 3. Homer's expression, ἐννέωρος βασίλευε, has been variously explained.

that at the end of every eight years the king's sacred powers needed to be renewed by intercourse with the godhead, and that without such a renewal he would have forfeited his right to the throne. We may surmise that among the solemn ceremonies which marked the beginning or the end of the eight years' cycle the sacred marriage of the king with the queen played an important part, and that in this marriage we have the true explanation of the strange legend of Pasiphae and the bull. It was said that Pasiphae, the wife of King Minos, fell in love with a wondrous white bull which rose from the sea, and that in order to gratify her unnatural passion the artist Daedalus constructed a hollow wooden cow, covered with a cow's hide, in which the love-sick queen was hidden while the bull mounted it. The result of their union was the Minotaur, a monster with the body of a man and the head of a bull, whom the king shut up in the labyrinth, a building full of such winding and intricate passages that the prisoner might roam in it for ever without finding the way out.[1] The legend appears to reflect a mythical marriage of the sun and moon, which was acted as a solemn rite by the king and queen of Cnossus, wearing the masks of a bull and cow respectively.[2] To a

Sacred marriage of the king and queen of Cnossus in the form of bull and cow as symbols of the sun and moon.

I follow the interpretation which appears to have generally found favour both with the ancients, including Plato, and with modern scholars. See K. Hoeck, *Kreta*, i. 244 *sqq.*; K. O. Müller, *Die Dorier*,[2] ii. 96; G. F. Unger, "Zeitrechnung der Griechen und Römer," in Ivan Müller's *Handbuch der klassischen Altertumswissenschaft*, i. 569; A. Schmidt, *Handbuch der griechischen Chronologie* (Jena, 1888), p. 65; W. H. Roscher, "Die enneadischen und hebdomadischen Fristen und Wochen der ältesten Griechen," *Abhandlungen der philolog.-histor. Klasse der Königl. Sächsischen Gesellschaft der Wissenschaften*, xxi. No. 4 (Leipsic, 1903), pp. 22 *sq.*; E. Rohde, *Psyche*,[3] i. 128 *sq.* Literally interpreted, ἐννέωρος means "for nine years," not "for eight years." But see above, p. 59, note [1].

[1] Apollodorus, iii. 1. 3 *sq.*, iii. 15. 8; Diodorus Siculus, iv. 77; Schol. on Euripides, *Hippolytus*, 887; J. Tzetzes, *Chiliades*, i. 479 *sqq.*; Hyginus,

Fabulae, 40; Virgil, *Ecl.* vi. 45 *sqq.*; Ovid, *Ars amat.* i. 289 *sqq.*

[2] K. Hoeck, *Kreta*, ii. (Göttingen, 1828) pp. 63-69; L. Preller, *Griechische Mythologie*,[3] ii. 119-123; W. H. Roscher, *Über Selene und Verwandtes* (Leipsic, 1890), pp. 135-139; *id.*, *Nachträge zu meiner Schrift über Selene* (Leipsic, 1895), p. 3; Türk, in W. H. Roscher's *Lexikon der griech. und röm. Mythologie*, iii. 1666 *sq.*; A. J. Evans, "Mycenaean Tree and Pillar Cult," *Journal of Hellenic Studies*, xxi. (1901) p. 181; A. B. Cook, "Zeus, Jupiter, and the Oak," *Classical Review*, xvii. (1903) pp. 406-412; compare *id.*, "The European Sky-god," *Folklore*, xv. (1904) p. 272. All these writers, except Mr. Cook, regard Minos and Pasiphae as representing the sun and moon. Mr. Cook agrees so far as relates to Minos, but he supposes Pasiphae to be a sky-goddess or sun-goddess rather than a goddess of the moon. On the other hand, he was

pastoral people a bull is the most natural type of vigorous reproductive energy,[1] and as such is a fitting emblem of the sun. Islanders who, like many of the Cretans, see the sun daily rising from the sea, might readily compare him to a white bull issuing from the waves. Indeed, we are expressly told that the Cretans called the sun a bull.[2] Similarly in ancient Egypt the sacred bull Mnevis of Heliopolis (the City of the Sun) was deemed an incarnation of the Sun-god,[3] and for thousands of years the kings of Egypt delighted to be styled " mighty bull "; many of them inscribed the title on their *serekh* or cognisance, which set forth their names in their character of descendants of Horus.[4] The identification of Pasiphae, " she who shines on all," with the moon was made long ago by Pausanias, who saw her image along with that of the sun in a sanctuary on that wild rocky coast of Messenia where the great range of Taygetus descends seaward in a long line of naked crags.[5] The horns of the waxing or waning moon naturally suggest the resemblance of the luminary to a white cow ; hence the ancients represented the goddess of the moon drawn by a team of white cattle.[6] When we remember that at the court of Egypt the king and queen figured as god and goddess in solemn masquerades, where the parts of animal-headed deities were played by masked men and women,[7] we need have no difficulty in imagining that similar dramas may have been performed at the court of a Cretan king, whether we suppose them to have been imported from Egypt or to have had an independent origin.

the first to suggest that the myth was periodically acted by the king and queen of Cnossus disguised in bovine form.

[1] Compare *The Magic Art and the Evolution of Kings*, ii. 368 *sq.*

[2] Bekker's *Anecdota Graeca*, i. 344, *s.v.* 'Αδιούνιος ταῦρος.

[3] Eusebius, *Praeparatio Evangelii*, iii. 13. 1 *sq.* ; Diodorus Siculus, i. 84. 4, i. 88. 4 ; Strabo, xvii. 1. 22 and 27, pp. 803, 805 ; Aelian, *De natura animalium*, xi. 11 ; Suidas, *s.v.* Ἄπις ; Ammianus Marcellinus, xxii. 14. 7 ; A. Wiedemann, *Herodots Zweites Buch*, p. 552 ; A. Erman, *Die ägyptische Religion* (Berlin, 1905), p. 26 ;

E. A. Wallis Budge, *The Gods of the Egyptians* (London, 1904), i. 330.

[4] E. A. Wallis Budge, *The Gods of the Egyptians*, i. 25.

[5] Pausanias, i. 26. 1. For a description of the scenery of this coast, see Morritt, in Walpole's *Memoirs relating to European Turkey*, i.[2] p. 54.

[6] W. H. Roscher, *Über Selene und Verwandtes*, pp. 30-33.

[7] See *The Magic Art and the Evolution of Kings*, ii. 130 *sqq.* We are told that Egyptian sovereigns assumed the masks of lions, bulls, and serpents as symbols of power (Diodorus Siculus, i. 62. 4).

The stories of Zeus and Europa, and of Minos and The same myth and custom of the marriage of the sun and moon appear in the stories of Zeus and Europa, of Minos and Brito- martis. Britomartis or Dictynna appear to be only different expressions of the same myth, different echoes of the same custom. The moon rising from the sea was the fair maiden Europa coming across the heaving billows from the far eastern land of Phoenicia, borne or pursued by her suitor the solar bull. The moon setting in the western waves was the coy Britomartis or Dictynna, who plunged into the sea to escape the warm embrace of her lover Minos, himself the sun. The story how the drowning maiden was drawn up in a fisherman's net may well be, as some have thought, the explanation given by a simple seafaring folk of the moon's reappearance from the sea in the east after she had sunk into it in the west.[1] To the mythical fancy of the ancients the moon was a coy or a wanton maiden, who either fled from or pursued the sun every month till the fugitive was overtaken and the lovers enjoyed each other's company at the time when the luminaries are in conjunction, namely, in the interval between the old and the new moon. Hence on The con- junction of the sun and moon regarded as the best time for marriages. the principles of sympathetic magic that interval was considered the time most favourable for human marriages. When the sun and moon are wedded in the sky, men and women should be wedded on earth. And for the same reason the ancients chose the interlunar day for the celebration of the Sacred Marriages of gods and goddesses. Similar beliefs and customs based on them have been noted among other peoples.[2] It is likely, therefore, that a king and queen

---

[1] As to Minos and Britomartis or Dictynna, see Callimachus, *Hymn to Diana*, 189 *sqq.*; Pausanias, ii. 30. 3 ; Antoninus Liberalis, *Transform.* 40 ; Diodorus Siculus, v. 76. On Britomartis as a moon - goddess, see K. Hoeck, *Kreta*, ii. 170 ; W. H. Roscher, *Über Selene und Verwandtes*, pp. 45 *sq.*, 116-118. Hoeck acutely perceived that the pursuit of Britomartis by Minos "is a trait of old festival customs in which the conceptions of the sun-god were transferred to the king of the island." As to the explanation here adopted of the myth of Zeus and Europa, see K. Hoeck, *Kreta*, i. 90 *sqq.*; W. H. Roscher, *op. cit.* pp. 128-135.

Moschus describes (ii. 84 *sqq.*) the bull which carried off Europa as yellow in colour with a silver circle shining on his forehead, and he compares the bull's horns to those of the moon.

[2] See W. H. Roscher, *op. cit.* pp. 76-82. Amongst the passages of classical writers which he cites are Plutarch, *De facie in orbe lunae*, 30 ; *id.*, *Isis et Osiris*, 52 ; Cornutus, *Theologiae Graecae compendium*, 34, p. 72, ed. C. Lang ; Proclus, on Hesiod, *Works and Days*, 780 ; Macrobius, *Commentar. in Somnium Scipionis*, i. 18. 10 *sq.*; Pliny, *Nat. hist.* ii. 45. When the sun and moon were eclipsed, the Tahitians supposed that the lumin-

who represented the sun and moon may have been expected
to exercise their conjugal rights above all at the time when
the moon was thought to rest in the arms of the sun.

Octennial
marriage
of the
king and
queen as
representa-
tives of the
sun and
moon.

However that may have been, it would be natural that their
union should be consummated with unusual solemnity every
eight years, when the two great luminaries, so to say, meet
and mark time together once more after diverging from
each other more or less throughout the interval. It is true
that sun and moon are in conjunction once every month,
but every month their conjunction takes place at a different
point in the sky, until eight revolving years have brought
them together again in the same heavenly bridal chamber
where first they met.

Octennial
tribute of
youths and
maidens
probably
required as
a means of
renewing
the sun's
fire by
human
sacrifices.

Without being unduly rash we may surmise that the
tribute of seven youths and seven maidens whom the
Athenians were bound to send to Minos every eight years
had some connexion with the renewal of the king's power
for another octennial cycle. Traditions varied as to the
fate which awaited the lads and damsels on their arrival in
Crete ; but the common view appears to have been that
they were shut up in the labyrinth, there to be devoured
by the Minotaur, or at least to be imprisoned for life.[1]

The
Minotaur
a bull-
headed
image of
the sun.

Perhaps they were sacrificed by being roasted alive in a
bronze image of a bull, or of a bull-headed man, in order to
renew the strength of the king and of the sun, whom he
personated. This at all events is suggested by the legend
of Talos, a bronze man who clutched people to his breast
and leaped with them into the fire, so that they were roasted
alive. He is said to have been given by Zeus to Europa,
or by Hephaestus to Minos, to guard the island of Crete,
which he patrolled thrice daily.[2] According to óne
account he was a bull,[3] according to another he was the

aries were in the act of copulation
(J. Wilson, *Missionary Voyage to the
Southern Pacific Ocean* (London, 1799),
p. 346).

[1] Plutarch, *Theseus*, 15 sq.; Diodorus Siculus, iv. 61 ; Pausanias, i. 27.
10 ; Ovid, *Metam.* viii. 170 sq. According to another account, the tribute
of youths and maidens was paid every
year. See Virgil, *Aen.* vi. 14 sqq.,
with the commentary of Servius ;

Hyginus, *Fabulae*, 41.

[2] Apollodorus, i. 9. 26 ; Apollonius
Rhodius, *Argon.* iv. 1638 sqq., with the
scholium ; Agatharchides, in Photius,
Bibliotheca, p. 443 b, lines 22-25, ed.
Bekker ; Lucian, *De saltatione*, 49 ;
Zenobius, v. 85 ; Suidas, s.v. Σαρδάνιος
γέλως ; Eustathius on Homer, *Odyssey*,
xx. 302, p. 1893 ; Schol. on Plato,
Republic, i. p. 337 A.

[3] Apollodorus. i. 9. 26.

sun.[1] Probably he was identical with the Minotaur, and stripped of his mythical features was nothing but a bronze image of the sun represented as a man with a bull's head. In order to renew the solar fires, human victims may have been sacrificed to the idol by being roasted in its hollow body or placed on its sloping hands and allowed to roll into a pit of fire. It was in the latter fashion that the Carthaginians sacrificed their offspring to Moloch. The children were laid on the hands of a calf-headed image of bronze, from which they slid into a fiery oven, while the people danced to the music of flutes and timbrels to drown the shrieks of the burning victims.[2] The resemblance which the Cretan traditions bear to the Carthaginian practice suggests that the worship associated with the names of Minos and the Minotaur may have been powerfully influenced by that of a Semitic Baal.[3] In the tradition of Phalaris, tyrant of Agrigentum, and his brazen bull[4] we may have an echo of similar rites in Sicily, where the Carthaginian power struck deep roots.

But perhaps the youths and maidens who were sent across the sea to Cnossus had to perform certain religious duties before they were cast into the fiery furnace. The same cunning artist Daedalus who planned the labyrinth and contrived the wooden cow for Pasiphae was said to have made a dance for Ariadne, daughter of Minos. It represented youths and maidens dancing in ranks, the youths armed with golden swords, the maidens crowned with garlands.[5] Moreover, when Theseus landed with Ariadne in Delos on his return from Crete, he and the young companions whom he had rescued from the Minotaur are said to have danced a mazy dance in imitation of the intricate windings of the labyrinth ; on account of its sinuous turns the dance was called " the Crane."[6] Taken together, these two traditions suggest that the youths and maidens who

Dance of the youths and maidens at Cnossus.

---

[1] Hesychius, *s.v.* Ταλῶς.
[2] Diodorus Siculus, xx. 14 ; Clitarchus, cited by Suidas, *s.v.* Σαρδάνιος γέλως, and by the Scholiast on Plato, *Republic*, p. 337 A ; Plutarch, *De superstitione*, 13 ; Paulus Fagius, quoted by Selden, *De dis Syris* (Leipsic, 1668), pp. 169 *sq.* The calf's head of the idol is mentioned only by P. Fagius,

who drew his account from a book Jalkut by Rabbi-Simeon.
[3] Compare M. Mayer, *s.v.* "Kronos," in W. H. Roscher's *Lexikon d. griech. u. röm. Mythologie*, iii. 1501 *sqq.*
[4] J. Tzetzes, *Chiliades*, i. 646 *sqq.*
[5] Homer, *Iliad*, xviii. 590 *sqq.*
[6] Plutarch, *Theseus*, 21 ; Julius Pollux, iv. 101.

were sent to Cnossus had to dance in the labyrinth before they were sacrificed to the bull-headed image. At all events there are good grounds for thinking that there was a famous dance which the ancients regularly associated with the Cretan labyrinth.

The game of Troy.

Among the Romans that dance appears to have been known from the earliest times by the name of Troy or the Game of Troy. Tradition ran that it was imported into Italy by Aeneas, who transmitted it through his son Ascanius to the Alban kings, who in their turn handed it down to the Romans. It was performed by bands of armed youths on horseback. Virgil compares their complicated evolutions to the windings of the Cretan labyrinth;[1] and that the comparison is more than a mere poetical flourish appears from a drawing on a very ancient Etruscan vase found at Tragliatella. The drawing represents a procession of seven beardless warriors dancing, accompanied by two armed riders on horseback, who are also beardless. An inscription proves that the scene depicted is the Game of Troy; and attached to the procession is a figure of the Cretan labyrinth,[2] the pattern of which is well known from coins of Cnossus on which it is often represented.[3] The same pattern, identified by an inscription, "*Labyrinthus, hic habitat Minotaurus*," is scratched on a wall at Pompeii; and it is also worked in mosaic on the floor of Roman apartments, with the figures of Theseus and the Minotaur in the middle.[4] Roman boys appear to have drawn the very same pattern on the ground and to have played a game on it, probably a miniature Game of Troy.[5] Labyrinths of similar type occur as decorations on the floors of old churches, where they are known as "the Road of Jerusalem"; they were used for processions. The garden mazes of the Renaissance were modelled on them. Moreover, they are found very commonly in the north of Europe, marked out either by raised bands of turf or by

[1] As to the Game of Troy, see Virgil, *Aen.* v. 545-603; Plutarch, *Cato*, 3; Tacitus, *Annals*, xi. 11; Suetonius, *Augustus*, 43; *id.*, *Tiberius*, 6; *id.*, *Caligula*, 18; *id.*, *Nero*, 6; W. Smith's *Dictionary of Greek and Roman Antiquities*,[3] *s.v.* "Trojae ludus"; O. Benndorf, "Das Alter des Troja-

spieles," appended to W. Reichel's *Über homerische Waffen* (Vienna, 1894), pp. 133-139.

[2] O. Benndorf, *op. cit.* pp. 133 *sq.*

[3] B. V. Head, *Historia numorum* (Oxford, 1887), pp. 389-391.

[4] O. Benndorf, *op. cit.* pp. 134 *sq.*

[5] Pliny, *Nat. hist.* xxxvi. 85.

rows of stones.   Such labyrinths may be seen in Norway, Sweden, Denmark, Finnland, the south coast of Russian Lappland, and even in Iceland.   They go by various names, such as Babylon, Wieland's House, Trojeborg, Tröburg, and so forth, some of which clearly indicate their connexion with the ancient Game of Troy.   They are used for children's games.[1]

A dance or game which has thus spread over Europe and survived in a fashion to modern times must have been very popular, and bearing in mind how often with the decay of old faiths the serious rites and pageants of grown people have degenerated into the sports of children, we may reasonably ask whether Ariadne's Dance or the Game of Troy may not have had its origin in religious ritual.   The ancients connected it with Cnossus and the Minotaur.   Now we have seen reason to hold, with many other scholars, that Cnossus was the seat of a great worship of the sun, and that the Minotaur was a representative or embodiment of the sungod.   May not, then, Ariadne's dance have been an imitation of the sun's course in the sky? and may not its intention have been, by means of sympathetic magic, to aid the great luminary to run his race on high?   We have seen that during an eclipse of the sun the Chilcotin Indians walk in a circle, leaning on staves, apparently to assist the labouring orb.   In Egypt also the king, who embodied the sun-god, seems to have solemnly walked round the walls of a temple for the sake of helping the sun on his way.[2]   If there is any truth in this conjecture, it would seem to follow that the sinuous lines of the labyrinth which the dancers followed in their evolutions may have represented the ecliptic, the sun's apparent annual path in the sky.   It is some confirmation of this view that on coins of Cnossus the sun or a star appears in the middle of the labyrinth, the place which on other coins is occupied by the Minotaur.[3]

On the whole the foregoing evidence, slight and fragmentary as it is, points to the conclusion that at Cnossus the

The dance at Cnossus perhaps an imitation of the sun's course in the sky.

---

[1] O. Benndorf, *op. cit.* p. 135 ; W. Meyer, "Ein Labyrinth mit Versen," *Sitzungsberichte der philosoph. philolog. und histor. Classe der k. b. Akademie der Wissenschaften zu München*, 1882, vol. ii. pp. 267-300.

[2] See *The Magic Art and the Evolution of Kings*, i. 312.

[3] B. V. Head, *Historia numorum*, p. 389.

Con-
clusions as
to the king
of Cnossus.

king represented the sun-god, and that every eight years his divine powers were renewed at a great festival, which comprised, first, the sacrifice of human victims by fire to a bull-headed image of the sun, and, second, the marriage of the king disguised as a bull to the queen disguised as a cow, the two personating respectively the sun and the moon.

Octennial
festivals
of the
Crowning
at Delphi
and the
Laurel-
bearing at
Thebes.

Whatever may be thought of these speculations, we know that many solemn rites were celebrated by the ancient Greeks at intervals of eight years.[1] Amongst them, two deserve to be noticed here, because it has been recently suggested, with some appearance of probability, that they were based on an octennial tenure of the kingship.[2] One was the Festival of the Crowning at Delphi; the other was the Festival of the Laurel-bearing at Thebes. In their general features the two festivals seem to have resembled each other very closely. Both represented dramatically the slaying of a great water-dragon by a god or hero; in both, the lad who played the part of the victorious god or hero crowned his brows with a wreath of sacred laurel and had to submit to a penance and purification for the slaughter of the beast. At Delphi the legendary slayer of the dragon was Apollo; at Thebes he was Cadmus.[3] At both places the legendary penance for the slaughter seems to have been servitude for eight years.[4] The evidence for the rites of the Delphic festival is fairly complete, but for the Theban festival it has to be eked out by vase-paintings, which represent Cadmus crowned with laurel preparing to

Both
represented
dramati-
cally the
slaying of
a water-
dragon.

---

[1] Censorinus, *De die natali*, 18. 6.

[2] The suggestion was made by Mr. A. B. Cook. The following discussion of the subject is founded on his ingenious exposition. See his article, "The European Sky-god," *Folklore*, xv. (1904) pp. 402-424.

[3] As to the Delphic festival see Plutarch, *Quaest. Graec.* 12; *id.*, *De defectu oraculorum*, 15; Strabo, ix. 3. 12, pp. 422 *sq.*; Aelian, *Var. hist.* iii. 1; Stephanus Byzantius, *s.v.* Δειπνίας; K. O. Müller, *Die Dorier*,[2] i. 203 *sqq.*, 321-324; Aug. Mommsen, *Delphika* (Leipsic, 1878), pp. 206 *sqq.*; Th. Schreiber, *Apollo Pythoktonos*, pp. 9 *sqq.*; my note on Pausanias, ii. 7. 7 (vol. ii. 53 *sqq.*). As to the Theban

festival, see Pausanias, ix. 10. 4, with my note; Proclus, quoted by Photius, *Bibliotheca*, p. 321, ed. Bekker; Aug. Boeckh, in his edition of Pindar, *Explicationes*, p. 590; K. O. Müller, *Orchomenus und die Minyer*,[2] pp. 215 *sq.*; *id.*, *Dorier*,[2] i. 236 *sq.*, 333 *sq.*; C. Boetticher, *Der Baumkultus der Hellenen*, pp. 386 *sqq.*; G. F. Schömann, *Griechische Alterthümer*,[4] ii. 479 *sq.*

[4] Apollodorus, iii. 4. 2, iii. 10. 4; Servius, on Virgil, *Aen.* vii. 761. The servitude of Apollo is traditionally associated with his slaughter of the Cyclopes, not of the dragon. But see my note on Pausanias, ii. 7. 7 (vol. ii. pp. 53 *sqq.*).

attack the dragon or actually in combat with the monster, while goddesses bend over the champion, holding out wreaths of laurel to him as the mede of victory.[1] It is true that in historical times Apollo appears to have ousted Cadmus from the festival, though not from the myth. But at Thebes the god was plainly a late intruder, for his temple lay outside the walls, whereas the most ancient sanctuaries stood in the oldest part of the city, the low hill which took its name of Cadmea from the genuine Theban hero Cadmus.[2] It is not impossible that at Delphi also, and perhaps at other places where the same drama was acted,[3] Apollo may have displaced an old local hero in the honourable office of dragon-slayer.

Both at Thebes and at Delphi the dragon guarded a spring,[4] the water of which was probably deemed oracular. At Delphi the sacred spring may have been either Cassotis or the more famed Castaly, which issues from a narrow gorge, shut in by rocky walls of tremendous height, a little to the east of Apollo's temple. The waters of both were thought to be endowed with prophetic power.[5] Probably, too, the monster was supposed to keep watch and ward over the sacred laurel, from which the victor in the combat wreathed his brows ; for in vase-paintings the Theban dragon appears coiled beside the holy tree,[6] and Euripides describes the Delphic dragon as covered by a leafy laurel.[7] At all

Both at Delphi and at Thebes the dragon seems to have guarded the oracular spring and the oracular tree.

The crown of laurel and the crown of oak.

[1] W. H. Roscher's *Lexikon d. griech. und röm. Mythologie*, ii. 830, 838, 839. On an Etruscan mirror the scene of Cadmus's combat with the dragon is surrounded by a wreath of laurel (Roscher, *op. cit.* ii. 862). Mr. A. B. Cook was the first to call attention to these vase-paintings in confirmation of my view that the Festival of the Laurel-bearing celebrated the destruction of the dragon by Cadmus (*Folklore*, xv. (1904) p. 411, note [224]).

[2] Pausanias, ix. 10. 2 ; K. O. Müller, *Die Dorier*,[2] i. 237 *sq.*

[3] For evidence of the wide diffusion of the myth and the drama, see Th. Schreiber, *Apollon Pythoktonos*, pp. 39-50. The Laurel-bearing Apollo was worshipped at Athens, as we know from an inscription carved on one of the seats in the theatre. See E. S.

Roberts and E. A. Gardner, *Introduction to Greek Epigraphy*, ii. (Cambridge, 1905) p. 467, No. 247.

[4] Apollodorus, iii. 4. 3 ; Schol. on Homer, *Iliad*, ii. 494 ; Pausanias, ix. 10. 5 ; *Homeric Hymn to Apollo*, 300 *sq.* The writer of the Homeric hymn merely says that Apollo slew the Delphic dragon at a spring ; but Pausanias (x. 6. 6) tells us that the beast guarded the oracle.

[5] Pausanias, x. 8. 9, x. 24. 7, with my notes ; Ovid, *Amores*, i. 15. 35 *sq.*; Lucian, *Jupiter tragoedus*, 30 ; Nonnus, *Dionys.* iv. 309 *sq.*; Suidas, *s.v.* Κασταλία.

[6] W. H. Roscher, *Lexikon d. griech. u. röm. Mythologie*, ii. 830, 838.

[7] Euripides, *Iphigenia in Tauris*, 1245 *sq.*, where the reading κατάχαλ-κος is clearly corrupt.

oracular seats of Apollo his priestess drank of the sacred spring and chewed the sacred laurel before she prophesied.[1] Thus it would seem that the dragon, which at Delphi is expressly said to have been the guardian of the oracle,[2] had in its custody both the instruments of divination, the holy tree and the holy water. We are reminded of the dragon or serpent, slain by Hercules, which guarded the golden apples of the Hesperides in the happy garden.[3] But at Delphi the oldest sacred tree appears, as Mr. A. B. Cook has pointed out,[4] to have been not a laurel but an oak. For we are told that originally the victors in the Pythian games at Delphi wore crowns of oak leaves, since the laurel had not yet been created.[5] Now, like the Festival of Crowning, the Pythian games were instituted to commemorate the slaughter of the dragon ;[6] like it they were originally held every eighth year ;[7] the two festivals were celebrated nearly at the same time of the year ;[8] and the representative of Apollo in the one and the victors in the other were adorned with crowns made from the same sacred laurel.[9] In short, the two festivals appear to have been in origin substantially identical ; the distinction between them may have arisen when the Delphians decided to hold the Pythian games every fourth, instead of every eighth year.[10] We may fairly suppose,

The Festival of Crowning at Delphi originally identical with the Pythian games.

---

[1] Lucian, *Bis accusatus*, 1. So the priest of the Clarian Apollo at Colophon drank of a secret spring before he uttered oracles in verse (Tacitus, *Annals*, ii. 54 ; Pliny, *Nat. hist.* ii. 232).

[2] Euripides, *Iphigenia in Tauris*, 1245 *sqq.*; Apollodorus, i. 4. 1 ; Pausanias, x. 6. 6 ; Aelian, *Var. hist.* iii. 1 ; Hyginus, *Fabulae*, 140; Schol. on Homer, *Iliad*, ii. 519; Schol. on Pindar, *Pyth.* Argument, p. 298, ed. Boeckh.

[3] Euripides, *Hercules Furens*, 395 *sqq.*; Apollodorus, ii. 5. 11 ; Diodorus Siculus, iv. 26 ; Eratosthenes, *Catasterism.* 3 ; Schol. on Euripides, *Hippolytus*, 742 ; Schol. on Apollonius Rhodius, *Argon.* iv. 1396.

[4] A. B. Cook, "The European Sky-god," *Folklore*, xv. (1904) p. 413.

[5] Ovid, *Metam.* i. 448 *sqq.*

[6] Clement of Alexandria, *Protrept.* i. 1, p. 2, and ii. 34, p. 29, ed. Potter: Aristotle, *Peplos*, Frag. (*Fragmenta*

historicorum Graecorum, ii. p. 189, No. 282, ed. C. Müller) ; John of Antioch, Frag. i. 20 (*Frag. histor. Graec.* iv. p. 539, ed. C. Müller) ; Jamblichus, *De Pythagor. vit.* x. 52 ; Schol. on Pindar, *Pyth.* Argum. p. 298, ed. Boeckh ; Ovid, *Metam.* i. 445 *sqq.*; Hyginus, *Fabulae*, 140.

[7] Schol. on Pindar, *l.c.*; Censorinus, *De die natali*, 18. 6 ; compare Eustathius on Homer, *Od.* iii. 267, p. 1466. 29.

[8] Plutarch, *De defectu oraculorum*, 3, compared with *id.* 15 ; Aug. Mommsen, *Delphika*, pp. 211, 214 ; Th. Schreiber, *Apollon Pythoktonos* (Leipsic, 1879), pp. 32 *sqq.*

[9] Aelian, *Var. hist.* iii. 1 ; Schol. on Pindar, *l.c.*

[10] On the original identity of the festivals see Th. Schreiber, *Apollon Pythoktonus*, pp. 37 *sq.*; A. B. Cook, in *Folklore*, xv. (1904) pp. 404 *sq.*

therefore, that the leaf-crowned victors in the Pythian games, like the laurel-wreathed boy in the Festival of Crowning, formerly acted the part of the god himself. But if in the beginning these actors in the sacred drama wore wreaths of oak instead of laurel, it seems to follow that the deity whom they personated was the oak-god Zeus rather than the laurel-god Apollo ; from which again we may infer that Delphi was a sanctuary of Zeus and the oak before it became the shrine of Apollo and the laurel.[1]

But why should the crown of oak have ceased to be the badge of victory ? and why should a wreath of laurel have taken its place ? The abandonment of the oak crown may have been a consequence of the disappearance of the oak itself from the neighbourhood of Delphi ; in Greece, as in Italy, the deciduous trees have for centuries been retreating up the mountain sides before the advance of the evergreens.[2] When the last venerable oak, the rustling of whose leaves in the breeze had long been listened to as oracular, finally succumbed through age, or was laid low by a storm, the priests may have cast about for a tree of another sort to take its place. Yet they sought it neither in the lower woods of the valley nor in the dark forests which clothe the upper slopes of Parnassus above the frowning cliffs of Delphi. Legend ran that after the slaughter of the dragon, Apollo had purged himself from the stain of blood in the romantic Vale of Tempe, where the Peneus flows smoothly in a narrow defile between the lofty wooded steeps of Olympus and Ossa. Here the god crowned himself with a laurel wreath, and thither accordingly at the Festival of Crowning his human representative went to pluck the laurel for his brows.[3] The custom, though doubtless ancient, can hardly have been original. We must suppose that in the beginning the dragon-guarded tree, whether an oak or a laurel, grew at Delphi itself. But why should the laurel be chosen as a substitute for the oak ? Mr. A. B. Cook has suggested a plausible answer. The laurel leaf resembles so closely the leaf of the ilex or holm-

Substitution of the laurel for the oak.

---

[1] The inference was drawn by Mr. A. B. Cook, whom I follow. See his article, "The European Sky-god," *Folk-lore*, xv. (1904) pp. 412 *sqq.*

[2] See *The Magic Art and the Evolution of Kings*, vol. i. p. 8.

[3] Aelian, *Var. hist.* iii. 1 ; Schol. on Pindar, *Pyth.* Argum. p. 298, ed. Boeckh.

oak in both shape and colour that an untrained observer may easily confuse the two. The upper surface of both is a dark glossy green, the lower surface shews a lighter tint. Nothing, therefore, could be more natural than to make the new wreath out of leaves which looked so like the old oak leaves that the substitution might almost pass undetected.[1]

Whether at Thebes, as at Delphi, the laurel had ousted the oak from the place of honour at the festival of the Slaying of the Dragon, we cannot say. The oak has long disappeared from the low hills and flat ground in the neighbourhood of Thebes, but as late as the second century of our era there was a forest of ancient oaks not many miles off at the foot of Mount Cithaeron.[2]

Hypothesis of octennial kings at Delphi and Thebes, who personated dragons or serpents.

It has been conjectured that in ancient days the persons who wore the wreath of laurel or oak at the octennial festivals of Delphi and Thebes were no other than the priestly kings, who personated the god, slew their predecessors in the guise of dragons, and reigned for a time in their stead.[3] The theory certainly cannot be demonstrated, but there is a good deal of analogy in its favour. An eight years' tenure of the kingship at Delphi and Thebes would accord with the similar tenure of the office at Sparta and Cnossus. And if the kings of Cnossus disguised themselves as bulls, there seems no reason why the kings of Delphi and Thebes should not have personated dragons or serpents. In all these cases the animal whose guise the king assumed would be sacred to the royal family. At first the relation of the beast to the man would be direct and simple ; the creature would be revered for some such reason as that for which a savage respects a certain species of animals, for example, because he believes that his ancestors were beasts of the same sort, or that the souls of his dead are lodged in them. In later times the sanctity of the species would be explained by saying that a god had at some time, and for some reason or other, assumed the form of the animal. It is probably not without significance that in Greek mythology the gods in general, and Zeus in particular,

Animals sacred to royal families.

Greek stories of the trans-

---

[1] A. B. Cook, "The European Sky-god," *Folk-lore*, xv. (1904) pp. 423 *sq.*

[2] Pausanias, ix. 3. 4. See *The*

Magic Art and the Evolution of Kings, vol. ii. p. 140.

[3] A. B. Cook, "The European Sky-god," *Folk-lore*, xv. (1904) pp. 402 *sqq.*

are commonly said to have submitted to this change of shape formation of gods into beasts point to a custom of a sacred marriage in which the actors masqueraded as animals.
for the purpose of prosecuting a love adventure. Such
stories may well reflect a custom of a Sacred Marriage at
which the actors played the parts of the worshipful animals.
With the growth of culture these local worships, the relics of
a barbarous age, would be explained away by tales of the
loves of the gods, and, gradually falling out of practice, would
survive only as myths.

It is said that at the festival of the Wolf-god Zeus, held Analogy of the Wolf Society of Arcadia to the Leopard Society of west Africa.
every nine years on the Wolf-mountain in Arcadia, a man
tasted of the bowel of a human victim mixed with the bowels
of animals, and having tasted it he was turned into a wolf, and
remained a wolf for nine years, when he changed back again
into a man if in the interval he had abstained from eating
human flesh.[1] The tradition points to the existence of a
society of cannibal wolf-worshippers, one or more of whom
personated, and were supposed to embody, the sacred animal
for periods of nine years together. Their theory and practice
would seem to have agreed with those of the Human Leopard
Societies of western Africa, whose members disguise themselves in the skins of leopards with sharp claws of steel. In
that guise they attack and kill men in order to eat their
flesh or to extract powerful charms from their bodies.[2]
Their mode of gaining recruits is like that of the Greek
Wolf Society. When a visitor came to a village inhabited
by a Leopard Society, "he was invited to partake of food,
in which was mixed a small quantity of human flesh. The
guest all unsuspectingly partook of the repast, and was afterwards told that human flesh formed one of the ingredients of
the meal, and that it was then necessary that he should join
the society, which was invariably done."[3] As the ancient
Greeks thought that a man might be turned into a wolf, so
these negroes believe that he can be changed into a leopard;
and, like the Greeks, some of them fancy that if the transformed man abstains during his transformation from preying

[1] Plato, *Republic*, viii. p. 565 D E; Polybius, vii. 13; Pliny, *Nat. hist.* viii. 81; Varro, cited by Augustine, *De civitate Dei*, xviii. 17; Pausanias, vi. 8. 2, viii. 2. 3-6.

[2] Mary H. Kingsley, *Travels in West Africa*, pp. 536-543; T. J. Alldridge, *The Sherbro and its Hinterland* (London, 1901), pp. 153-159; compare R. H. Nassau, *Fetichism in West Africa* (London, 1904), pp. 200-203.

[3] T. J. Alldridge, *op. cit.* p. 154.

on his fellows he can regain his human shape, but that if he once laps human blood he must remain a leopard for ever.[1]

Legend of the transformation of Cadmus and Harmonia into serpents.

The hypothesis that the ancient kings of Thebes and Delphi had for their sacred animal the serpent or dragon, and claimed kinship with the creature, derives some countenance from the tradition that at the end of their lives Cadmus and his wife Harmonia quitted Thebes and went to reign over a tribe of Encheleans or Eel-men in Illyria, where they were both finally transformed into dragons or serpents.[2]   To the primitive mind an eel is a water-serpent;[3] it can hardly, therefore, be an accident that the serpent-killer afterwards reigned over a tribe of eel-men and himself became a serpent at last.   Moreover, according to one account, his wife Harmonia was a daughter of the very dragon which he slew.[4]   The tradition would fit in well with the hypothesis that the dragon or serpent was the sacred animal of the old royal house of Thebes, and that the kingdom fell to him who slew his predecessor and married his daughter.   We have seen reason to think that such a mode of succession to the throne was common in antiquity.[5]   The story of the final transformation of Cadmus and Harmonia into snakes may be a relic of a belief that the souls of the dead kings and queens of Thebes transmigrated into the bodies of serpents, just as Caffre kings turn at death into boa-constrictors or deadly black snakes.[6]   Indeed the notion that the souls of the dead lodge in serpents is widely spread in Africa and Madagascar.[7]   Other African tribes believe that their dead kings and chiefs turn into lions, leopards, hyaenas, pythons, hippopotamuses, or other creatures, and the animals are respected and spared accordingly.[8]   In

Transmigration of the souls of the dead into serpents.

[1] A. Bastian, Die deutsche Expedition an der Loango-Küste, ii. 248.

[2] Apollodorus, iii. 5. 4 ; Strabo, vii. 7. 8, p. 326 ; Ovid, Metam. iv. 563-603 ; Hyginus, Fabulae, 6 ; Nicander, Theriaca, 607 sqq.

[3] A. van Gennep, Tabou et totémisme à Madagascar (Paris, 1904), p. 326.

[4] Dercylus, quoted by a scholiast on Euripides, Phoenissae, 7 ; Fragmenta historicorum Graecorum, ed. C. Müller, iv. 387. The writer rationalises the legend by representing the dragon as a Theban man of that name whom

Cadmus slew. On the theory here suggested this Euhemeristic version of the story is substantially right.

[5] See The Magic Art and the Evolution of Kings, ii. 268 sqq.

[6] David Leslie, Among the Zulus and Amatongas, Second Edition (Edinburgh, 1875), p. 213. Compare H. Callaway, The Religious System of the Amazulu, Part II., pp. 196, 211.

[7] See Adonis, Attis, Osiris, Second Edition, pp. 73 sqq.

[8] D. Livingstone, Missionary Travels and Researches in South Africa, p. 615 ; Miss A. Werner,

like manner the Semang and other wild tribes of the Malay
Peninsula imagine that the souls of their chiefs, priests, and
magicians transmigrate at death into the bodies of certain
wild beasts, such as elephants, tigers, and rhinoceroses, and
that in their bestial form the dead men extend a benign
protection to their living human kinsfolk.[1] Even during their
lifetime kings in rude society sometimes claim kinship with
the most formidable beasts of the country.   Thus the royal
family of Dahomey specially worships the leopard ; some of
the king's wives are distinguished by the title of Leopard
Wives, and on state occasions they wear striped cloths
to resemble the animal.[2]   One king of Dahomey, on
whom the French made war, bore the name of Shark ;
hence in art he was represented sometimes with a shark's
body and a human head, sometimes with a human
body and the head of a shark.[3]   The Trocadero Museum
at Paris contains the wooden images of three kings of
Dahomey who reigned during the nineteenth century, and
who are all represented partly in human and partly in animal
form.   One of them, Guezo, bore the surname of the Cock,
and his image represents him as a man covered with feathers.
His son Guelelé, who succeeded him on the throne, was
surnamed the Lion, and his effigy is that of a lion rampant
with tail raised and hair on his body, but with human feet
and hands.   Guelelé was succeeded on the throne by his
son Behanzin, who was surnamed the Shark, and his effigy
portrays him standing upright with the head and body of
a fish, the fins and scales being carefully represented, while
his arms and legs are those of a man.[4]   Again, a king of

*Kings
claim kin-
ship with
the most
powerful
animals.*

The Natives of British Central Africa
(London, 1906), p. 64 ; L. Decle,
Three Years in Savage Africa (London, 1898), p. 74 ; J. Roscoe, "The
Bahima," Journal of the Anthropological Institute, xxxvii. (1907) pp. 101
sq. ; Major J. A. Meldon, "Notes on
the Bahima," Journal of the African
Society, No. 22 (January, 1907), pp.
151-153 ; J. A. Chisholm, "Notes on
the Manners and Customs of the
Winamwanga and Wiwa," Journal of
the African Society, No. 36 (July,
1910), pp. 374, 375 ; P. Alois Ham-
berger, in Anthropos, v. (1910) p. 802.

[1] W. W. Skeat and C. O. Blagden,
Pagan Races of the Malay Peninsula
(London, 1906), ii. 194, 197, 221,
227, 305.
[2] A. B. Ellis, The Ewe-speaking
Peoples of the Slave Coast, pp. 74 sq.
[3] This I learned from Professor
F. von Luschan in the Anthropological
Museum at Berlin.
[4] M. Delafosse, in La Nature, No.
1086 (March 24th, 1894), pp. 262-266 ;
J. G. Frazer, "Statues of Three
Kings of Dahomey," Man, viii. (1908)
pp. 130-132. King Behanzin, surnamed the Shark, is doubtless the

Benin was called Panther, and a bronze statue of him, now in the Anthropological Museum at Berlin, represents him with a panther's whiskers.[1]	Such portraits furnish an exact parallel to what I conceive to be the true story of the Minotaur.	On the Gold Coast of Africa a powerful ruler is commonly addressed as " O Elephant ! " or " O Lion ! " and one of the titles of the king of Ashantee, mentioned at great ceremonies, is *borri*, the name of a venomous snake.[2]	It has been argued that King David belonged to a serpent family, and that the brazen serpent, which down to the time of Hezekiah was worshipped with fumes of burning incense,[3] represented the old sacred animal of his house.[4]	In Europe the bull, the serpent, and the wolf would naturally be on the list of royal beasts.

The serpent the royal animal at Athens and Salamis.

If the king's soul was believed to pass at death into the sacred animal, a custom might arise of keeping live creatures of the species in captivity and revering them as the souls of dead rulers.	This would explain the Athenian practice of keeping a sacred serpent on the Acropolis and feeding it with honey cakes ; for the serpent was identified with Erichthonius or Erechtheus, one of the ancient kings of Athens, of whose palace some vestiges have been discovered in recent times.	The creature was supposed to guard the citadel.	During the Persian invasion a report that the serpent had left its honey-cake untasted was one of the strongest reasons which induced the people to abandon Athens to the enemy ; they thought that the holy reptile had forsaken the city.[5]	Again, Cecrops, the first king of Athens,

King of Dahomey referred to by Professor von Luschan (see the preceding note).

[1] The statue was pointed out to me and explained by Professor F. von Luschan.

[2] A. B. Ellis, *The Tshi-speaking Peoples of the Gold Coast*, pp. 205 *sq.*

[3] 2 Kings xviii. 4.

[4] W. Robertson Smith, "Animal Worship and Animal Tribes," *Journal of Philology*, ix. (1880) pp. 99 *sq.* Professor T. K. Cheyne prefers to suppose that the brazen serpent and the brazen "sea" in the temple at Jerusalem were borrowed from Babylon and represented

the great dragon, the impersonation of the primaeval watery chaos.	See *Encyclopaedia Biblica, s.v.* "Nehushtan," vol. i. coll. 3387.	The two views are perhaps not wholly irreconcilable.	See below, pp. 111 *sq.*

[5] Herodotus, viii. 41 ; Plutarch, *Themistocles*, 10 ; Aristophanes, *Lysistrata*, 758 *sq.*, with the Scholium ; Philostratus, *Imagines*, ii. 17. 6.	Some said that there were two serpents (Hesychius and Photius, *Lexicon, s.v.* οἰκουρὸν ὄφιν).	For the identity of the serpent with Erichthonius, see Pausanias, i. 24. 7 ; Hyginus, *Astronomica*, ii. 13 ; Tertullian, *De spectaculis*, 9 ; compare

is said to have been half-serpent and half-man ;[1] in art he is represented as a man from the waist upwards, while the lower part of his body consists of the coils of a serpent.[2] It has been suggested that like Erechtheus he was identical with the serpent on the Acropolis.[3] Once more, we are told that Cychreus gained the kingdom of Salamis by slaying a snake which ravaged the island,[4] but that after his death he, like Cadmus, appeared in the form of the reptile.[5] Some said that he was a man who received the name of Snake on account of his cruelty.[6] Such tales may preserve reminiscences of kings who assumed the style of serpents in their lifetime and were believed to transmigrate into serpents after death. Like the dragons of Thebes and Delphi, the Athenian serpent appears to have been conceived as a creature of the waters ; for the serpent-man Erechtheus was identified with the water-god Poseidon,[7] and in his temple, the Erechtheum, where the serpent lived, there was a tank which went by the name of " the sea of Erechtheus." [8]

If the explanation of the eight years' cycle which I have adopted holds good for Thebes and Delphi, the octennial festivals held at these places probably had some reference to the sun and moon, and may have comprised a sacred marriage of these luminaries. The solar character of Apollo,

The wedding of Cadmus and Harmonia at Thebes may have

Philostratus, *Vit. Apoll.* vii. 24 ; and for the identity of Erichthonius and Erechtheus, see Schol. on Homer, *Iliad*, ii. 547 ; *Etymologicum magnum*, p. 371, *s.v.* Ἐρεχθεύς. According to some, the upper part of Erichthonius was human and the lower part or only the feet serpentine. See Hyginus, *Fabulae*, 166 ; *id., Astronomica*, ii. 13 ; Schol. on Plato, *Timaeus*, p. 23 D ; *Etymologicum magnum*, *l.c.* ; Servius on Virgil, *Georg.* iii. 13. See further my notes on Pausanias i. 18. 2 and i. 26. 5, vol. ii. pp. 168 *sqq.*, 330 *sqq.*

[1] Apollodorus, iii. 14. 1 ; Aristophanes, *Wasps*, 438. Compare J. Tzetzes, *Chiliades*, v. 641.

[2] W. H. Roscher, *Lexikon d. griech. und röm. Mythologie*, ii. 1019. Compare Euripides, *Ion*, 1163 *sqq.*

[3] O. Immisch, in W. H. Roscher's *Lexikon d. griech. und röm. Mythologie*, ii. 1023.

[4] Apollodorus, iii. 12. 7 ; Diodorus Siculus, iv. 72 ; J. Tzetzes, *Schol. on Lycophron*, 110, 175, 451.

[5] Pausanias, i. 36. 1.   Another version of the story was that Cychreus bred a snake which ravaged the island and was driven out by Eurylochus, after which Demeter received the creature at Eleusis as one of her attendants (Hesiod, quoted by Strabo, ix. 1. 9, p. 393).

[6] Stephanus Byzantius, *s.v.* Κυχρεῖος πάγος ; Eustathius, *Commentary on Dionysius*, 507, in *Geographi Graeci minores*, ed. C. Müller, ii. 314.

[7] Hesychius, *s.v.* Ἐρεχθεύς ; Athenagoras, *Supplicatio pro Christianis*, 1 ; [Plutarch], *Vit. X. Orat.* p. 843 B C ; *Corpus inscriptionum Atticarum*, i. No. 387, iii. Nos. 276, 805 ; compare Pausanias, i. 26. 5.

[8] Apollodorus, iii. 14. 1 ; Herodotus, viii. 55 : compare Pausanias, viii. 10. 4.

been a
dramatic
representa-
tion of
the
marriage
of the sun
and moon
at the end
of the eight
years cycle.

whether original or adventitious, lends some countenance to this view, but at both Delphi and Thebes the god was apparently an intruder who usurped the place of an older god or hero at the festival. At Thebes that older hero was Cadmus. Now Cadmus was a brother of Europa, who appears to have been a personification of the moon conceived in the form of a cow.[1] He travelled westward seeking his lost sister till he came to Delphi, where the oracle bade him give up the search and follow a cow which had the white mark of the full moon on its flank; wherever the cow fell down exhausted, there he was to take up his abode and found a city. Following the cow and the directions of the oracle he built Thebes.[2] Have we not here in another form the myth of the moon pursued and at last overtaken by the sun? and the famous wedding of Cadmus and Harmonia, to attend which all the gods came down from heaven,[3] may it not have been at once the mythical marriage of the great luminaries and the ritual marriage of the king and queen of Thebes masquerading, like the king and queen of Cnossus, in the character of the lights of heaven at the octennial festival which celebrated and symbolised the conjunction of the sun and moon after their long separation, their harmony after eight years of discord? A better name for the bride at such a wedding could hardly have been chosen than Harmonia.

This
theory
confirmed
by the
astronomi-
cal symbols
carried by
the Laurel-
bearer
at the
octennial
festival of
Laurel-
bearing.

This theory is supported by a remarkable feature of the festival. At the head of the procession, immediately in front of the Laurel-bearer, walked a youth who carried in his hands a staff of olive-wood draped with laurels and flowers. To the top of the staff was fastened a bronze globe, with smaller globes hung from it; to the middle of the staff were attached a globe of medium size and three hundred and sixty-five purple ribbands, while the lower part of the staff was swathed in a saffron pall. The largest globe, we are told, signified the sun, the smaller the moon, and the smallest

---

[1] See above, p. 73.
[2] Apollodorus, iii. 4. 1 *sq.*; Pausanias, ix. 12. 1 *sq.*; Schol. on Homer, *Iliad*, ii. 494; Hyginus, *Fabulae*, 178. The mark of the moon on the cow is mentioned only by Pausanias and

Hyginus.
[3] Apollodorus, iii. 4. 2; Euripides, *Phoenissae*, 822 *sq.*; Pindar, *Pyth.* iii. 155 *sqq.*; Diodorus Siculus, v. 49. 1; Pausanias, iii. 18. 12, ix. 12. 3; Schol. on Homer, *Iliad*, ii. 494.

the stars, and the purple ribbands stood for the course of the year, being equal in number to the days comprised in it.[1] The choir of virgins who followed the Laurel-bearer singing hymns[2] may have represented the Muses, who are said to have sung and played at the marriage of Cadmus and Harmonia ; down to late times the very spot in the market-place was shewn where they had discoursed their heavenly music.[3] We may conjecture that the procession of the Laurel-bearing was preceded by a dramatic performance of the Slaying of the Dragon, and that it was followed by a pageant representative of the nuptials of Cadmus and Harmonia in the presence of the gods. On this hypothesis Harmonia, the wife of Cadmus, is only another form of his sister Europa, both of them being personifications of the moon. Accordingly in the Samothracian mysteries, in which the marriage of Cadmus and Harmonia appears to have been celebrated, it was Harmonia and not Europa whose wanderings were dramatically represented.[4] The gods who quitted Olympus to grace the wedding by their presence were probably represented in the rites, whether celebrated at Thebes or in Samothrace, by men and women attired as deities. In like manner at the marriage of a Pharaoh the courtiers masqueraded in the likeness of the animal-headed Egyptian gods.[5]

Within historical times the great Olympic festival was

---

[1] Proclus, quoted by Photius, *Bibliotheca*, p. 321, ed. Bekker.

[2] Proclus, *l.c.*

[3] Pindar, *Pyth.* iii. 155 *sqq.* ; Diodorus Siculus, v. 49. 1 ; Pausanias, ix. 12. 3 ; Schol. on Homer, *Iliad*, ii. 494.

[4] Schol. on Euripides, *Phoenissae*, 7 καὶ νῦν ἔτι ἐν τῇ Σαμοθρᾴκῃ ζητοῦσιν αὐτὴν [scil. 'Αρμονίαν] ἐν ταῖς ἑορταῖς. According to the Samothracian account, Cadmus in seeking Europa came to Samothrace,. and there, having been initiated into the mysteries, married Harmonia (Diodorus Siculus, v. 48 *sq.*). It is probable, though it cannot be proved, that the legend was acted in the mystic rites.

[5] See *The Magic Art and the Evolution of Kings*, ii. 133. Mr. A. B. Cook has suggested that the central

scene on the eastern frieze of the Parthenon represents the king and queen of Athens about to take their places among the enthroned deities. See his article "Zeus, Jupiter, and the Oak," *Classical Review*, xviii. (1904) p. 371. As the scenes on the frieze appear to have been copied from the Panathenaic festival, it would seem, on Mr. Cook's hypothesis, that the sacred marriage of the King and Queen was celebrated on that occasion in presence of actors who played the parts of gods and goddesses. In this connexion it may not be amiss to remember that in the eastern gable of the Parthenon the pursuit of the moon by the sun was mythically represented by the horses of the sun emerging from the sea on the one side, and the horses of the moon plunging into it on the other.

The Olympic festival seems to have been based on the octennial cycle.

always held at intervals of four, not of eight, years. Yet it too would seem to have been based on the octennial cycle. For it always fell on a full moon, at intervals of fifty and of forty-nine lunar months alternately.[1] Thus the total number of lunar months comprised in two successive Olympiads was ninety-nine, which is precisely the number of lunar months in the octennial cycle.[2] It is possible that, as K. O. Müller conjectured,[3] the Olympic games may, like the Pythian, have originally been celebrated at intervals of eight instead of four years. If that was so, analogy would lead us to infer that the festival was associated with a mythical marriage of the sun and moon. A reminiscence of such a marriage appears to survive in the legend that Endymion, the son of the first king of Elis, had fifty daughters by the Moon, and that he set his sons to run a race for the kingdom at Olympia.[4] For, as scholars have already perceived, Endymion is the sunken sun overtaken by the moon below the horizon, and his fifty daughters by her are the fifty lunar months of an Olympiad or, more strictly speaking, of every alternate Olympiad.[5] If the Olympic festival always fell, as many authorities have maintained, at the first full moon after the summer solstice,[6] the time would be eminently appropriate for a marriage of the luminaries, since both of them might then be conceived to be at the prime of their vigour.

Mythical marriage of the sun and moon at Olympia.

The Olympic victors, male and

It has been ingeniously argued by Mr. A. B. Cook[7] that the Olympic victors in the chariot-race were the lineal successors of the old rulers, the living embodiments of Zeus,

[1] Schol. on Pindar, *Olymp.* iii. 35 (20).

[2] Compare Aug. Boeckh, on Pindar, *l.c., Explicationes,* p. 138 ; L. Ideler, *Handbuch der mathematischen und technischen Chronologie,* i. 366 *sq.*; G. F. Unger, "Zeitrechnung der Griechen und Römer," in Iwan Müller's *Handbuch der classischen Altertumswissenschaft,* i. 605 *sq.* All these writers recognise the octennial cycle at Olympia.

[3] K. O. Müller, *Die Dorier,*[2] ii. 483; compare *id.* i. 254 *sq.*

[4] Pausanias, v. 1. 4.

[5] Aug. Boeckh, *l.c.*; A. Schmidt, *Handbuch der griechischen Chronologie* (Jena, 1888), pp. 50 *sqq.* ; K. O.

Müller, *Die Dorier,*[2] i. 438 ; W. H. Roscher, *Selene und Verwandtes,* pp. 2 *sq.,* 80 *sq.,* 101.

[6] See Aug. Boeckh and L. Ideler, *ll.cc.* More recent writers would date it on the second full moon after the summer solstice, hence in August or the last days of July. See G. F. Unger, *l.c.*; E. F. Bischoff, "De fastis Graecorum antiquioribus," *Leipziger Studien zur classischen Philologie,* vii. (1884) pp. 347 *sq.*; Aug. Mommsen, *Über die Zeit der Olympien* (Leipsic, 1891); and my note on Pausanias, v. 9. 3 (vol. iii. pp. 488 *sq.*).

[7] A. B. Cook, "The European Sky-God," *Folk-lore,* xv. (1904) pp. 398-402.

whose claims to the kingdom were decided by a race, as in the legend of Endymion and his sons, and who reigned for a period of four, perhaps originally of eight years, after which they had again, like Oenomaus, to stake their right to the throne on the issue of a chariot-race.   Certainly the four-horse car in which they raced assimilated them to the sun-god, who was commonly supposed to drive through the sky in a similar fashion ;[1] while the crown of sacred olive which decked their brows[2] likened them to the great god Zeus himself, whose glorious image at Olympia wore a similar wreath.[3]   But if the olive-crowned victor in the men's race at Olympia represented Zeus, it becomes probable that |the olive-crowned victor in the girls' race, which was held every fourth year at Olympia in honour of Hera,[4] represented in like manner the god's wife ; and that in former days the two together acted the part of the god and goddess in that sacred marriage of Zeus and Hera which is known to have been celebrated in many parts of Greece.[5]   This conclusion is confirmed by the legend that the girls' race was instituted by Hippodamia in gratitude for her marriage with Pelops ;[6] for if Pelops as victor in the chariot-race represented Zeus, his bride would naturally play the part of Hera.   But under the names of Zeus and Hera the pair of Olympic victors would seem to have really personated the Sun and Moon, who were the true heavenly bridegroom and bride of the ancient octennial festival.[7]   In the decline of ancient civilisation the old myth of the marriage of the great luminaries

[Marginal note:] female, may originally have represented Zeus and Hera or the Sun and Moon, and have reigned as divine king and queen for four or eight years.

[1] Rapp, in W. H. Roscher's *Lexikon d. griech. und röm. Mythologie,* i. 2005 *sqq.*

[2] Pausanias, v. 15. 3, with my note; Schol. on Pindar, *Olymp.* iii. 60.

[3] Pausanias, v. 11. 1.

[4] Pausanias, v. 16. 2 *sqq.*

[5] See *The Magic Art and the Evolution of Kings,* vol. ii. p. 143.

[6] Pausanias, v. 16. 4.

[7] Many years after the theory in the text was printed (for the present volume has been long in the press) I accidentally learned that my friend Mr. F. M. Cornford, Fellow and Lecturer of Trinity College, Cambridge, had quite independently arrived at a similar conclusion with regard to the mythical and dramatic parts played by the Olympic victors, male and female, as representatives of the Sun and Moon, and I had the pleasure of hearing him expound the theory in a brilliant lecture delivered before the Classical Society of Cambridge, 28th February 1911.   The coincidence of two independent enquirers in conclusions, which can hardly be called obvious, seems to furnish a certain confirmation of their truth.   In Mr. Cornford's case the theory in question forms part of a more elaborate and comprehensive hypothesis as to the origin of the Olympic games, concerning which I must for the present suspend my judgment.

was revived by the crazy fanatic and libertine, the emperor Heliogabalus, who fetched the image of Astarte, regarded as the moon-goddess, from Carthage to Rome and wedded it to the image of the Syrian sun-god, commanding all men at Rome and throughout Italy to celebrate with joy and festivity the solemn nuptials of the God of the Sun with the Goddess of the Moon.[1]

§ 5. Funeral Games

Tradition that the great games of Greece originated in funeral celebrations.

But a different and at first sight inconsistent explanation of the Olympic festival deserves to be considered. Some of the ancients held that all the great games of Greece—the Olympic, the Nemean, the Isthmian, and the Pythian—were funeral games celebrated in honour of the dead.[2] Thus the Olympic games were supposed to have been founded in honour of Pelops,[3] the great legendary hero, who had a sacred precinct at Olympia, where he was honoured above all the other heroes and received annually the sacrifice of a black ram.[4] Once a year, too, all the lads of Peloponnese are said to have lashed themselves on his grave at Olympia, till the blood streamed down their backs as a libation to the departed hero.[5] Similarly at Roman funerals the women scratched their faces till they bled for the purpose, as Varro tells us, of pleasing the ghosts with the sight of the flowing blood.[6] So, too, among the aborigines of Australia mourners sometimes cut and hack themselves and allow the streaming blood to drip on the dead body of their kinsman or into the grave.[7] Among the eastern islanders of Torres Straits in like manner youths who had lately been initiated and girls who had attained to puberty used to have the lobes of their ears cut as a mourning ceremony, and the flowing blood was

[1] Herodian, v. 6. 3-5.

[2] Clement of Alexandria, Protrept. ii. 34, p. 29, ed. Potter. The following account of funeral games is based on my note on Pausanias i. 44. 8 (vol. ii. pp. 549 sq.). Compare W. Ridgeway, The Origin of Tragedy (Cambridge, 1910), pp. 32 sqq.

[3] Clement of Alexandria, l.c.

[4] Pausanias, v. 13. 1 sq.

[5] Scholiast on Pindar, Olymp. i. 146.

[6] Varro, cited by Servius, on Virgil, Aen. iii. 67.

[7] F. Bonney, "On some Customs of the Aborigines of the River Darling," Journal of the Anthropological Institute, xiii. (1884) pp. 134 sq. ; Spencer and Gillen, Native Tribes of Central Australia, pp. 507, 509 sq. ; (Sir) G. Grey, Journals of Two Expeditions of Discovery in North - West and Western Australia (London, 1841), ii. 332.

allowed to drip on the feet of the corpse as a mark of pity
or sorrow; moreover, young adults of both sexes had patterns
cut in their flesh with a sharp shell so that the blood fell on
the dead body.[1]   The similarity of these savage rites to the
Greek custom observed at the grave of Pelops suggests that
the tomb was not a mere cenotaph, but that it contained the
actual remains of the dead hero, though these have not been
discovered by the German excavators of Olympia.   In like
manner the Nemean games are said to have been celebrated
in honour of the dead Opheltes, whose grave was shewn at
Nemea.[2]   According to tradition, the Isthmian games were
instituted in honour of the dead Melicertes, whose body had
been washed ashore at the Isthmus of Corinth.   It is said
that when this happened a famine fell upon the Corinthians,
and an oracle declared that the evil would not cease until
the people paid due obsequies to the remains of the drowned
Melicertes and honoured him with funeral games.   The
Corinthians complied with the injunction for a short time;
but as soon as they omitted to celebrate the games, the
famine broke out afresh, and the oracle informed them that
the honours paid to Melicertes must be eternal.[3]   Lastly,
the Pythian games are said to have been celebrated in
honour of the dead dragon or serpent Python.[4]

These Greek traditions as to the funeral origin of the
great games are strongly confirmed by Greek practice in
historical times.   Thus in the Homeric age funeral games,
including chariot-races, foot-races, wrestling, boxing, spear-
throwing, quoit-throwing, and archery, were celebrated in
honour of dead kings and heroes at their barrows.[5]   In the
fifth century before Christ, when Miltiades, the victor of
Marathon, died in the Thracian Chersonese, the people
offered sacrifices to him as their founder and instituted

The
tradition is
confirmed
by Greek
practice,
for in
historical
times
games were
instituted
to do
honour
to many

---

[1] *Reports of the Cambridge Anthropological Expedition to Torres Straits*,
vi. (Cambridge, 1908) pp. 135, 154.

[2] Hyginus, *Fabulae*, 74; Apollodorus, iii. 6. 4; Schol. on Pindar,
Pyth., Introduction; Pausanias, ii. 15.
2 *sq.*; Clement of Alexandria, *Protrept.* ii. 34, p. 29, ed. Potter.

[3] Scholiast on Pindar, *Isthm.*, Introduction, p. 514, ed. Boeckh; Pausanias,

i. 44. 8; Apollodorus, iii. 4. 3:
Zenobius, iv. 38; Clement of Alex-
andria, *l.c.*; J. Tzetzes, *Scholia on
Lycophron*, 107, 229; Scholia on
Euripides, *Medea*, 1284; Hyginus,
Fabulae, 2.

[4] Clement of Alexandria, *l.c.*;
Hyginus, *Fabulae*, 140.

[5] Homer, *Iliad*, xxiii. 255 *sqq.*, 629
sqq., 651 *sqq.*

equestrian and athletic games in his honour, in which no
citizen of Lampsacus was allowed to contend.[1] Near the
theatre at Sparta there were two graves ; one contained the
bones of the gallant Leonidas which had been brought back
from the pass of Thermopylae to rest in Spartan earth; the
other held the dust of King Pausanias, who commanded the
Greek armies on the great day when they routed the Persian
host at Plataea, but who lived to tarnish his laurels and to
die a traitor's death. Every year speeches were spoken
over these graves and games were held in which none but
Spartans might compete.[2] Perhaps in the case of Pausanias
the games were intended rather to avert his anger than
to do him honour ; for we are told that wizards were fetched
even from Italy to lay the traitor's unquiet ghost.[3] Again,
when the Spartan general Brasidas, defending Amphipolis
in Thrace against the Athenians, fell mortally wounded
before the city and just lived, like Wolfe on the Heights of
Abraham, to learn that his men were victorious, all the
allies in arms followed the dead soldier to the grave ; and
the grateful citizens fenced his tomb about, sacrificed to
him as a hero, and decreed that his memory should be
honoured henceforth with games and annual sacrifices.[4]
So, too, when Timoleon, the saviour of Syracuse, died in
the city which he had delivered from tyrants within and
defended against enemies without, vast multitudes of men
and women, crowned with garlands and clad in clean
raiment, attended all that was mortal of their benefactor
to the funeral pyre, the voices of praise and benedic-
tion mingling with the sound of lamentations and sobs ;
and when at last the bier was laid on the pyre a herald
chosen for his sonorous voice proclaimed that the people
of Syracuse were burying Timoleon, and that they would
honour him for all time to come with musical, equestrian,
and athletic games, because he had put down the tyrants,
conquered the foreign foe, rebuilt the cities that had been
laid waste, and restored their free constitutions to the
Sicilians.[5] In dedicating the great Mausoleum at Hali-

---

[1] Herodotus, vi. 38.
[2] Pausanias, iii. 14. 1.
[3] Plutarch, *De sera numinis vin-*
dicta, 17.
[4] Thucydides, v. 10 *sq.*
[5] Plutarch, *Timoleon*, 39.

carnassus to the soul of her dead husband Mausolus, his widow Artemisia instituted a contest of eloquence in his memory, prizes of money and other valuables being offered to such as should pronounce the most splendid panegyrics on the departed. Isocrates himself is said to have entered for the prize but to have been vanquished by his pupil Theopompus.[1] Alexander the Great prepared to pay honour to his dead friend Hephaestion by celebrating athletic and musical contests on a greater scale than had ever been witnessed before, and for this purpose he actually assembled three thousand competitors, who shortly afterwards contended at the funeral games of the great conqueror himself.[2]

Nor were the Greeks in the habit of instituting games in honour only of a few distinguished individuals; they sometimes established them to perpetuate the memory or to appease the ghosts of large numbers of men who had perished on the field of battle or been massacred in cold blood. When the Carthaginians and Tyrrhenians together had beaten the Phocaeans in a sea-fight, they landed their prisoners near Agylla in Etruria and stoned them all to death. After that, whenever the people of Agylla or their oxen or their sheep passed the scene of the massacre, they were attacked by a strange malady, which distorted their bodies and deprived them of the use of their limbs. So they consulted the Delphic oracle, and the priestess told them that they must offer great sacrifices to the dead Phocaeans and institute equestrian and athletic games in their honour,[3] no doubt to appease the angry ghosts of the murdered men, who were supposed to be doing the mischief. At Plataea down to the second century of our era might be seen the graves of the men who fell in the great battle with the Persians. Sacrifices were offered to them every year with great solemnity. The chief magistrate of Plataea, clad in a purple robe, washed with his own hands the tombstones and anointed them with scented oil. He slaughtered a black bull over a burning pyre and called upon the dead warriors to come and partake of the banquet and the blood. Then filling a bowl of wine and pouring a libation he said, " I drink

The Greeks also instituted games in honour of large numbers of men who had perished in battle or a massacre.

---

[1] Aulus Gellius, x. 18. 5 *sq.*   [2] Arrian, vii. 14. 10.
[3] Herodotus, i. 167.

to the men who died for the freedom of Greece." Moreover, games were celebrated every fourth year in honour of these heroic dead, the principal prizes being offered for a race in armour.[1] At Athens funeral games were held in the Academy to commemorate the men slain in war who were buried in the neighbouring Ceramicus, and sacrifices were offered to them at a pit: the games were superintended and the sacrifices offered by the Polemarch or minister of war.[2]

Funeral games have been celebrated in honour of the dead by other peoples both in ancient and modern times.

Similar honours have been paid to the spirits of the departed by many other peoples both ancient and modern. Thus in antiquity the Thracians burned or buried their dead, and having raised mounds over their remains they held games of all kinds on the spot, assigning the principal prizes to victory in single combat.[3]   At Rome funeral games were celebrated and gladiators fought in honour of distinguished men who had just died.   The games were sometimes held in the forum.   Thus in the year 216 B.C., when Marcus Aemilius Lepidus died, who had been twice consul, his three sons celebrated funeral games in the forum for three days, and two-and-twenty pairs of gladiators fought on the occasion.[4] Again, in the year 200 B.C. funeral games were held for four days in the forum, and five-and-twenty pairs of gladiators fought in honour of the deceased M. Valerius Laevinus, the expense of the ceremonies being defrayed by the two sons of the dead man.[5]   Once more, when the Pontifex Maximus, Publicius Licinius Crassus, died at the beginning of the year 183 B.C., funeral games were celebrated in his honour for three days, a hundred and twenty gladiators fought, and the ceremonies concluded with a banquet, for which the tables were spread in the forum.[6]   These games and combats were doubtless intended to please and soothe the ghost of the recently departed, just as we saw that Roman women lacerated their faces for a similar purpose.   Similarly, when the Southern Nicobarese dig up the bones of their dead, clean them, and bury them again, they hold a feast at which sham-fights with quarter-staves take place " to gratify the departed

[1] Plutarch, *Aristides*, 21 ; Strabo, ix. 2. 31, p. 412 ; Pausanias, ix. 2. 5 *sq*.
[2] Philostratus, *Vit. Sophist.* ii. 30 ; Heliodorus, *Aethiopica*, i. 17 ; compare Aristotle, *Constitution of Athens*, 58.
[3] Herodotus, v. 8.
[4] Livy, xxiii. 30. 15.
[5] Livy, xxxi. 50. 4.
[6] Livy, xxxix. 46. 2 *sq*.

spirit." [1]   In Futuna, an island of the South Pacific, when a
death has taken place friends express their grief by cutting
their faces, breast, and arms with shells, and at the funeral
festival which follows pairs of boxers commonly engage in
combats by way of honouring the deceased.[2]   In Laos, a
province of Siam, boxers are similarly engaged to bruise
each other at the festival which takes place when the remains
of a chief or other important person are cremated.   The
festival lasts three days, but it is while the pyre is actually
blazing that the combatants are expected to batter each
other's heads with the utmost vigour.[3]   Among the Kirghiz
the anniversary of the death of a rich man is celebrated with
a great feast and with horse-races, shooting-matches, and
wrestling-matches.   It is said that thousands of sheep and
hundreds of horses, besides slaves, coats of mail, and a great
many other objects, are sometimes distributed as prizes
among the winners.[4]   The Bashkirs, a Tartar people of
mixed extraction, bury their dead, and always end the
obsequies with horse-races.[5]   Among some of the North
American Indians contests in running, shooting, and so forth
formed part of the funeral celebration.[6]

The Bedouins of the Sinaitic peninsula observe a great
annual festival at the grave of the prophet Salih, and camel-
races are included in the ceremonies.   At the end of the races a
procession takes place round the prophet's grave, after which
the sacrificial victims are led to the door of the mortuary
chapel, their ears are cut off, and the doorposts are smeared
with their streaming blood.[7]   The custom of holding funeral

Funeral games among the Bedouins and among the peoples of the Caucasus.

[1] *Census of India, 1901*, vol. iii.,
The Andaman and Nicobar Islands, by
Lieut.-Col. Sir Richard C. Temple
(Calcutta, 1903), p. 209.
[2] Letter of the missionary Chevron,
in *Annales de la Propagation de la Foi*,
xv. (1843) pp. 40 *sq.*
[3] É. Aymonier, *Voyage dans le Laos*
(Paris, 1895-1897), ii. 325 *sq.* ; C.
Bock, *Temples and Elephants* (London,
1884), p. 262.
[4] A. de Levchine, *Description des
hommes et des steppes des Kirghiz-
Kazaks ou Kirghiz-Kaisaks* (Paris,
1840), pp. 367 *sq.* ; H. Vambery, *Das
Türkenvolk* (Leipsic, 1885), p. 255 ; P.

von Stenin, "Die Kirgisen des Kreises
Saissanak im Gebiete von Ssemipala-
tinsk," *Globus*, lxix. (1906) p. 228.
[5] T. de Pauly, *Description ethno-
graphique des peuples de la Russie* (St.
Petersburg, 1862), *Peuples ouralo-
altaïques*, p. 29.
[6] Charlevoix, *Histoire de la Nouvelle
France* (Paris, 1744), vi. 111.
[7] I. Goldziher, *Muhammedanische
Studien* (Halle a. S., 1888-1890), ii.
328 *sq.*   However, Prof. Goldziher believes that the festival is an ancient
heathen one which has been subsequently grafted upon the tradition of
the orthodox prophet Salih.

games in honour of the dead appears to be common among the people of the Caucasus. Thus in Circassia the anniversary of the death of a distinguished warrior or chief is celebrated for years with horse-races, foot-races, and various kinds of martial and athletic exercises, for which prizes are awarded to the successful competitors.[1] Among the Chewsurs, another people of the Caucasus, horse-races are held at the funeral of a rich man, and prizes of cattle and sheep are given to the winners; poorer folk content themselves with a competition in shooting and with more modest prizes. Similar celebrations take place on the anniversary of the death.[2] In like manner shooting-matches form a feature of an annual Festival of All Souls, when the spirits of departed Chewsurs are believed to revisit their old village. Adults and children alike take part in the matches, the adults shooting with guns and the children with bows and arrows. The prizes consist of loaves, stockings, gloves, and so forth.[3] Among the Abchases, another people of the Caucasus, two years after a death a memorial feast is held in honour of the deceased, at which animals are killed and measures taken to appease the soul of the departed. For they believe that if the ghost is discontented he can injure them and their property. The horse of the deceased figures prominently at the festival. After the guests have feasted at a long table spread in the open air, the young men perform evolutions on horseback which are said to recall the tournaments of the Middle Ages, and children of eight or nine years of age ride races on horseback.[4]

Games periodically held in honour of some famous man might in time assume the Thus it appears that many different peoples have been in the habit of holding games, including horse-races, in honour of the dead ; and as the ancient Greeks unquestionably did so within historical times for men whose existence is as little open to question as that of Wellington and Napoleon, we cannot dismiss as improbable the tradition that the Olympic

[1] J. Potocki, *Voyage dans les steps d'Astrakhan et du Caucase* (Paris, 1829), i. 275 *sq.*; Edmund Spencer, *Travels in Circassia, Krim Tartary*, etc. (London, 1836) ii. 399.

[2] G. Radde, *Die Chews'uren und ihr Land* (Cassel, 1878), pp. 95 *sq.* ; Prince Eristow, "Die Pschawen und Chewsurier im Kaukasus," *Zeitschrift*

für allgemeine Erdkunde, Neue Folge, ii. (1857) p. 77.

[3] C. v. Hahn, "Religiöse Anschauungen und Totengedächtnisfeier der Chewsuren," *Globus*, lxxvi. (1899) pp. 211 *sq.*

[4] N. v. Seidlitz, "Die Abchasen," *Globus*, lxvi. (1894) pp. 42 *sq.*

and perhaps other great Greek games were instituted to character of a great fair. commemorate real men who once lived, died, and were buried on the spot where the festivals were afterwards held.   When the person so commemorated had been great and powerful in his lifetime, his ghost would be deemed great and powerful after death, and the games celebrated in his honour might naturally attract crowds of spectators.   The need of providing food and accommodation for the multitude which assembled on these occasions would in turn draw numbers of hucksters and merchants to the spot, and thus what in its origin had been a solemn religious ceremony might gradually assume more and more the character of a fair, that is, of a concourse of people brought together mainly for purposes of trade and amusement.   This theory might account for the origin not only of the Olympic and other Greek games, but also for that of the great fairs or public assemblies of ancient Ireland which have been compared, not without reason, to the Greek games.   Indeed the two most The great Irish fairs of Tailltin and Carman, in which horse-races played a prominent part, are said to have been instituted in honour of the dead. famous of these Irish festivals, in which horse-races played a prominent part, are actually said to have been instituted in honour of the dead.   Most celebrated of all was the fair of Tailltiu or Tailltin, held at a place in the county of Meath which is now called Teltown on the Blackwater, midway between Navan and Kells.   The festival lasted for a fortnight before Lammas (the first of August) and a fortnight after it. Among the manly sports and contests which formed a leading feature of the fair horse-races held the principal place.   But trade was not neglected, and among the wares brought to market were marriageable women, who, according to a tradition which survived into the nineteenth century, were bought and sold as wives for one year.   The very spot where the marriages took place is still pointed out by the peasantry; they call it " Marriage Hollow."   Multitudes flocked to the fair not only from all parts of Ireland, but even from Scotland ; it is officially recorded that in the year 1169 A.D. the horses and chariots alone, exclusive of the people on foot, extended in a continuous line for more than six English miles, from Tailltin to Mullach-Aiti, now the Hill of Lloyd near Kells. The Irish historians relate that the fair of Tailltin was instituted by Lug in honour of his foster-mother Tailltiu, whom he buried under a great sepulchral mound on the spot, ordering that a commemorative festival with games and sports should be celebrated there annually for ever.[1] The other great fair of ancient Ireland was held only once in three years at Carman, now called Wexford, in Leinster. It began on Lammas Day (the first of August) and lasted six days. A horse-race took place on each day of the festival. In different parts of the green there were separate markets for victuals, for cattle and horses, and for gold and precious stuffs of the merchants. Harpers harped and pipers piped for the entertainment of the crowds, and in other parts of the fair bards recited in the ears of rapt listeners old romantic tales of forays and cattle-raids, of battles and murders, of love and courtship and marriage. Prizes were awarded to the best performers in every art. In the Book of Ballymote the fair of Carman or Garman is said to have been founded in accordance with the dying wish of a chief named Garman, who was buried on the spot, after begging that a fair of mourning (*aenach n-guba*) should be instituted for him and should bear his name for ever. " It was considered an institution of great importance, and among the blessings promised to the men of Leinster from holding it and duly celebrating the established games, were plenty of corn, fruit and milk, abundance of fish in their lakes and rivers, domestic prosperity, and immunity from the yoke of any other province. On the other hand, the evils to follow from the neglect of this institution were to be failure and early greyness on them and their kings." [2]

Indeed most of the great Irish fairs are said to have

Nor were these two great fairs the only ancient Irish festivals of the sort which are reported to have been founded in honour of the dead. The annual fair at Emain is said to have been established to lament the death of Queen Macha

[1] (Sir) John Rhys, *Celtic Heathendom* (London, 1888), pp. 409 *sq.* ; H. d'Arbois de Jubainville, *Cours de littérature celtique*, vii. (Paris, 1895) pp. 309 *sqq.* ; P. W. Joyce, *Social History of Ancient Ireland* (London, 1903), ii. 438 *sqq.* " The *aenach* or fair was an assembly of the people of every grade without distinction ; it was the most common kind of large public meeting, and its main object was the celebration of games, athletic exercises, sports, and pastimes of all kinds " (P. W. Joyce, *op. cit.* ii. 438). The Irish name is *Tailltiu*, genitive *Taillten*, accusative and dative *Tailltin* (Sir J. Rhys, *op. cit.* p. 409 note [1]).

[2] (Sir) John Rhys, *Celtic Heathendom*, p. 411 ; H. d'Arbois de Jubainville, *Cours de littérature celtique*, vii. 313 *sqq.* ; P. W. Joyce, *Social History of Ancient Ireland*, ii. 434 *sq.*, 441 *sqq.*

of the Golden Hair, who had her palace on the spot.[1] In originated
in funeral
games.
short " most of the great meetings, by whatever name known,
had their origin in funeral games. Tara, Tailltenn, Tlachtga,
Ushnagh, Cruachan, Emain Macha and other less prominent
meeting-places, are well known as ancient pagan cemeteries,
in all of which many illustrious semi-historical personages
were interred : and many sepulchral monuments remain in
them to this day." [2]   " There was a notion that Carman
was a cemetery, that there kings and queens had been
buried, and that the games and horse-races, which formed
the principal attraction of the fair, had been instituted in
honour of the dead folk on whose graves the feet of the
assembled multitude were treading. The same view is taken
of the fairs of Tailltiu and Cruachan : Tailltiu and Cruachan
were cemeteries before they served periodically as places of
assembly for business and pleasure." [3]   The tombs of the
first kings of Ulster were at Tailltin.[4]

If we ask whether the tradition as to the funeral origin The
great Irish
fairs were
of these great Irish fairs is true or false, it is important to
observe the date at which they were commonly celebrated. held on
The date was the first of August, or Lugnasad, that is, the the first of
August
nasad or games of Lug, as the day is still called in every part (Lammas),
of Ireland.[5] This was the date of the great fair of Cruachan [6] which
seems to
as well as of Tailltin and Carman. Now the first of August have been
an old
is our Lammas Day, a name derived from the Anglo-Saxon harvest
hlafmaesse, that is, " Loaf-mass " or " Bread-mass," and the festival of
first-fruits.
name marks the day as a mass or feast of thanksgiving for
the first-fruits of the corn-harvest, which in England and
Ireland usually ripen about that time. The feast " seems
to have been observed with bread of new wheat, and therefore in some parts of England, and even in some near Oxford,
the tenants are bound to bring in wheat of that year to their
lord, on or before the first of August." [7]   But if the festival
of the first of August was in its origin an offering of the

---

[1] P. W. Joyce, *op. cit.* ii. 435.
[2] P. W. Joyce, *op. cit.* ii. 434.
Compare (Sir) J. Rhys, *Celtic Heathendom*, p. 411.
[3] H. d'Arbois de Jubainville, *Cours
de littérature celtique*, vii. 313.
[4] H. d'Arbois de Jubainville, *op.
cit.* vii. 310.

[5] P. W. Joyce, *op. cit.* ii. 389, 439.
[6] (Sir) J. Rhys, *Celtic Heathendom*,
p. 410.
[7] (Sir) J. Rhys, *Celtic Heathendom*,
pp. 411 *sq.*, quoting the substance of
a note by Thos. Hearne, in his edition
of *Robert of Gloucester's Chronicles*
(Oxford, 1724), p. 679. As to the

first-fruits of the corn-harvest, we can easily understand the great importance which the ancient Irish attached to it, and why they should have thought that its observance ensured a plentiful crop of corn as well as abundance of fruit and milk and fish, whereas the neglect of the festival would entail the failure of these things and cause the hair of their kings to turn prematurely grey.[1]   For it is a widespread custom among primitive agricultural peoples to offer the first-fruits of the harvest to divine beings, whether gods or spirits, before any person may eat of the new crops,[2] and wherever such customs are observed we may assume that an omission to offer the first-fruits must be supposed to endanger the crops and the general prosperity of the community, by exciting the wrath of the gods or spirits, who conceive themselves to be robbed of their dues.   Now among the divine beings who are thus propitiated the souls of dead ancestors take in many tribes a prominent or even exclusive place, and that these ancestors are not creations of the mythical fancy but were once men of flesh and blood is sometimes demonstrated by the substantial evidence of their skulls, to which the offerings are made and in which the spirits are supposed to take up their abode for the purpose of partaking of the food presented to them.   Sometimes the ceremony is designated by the expressive name of "feeding the dead."[3]

If the great Irish fairs were instituted in honour of the dead, we can understand why their observance was supposed to ensure plenty of corn, fruit, milk, and fish.   All this tends to support the traditional explanation of the great Irish fairs held at the beginning of August, when the first corn is ripe; for if these festivals were indeed celebrated, as they are said to have been, at cemeteries where kings and other famous men were buried, and if the horse-races and other games, which formed the most prominent feature of the celebrations, were indeed instituted, as they are said to have been, in honour of dead men and women, we can perfectly understand why the observance of the festivals and the games was supposed to ensure a plentiful harvest and abundance of fruit and fish, whereas the neglect to celebrate them was believed to entail the

derivation of the word see *New English Dictionary* (Oxford, 1888-   ) and W. W. Skeat, *Etymological Dictionary of the English Language* (Oxford, 1910), *s.v.* "Lammas."

[1] See above, p. 100.
[2] See *The Golden Bough*, Second Edition, ii. 459 *sqq.*
[3] See *The Golden Bough*, Second Edition, ii. 460, 463, 464 *sq.*

failure of these things. So long as the spirits of the dead men and women, who were buried on the spot, received the homage of their descendants in the shape of funeral games and perhaps of first-fruits, so long would they bless their people with plenty by causing the earth to bring forth its fruits, the cows to yield milk, and the waters to swarm with fish ; whereas if they deemed themselves slighted and neglected, they would avenge their wrongs by cutting off the food supply and afflicting the people with dearth and other calamities. Among these threatened calamities the premature greyness of the kings is specially mentioned, and was probably deemed not the least serious ; for we have seen that the welfare of the whole people is often deemed to be bound up with the physical vigour of the king, and that the appearance of grey hairs on his head and wrinkles on his face is sometimes viewed with apprehension and proves the signal for putting him to death.[1] Similarly the Abchases of the Caucasus imagine that if they do not honour a dead man by horse-races and other festivities, his ghost will be angry with them and visit his displeasure on their persons and their property.[2] In this connexion it is significant that the celebration of the Isthmian games at Corinth in honour of the dead Melicertes is said to have been instituted for the purpose of staying a famine, and that the intermission of the games was immediately followed by a fresh visitation of the calamity.[3] Analogy suggests that the famine may have been ascribed to the anger of the ghost of Melicertes at the neglect of his funeral honours.

Thus on the whole the theory of the funeral origin of the great Greek games is supported not only by Greek tradition and Greek custom but by the evidence of parallel customs observed in many lands. Yet the theory seems hardly adequate to explain all the features in the legends of the foundation and early history of the Olympic games. For if these contests were instituted merely to please and propitiate the soul of a prince named Pelops who was buried on the spot, what are we to make of the tradition that the foot-race was founded in order to determine the successor to

But the theory of the funeral origin of the Olympic games does not explain all the legends connected with them.

---

[1] See above, pp. 14 *sqq.*, 21, 27, 33, 36 *sq.*
[2] See above, p. 98.   [3] See above, p. 93.

the kingdom?[1] or of the similar, though not identical, tradition that the kingdom and the hand of the king's daughter were awarded as the prize to him who could vanquish the king in a chariot race, while death was the penalty inflicted on the beaten charioteer?[2]   Such legends can hardly have been pure fictions; they probably reflect some real custom observed at Olympia.   We may perhaps combine them with the tradition of the funeral origin of the games by supposing that victory in the race entitled the winner to reign as a divine king, the embodiment of a god, for a term of years, whether four or eight years according to the interval between successive celebrations of the festival; that when the term had expired the human god must again submit his title to the crown to the hazard of a race for the purpose of proving that his bodily vigour was unimpaired; that if he failed to do so he lost both his kingdom and his life; and lastly that the spirits of these divine kings, like those of the divine kings of the Shilluk, were worshipped with sacrifices at their graves and were thought to delight in the spectacle of the games which reminded them of the laurels they had themselves won long ago, amid the plaudits of a vast multitude, in the sunshine and dust of the race-course, before they joined the shadowy company of ghosts in the darkness and silence of the tomb.   The theory would explain the existence of the sacred precinct of Pelops at Olympia, where the black rams, the characteristic offerings to the dead,[3] were sacrificed to the hero, and where the young men lashed themselves till the blood dripped from their backs on the ground—a sight well-pleasing to the grim bloodthirsty ghost lurking unseen below.   Perhaps, too, the theory may explain the high mound, at some distance from Olympia, which passed for the grave of the suitors of Hippodamia, to whose shades Pelops is said to have sacrificed as to heroes every year.[4] It is possible that the men buried in this great barrow were not, as tradition had it, the suitors who contended in the

Marginal note: Suggested theory of the origin of the Olympic games.

---

[1] Pausanias, v. 1. 4, v. 8. 1.

[2] Apollodorus, *Bibliotheca*, pp. 183-185 ed. R. Wagner (*Epitoma*, ii. 3-9); Diodorus Siculus, iv. 73; Hyginus, *Fabulae*, 84; Schol. on Pindar, *Olymp.* i. 114; Servius on Virgil, *Georg.*

iii. 7.   See *The Magic Art and the Evolution of Kings*, ii. 299 *sq.*

[3] Strabo, vi. 3. 9, p. 284; K. O. Müller, *Aeschylos Eumeniden* (Göttingen, 1833), p. 144.

[4] Pausanias, vi. 21. 9-11.

chariot-race for the hand of Hippodamia and being defeated were slain by her relentless father; they may have been men who, like Pelops himself, had won the kingdom and a bride in the chariot-race, and, after enjoying the regal dignity and posing as incarnate deities for a term of years, had been finally defeated in the race and put to death.

Whatever may be thought of these speculations, the great Olympic festival cannot have been, like our Lammas, a harvest festival: the quadrennial period of the celebration and the season of the year at which it fell, about halfway between the corn-reaping of early summer and the vintage of mid-autumn, alike exclude the supposition and alike point to an astronomical, not an agricultural, basis of the solemnity. Accordingly we seem driven to conclude that if the winners, male and female, in the Olympic games indeed represented divinities, these divinities must have been personifications of astronomical, not agricultural, powers; in short that the victors posed as embodiments of the Sun and Moon, then at the prime of their radiant power and glory, whose meeting in the heavenly bridechamber of the sky after years of separation was mimicked and magically promoted by the nuptials of their human representatives on earth.

The Olympic games not a harvest festival, but based on astronomical considerations.

§ 6. *The Slaughter of the Dragon*

In the foregoing discussion it has been suggested that Delphi, Thebes, Salamis, and Athens were once ruled by kings who had, in modern language, a serpent or dragon for their crest, and were believed to migrate at death into the bodies of the beasts. But these legends of the dragon admit of another and, at first sight at least, discrepant explanation. It is difficult to separate them from those similar tales of the slaughter of a great dragon which are current in many lands, and have commonly been interpreted as nature-myths, in other words, as personifications of physical phenomena. Of such tales the oldest known versions are the ancient Baby-lonian and the ancient Indian. The Babylonian myth relates how in the beginning the mighty god Marduk fought and killed the great dragon Tiamat, an embodiment of the primaeval watery chaos, and how after his victory he created

Wide-spread myth of the slaughter of a great dragon.

The Babylonian story of the slaying of Tiamat by Marduk is

a myth of the creation of cosmos out of chaos. the present heaven and earth by splitting the huge carcase of the monster into halves and setting one of them up to form the sky, while the other half apparently he used to fashion the earth. Thus the story is a myth of creation. In language which its authors doubtless understood literally, but which more advanced thinkers afterwards interpreted figuratively, it describes how confusion was reduced to order, how a cosmos emerged from chaos.[1] The account of creation given in the first chapter of Genesis, which has been so much praised for its simple grandeur and sublimity, is merely a rationalised version of the old myth of the fight with the dragon,[2] a myth which for crudity of thought deserves to rank with the quaint fancies of the lowest savages.

Indian story of the slaying of Vṛtra by Indra. Again, the Indian myth embodied in the hymns of the Rigveda tells how the strong and valiant god Indra conquered a great dragon or serpent named Vrtra, which had obstructed the waters so that they could not flow. He slew the monster with his bolt, and then the pent-up springs gushed in rivers to the sea. And what he did once, he continues to do. Again and again he renews the conflict ; again and again he slays the dragon and releases the imprisoned waters. Prayers are addressed to him that he would be pleased to do so in the future. Even priests on

---

[1] P. Jensen, *Die Kosmologie der Babylonier* (Strasburg, 1890), pp. 263 *sqq.* ; *id.*, *Assyrisch - babylonische Mythen und Epen* (Berlin, 1900), pp. 3 *sqq.* ; M. Jastrow, *The Religion of Babylonia and Assyria*, pp. 407 *sqq.* ; L. W. King, *Babylonian Religion and Mythology*, pp. 53 *sqq.* ; H. Zimmern, in E. Schrader's *Die Keilinschriften und das Alte Testament* (Berlin, 1902), pp. 488 *sqq.* ; M. J. Lagrange, *Études sur les religions sémitiques* [2] (Paris, 1905), pp. 366 *sqq.*

[2] P. Jensen, *Die Kosmologie der Babylonier*, pp. 304-306 ; H. Gunkel, *Schöpfung und Chaos in Urzeit und Endzeit* (Göttingen, 1895), pp. 114 *sqq.* ; *id.*, *Genesis übersetzt und erklärt* (Göttingen, 1901), pp. 107 *sqq.* ; *Encyclopaedia Biblica*, *s.v.* "Creation," i. coll. 938 *sqq.* ; S. R. Driver, *The Book of Genesis* [4] (London, 1905), pp.

27 *sqq.* The myth is clearly alluded to in several passages of Scripture, where the dragon of the sea is spoken of as Rahab or Leviathan. See Isaiah li. 9, " Art thou not it that cut Rahab in pieces, that pierced the dragon ? " : *id.* xxvii. 1, " In that day the Lord with his sore and great and strong sword shall punish leviathan the swift serpent, and leviathan the crooked serpent ; and he shall slay the dragon that is in the sea " : Job xxvi. 12, " He stirreth up the sea with his power, and by his understanding he smiteth through Rahab " : Psalm lxxxix. 10, " Thou hast broken Rahab in pieces as one that is slain " : Psalm lxxiv. 13 *sq.*, " Thou didst divide the sea by thy strength : thou brakest the heads of the dragons in the waters. Thou brakest the heads of leviathan in pieces." See further H. Gunkel, *Schöpfung und Chaos*, pp. 29 *sqq.*

earth sometimes associate themselves with Indra in his battles with the dragon. The worshipper is said to have placed the bolt in the god's hands, and the sacrifice is spoken of as having helped the weapon to slay the monster.[1] Thus the feat attributed to Indra would seem to be a mythical account not so much of creation as of some regularly recurring phenomenon. It has been plausibly interpreted as a description of the bursting of the first storms of rain and thunder after the torrid heat of an Indian summer.[2] At such times all nature, exhausted by the drought, longs for coolness and moisture. Day after day men and cattle may be tormented by the sight of clouds that gather and then pass away without disburdening themselves of their contents. At last the long-drawn struggle between the rival forces comes to a crisis. The sky darkens, thunder peals, lightning flashes, and the welcome rain descends in sheets, drenching the parched earth and flooding the rivers. Such a battle of the elements might well present itself to the primitive mind in the guise of a conflict between a maleficent dragon of drought and a beneficent god of thunder and rain. The cloud-dragon has swallowed the waters and keeps them shut up in the black coils of his sinuous body ; the god cleaves the monster's belly with his thunder-bolt, and the imprisoned waters escape, in the form of dripping rain and rushing stream.

The story may be a myth descriptive of the beginning of the rainy season in India.

In other countries a similar myth might, with appropriate variations of detail, express in like manner the passage of one season into another. For example, in more rigorous climates the dragon might stand for the dreary winter and the dragon-slayer for the genial summer. The myths of Apollo and the Python, of St. George and the Dragon have thus been interpreted as symbolising the victory of summer over winter.[3] Similarly it has been held with much probability that the Babylonian legend of Marduk and Tiamat reflects the annual change which transforms the valley of the

Similarly the other tales of the slaughter of the dragon may be mythical descriptions of the changes of the seasons.

---

[1] A. A. Macdonell, *Vedic Mythology*, pp. 58-60, 158 *sq.* Compare H. Oldenberg, *Die Religion des Veda*, pp. 134 *sqq.*

[2] See M. Winternitz, "Der Sarpa-bali, ein altindischer Schlangencult,"

Mittheilungen der Anthropologischen Gesellschaft in Wien, xviii. (1888) pp. 44 *sq.*

[3] A. Kuhn, "Wodan," *Zeitschrift für deutsches Alterthum*, v. (1845) pp. 484-488.

Euphrates in spring. During the winter the wide Babylonian plain, flooded by the heavy rains, looks like a sea, for which the Babylonian word is *tiamtu, tiamat*. Then comes the spring, when with the growing power of the sun the clouds vanish, the waters subside, and dry land and vegetation appear once more. On this hypothesis the dragon Tiamat represents the clouds, the rain, the floods of winter, while Marduk stands for the vernal or summer sun which dispels the powers of darkness and moisture.[1]

The cosmogonical significance of the Babylonian myth may have been an afterthought, the early philosophers picturing the creation of the world on the analogy of the change from winter to summer.

But if the combat of Marduk and Tiamat was primarily a mythical description of the Babylonian spring, it would seem that its cosmogonical significance as an account of creation must have been an after-thought. The early philosophers who meditated on the origin of things may have pictured to themselves the creation or evolution of the world on the analogy of the great changes which outside the tropics pass over the face of nature every year. In these changes it is not hard to discern or to imagine a conflict between two hostile forces or principles, the principle of construction or of life and the principle of destruction or of death, victory inclining now to the one and now to the other, according as winter yields to spring or summer fades into autumn. It would be natural enough to suppose that the same mighty rivals which still wage war on each other had done so from the beginning, and that the formation of the universe as it now exists had resulted from the shock of their battle. On this theory the creation of the world is repeated every spring, and its dissolution is threatened every autumn : the one is proclaimed by summer's gay heralds, the opening flowers ; the other is whispered by winter's sad harbingers, the yellow leaves. Here as elsewhere the old creed is echoed by the poet's fancy :—

> " *Non alios prima crescentis origine mundi*
> *Inluxisse dies aliumve habuisse tenorem*
> *Crediderim : ver illud erat, ver magnus agebat*

[1] P. Jensen, *Die Kosmologie der Babylonier*, pp. 315 *sq.* ; H. Gunkel, *Schöpfung und Chaos*, p. 25 ; *id.*, *Genesis übersetzt und erklärt*, pp. 115 *sq.* ; M. Jastrow, *The Religion of Babylonia and Assyria*, pp. 411 *sq.*, 429 *sq.*, 432 *sq.* ; H. Zimmern, in *Encyclopaedia Biblica*, *s.v.* " Creation," i. coll. 940 *sq.* ; *id.*, in E. Schrader's *Die Keilinschriften und das Alte Testament*,[3] pp. 370 *sq.*, 500 *sq.* ; S. R. Driver, *The Book of Genesis*[4] (London, 1905), p. 28.

Orbis, et hibernis parcebant flatibus Euri :
Cum primae lucem pecudes hausere, virumque
Ferrea progenies duris caput extulit arvis,
Inmissaeque ferae silvis et sidera caelo." [1]

Thus the ceremonies which in many lands have been performed to hasten the departure of winter or stay the flight of summer are in a sense attempts to create the world afresh, to " re-mould it nearer to the Heart's desire." But if we would set ourselves at the point of view of the old sages who devised means so feeble to accomplish a purpose so immeasurably vast, we must divest ourselves of our modern conceptions of the immensity of the universe and of the pettiness and insignificance of man's place in it. We must imagine the infinitude of space shrunk to a few miles, the infinitude of time contracted to a few generations. To the savage the mountains that bound the visible horizon, or the sea that stretches away to meet it, is the world's end. Beyond these narrow limits his feet have never strayed, and even his imagination fails to conceive what lies across the waste of waters or the far blue hills. Of the future he hardly thinks, and of the past he knows only what has been handed down to him by word of mouth from his savage forefathers. To suppose that a world thus circumscribed in space and time was created by the efforts or the fiat of a being like himself imposes no great strain on his credulity ; and he may without much difficulty imagine that he himself can annually repeat the work of creation by his charms and incantations. And once a horde of savages had instituted magical ceremonies for the renewal or preservation of all things, the force of custom and tradition would tend to maintain them in practice long after the old narrow ideas of the universe had been superseded by more adequate conceptions, and the tribe had expanded into a nation.

Neither in Babylonia nor in India, indeed, so far as I am aware, is there any direct evidence that the story of the Slaughter of the Dragon was ever acted as a miracle-play or magical rite for the sake of bringing about those natural events which it describes in figurative language. But analogy leads us to conjecture that in both countries the myth may

Thus ceremonies intended to hasten the departure of winter are in a sense attempts to repeat the creation of the world.

In Babylon and India the myth of the slaughter of the dragon may have been acted

[1] Virgil, *Georgics*, ii. 336-342.

as a
magical
ceremony
to hasten
the advent
of summer
or of the
rainy
season.

New-year
festival of
Zagmuk at
Babylon.

have been recited, if not acted, as an incantation, for the
purpose I have indicated.   At Babylon the recitation may
have formed part of the great New Year festival of Marduk,
which under the name of Zagmuk was celebrated with great
pomp about the vernal equinox.[1]   In this connexion it may
not be without significance that one version of the Babylonian
legend of creation has been found inscribed on a tablet, of
which the reverse exhibits an incantation intended to be
recited for the purification of the temple of E-zida in
Borsippa.[2]   Now E-zida was the temple of Nabu or Nebo,
a god closely associated, if not originally identical, with
Marduk ; indeed Hammurabi, the great king of Babylon,
dedicated the temple in question to Marduk and not to
Nabu.[3]   It seems not improbable, therefore, that the creation
legend, in which Marduk played so important a part, was
recited as an incantation at the purification of the temple
E-zida.   The ceremony perhaps took place at the Zagmuk
festival, when the image of Nabu was solemnly brought in
procession from his temple in Borsippa to the great temple
of Marduk in Babylon.[4]   Moreover, it was believed that at
this great festival the fates were determined by Marduk or
Nabu for the ensuing year.[5]   Now, the creation myth
relates how, after he had slain the dragon, Marduk wrested
the tablets of destiny from Ningu, the paramour of Tiamat,
sealed them with a seal, and laid them on his breast.[6]   We
may conjecture that the dramatic representation of this

[1] P. Jensen, *Die Kosmologie der
Babylonier*, pp. 84 *sqq.*; M. Jastrow,
The Religion of Babylonia and Assyria,
pp. 677 *sqq.*; H. Zimmern, in E.
Schrader's *Die Keilinschriften und das
Alte Testament*,[3] pp. 371, 384 note [4],
402, 427, 515 *sqq.*; R. F. Harper,
Babylonian and Assyrian Literature
(New York, 1901), pp. 136 *sq.*, 137,
140, 149 ; M. J. Lagrange, *Etudes sur
les religions sémitiques*[2] (Paris, 1905),
pp. 285 *sqq.*

[2] L. W. King, *Babylonian Religion
and Mythology*, pp. 88 *sqq.*

[3] See C. P. Tiele, *Geschiedenis van
den Godsdienst in de Oudheid*, i.
(Amsterdam, 1903) pp. 159 *sq.* ;
L. W. King, *op. cit.* p. 21 ; H. Zimmern, in E. Schrader's *Die Keil-*

inschriften und das Alte Testament,[3]
p. 399 ; M. Jastrow, *Die Religion
Babyloniens und Assyriens*, i (Giessen,
1905) pp. 117 *sqq.*

[4] P. Jensen, *op. cit.* pp. 85 *sqq.*;
M. Jastrow, *The Religion of Babylonia
and Assyria*, p. 679 ; H. Zimmern, *op.
cit.* p. 515 ; M. J. Lagrange, *op. cit.*
p. 286.

[5] P. Jensen, *op. cit.* p. 87 ; M.
Jastrow, *The Religion of Babylonia and
Assyria*, p. 681 ; H. Zimmern, *op. cit.*
pp. 402, 415 ; R. F. Harper, *op. cit.*
p. 136.

[6] P. Jensen, *Assyrisch-babylonische
Mythen und Epen*, p. 29 ; L. W.
King, *Babylonian Religion and Mytho-
logy*, p. 74.

incident formed part of the annual determination of the fates at Zagmuk. In short, it seems probable that the whole myth of creation was annually recited and acted at this great spring festival as a charm to dispel the storms and floods of winter, and to hasten the coming of summer.[1]

Wherever sacred dramas of this sort were acted as magical rites for the regulation of the seasons, it would be natural that the chief part should be played by the king, at first in his character of head magician, and afterwards as representative and embodiment of the beneficent god who vanquishes the powers of evil. If, therefore, the myth of the Slaughter of the Dragon was ever acted with this intention, the king would appropriately figure in the play as the victorious champion, while the defeated monster would be represented by an actor of inferior rank. But it is possible that under certain circumstances the distribution of parts in the drama might be somewhat different. Where the tenure of the regal office was limited to a fixed time, at the end of which the king was inexorably put to death, the fatal part of the dragon might be assigned to the monarch as the representative of the old order, the old year, or the old cycle which was passing away, while the part of the victorious god or hero might be supported by his successor and executioner.

Part played by the king in the drama of the Slaughter of the Dragon.

An hypothesis of this latter sort would to a certain extent reconcile the two apparently discrepant interpretations of the myth which have been discussed in the preceding pages, and which for the sake of distinction may be called the totemic and the cosmological interpretations respectively. The serpent or dragon might be the sacred animal or totem of the royal house at the same time that it stood mythically for certain cosmological phenomena, whether moisture or drought, cold or heat, winter or summer. In like manner any other species of animal which served as the totem of the royal family might simultaneously possess a cosmological significance as the symbol of an elemental power. Thus at Cnossus, as we have seen reason to think, the bull was at

Suggested reconciliation of the totemic with the cosmological interpretation of the Slaughter of the Dragon.

---

[1] This appears to be substantially the view of H. Zimmern (*op. cit.* p. 501) and of Karppe (referred to in *Encyclopaedia Biblica, s.v.* "Creation," i. coll. 941 note [1]).

once the king's crest and an emblem of the sun. Similarly in Egypt the hawk was the symbol both of the sun and of the king. The oldest royal capital known to us was Hieraconpolis or Hawk-town, and the first Egyptian king of whom we hear had for his only royal title the name of hawk.[1] At the same time the hawk was with the Egyptians an emblem of the sun.[2] Hawks were kept in the sun-god's temple, and the deity himself was commonly represented in art as a man with a hawk's head and the disc of the sun above it.[3] However, I am fully sensible of the slipperiness and uncertainty of the ground I am treading, and it is with great diffidence that I submit these speculations to the judgment of my readers. The subject of ancient mythology is involved in dense mists which it is not always possible to penetrate and illumine even with the lamp of the Comparative Method. Demonstration in such matters is rarely, if ever, attainable ; the utmost that a candid enquirer can claim for his conclusions is a reasonable degree of probability. Future researches may clear up the obscurity which still rests on the myth of the Slaughter of the Dragon, and may thereby ascertain what measure of truth, if any, there is in the suggested interpretations.

§ 7. *Triennial Tenure of the Kingship*

In the province of Lagos, which forms part of Southern Nigeria, the Ijebu tribe of the Yoruba race is divided into two branches, which are known respectively as the Ijebu Ode and the Ijebu Remon. The Ode branch of the tribe is ruled by a chief who bears the title of Awujale and is surrounded by a great deal of mystery. Down to recent times his face might not be seen even by his own subjects, and if circumstances obliged him to communicate with them he did so through a screen which hid him from view. The other or Remon branch of the Ijebu tribe is governed by a chief, who ranks below the Awujale. Mr. John Parkinson

---

[1] A. Moret, *Du caractère religieux de la royauté Pharaonique* (Paris, 1902), pp. 18 *sqq.*, 33 *sqq.*

[2] Clement of Alexandria, *Strom.* v.

7. p. 671, ed. Potter.

[3] A. Erman, *Die ägyptische Religion* (Berlin, 1905), pp. 10, 25.

was informed that in former times this subordinate chief used to be killed with ceremony after a rule of three years. As the country is now under British protection the custom of putting the chief to death at the end of a three years' reign has long been abolished, and Mr. Parkinson was unable to ascertain any particulars on the subject.[1]

§ 8. *Annual Tenure of the Kingship*

At Babylon, within historical times, the tenure of the kingly office was in practice lifelong, yet in theory it would seem to have been merely annual. For every year at the festival of Zagmuk the king had to renew his power by seizing the hands of the image of Marduk in his great temple of Esagil at Babylon. Even when Babylon passed under the power of Assyria, the monarchs of that country were expected to legalise their claim to the throne every year by coming to Babylon and performing the ancient ceremony at the New-year festival, and some of them found the obligation so burdensome that rather than discharge it they renounced the title of king altogether and contented themselves with the humbler one of Governor.[2] Further, it would appear that in remote times, though not within the historical period, the kings of Babylon or their barbarous predecessors forfeited not merely their crown but their life at the end of a year's tenure of office. At least this is the conclusion to which the following evidence seems to point. According to the historian Berosus, who as a Babylonian priest spoke with ample knowledge, there was annually celebrated in Babylon a festival called the Sacaea. It began on the sixteenth day of the month Lous, and lasted for five days. During these five days masters and servants changed places, the servants giving orders and the masters obeying them. A

Marginal notes: Evidence of an annual tenure of the king-ship at Babylon.

Further, it would seem that in very early times the kings of Babylon were put to death at the end of a year's reign.

The mock king put to death at the festival of the Sacaea was

---

[1] John Parkinson (late Principal of the Mineral Survey of Southern Nigeria), "Southern Nigeria, the Lagos Province," *The Empire Review*, vol. xv. May 1908, pp. 290 *sq.* The account in the text of the mystery surrounding the Awujale is taken from A. B. Ellis, *The Yoruba-speaking Peoples of the Slave Coast of West*

Africa (London, 1894), p. 170.
[2] M. Jastrow, *The Religion of Babylonia and Assyria*, p. 680; H. Zimmern, in E. Schrader's *Die Keilinschriften und das Alte Testament*,[3] pp. 374, 515; C. Brockelmann, "Wesen und Ursprung des Eponymats in Assyrien," *Zeitschrift für Assyriologie*, xvi. (1902) pp. 391 *sq.*, 396 *sq.*

prisoner condemned to death was dressed in the king's robes, seated on the king's throne, allowed to issue whatever commands he pleased, to eat, drink, and enjoy himself, and to lie with the king's concubines. But at the end of the five days he was stripped of his royal robes, scourged, and hanged or impaled. During his brief term of office he bore the title of Zoganes.[1] This custom might perhaps have been explained as merely a grim jest perpetrated in a season of jollity at the expense of an unhappy criminal. But one circumstance—the leave given to the mock king to enjoy the king's concubines—is decisive against this interpretation. Considering the jealous seclusion of an oriental despot's harem we may be quite certain that permission to invade it would never have been granted by the despot, least of all to a condemned criminal, except for the very gravest cause. This cause could hardly be other than that the condemned man was about to die in the king's stead, and that to make the substitution perfect it was necessary he should enjoy the full rights of royalty during his brief reign. There is nothing surprising in this substitution. The rule that the king must be put to death either on the appearance of any symptom of bodily decay or at the end of a fixed period is certainly one which, sooner or later, the kings would seek to abolish or modify. We have seen that in Ethiopia, Sofala, and Eyeo the

---

[1] Athenaeus, xiv. 44, p. 639 c ; Dio Chrysostom, *Or.* iv. pp. 69 *sq.* (vol. i. p. 76, ed. L. Dindorf). Dio Chrysostom does not mention his authority, but it was probably either Berosus or Ctesias. The execution of the mock king is not noticed in the passage of Berosus cited by Athenaeus, probably because the mention of it was not germane to Athenaeus's purpose, which was simply to give a list of festivals at which masters waited on their servants. A passage of Macrobius (*Saturn.* iii. 7. 6) which has sometimes been interpreted as referring to this Babylonian custom (F. Liebrecht, in *Philologus*, xxii. 710 ; J. J. Bachofen, *Die Sage von Tanaquil*, p. 52, note [16]) has in fact nothing to do with it. See A. B. Cook, in *Classical Review*, xvii. (1903) p. 412 ; *id.* in *Folk-lore*, xv. (1904) pp. 304, 384. In the passage of Dio Chrysostom ἐκρέμασαν should strictly mean "hanged," but the verb was applied by the Greeks to the Roman punishment of crucifixion (Plutarch, *Caesar*, 2). It may have been extended to include impalement, which was often inflicted by the Assyrians, as we may see by the representations of it on the Assyrian monuments in the British Museum. See also R. F. Harper, *Assyrian and Babylonian Literature*, p. 41, with the plate facing p. 54. The proper word for impalement in Greek is ἀνασκολοπίζειν (Herodotus, iv. 202). Hanging was also an Oriental as well as Roman mode of punishment. The Hebrew word for it (תלה) seems unambiguous. See Esther, v. 14, vii. 9 *sq.* ; Deuteronomy, xxi. 22 *sq.* ; Joshua, viii. 29, x. 26 ; Livy, i. 26. 6.

rule was boldly set aside by enlightened monarchs ; and that in Calicut the old custom of killing the king at the end of twelve years was changed into a permission granted to any one at the end of the twelve years' period to attack the king, and, in the event of killing him, to reign in his stead ; though, as the king took care at these times to be surrounded by his guards, the permission was little more than a form. Another way of modifying the stern old rule is seen in the Babylonian custom just described. When the time drew near for the king to be put to death (in Babylon this appears to have been at the end of a single year's reign) he abdicated for a few days, during which a temporary king reigned and suffered in his stead. At first the temporary king may have been an innocent person, possibly a member of the king's own family ; but with the growth of civilisation the sacrifice of an innocent person would be revolting to the public sentiment, and accordingly a condemned criminal would be invested with the brief and fatal sovereignty. In the sequel we shall find other examples of a dying criminal representing a dying god. For we must not forget that, as the case of the Shilluk kings clearly shews,[1] the king is slain in his character of a god or a demigod, his death and resurrection, as the only means of perpetuating the divine life unimpaired, being deemed necessary for the salvation of his people and the world.

If at Babylon before the dawn of history the king himself used to be slain at the festival of the Sacaea, it is natural to suppose that the Sacaea was no other than Zagmuk or Zakmuk, the great New-year festival at which down to historical times the king's power had to be formally renewed by a religious ceremony in the temple of Marduk. The theory of the identity of the festivals is indeed strongly supported by many considerations and has been accepted by some eminent scholars,[2] but it has to encounter a serious chronological difficulty, since Zagmuk fell about the equinox

The festival of the Sacaea was perhaps identical with Zagmuk.

---

[1] See above, pp. 21, 26 *sqq.*

[2] Bruno Meissner, " Zur Entstehungsgeschichte des Purimfestes," *Zeitschrift der deutschen morgenländischen Gesellschaft*, l. (1896) pp. 296-301 ;

H. Winckler, *Altorientalische Forschungen*, Zweite Reihe, Bd. ii. p. 345 ; C. Brockelmann, " Wesen und Ursprung des Eponymats in Assyrien," *Zeitschrift für Assyriologie*, xvi. (1902) pp. 391 *sq.*

in spring, whereas the Sacaea according to Berosus was held on the sixteenth of the month Lous, which was the tenth month of the Syro-Macedonian calendar and appears to
Festival of Zagmuk in Assyria. have nearly coincided with July. The question of the sameness or difference of these festivals will be discussed later on.[1] Here it is to be observed that Zagmuk was apparently celebrated in Assyria as well as in Babylonia. For at the end of his great inscription Esarhaddon, king of Assyria, expresses a wish that it may be granted to him to muster all his riding-horses and so *Trace of an annual tenure of the king-ship in Assyria.* forth every year at Zagmuk in his palace.[2] But whether the power of the Assyrian kings had, like that of the Babylonian monarchs, to be annually renewed at this festival, we do not know. However, a trace of an annual tenure of the kingly office in Assyria may perhaps, as Dr. C. Brockelmann thinks,[3] be detected in the rule that an Assyrian king regularly gave his name only to a single year of his reign, while all the other years were named after certain officers and provincial governors, about thirty in number, who were appointed for this purpose and succeeded each other according to a fixed rotation.[4] But we know too little about

---

[1] Meantime I may refer the reader to *The Golden Bough*, Second Edition, ii. 254, iii. 151 *sqq.* As I have there pointed out (iii. 152 *sq.*) the identification of the months of the Syro-Macedonian calendar (that is, the ascertainment of their astronomical dates in the solar year) is a matter of some uncertainty, the dates appearing to have varied considerably in different places. The month Lous in particular is variously said to have corresponded in different places to July, August, September, and October. Until we have ascertained beyond the reach of doubt when Lous fell at Babylon in the time of Berosus, it would be premature to allow much weight to the seeming discrepancy in the dates of Zagmuk and the Sacaea. On the whole difficult question of the identification or dating of the months of the Syro-Macedonian calendar see L. Ideler, *Handbuch der mathematischen und technischen Chronologie*, i. 393 *sqq.*; K. F. Hermann, "Über griechische

Monatskunde," *Abhandlungen der histor.-philolog. Classe d. kön. Gesellschaft der Wissenschaften zu Göttingen*, ii. (1843-44) pp. 68 *sqq.*, 95, 109, 111 *sqq.*; H. F. Clinton, *Fasti Hellenici*, iii.[2] 351 *sqq.*; article "Calendarium," in W. Smith's *Dictionary of Greek and Roman Antiquities*,[3] i. 339. The distinction between the dates of the Syro-Macedonian months, which differed in different places, and their order, which was the same in all places (Dius, Apellaeus, etc.), appears to have been overlooked by some of my former readers.

[2] P. Jensen, *Die Kosmologie der Babylonier*, p. 84; C. Brockelmann, "Wesen und Ursprung des Eponymats in Assyrien," *Zeitschrift für Assyriologie*, xvi. (1902) p. 392. However, there is no mention of Zagmuk in Prof. R. F. Harper's translation of the inscription (*Assyrian and Babylonian Literature*, p. 87).

[3] C. Brockelmann, *op. cit.* pp. 389-401.

[4] H. Winckler, *Geschichte Baby-*

the institution of the *limu* or eponymate to allow us to press this argument for an annual tenure of the kingship in Assyria.[1] A reminiscence of Zagmuk seems to linger in the belief of the Yezidis that on New-year's day God sits on his throne arranging the decrees for the coming year, assigning to dignitaries their various offices, and delivering to them their credentials under his signature and seal.[2]

The view that at Babylon the condemned prisoner who wore the royal robes was slain as a substitute for the king may be supported by the practice of West Africa, where at the funeral of a king slaves used sometimes to be dressed up as ministers of state and then sacrificed in that character instead of the real ministers, their masters, who purchased for a sum of money the privilege of thus dying by proxy. Such vicarious sacrifices were witnessed by Catholic missionaries at Porto Novo on the Slave Coast.[3]

A vestige of a practice of putting the king to death at the end of a year's reign appears to have survived in the festival called Macahity, which used to be celebrated in Hawaii during the last month of the year. About a hundred years ago a Russian voyager described the custom as follows: "The taboo Macahity is not unlike to our festival of Christmas. It continues a whole month, during which the people amuse themselves with dances, plays, and sham-

Slaves sacrificed instead of their masters in West Africa.

Trace of custom of killing the kings of Hawaii at the end of a year's reign.

Ioniens und Assyriens (Leipsic, 1902), p. 212; R. F. Harper, *Assyrian and Babylonian Literature*, pp. xxxviii. *sq.*, 206-216; E. Meyer, *Geschichte des Altertums*[2], i. 2 (Stuttgart and Berlin, 1909), pp. 331 *sq.* It was the second, not the first, year of a king's reign which in later times at all events was named after him. For the explanation see C. Brockelmann, *op. cit.* pp. 397 *sq.*

[1] The eponymate in Assyria and elsewhere may have been the subject of superstitions which we do not yet understand. Perhaps the eponymous magistrate may have been deemed in a sense responsible for everything that happened in the year. Thus we are told that "in Manipur they have a noteworthy system of keeping count of the years. Each year is named after some man, who—for a consideration—undertakes to bear the fortune, good or

bad, of the year. If the year be good, if there be no pestilence and a good harvest, he gets presents from all sorts of people, and I remember hearing that in 1898, when the cholera was at its worst, a deputation came to the Political Agent and asked him to punish the name-giver, as it was obvious that he was responsible for the epidemic. In former times he would have got into trouble" (T. C. Hodson, "The Native Tribes of Manipur," *Journal of the Anthropological Institute*, xxxi. 1901, p. 302).

[2] C. Brockelmann, "Das Neujahrs-fest der Jezîdîs," *Zeitschrift der deutschen morgenländischen Gesellschaft*, lv. (1901) pp. 388-390.

[3] Letter of the missionary N. Baudin, dated 16th April 1875, in *Missions Catholiques*, vii. (1875) pp. 614-616, 627 *sq.*; *Annales de la Propagation de la Foi*, xlviii. (1876) pp. 66-76.

fights of every kind. The king must open this festival wherever he is. On this occasion his majesty dresses himself in his richest cloak and helmet, and is paddled in a canoe along the shore, followed sometimes by many of his subjects. He embarks early, and must finish his excursion at sun-rise. The strongest and most expert of the warriors is chosen to receive him on his landing. This warrior watches the canoe along the beach; and as soon as the king lands, and has thrown off his cloak, he darts his spear at him, from a distance of about thirty paces, and the king must either catch the spear in his hand, or suffer from it: there is no jesting in the business. Having caught it, he carries it under his arm, with the sharp end downwards, into the temple or *heavoo*. On his entrance, the assembled multitude begin their sham-fights, and immediately the air is obscured by clouds of spears, made for the occasion with blunted ends. Hamamea [the king] has been frequently advised to abolish this ridiculous ceremony, in which he risks his life every year; but to no effect. His answer always is, that he is as able to catch a spear as any one on the island is to throw it at him. During the Macahity, all punishments are remitted throughout the country; and no person can leave the place in which he commences these holidays, let the affair be ever so important." [1]

§ 9. *Diurnal Tenure of the Kingship*

The reign and life of the king limited to a single day in Ngoio, a province of Congo.

That a king should regularly have been put to death at the close of a year's reign will hardly appear improbable when we learn that to this day there is still a kingdom in which the reign and the life of the sovereign are limited to a single day. In Ngoio, a province of the ancient kingdom of Congo in West Africa, the rule obtains that the chief who assumes the cap of sovereignty is always killed on the night

[1] U. Lisiansky, *A Voyage Round the World in the Years 1803, 4, 5, and 6* (London, 1814), pp. 118 *sq.* The same ceremony seems to be more briefly described by the French voyager Freycinet, who says that after the principal idol had been carried in procession about the island for twenty-three days it was brought back to the temple, and that thereupon the king was not allowed to enter the precinct until he had parried a spear thrown at him by two men. See L. de Freycinet, *Voyage autour du monde*, vol. ii. Première Partie (Paris, 1829), pp. 596 *sq.*

after his coronation. The right of succession lies with the chief of the Musurongo ; but we need not wonder that he does not exercise it, and that the throne stands vacant. " No one likes to lose his life for a few hours' glory on the Ngoio throne." [1]

[1] R. E. Dennett, *Notes on the Folk-lore of the Fjort*, with an introduction by Mary H. Kingsley (London, 1898), p. xxxii ; *id., At the Back of the Black Man's Mind* (London, 1906), p. 120. Miss Kingsley in conversation called my attention to this particular custom, and informed me that she was personally acquainted with the chief, who possesses but declines to exercise the right of succession.

CHAPTER III

THE SLAYING OF THE KING IN LEGEND

Reminiscences of a custom of regicide in popular tales. IF a custom of putting kings to death at the end of a set term has prevailed in many lands, it is natural enough that reminiscences of it should survive in tradition long after the custom itself has been abolished. In the *High History of the Holy Graal* Story how Lancelot came to a city where the king had to perish in the fire on New Year's Day. we read how Lancelot roamed through strange lands and forests seeking adventures till he came to a fair and wide plain lying without a city that seemed of right great lordship. As he rode across the plain the people came forth from the city to welcome him with the sound of flutes and viols and many instruments of music. When he asked them what meant all this joy, "'Sir,' said they, 'all this joy is made along of you, and all these instruments of music are moved to joy and sound of gladness for your coming.' 'But wherefore for me?' saith Lancelot. 'That shall you know well betimes,' say they. 'This city began to burn and to melt in one of the houses from the very same hour that our king was dead, nor might the fire be quenched, nor ever will be quenched until such time as we have a king that shall be lord of the city and of the honour thereunto belonging, and on New Year's Day behoveth him to be crowned in the midst of the fire, and then shall the fire be quenched, for otherwise may it never be put out nor extinguished. Wherefore have we come to meet you to give you the royalty, for we have been told that you are a good knight.' 'Lords,' saith Lancelot, 'of such a kingdom have I no need, and God defend me from it.' 'Sir,' say they, 'you may not be defended thereof, for you come into this land at hazard, and great grief would it be that so good a land as you see this

is were burnt and melted away by the default of one single
man, and the lordship is right great, and this will be right
great worship to yourself, that on New Year's Day you
should be crowned in the fire and thus save this city and
this great people, and thereof shall you have great praise.'
Much marvelleth Lancelot of this that they say. They come
round about him on all sides and lead him into the city.
The ladies and damsels are mounted to the windows of the
great houses and make great joy, and say the one to another,
'Look at the new king here that they are leading in. Now
will he quench the fire on New Year's Day.' 'Lord!' say
the most part, 'what great pity is it of so comely a knight
that he shall end on such-wise!' 'Be still!' say the others.
'Rather should there be great joy that so fair city as is
this should be saved by his death, for prayer will be made
throughout all the kingdom for his soul for ever!' There-
with they lead him to the palace with right great joy and
say that they will crown him. Lancelot found the palace
all strown with rushes and hung about with curtains of rich
cloths of silk, and the lords of the city all apparelled to do
him homage. But he refuseth right stoutly, and saith that
their king nor their lord will he never be in no such sort.
Thereupon behold you a dwarf that entereth into the city,
leading one of the fairest dames that be in any kingdom,
and asketh whereof this joy and this murmuring may be.
They tell him they are fain to make the knight king,
but that he is not minded to allow them, and they tell him
the whole manner of the fire. The dwarf and the damsel
are alighted, then they mount up to the palace. The dwarf
calleth the provosts of the city and the greater lords.
'Lords,' saith he, 'sith that this knight is not willing to be
king, I will be so willingly, and I will govern the city at
your pleasure and do whatsoever you have devised to do.'
'In faith, sith that the knight refuseth this honour and you
desire to have it, willingly will we grant it you, and he may
go his way and his road, for herein do we declare him wholly
quit.' Therewithal they set the crown on the dwarf's head,
and Lancelot maketh great joy thereof. He taketh his leave,
and they commend him to God, and so remounteth he on
his horse and goeth his way through the midst of the city

all armed. The dames and damsels say that he would not be king for that he had no mind to die so soon."[1]

Story of King Vikramditya of Ujjain in India. A story of the same sort is told of Ujjain, the ancient capital of Malwa in western India, where the renowned King Vikramaditya is said to have held his court, gathering about him a circle of poets and scholars.[2] Tradition has it that once on a time an arch-fiend, with a legion of devils at his command, took up his abode in Ujjain, the inhabitants of which he vexed and devoured. Many had fallen a prey to him, and others had abandoned the country to save their lives. Kings of Ujjain devoured by a demon after a reign of a single day. The once populous city was fast being converted into a desert. At last the principal citizens, meeting in council, besought the fiend to reduce his rations to one man a day, who would be duly delivered up to him in order that the rest might enjoy a day's repose. The demon closed with the offer, but required that the man whose turn it was to be sacrificed should mount the throne and exercise the royal power for a single day, all the grandees of the kingdom submitting to his commands, and everybody yielding him the most absolute obedience. Necessity obliged the citizens to accept these hard terms; their names were entered on a list; every day one of them in his turn ruled from morning to night, and was then devoured by the demon.

Vikramaditya puts an end to the custom by vanquishing the demon, after which he reigns as king of Ujjain. Now it happened by great good luck that a caravan of merchants from Gujerat halted on the banks of a river not far from the city. They were attended by a servant who was no other than Vikramaditya. At nightfall the jackals began to howl as usual, and one of them said in his own tongue, "In two hours a human corpse will shortly float down this river, with four rubies of great price at his belt,

---

[1] *The High History of the Holy Graal*, translated from the French by Sebastian Evans (London, 1898), i. 200-203. I have to thank the translator, Mr. Sebastian Evans, for his kindness in indicating this passage to me.

[2] For a discussion of the legends which gather round Vikramaditya see Captain Wilford, "Vicramaditya and Salivahana," *Asiatic Researches*, ix. (London, 1809) pp. 117 *sqq.*; Chr. Lassen, *Indische Alterthumskunde*, ii.[2] 752 *sqq.*, 794 *sqq.*; E. T. Atkinson, *The Himalayan Districts of the North-Western Provinces of India*, ii. (Allahabad, 1884), pp. 410 *sqq.* Vikramaditya is commonly supposed to have lived in the first century B.C. and to have founded the *Samvat* era, which began with 57 B.C., and is now in use all over India. But according to Professor H. Oldenberg it is now certain that this Vikramaditya was a purely legendary personage (H. Oldenberg, *Die Literatur des alten Indien*, Stuttgart and Berlin, 1903, pp. 215 *sq.*).

and a turquois ring on his finger. He who will give me that corpse to devour will bear sway over the seven lands." Vikramaditya, knowing the language of birds and beasts, understood what the jackal said, gave the corpse to the beast to devour, and took possession of the ring and the rubies. Next day he entered the town, and, traversing the streets, observed a troop of horse under arms, forming a royal escort, at the door of a potter's house. The grandees of the city were there, and with them was the garrison. They were in the act of inducing the son of the potter to mount an elephant and proceed in state to the palace. But strange to say, instead of being pleased at the honour conferred on their son, the potter and his wife stood on the threshold weeping and sobbing most bitterly. Learning how things stood, the chivalrous Vikramaditya was touched with pity, and offered to accept the fatal sovereignty instead of the potter's son, saying that he would either deliver the people from the tyranny of the demon or perish in the attempt. Accordingly he donned the kingly robes, assumed all the badges of sovereignty, and, mounting the elephant, rode in great pomp to the palace, where he seated himself on the throne, while the dignitaries of the kingdom discharged their duties in his presence. At night the fiend arrived as usual to eat him up. But Vikramaditya was more than a match for him, and after a terrific combat the fiend capitulated and agreed to quit the city. Next morning the people on coming to the palace were astonished to find Vikramaditya still alive. They thought he must be no common mortal, but some superhuman being, or the descendant of a great king. Grateful to him for their deliverance they bestowed the kingdom on him, and he reigned happily over them.[1]

According to one account, the dreadful being who ravaged Ujjain and devoured a king every day was the bloodthirsty goddess Kali. When she quitted the city she left behind her two sisters, whose quaint images still frown on

Yearly human sacrifices formerly offered at Ujjain.

---

[1] "Histoire des rois de l'Hindoustan après les Pandaras, traduite du texte hindoustani de Mîr Cher-i Alî Afsos, par M. l'abbé Bertrand," *Journal Asiatique*, IVème Série, iii. (Paris, 1844) pp. 248-257. The story is told more briefly by Mrs. Postans, *Cutch* (London, 1839), pp. 21 *sq.* Compare Chr. Lassen, *Indische Alterthumskunde*, ii.[2] 798.

the spectator from the pillared portal known as Vikramaditya's Gate at Ujjain.   To these her sisters she granted the
privilege of devouring as many human beings as they pleased
once every twelve years.   That tribute they still exact,
though the European in his blindness attributes the deaths
to cholera.   But in addition seven girls and five buffaloes
were to be sacrificed to them every year, and these sacrifices
used to be offered regularly until the practice was put down
by the English Government.   It is said that the men who
gave their five-year-old daughters to be slain received grants
of land as a reward of their piety.   Nowadays only buffaloes
are killed at the Daçaratha festival, which is held in October
on the ninth day of the month Açvina.   The heads of the
animals are buried at Vikramaditya's gateway, and those of
the last year's victims are taken up.   The girls who would
formerly have been sacrificed are now released, but they are
not allowed to marry, and their fathers still receive grants
of lands just as if the cruel sacrifice had been consummated.[1]
The persistence of these bloody rites at Ujjain down to
recent times raises a presumption that the tradition of the
daily sacrifice of a king in the same city was not purely
mythical.

Story of
the birth
of Vik-
ramaditya.
His father
Gand-
harva-Sena
was an
ass by day
and a man
by night,
until his
ass's skin
was burnt,
when he
left his wife
for ever.

It is worth while to consider another of the stories which
are told of King Vikramaditya.   His birth is said to have
been miraculous, for his father was Gandharva-Sena, who
was the son of the great god Indra.   One day Gandharva-
Sena had the misfortune to offend his divine father, who
was so angry that he cursed his son and banished him from
heaven to earth, there to remain under the form of an ass
by day and of a man by night until a powerful king should
burn his ass's body, after which Gandharva-Sena would
regain his proper shape and return to the upper world.   All
this happened according to the divine word.   In the shape
of an ass the son of the god rendered an important service
to the King of Dhara, and received the hand of the king's
daughter as his reward.   By day he was an ass and ate hay

---

[1] A. V. Williams Jackson, "Notes
from India, Second Series," *Journal of
the American Oriental Society*, xxiii.
(1902) pp. 308, 316 *sq.* I have to
thank my friend the Rev. Professor J.
H. Moulton for referring me to Prof.
Williams Jackson's paper.

in the stables; by night he was a man and enjoyed the company of the princess his wife. But the king grew tired of the taunts of his enemies, as well as of the gibes which were levelled by unfeeling wits at his asinine son-in-law. So one night, while Gandharva-Sena in human shape was with his wife, the king got hold of the ass's body which his son-in-law had temporarily quitted, and throwing it on a fire burned it to ashes. On the instant Gandharva - Sena appeared to him, and thanking him for undoing the spell announced that he was about to return to heaven, but that his wife was with child by him, and that she would bring forth a son who would bear the name of Vikramaditya and be endowed with the strength of a thousand elephants. The deserted wife was filled with sorrow at his departure, and died in giving birth to Vikramaditya.[1]

This story belongs to a widely diffused type of tale which in England is known by the name of Beauty and the Beast. It relates how a beast, doffing its animal shape, lives as a human husband or wife with a human spouse. Often, though not always, their marriage has a tragic ending. The couple live lovingly together for years and children are born to them. But it is a condition of their union that the transformed husband or wife should never be reminded of his or her old life in furry, feathered, or finny form. At last one unhappy day the fairy spouse finds his or her beast skin, which had been carefully hidden away by her or his loving partner; or husband and wife quarrel and the real man or woman taunts the other with her or his kinship with the beasts. The sight of the once familiar skin awakens old memories and stirs yearnings that had been long suppressed : the cruel words undo the kindness of years. The sometime animal resumes its native shape and disappears, and the human husband or wife is left lamenting. Sometimes, as in the story of Gandharva-Sena, the destruction of the beast's skin causes the fairy mate to vanish for ever; sometimes it enables him or her to remain thenceforth in human form

Stories of the type of Beauty and the Beast, which tell how human beings are married to beasts or to animals which temporarily assume human form.

[1] "Histoire des rois de l'Hindoustan," *Journal Asiatique*, IVème Série, iii. (1844) pp. 239-243. The legend is told with modifications by Captain Wilford ("Vicramaditya and Salivahana," *Asiatic Researches*, ix. London, 1809, pp. 148 *sq.*), Mrs. Postans (*Cutch*, London, 1839, pp. 18-20), and Prof. Williams Jackson (*op. cit.* pp. 314 *sq.*).

with the human wife or husband.   Tales of this sort are told by savages in many parts of the world, and many of them have survived in the folk-lore of civilised peoples.   With their implied belief that beasts can turn into men or men into beasts, they must clearly have originated among savages who see nothing incredible in such transformations.

Stories of this kind are told by savages to explain why they abstain from eating certain animals.

Now it is to be observed that stories of this sort are told by savage tribes to explain why they abstain from eating certain creatures.   The reason they assign for the abstinence is that they themselves are descended from a creature of that sort, who was changed for a time into human shape and married a human husband or wife.   Thus in the rivers of Sarawak there is a certain fish called a *puttin*, which some of the Dyaks will on no account eat, saying that if they did so they would be eating their relations.

Dyak stories of this type.

Tradition runs that a solitary old man went out fishing and caught a *puttin*, which he dragged out of the water and laid down in his boat.   On turning round he perceived that it had changed into a very pretty girl.   He thought she would make a charming wife for his son, so he took her home and brought her up till she was of an age to marry.   She consented to be his son's wife, but cautioned her husband to use her well.   Some time after marriage, however, he was angry and struck her.   She screamed and rushed away into the water, leaving behind her a beautiful daughter who became the mother of the race.   Other Dyak tribes tell similar stories of their ancestors.[1]   Thus the Sea Dyaks relate how the white-headed hawk married a Sea Dyak woman, and how he gave all his daughters in marriage to the various omen-birds.   Hence if a Sea Dyak kills an omen-bird by mistake, he wraps it in a cloth and buries it carefully in the earth along with rice, flesh, and money, entreating the bird not to be vexed, and to forgive him, because it was all an accident.[2]   Again, a Kalamantan chief and all his people refrain from killing and eating deer of a certain species (*cervulus muntjac*), because one of their

[1] The Bishop of Labuan, "Wild Tribes of Borneo," *Transactions of the Ethnological Society of London,* New Series, ii. (1863) pp. 26 *sq.*
[2] Ch. Hose and W. McDougall, "The Relations between Men and Animals in Sarawak," *Journal of the Anthropological Institute,* xxxi. (1901) pp. 197 *sq.*

ancestors became a deer of that kind, and as they cannot distinguish his incarnation from common deer they spare them all.[1]   In these latter cases the legends explaining the kinship of the men with the animals are not given in full; we can only conjecture, therefore, that they conform to the type here discussed.

The Sea Dyaks also tell a story of the same sort to explain how they first came to plant rice and to revere the omen-birds which play so important a part in Dyak life. Long, long ago, so runs the tale, when rice was yet unknown, and the Dyaks lived on tapioca, yams, potatoes, and such fruits as they could procure, a handsome young chief named Siu went out into the forest with his blow-pipe to shoot birds. He wandered without seeing a bird or meeting an animal till the sun was sinking in the west. Then he came to a wild fig-tree covered with ripe fruit, which a swarm of birds of all kinds were busy pecking at. Never in his life had he seen so many birds together! It seemed as if all the fowls of the forest were gathered in the boughs of that tree. He killed a great many with the poisoned darts of his blow-pipe, and putting them in his basket started for home. But he lost his way in the wood, and the night had fallen before he saw the lights and heard the usual sounds of a Dyak house. Hiding his blow-pipe and the dead birds in the jungle, he went up the ladder into the house, but what was his surprise to find it apparently deserted. There was no one in the long verandah, and of the people whose voices he had heard a minute before not one was to be seen. Only in one of the many rooms, dimly lighted, he found a beautiful girl, who prepared for him his evening meal. Now though Siu did not know it, the house was the house of the great Singalang Burong, the Ruler of the Spirit World. He could turn himself and his followers into any shape. When they went forth against an enemy they took the form of birds for the sake of speed, and flew over the tall trees, the broad rivers, and even the sea. But in his own house and among his own people Singalang Burong appeared as a man. He had eight daughters, and the girl who cooked Siu's food for him was the youngest. The

Story told by the Sea Dyaks to explain how they came to plant rice and to revere the omen-birds. It describes how the young chief Siu married a woman of the bird-family, and promised her never to hurt or even touch a bird.

[1] Ch. Hose and W. McDougall, *op. cit.* p. 193.

reason why the house was so still and deserted was that the people were in mourning for some of their relatives who had just been killed, and the men had gone out to take human heads in revenge. Siu stayed in the house for a week, and then the girl, whose pet name was Bunsu Burong or "the youngest of the bird family," agreed to marry him; but she said he must promise never to kill or hurt a bird or even to hold one in his hands; for if he did, she would be his wife no more. Siu promised, and together they returned to his people.

But one day he broke his word, and his bird-wife left him and returned to the bird-people.

There they lived happily, and in time Siu's wife bore him a son whom they named Seragunting. One day when the boy had grown wonderfully tall and strong for his years and was playing with his fellows, a man brought some birds which he had caught in a trap. Forgetting the promise he had made to his wife, Siu asked the man to shew him the birds, and taking one of them in his hand he stroked it. His wife saw it and was sad at heart. She took the pitchers and went as though she would fetch water from the well. But she never came back. Siu and his son sought her, sorrowing, for days. At last after many adventures they came to the house of the boy's grandfather, Singalang Burong, the Ruler of the Spirit World. There they found the lost wife and mother, and there they stayed for a time. But the heart of Siu yearned to his old home. He would fain have persuaded his wife to return with him, but she would not. So at last he and his son went back alone. But before he went he learned from his father-in-law how to plant rice, and how to revere the sacred birds and to draw omens from them. These birds were named after the sons-in-law of the Ruler of the Spirit World and were the appointed means whereby he made known his wishes to mankind. That is how the Sea Dyaks learned to plant rice and to honour the omen-birds.[1]

Stories of the same kind meet us on the west coast of Africa. Thus the Tshi-speaking negroes of the Gold Coast

[1] Rev. E. H. Gomes, "Two Sea Dyak Legends," *Journal of the Straits Branch of the Royal Asiatic Society*, No. 41 (January 1904, Singapore), pp. 12-28; *id.*, *Seventeen Years among the Sea Dyaks of Borneo* (London, 1911), pp. 278 *sqq.*

are divided into a number of great families or clans, mostly Stories of the same sort are told by the Tshi-speaking negroes of the Gold Coast to explain why they do not eat their totemic animals. named after animals or plants, and the members of a clan refrain from eating animals of the species whose name they bear. In short, the various animals or plants are the totems of their respective clans. Now some of the more recent of these clans possess traditions of their origin, and in such cases the founder of the family, from whom the name is derived, is always represented as having been a beast, bird, or fish, which possessed the power of assuming human shape at will. Thus, for instance, at the town of Chama there resides a family or clan who take their name from the *sarfu* or horse-mackerel, which they may not eat because they are descended from a horse-mackerel. One day, so runs the story, a native of Chama who had lost his wife was walking sadly on the beach, when he met a beautiful young woman whom he persuaded to be his wife. She consented, but told him that her home lay in the sea, that her people were fishes, and that she herself was a fish, and she made him swear that he would never allude to her old home and kinsfolk. All went well for a time till her husband took a second wife, who quarrelled with the first wife and taunted her with being a fish. That grieved her so that she bade her husband good-bye and plunged into the sea with her youngest child in her arms. But she left her two elder children behind, and from them are descended the Horse-mackerel people of Chama. A similar story is told of another family in the town of Appam. Their ancestor caught a fine fish of the sort called *appei*, which turned into a beautiful woman and became his wife. But she told him that in future neither they nor their descendants might eat the *appei* fish or else they would at once return to the sea. The family, duly observing the prohibition, increased and multiplied till they occupied the whole country, which was named after them Appeim or Appam.[1]

We may surmise that stories of this sort, wherever found, Stories of this sort were probably at first always told to had a similar origin; in other words, that they reflect and are intended to explain a real belief in the kinship of certain families with certain species of animals. Hence if the name

[1] A. B. Ellis, *The Tshi-speaking Peoples of the Gold Coast* (London, 1887), pp. 204-212.

explain
the totemic
belief in
the kinship
of certain
families
with certain
species of
animals.

When
husband
and wife
had differ-
ent totems,
a violation
of the
totemic
taboos by
husband
or wife
might lead
to the
separation
of the

totemism may be used to include all such beliefs and the practices based on them, the origin of this type of story may be said to be totemic.[1] Now, wherever the totemic clans have become exogamous, that is, wherever a man is always obliged to marry a woman of a totem different from his own, it is obvious that husband and wife will always have to observe different totemic taboos, and that a want of respect shewn by one of them for the sacred animal or plant of the other would tend to domestic jars, which might often lead to the permanent separation of the spouses, the offended wife or husband returning to her or his native clan of the fish-people, the bird-people, or what not. That, I take it, was the origin of the sad story of the man or woman happily mated with a transformed animal and then parted for ever. Such tales, if I am right, were not wholly fictitious. Totemism may have broken many loving hearts. But when that ancient

---

[1] The type of story in question has been discussed by Mr. Andrew Lang in a well-known essay "Cupid, Psyche, and the Sun-Frog," *Custom and Myth* (London, 1884), pp. 64-86. He rightly explains all such tales as based on savage taboos, but so far as I know he does not definitely connect them with totemism. For other examples of these tales told by savages see W. Lederbogen, "Duala Märchen," *Mittheilungen des Seminars für Orientalische Sprachen zu Berlin*, v. (1902) Dritte Abtheilung, pp. 139-145 (the Duala tribe of Cameroons ; in one tale the wife is a palm-rat, in the other a *mpondo*, a hard brown fruit as large as a coco-nut) ; R. H. Nassau, *Fetichism in West Africa* (London, 1904), pp. 25-28 (West Africa ; wife a forest-rat) ; G. H. Smith, "Some Betsimisaraka Superstitions," *The Antananarivo Annual and Madagascar Magazine*, No. 10 (Christmas, 1886), pp. 241 *sq.* ; R. H. Codrington, *The Melanesians*, pp. 172, 397 *sq.* (Melanesia ; wife a bird, husband an owl) ; A. F. van Spreeuwenberg, "Een blik op Minahassa," *Tijdschrift voor Neêrland's Indië*, 1846, Erste deel, pp. 25-28 (the Bantiks of Celebes; wife a white dove); J. H. F. Kohlbrugge, "Die Tenggeresen, ein alter Javanischer Volks-

staam," *Bijdragen tot de Taal- Land- en Volkenkunde van Nederlandsch-Indië*, liii. (1901) pp. 97-99 (the Tenggeres of Java ; wife a bird) ; J. Fanggidaej, "Rottineesche Verhalen," *Bijdragen tot de Taal- Land- en Volkenkunde van Nederlandsch-Indië*, lviii. (1905), pp. 430-436 (island of Rotti ; husband a crocodile) ; J. Kubary, "Die Religion der Pelauer," in A. Bastian's *Allerlei aus Volkes- und Menschenkunde* (Berlin, 1888), i. 60 *sq.* (Pelew Islands ; wife a fish) ; A. R. McMahon, *The Karens of the Golden Chersonese*, pp. 248-250 (Karens of Burma ; husband a tree-lizard) ; Landes, "Contes Tjames," *Cochinchine française, excursions et reconnaissances*, No. 29 (Saigon, 1887), pp. 53 *sqq.* (Chams of Cochin-China ; husband a coco-nut) ; A. Certeux and E. H. Carnoy, *L'Algérie traditionnelle* (Paris and Algiers, 1884), pp. 87-89 (Arabs of Algeria ; wife a dove) ; J. G. Kohl, *Kitschi-Gami* (Bremen, 1858), i. 140-145 (Ojebway Indians ; wife a beaver) ; Franz Boas and George Hunt, *Kwakiutl Texts*, ii. 322-330 (*The Jesup North Pacific Expedition, Memoir of the American Museum of Natural History*) (Kwakiutl Indians ; wife a salmon) ; J. R. Swanton, *Haida Texts and Myths* (*Bureau of American Ethnology, Bulletin*, No. 29, Washington, system of society had fallen into disuse, and the ideas on spouses. which it was based had ceased to be understood, the quaint This would explain the stories of mixed marriages to which it had given birth would separation not be at once forgotten. They would continue to be told, of husband and wife no longer indeed as myths explanatory of custom, but merely in the type of tale here as fairy tales for the amusement of the listeners. The discussed. barbarous features of the old legends, which now appeared too monstrously incredible even for story-tellers, would be gradually discarded and replaced by others which fitted in better with the changed beliefs of the time. Thus in particular the animal husband or animal wife of the story might drop the character of a beast to assume that of a fairy. This is the stage of decay exhibited by the two most famous tales of the class in question, the Greek fable of Cupid and Psyche and the Indian story of King Pururavas and the nymph Urvasi, though in the latter we can still detect hints that the fairy wife was once a bird-woman.[1]

1905), pp. 286 *sq.* (Haida Indians; wife a killer-whale); H. Rink, *Tales and Traditions of the Eskimo*, pp. 146 *sq.* (Esquimaux; wife a sea-fowl). The Bantik story is told to explain the origin of the people; the Tenggeres story is told to explain why it is forbidden to lift the lid of a basket in which rice is being boiled. The other stories referred to in this note are apparently told as fairy tales only, but we may conjecture that they too were related originally to explain a supposed relationship of human beings to animals or plants. I have already illustrated and explained this type of story in *Totemism and Exogamy*, vol. ii. pp. 55, 206, 308, 565-571, 589, iii. 60-64, 337 *sq.*

[1] The fable of Cupid and Psyche is only preserved in the Latin of Apuleius (*Metamorph.* iv. 28-vi. 24), but we cannot doubt that the original was Greek. For the story of Pururavas and Urvasi, see *The Rigveda*, x. 95 (*Hymns of the Rigveda*, translated by R. T. H. Griffith, vol. iv. Benares, 1892, pp. 304 *sqq.*); *Satapatha Brahmana*, translated by J. Eggeling, part v. pp. 68-74 (*Sacred Books of the East*, vol. xliv.); and the references in *The*

Magic Art and the Evolution of Kings, vol. ii. p. 250, note [4]. A clear trace of the bird-nature of Urvasi occurs in the *Satapatha Brahmana* (Part v. p. 70 of J. Eggeling's translation), where the sorrowing husband finds his lost wife among nymphs who are swimming about in the shape of swans or ducks on a lotus-covered lake. This has been already pointed out by Th. Benfey (*Pantschatantra*, i. 264). In English the type of tale is known as "Beauty and the Beast," which ought to include the cases in which the wife, as well as those in which the husband, appears as an animal. On stories of this sort, especially in the folklore of civilised peoples, see Th. Benfey, *Pantschatantra*, i. 254 *sqq.*; W. R. S. Ralston, Introduction to F. A. von Schiefner's *Tibetan Tales*, pp. xxxvii.-xxxix.; A. Lang, *Custom and Myth* (London, 1884), pp. 64 *sqq.*; S. Baring-Gould, *Curious Myths of the Middle Ages*, pp. 561-578; E. Cosquin, *Contes populaires de Lorraine*, ii. 215-230; W. A. Clouston, *Popular Tales and Fictions*, i. 182-191; Miss M. Roalfe Cox, *Introduction to Folklore* (London, 1895), pp. 120-123.

It would, no doubt, be a mistake to suppose that totemism, or a system of taboos resembling it, must have existed wherever such stories are told ; for it is certain that popular tales spread by diffusion from tribe to tribe and nation to nation, till they may be handed down by oral tradition among people who neither practise nor even understand the customs in which the stories originated.   Yet the legend of the miraculous parentage of Vikramaditya may very well have been based on the existence at Ujjain of a line of rajahs who had the ass for their crest or totem.[1]   Such a custom is not without analogy in India.   The crest of the Maharajah of Nagpur is a cobra with a human face under its expanded hood, surrounded by all the insignia of royalty. Moreover, the Rajah and the chief members of his family always wear turbans so arranged that they resemble a coiled serpent with its head projecting over the wearer's brow.   To explain this serpent badge a tale is told which conforms to the type of Beauty and the Beast.   Once upon a time a Nag or serpent named Pundarika took upon himself the likeness of a Brahman, and repaired in that guise to the house of a real Brahman at Benares, in order to perfect himself in a knowledge of the sacred books.   The teacher was so pleased with the progress made by his pupil that he gave him his only child, the beautiful Parvati, to wife.   But the subtle serpent, though he could assume any form at pleasure, was unable to rid himself of his forked tongue and foul breath.   To conceal these personal blemishes from his wife he always slept with his back to her.   One night, however, she got round him and discovered his unpleasant peculiarities.   She questioned him sharply, and to divert her attention he proposed that they should make a pilgrimage to Juggernaut.   The idea of visiting that fashionable watering-place so raised the lady's spirits that she quite forgot to pursue the enquiry.   However, on their way home her curiosity revived, and she repeated her questions under circumstances which rendered it impossible for the serpent,

---

[1] In the ruins of Raipoor, supposed to be the ancient Mandavie, coins are found bearing the image of an ass ; and the legend of the transformation of Gandharva-Sena into an ass is told to explain their occurrence.   The coins are called Gandharva pice.   See Mrs. Postans, *Cutch* (London, 1839), pp. 17 *sq.*, 22.

as a tender husband, to evade them, though well he knew that the disclosure he was about to make would sever him, the immortal, at once and for ever from his mortal wife. He related the wondrous tale, and, plunging into a pool, disappeared from sight. His poor wife was inconsolable at his hurried departure, and in the midst of her grief and remorse her child was born. But instead of rejoicing at the birth, she made for herself a funeral pyre and perished in the flames. At that moment a Brahman appeared on the scene, and perceived the forsaken babe lying sheltered and guarded by a great hooded snake. It was the serpent father protecting his child. Addressing the Brahman, he narrated his history, and foretold that the child should be called Phani-Makuta Raya, that is, "the snake crowned," and that he should reign as rajah over the country to be called Nagpur. That is why the rajahs of Nagpur have the serpent for their crest.[1] Again, the rajahs of Manipur trace their descent from a divine snake. At his installation a rajah of Manipur used to have to pass with great solemnity between two massive dragons of stone which stood in front of the coronation house. Somewhere inside the building was a mysterious chamber, and in the chamber was a pipe, which, according to the popular belief, led down to the depths of a cavern where dwells the snake god, the ancestor of the royal family. The length and prosperity of the rajah's reign were believed to depend on the length of time he could sit on the pipe enduring the fiery breath of his serpentine forefather in the place below. Women are specially devoted to the worship of the ancestral snake, and great reverence is paid them in virtue of their sacred office.[2]

Again, the rajahs of Manipur trace their descent from a divine serpent.

The parallelism between the legends of Nagpur and Ujjain may be allowed to strengthen my conjecture that, if we have a race of royal serpents in the one place, there may well have been a race of royal asses in the other; indeed such dynasties have perhaps not been so rare as might be supposed.

[1] E. T. Dalton, *Descriptive Ethnology of Bengal*, pp. 165 *sq.*

[2] T. C. Hodson, "The Native Tribes of Manipur," *Journal of the Anthropological Institute*, xxxi. (1901) pp. 302, 304.

CHAPTER IV

THE SUPPLY OF KINGS

Stories of the type of Beauty and the Beast are not mere fictions, but rest on a real basis of belief and custom.

Similarly the legend of kings who were sacrificed after a reign of a single day has its analogy in actual custom.

Such stories indicate that the supply of kings may have been maintained by compelling men to accept the fatal sovereignty.

TALES of the foregoing sort might be dismissed as fictions designed to amuse a leisure hour, were it not for their remarkable agreement with beliefs and customs which, as we have seen, still exist, or are known to have existed in former times. That agreement can hardly be accidental. We seem to be justified, therefore, in assuming that stories of the kind really rest on a basis of facts, however much these facts may have been distorted or magnified in passing through the mind of the story-teller, who is naturally more concerned to amuse than instruct his hearers. Even the legend of a line of kings of whom each reigned for a single day, and was sacrified at night for the good of the people, will hardly seem incredible when we remember that to this day a kingdom is held on a similar tenure in west Africa, though under modern conditions the throne stands vacant.[1] And while it would be vain to rely on such stories for exact historical details, yet they may help us in a general way to understand the practical working of an institution which to civilised men seems at first sight to belong to the cloudland of fancy rather than to the sober reality of the workaday world. Remark, for example, how in these stories the supply of kings is maintained. In the Indian tradition all the men of the city are put on a list, and each of them, when his turn comes, is forced to reign for a day and to die the death. It is not left to his choice to decide whether he will accept the fatal sovereignty or not. In the *High History of the Holy Grail* the mode of filling the vacant

---

[1] See above, pp. 118 *sq.*

throne is different.   A stranger, not a citizen, is seized and
compelled to accept office.   In the end, no doubt, the dwarf
volunteers to be king, thus saving Lancelot's life ; but the
narrative plainly implies that if a substitute had not thus
been found, Lancelot would have been obliged, whether he
would or not, to wear the crown and to perish in the fire.

In thus representing the succession to a throne as compulsory, the stories may well preserve a reminiscence of a
real custom.   To us, indeed, who draw our ideas of kingship
from the hereditary and highly privileged monarchies of
civilised Europe, the notion of thrusting the crown upon
reluctant strangers or common citizens of the lowest rank is
apt to appear fantastic and absurd.   But that is merely
because we fail to realise how widely the modern type of
kingship has diverged from the ancient pattern.   In early
times the duties of sovereignty are more conspicuous than
its privileges.   At a certain stage of development the chief
or king is rather the minister or servant than the ruler of
his people.   The sacred functions which he is expected to
discharge are deemed essential to the welfare, and even the
existence, of the community, and at any cost some one must
be found to perform them.   Yet the burdens and restrictions
of all sorts incidental to the early kingship are such that not
merely in popular tales, but in actual practice, compulsion
has sometimes been found necessary to fill vacancies, while
elsewhere the lack of candidates has caused the office to fall
into abeyance, or even to be abolished altogether.[1]   And
where death stared the luckless monarch in the face at the
end of a brief reign of a few months or days, we need not
wonder that gaols had to be swept and the dregs of society
raked to find a king.

Our conceptions of the primitive kingship are apt to be coloured and falsified by ideas borrowed from the very different monarchies of modern Europe.

Yet we should doubtless err if we supposed that under
such hard conditions men could never be found ready and
even eager to accept the sovereignty.   A variety of causes
has led the modern nations of western Europe to set on
human life—their own life and that of others—a higher value
than is put upon it by many other races.   The result is a
fear of death which is certainly not shared in the same

In other races and other ages many men may have been willing to accept a kingdom on con-

[1] See *The Magic Art and the Evolution of Kings,* vol. ii. p. 4 ; *Taboo and the Perils of the Soul,* pp. 17 *sqq.*

dition of
being killed
at the end
of a short
reign.
Various
causes have
contributed
to intensify
the fear of
death in
modern
Europe.
degree of intensity by some peoples whom we in our self-complacency are accustomed to regard as our inferiors. Among the causes which thus tend to make us cowards may be numbered the spread of luxury and the doctrines of a gloomy theology, which by proclaiming the eternal damnation and excruciating torments of the vast majority of mankind has added incalculably to the dread and horror of death. The growth of humaner sentiments, which seldom fails to effect a corresponding amelioration in the character even of the gods, has indeed led many Protestant divines of late years to temper the rigour of the divine justice with a large infusion of mercy by relegating the fires of hell to a decent obscurity or even extinguishing them altogether. But these lurid flames appear to blaze as fiercely as ever in the more conservative theology of the Catholic Church.[1]

Evidence
of the com-
parative
indifference
to death
displayed
by other
races.
Absence of
the fear of
death in
India and
Annam.
It would be easy to accumulate evidence of the indifference or apathy exhibited in presence of death by races whom we commonly brand as lower. A few examples must here suffice. Speaking of the natives of India an English writer observes : " We place the highest value on life, while they, being blessed with a comfortable fatalism, which assumes that each man's destiny is written on his forehead in invisible characters, and being besides untroubled with any doubts or thoughts as to the nature of their reception in the next world, take matters of life and death a great deal more unconcernedly, and, compared with our ideas, they may be said to present an almost apathetic indifference on these subjects." [2]   To the same effect another English writer remarks that " the absence of that fear of death, which is so powerful in the hearts of civilised men, is the most remarkable trait in the Hindu character." [3]   Among the natives of Annam, according to a Catholic missionary, " the subject of death has nothing alarming for anybody. In presence of a sick man people will speak of his approaching end

[1] See Dr. Joseph Bautz, *Die Hölle,
im Anschluss an die Scholastik darge-
stellt* [2] (Mainz, 1905). Dr. Bautz holds
that the damned burn in eternal darkness and eternal fire somewhere in
the bowels of the earth. He is, let us
hope in more senses than one, an
extraordinary professor of theology at
the University of Münster, and his
book is published with the approbation
of the Catholic Church.

[2] R. H. Elliot, *Experiences of a
Planter in the Jungles of Mysore*
(London, 1871), i. 95.

[3] Mrs. Postans, *Cutch* (London,
1839), p. 168.

and of his funeral as readily as of anything else.   Hence
we never need to take the least verbal precaution in
warning the sick to prepare themselves to receive the
last sacraments.   Some time ago I was summoned to a
neophyte whose death, though certain, was still distant.   On
entering the house I found a woman seated at his bedside
sewing the mourning dresses of the family.   Moreover, the
carpenter was fitting together the boards of the coffin quite
close to the door of the house, so that the dying man could
observe the whole proceeding from his bed.   The worthy
man superintended personally all these details and gave
directions for each of the operations.   He even had for his
pillow part of the mourning costume which was already
finished.   I could tell you a host of anecdotes of the same
sort."   Among these people it is a mark of filial piety to
present a father or mother with a coffin ; the presentation is
the occasion of a family festival to which all friends are
invited.   Pupils display their respect for their masters in the
same fashion.   Bishop Masson, whose letter I have just
quoted, was himself presented with a fine coffin by some of
his converts as a New Year gift and a token of their respect
and affection ; they invited his attention particularly to the
quality of the wood and the beauty of the workmanship.[1]

With regard to the North American Indians a writer *Absence of*
who knew them well has said that among them "the idea *the fear of*
death
of immortality is strongly dwelt upon.   It is not spoken of *among the*
as a supposition or a mere belief, not fixed.   It is regarded *American*
Indians.
as an actuality,—as something known and approved by the
judgment of the nation.   During the whole period of my
residence and travels in the Indian country, I never knew
and never heard of an Indian who did not believe in it, and
in the reappearance of the body in a future state.   However
mistaken they are on the subject of accountabilities for acts
done in the present life, no small part of their entire mythology, and the belief that sustains the man in his vicissitudes
and wanderings here, arises from the anticipation of ease and
enjoyment in a future condition, after the soul has left the
body.   The resignation, nay, the alacrity with which an

[1] Mgr. Masson, in *Annales de la Propagation de la Foi*, xxiv. (1852) pp.
324 *sq.*

Indian frequently lies down and surrenders life, is to be ascribed to this prevalent belief. He does not fear to go to a land which, all his life long, he has heard abounds in rewards without punishments."[1]   Another traveller, who saw much of the South American Indians, asserts that they surpass the beasts in their insensibility to hardship and pain, never complaining in sickness nor even when they are being killed, and exhibiting in their last moments an apathetic indifference untroubled by any misgiving as to the future.[2]

Apathy of savages under sentence of death.
Wholesale butcheries of human beings were perpetrated till lately in the name of religion in the west African kingdom of Dahomey.   As to the behaviour of the victims we are told that "almost invariably, those doomed to die exhibit the greatest coolness and unconcern.   The natural dread of death which the instinct of self-preservation has implanted in every breast, often leads persons who are liable to be seized for immolation to endeavour to escape ; but once they are seized and bound, they resign themselves to their fate with the greatest apathy.   This is partly due to the less delicate nervous system of the negro ; but one reason, and that not the least, is that they have nothing to fear.   As has been said, they have but to undergo a surgical operation and a change of place of residence ; there is no uncertain future to be faced, and, above all, there is an entire absence of that notion of a place of terrible punishment which makes so many Europeans cowards when face to face with death."[3]   One of the earliest European settlers on the coast of Brazil has remarked on the indifference exhibited by the Indian prisoners who were about to be massacred by their enemies.   He conversed with the captives, men young, strong, and handsome.   To his question whether they did not fear the death that was so near and so appalling, they replied with laughter and mockery.   When he spoke of ransoming them from their foes, they jeered at the cowardice of Europeans.[4]   The

[1] H. R. Schoolcraft, *Indian Tribes of the United States*, ii. (Philadelphia, 1853), p. 68.
[2] F. de Azara, *Voyages dans l'Amérique Méridionale*, ii. 181.
[3] A. B. Ellis, *The Ewe-speaking Peoples of the Slave Coast*, p. 127. The testimony of a soldier on such a point is peculiarly valuable.
[4] A. Thevet, *Les Singularitez de la France Antarctique* (Antwerp, 1558), pp. 74 *sq.* ; *id.*, *Cosmographie*

Khonds of India practised an extensive system of human sacrifice, of which we shall hear more in the sequel. The victims, known as Meriahs, were kept for years to be sacrificed, and their manner of death was peculiarly horrible, since they were hacked to pieces or slowly roasted alive. Yet when these destined victims were rescued by the English officers who were engaged in putting down the custom, they generally availed themselves of any opportunity to escape from their deliverers and returned to their fate.[1] In Uganda there were formerly many sacrificial places where human victims used to be slaughtered or burned to death, sometimes in hundreds, from motives of superstition. "Those who have taken part in these executions bear witness how seldom a victim, whether man or woman, raised his voice to protest or appeal against the treatment meted out to him. The victims went to death (so they thought) to save their country and race from some calamity, and they laid down their lives without a murmur or a struggle."[2]

But it is not merely that men of other races and other religions submit to inevitable death with an equanimity which modern Europeans in general cannot match; they actually seek and find it for reasons which seem to us wholly inadequate. The motives which lead them to sacrifice their lives are very various. Among them religious fanaticism has probably been one of the commonest, and in the preceding pages we have met with many instances of voluntary deaths incurred under its powerful impulse.[3] But more secular motives, such as loyalty, revenge, and an excessive sensibility on the point of honour, have also driven multitudes to throw away their lives with a levity which may strike the average modern Englishman as bordering on insanity. It may be well to illustrate this comparative indifference to death by a few miscellaneous examples drawn from different races. Thus, when the king of Benin

Further, men of other races often sacrifice their lives voluntarily for reasons which seem to us wholly inadequate.

universelle (Paris, 1575), p. 945 [979].

[1] My informant was the late Captain W. C. Robinson, formerly of the 2nd Bombay Europeans (Company's Service), afterwards resident at 15 Chesterton Hall Crescent, Cambridge. He learned the facts in the year 1853 from his friend Captain Gore, of the 29th Madras Native Infantry, who rescued some of the victims.

[2] Rev. J. Roscoe, *The Baganda* (London, 1911), p. 338.

[3] See above, pp. 42 *sqq.*, 54 *sqq.*

Thus
people
have freely
allowed
themselves
to be killed
in order to
accompany
their dead
ruler to the
other
world.
died and was about to be lowered into the earth, his
favourites and servants used to compete with each other
for the privilege of being buried alive with his body in order
that they might attend and minister to him in the other
world. After the dispute was settled and the tomb had
closed over the dead and the living, sentinels were set to
watch it day and night. Next day the sepulchre would be
opened and some one would call down to the entombed
men to know what they were doing and whether any of
them had gone to serve the king. The answer was
commonly, " No, not yet." The third day the same question
would be put, and a voice would reply that so-and-so had
gone to join his Majesty. The first to die was deemed the
happiest. In four or five days when no answer came up to
the question, and all was silent in the grave, the heir to the
throne was informed, and he signalised his accession by
kindling a fire on the tomb, roasting flesh at it, and dis-
tributing the meat to the people.[1] The daughter of a
Mbaya chief in South America, having been happily baptized
at the very point of death, was accorded Christian burial in
the church by the Jesuit missionary who had rescued her
like a brand from the burning. But an old heathen woman
of the tribe took it sadly to heart that her chief's daughter
should not be honoured with the usual human sacrifices.
So, drawing an Indian aside, she implored him to be so kind
as to knock her on the head, that she might go and serve
her young mistress in the Land of Souls. The savage
obligingly complied with her request, and the whole horde
begged the missionary that her body might be buried with
that of the chief's daughter. The Jesuit sternly refused.
He informed them that the girl was now with the angels,
and stood in need of no such attendant. As for the old
woman, he observed grimly that she had gone to a very
different place and would move in a very different circle of
society.[2] When Otho committed suicide after the battle of
Bedriacum, some of his soldiers slew themselves at his pyre,
and their example was afterwards followed by many of their

[1] O. Dapper, *Description de l'A-
frique* (Amsterdam, 1686), p. 312 ; H.
Ling Roth, *Great Benin*, p. 43.

[2] R. Southey, *History of Brazil*,
iii. 391 *sq.*

comrades in the armies which had marched with Otho to meet Vitellius ; their motive was not fear of the conqueror, but purely loyalty and devotion to their emperor.[1]

In the East that indifference to human life which seems so strange to the Western mind often takes a peculiar form. A man will sometimes kill himself merely in order to be revenged on his foe, believing that his ghost will haunt and torment the survivor, or expecting that punishment of some sort will overtake the wretch who drove him to this extreme step.[2] Among some peoples etiquette requires that if a man commits suicide for this purpose, his enemy should at once follow his example. To take a single example. There is a caste of robbers in southern India among whom " the law of retaliation prevails in all its rigour. If a quarrel takes place, and somebody tears out his own eye or kills himself, his adversary must do the same either to himself or to one of his relations. The women carry this barbarity still further. For a slight affront put on them, a sharp word said to them, they will go and smash their head against the door of her who offended them, and the latter is obliged immediately to do the same. If a woman poisons herself by drinking the juice of a poisonous herb, the other woman who drove her to this violent death must poison herself likewise ; else her house will be burned, her cattle carried off, and injuries of all kinds done her until satisfaction is given. They extend this cruelty even to their own children. Not long ago, a few steps from the church in which I have the honour to write to you, two of these barbarians having quarrelled, one of them ran to his house, took from it a child of about four years, and crushed its head between two stones in the presence of his enemy. The latter, without exhibiting any emotion, took his nine-years' old daughter, and, plunging a dagger into her breast, said, ' Your child was only four years old, mine was nine years old. Give me a victim to equal her.' ' Certainly,' replied the other, and seeing at his side his eldest son, who was ready to be married, he stabbed him four or five times with his dagger :

In the East, persons sometimes commit suicide in order to avenge themselves on their enemies.

Law of retaliation in a robber caste of southern India.

---

[1] Tacitus, *Histor.* ii. 49 ; Plutarch, *Otho,* 17.

[2] R. Lasch, " Rache als Selbstmord-motiv," *Globus,* lxxiv. (1898) pp. 37-39.

and, not content with shedding the blood of his two sons, he killed his wife too, in order to oblige his enemy to murder his wife in like manner.   Lastly, a little girl and a baby at the breast had also their throats cut, so that in a single day seven persons were sacrificed to the vengeance of two blood-thirsty men, more cruel than the most ferocious brutes.   I have actually in my church a young man who sought refuge among us, wounded by a spear-thrust which his father inflicted on him in order to kill him and thus oblige his foe to slay his own son in like manner.   The barbarian had already stabbed two of his children on other occasions for the same purpose.   Such atrocious examples will seem to you to partake more of fable than of truth ; but believe me that far from exaggerating, I could produce many others not less tragical." [1]

Contempt of death exhibited in antiquity by the Thracians and the Gauls.

The same contempt of death which many races have exhibited in modern times was displayed in antiquity by the hardy natives of Europe before Christianity had painted the world beyond the grave in colours at which even their bold spirits quailed.   Thus, for example, at their banquets the rude Thracians used to suspend a halter over a movable stone and cast lots among themselves.   The man on whom the lot fell mounted the stone with a scimitar in his hand and thrust his head into the noose.   A comrade then rolled the stone from under him, and while he did so the other attempted to sever the rope with his scimitar.   If he succeeded he dropped to the ground and was saved ; if he failed, he was hanged, and his dying struggles were greeted with peals of laughter by his fellows, who regarded the whole thing as a capital joke.[2]   The Greek traveller Posidonius, who visited Gaul early in the first century before our era, records that among the Celts men were to be found who for a sum of money or a number of jars of wine, which they distributed among their kinsmen or friends, would allow themselves to be publicly slaughtered in a theatre.   They

---

[1] Father Martin, Jesuit missionary, in *Lettres édifiantes et curieuses*, Nouvelle Édition, xi. (Paris, 1781), pp. 246-248.   The letter was written at Marava, in the mission of Madura, 8th November 1709.   No doubt the English Government has long since done its best to suppress these practices.

[2] Seleucus, quoted by Athenaeus, iv. 42, p. 155 D E.

lay down on their backs upon a shield and a man came and cut their throats with a sword.[1]

A Greek author, Euphorion of Chalcis, who lived in the age when the eyes of all the world were turned on the great conflict between Rome and Carthage for the mastery of the Mediterranean, tells us that at Rome it was customary to advertise for men who would consent to be beheaded with an axe in consideration of receiving a sum of five *minae*, or about twenty pounds of our money, to be paid after their death to their heirs. Apparently there was no lack of applicants for this hard-earned bounty; for we are informed that several candidates would often compete for the privilege, each of them arguing that he had the best right to be cudgelled to death.[2] Why were these men invited to be beheaded for twenty pounds a piece? and why in response to the invitation did they gratuitously, as it would seem, express their readiness to suffer a much more painful death than simple decapitation? The reasons are not stated by Euphorion in the brief extract quoted from his work by Athenaeus, the Greek writer who has also preserved for us the testimony of Posidonius to the Gallic recklessness of life. But the connexion in which Athenaeus cites both these passages suggests that the intention of the Roman as of the Gallic practice was merely to minister to the brutal pleasure of the spectators; for he inserts his account of the customs in a dissertation on banquets, and he had just before described how hired ruffians fought and butchered each other at Roman dinner-parties for the amusement of the tipsy guests.[3] Or perhaps the men were wanted to be slaughtered at funerals, for we know that at Rome a custom formerly prevailed of sacrificing human beings at the tomb: the victims were commonly captives or slaves,[4] but they may sometimes have

In ancient Rome there were men willing to be beheaded for a sum of five minae.

[1] Posidonius, quoted by Athenaeus, iv. 40, p. 154 B C.

[2] Euphorion of Chalcis, quoted by Athenaeus, iv. 40, p. 154 C; Eustathius on Homer, *Odyssey*, xviii. 46, p. 1837.

[3] Athenaeus, iv. 39, p. 153 E F, quoting Nicolaus Damascenus.

[4] Tertullian, *De spectaculis*, 12. The custom of sacrificing human beings in honour of the dead, which has been practised by many savage and barbarous peoples, was in later times so far mitigated at Rome that the destined victims were allowed to fight each other, which gave some of them a chance of surviving. This mitigation of human sacrifice is said to have been introduced by D. Junius Brutus in the third century B.C. (Livy, *Epit.* xvi.). It resembles the change which I suppose to have taken place at Nemi and other places, where,

been obtained by advertisement from among the class of needy freemen. Such wretches in bidding against each other may have pleaded as a reason for giving them the preference that they really deserved for their crimes to die a slow and painful death under the cudgel of the executioner. This explanation of the custom, which I owe to my friend Mr. W. Wyse, is perhaps the most probable. But it is also possible, though the language of Euphorion does not lend itself so well to this interpretation, that a cudgelling preceded decapitation as part of the bargain. If that was so, it would seem that the men were wanted to die as substitutes for condemned criminals; for in old Rome capital punishment was regularly inflicted in this fashion, the malefactors being tied up to a post and scourged with rods before they were beheaded with an axe.[1] There is nothing improbable in the view that persons could be hired to suffer the extreme penalty of the law instead of the real culprits. We shall see that a voluntary substitution of the same sort is reported on apparently good authority to be still occasionally practised in China. However, it is immaterial to our purpose whether these men perished to save others, to adorn a funeral, or merely to gratify the Roman lust for blood. The one thing that concerns us is that in the great age of Rome there were to be found Romans willing, nay, eager to barter their lives for a paltry sum of money of which they were not even to have the enjoyment. No wonder that men made of that stuff founded a great empire, and spread the terror of the Roman arms from the Grampians to the tropics.[2]

Chinese indifference to death.

The comparative indifference with which the Chinese regard their lives is attested by the readiness with which they commit suicide on grounds which often seem to the European extremely trifling.[3] A still more striking proof

---

if I am right, kings were at first put to death inexorably at the end of a fixed period, but were afterwards permitted to defend themselves in single combat.

[1] Livy, ii. 5. 8, xxvi. 13. 15, xxviii. 29. 11 ; Polybius, i. 7. 12, xi. 30. 2 ; Th. Mommsen, *Römisches Strafrecht* (Leipsic, 1899), pp. 916 *sqq.*

[2] Hiera Sykaminos (*Maharraka*), the furthest point of the Roman dominion in southern Egypt, lies within the

tropics. The empire did not reach this its extreme limit till after the age of Augustus. See Th. Mommsen, *Römische Geschichte*, v. 594 *sq.* Strabo speaks (xvii. 1. 48, p. 817) as if Syene, which was held by a Roman garrison of three cohorts, were within the tropics ; but that is a mistake.

[3] For some evidence see J. H. Gray, *China*, i. 329 *sqq.* ; H. Norman, *The Peoples and Politics of the Far East*

of their apathy in this respect is furnished by the readiness with which in China a man can be induced to suffer death for a sum of money to be paid to his relatives. Thus, for example, "one of the most wealthy of the aboriginal tribes, called Shurii-Kia-Miau, is remarkable for the practice of a singular and revolting religious ceremony. The people possess a large temple, in which is an idol in the form of a dog. They resort to this shrine on a certain day every year to worship. At this annual religious festival it is, I believe, customary for the wealthy members of the tribe to entertain their poorer brethren at a banquet given in honour of one who has agreed, for a sum of money paid to his family, to allow himself to be offered as a sacrifice on the altar of the dog idol. At the end of the banquet the victim, having drunk wine freely, is put to death before the idol. This people believe that, were they to neglect this rite, they would be visited with pestilence, famine, or the sword."[1] Further, it is said that in China a man condemned to death can procure a substitute, who, for a small sum, will voluntarily consent to be executed in his stead. The money goes to the substitute's kinsfolk, and since to increase the family prosperity at the expense of personal suffering is regarded by the Chinese as an act of the highest virtue, there is reported to be, just as there used to be in ancient Rome, quite a competition among the candidates for death. Such a substitution is even recognised by the Chinese authorities, except in the case of certain grave crimes, as for instance parricide. The local mandarin is probably not averse to the arrangement, for he is said to make a pecuniary profit by the transaction,

(London, 1905), pp. 277 *sq.* On this subject the Rev. Dr. W. T. A. Barber, Headmaster of the Leys School, Cambridge, formerly a missionary in China, writes to me as follows (3rd February 1902) :—" Undoubtedly the Eastern, through his belief in Fate, has comparatively little fear of death. I have sometimes seen the Chinese in great fear; but, on the other hand, I have saved at least a hundred lives of people who had swallowed opium out of spite against some one else, the idea being, first, the trouble given by minions of the law to the survivor; second, that the dead would gain a vantage ground by becoming a ghost, and thus able to plague his enemy in the flesh. Probably blind anger has more to do with it than either of these causes. But the particular mode would not ordinarily occur to a Western. I am bound to say that in many cases the patient was ready enough to take my medicines, but mostly it was the friends who were most eager, and exceedingly rarely did I receive thanks from the rescued."

[1] J. H. Gray (Archdeacon of Hongkong), *China* (London, 1878), ii. 306.

engaging a substitute for a less sum than he received from the condemned man, and pocketing the difference.[1]

We must not judge of all men's love of life by our own.

The foregoing evidence may suffice to convince us that we should commit a grievous error were we to judge all men's love of life by our own, and to assume that others cannot hold cheap what we count so dear. We shall never understand the long course of human history if we persist in measuring mankind in all ages and in all countries by the standard, perhaps excellent but certainly narrow, of the modern English middle class with their love of material comfort and "their passionate, absorbing, almost bloodthirsty clinging to life." That class, of which I may say, in the words of Matthew Arnold, that I am myself a feeble unit, doubtless possesses many estimable qualities, but among them can hardly be reckoned the rare and delicate gift of historical imagination, the power of entering into the thoughts and feelings of men of other ages and other countries, of conceiving that they may regulate their life by principles which do not square with ours, and may throw it away for objects which to us might seem ridiculously inadequate.[2]

Hence it is probable that in some races and at some periods of history it would be easy to find

To return, therefore, to the point from which we started, we may safely assume that in some races, and at some periods of history, though certainly not in the well-to-do classes of England to-day, it might be easy to find men who would willingly accept a kingdom with the certainty of being put to death after a reign of a year or less. Where men are ready, as they have been in Gaul, in Rome, and in China, to

[1] The particulars in the text are taken, with Lord Avebury's kind permission, from a letter addressed to him by Mr. M. W. Lampson of the Foreign Office. See Note A at the end of the volume. Speaking of capital punishment in China, Professor E. H. Parker says : "It is popularly stated that substitutes can be bought for Taels 50, and most certainly this statement is more than true, so far as the price of human life is concerned ; but it is quite another question whether the gaolers and judges can always be bribed" (E. H. Parker, Professor of Chinese at the Owens College, Manchester, *China Past and Present*, London, 1903, pp. 378 *sq.*). However, from his personal enquiries Professor Parker is convinced that in such matters the local mandarin can do what he pleases, provided that he observes the form of law and gives no offence to his superiors.

[2] My friend, the late Sir Francis Galton, mentioned in conversation a phrase which described the fear of death as "the Western (or European) malady," but he did not remember where he had met with it. He wrote to me (18th October 1902) that "our fear of death is presumably much greater than that of the barbarians who were our far-back ancestors."

yield up their lives at once for a paltry sum of which they *men willing*
are themselves to reap no benefit, would they not be willing *to accept a kingdom*
to purchase at the same price a year's tenure of a throne? *on con-*
Among people of that sort the difficulty would probably be *dition of being killed*
not so much to find a candidate for the crown as to decide *at the end*
between the conflicting claims of a multitude of competitors. *of a short reign.*
In point of fact we have heard of a Shilluk clamouring
to be made king on condition of being killed at the end of
a brief reign of a single day, and we have read how in
Malabar a crowd scrambled for the bloody head which
entitled the lucky man who caught it to be decapitated after
five years of unlimited enjoyment, and how at Calicut many
men used to rush cheerfully on death, not for a kingship of
a year, or even of an hour, but merely for the honour of
displaying their valour in a fruitless attack on the king.[1]

[1] See above, pp. 23, 49 *sqq.*, 52 *sq.*

CHAPTER V

TEMPORARY KINGS

Annual abdication of kings and their places temporarily taken by nominal sovereigns.

Temporary kings in Cambodia.

IN some places the modified form of the old custom of regicide which appears to have prevailed at Babylon[1] has been further softened down. The king still abdicates annually for a short time and his place is filled by a more or less nominal sovereign ; but at the close of his short reign the latter is no longer killed, though sometimes a mock execution still survives as a memorial of the time when he was actually put to death. To take examples. In the month of Méac (February) the king of Cambodia annually abdicated for three days. During this time he performed no act of authority, he did not touch the seals, he did not even receive the revenues which fell due. In his stead there reigned a temporary king called Sdach Méac, that is, King February. The office of temporary king was hereditary in a family distantly connected with the royal house, the sons succeeding the fathers and the younger brothers the elder brothers, just as in the succession to the real sovereignty. On a favourable day fixed by the astrologers the temporary king was conducted by the mandarins in triumphal procession. He rode one of the royal elephants, seated in the royal palanquin, and escorted by soldiers who, dressed in appropriate costumes, represented the neighbouring peoples of Siam, Annam, Laos, and so on. In place of the golden crown he wore a peaked white cap, and his regalia, instead of being of gold encrusted with diamonds, were of rough wood. After paying homage to the real king, from whom he received the sovereignty for three days, together with all

[1] See above, pp. 113 *sqq.*

148

the revenues accruing during that time (though this last custom has been omitted for some time), he moved in procession round the palace and through the streets of the capital. On the third day, after the usual procession, the temporary king gave orders that the elephants should trample under foot the "mountain of rice," which was a scaffold of bamboo surrounded by sheaves of rice. The people gathered up the rice, each man taking home a little with him to secure a good harvest. Some of it was also taken to the king, who had it cooked and presented to the monks.[1]

In Siam on the sixth day of the moon in the sixth month (the end of April) a temporary king is appointed, who for three days enjoys the royal prerogatives, the real king remaining shut up in his palace. This temporary king sends his numerous satellites in all directions to seize and confiscate whatever they can find in the bazaar and open shops; even the ships and junks which arrive in harbour during the three days are forfeited to him and must be redeemed. He goes to a field in the middle of the city, whither they bring a gilded plough drawn by gaily-decked oxen. After the plough has been anointed and the oxen rubbed with incense, the mock king traces nine furrows with the plough, followed by aged dames of the palace scattering the first seed of the season. As soon as the nine furrows are drawn, the crowd of spectators rushes in and scrambles for the seed which has just been sown, believing that, mixed with the seed-rice, it will ensure a plentiful crop. Then the oxen are unyoked, and rice, maize, sesame, sago, bananas, sugar-cane, melons, and so on, are set before them; whatever they eat first will, it is thought, be dear in the year following, though some people interpret the omen in the opposite sense. During this time the temporary king stands leaning against a tree with his right foot resting on his left knee. From standing thus on one foot he is popularly known as King Hop; but his official title is Phaya Phollathep, "Lord of the Heavenly Hosts."[2] He is a sort of Minister of

Temporary kings in Siam in former days.

---

[1] E. Aymonier, *Notice sur le Cambodge* (Paris, 1875), p. 61; J. Moura, *Le Royaume du Cambodge* (Paris, 1883), i. 327 *sq.* For the connexion of the temporary king's family with the royal house,

see E. Aymonier, *op. cit.* pp. 36 *sq.*

[2] De la Loubère, *Du royaume de Siam* (Amsterdam, 1691), i. 56 *sq.*; Turpin, "History of Siam," in Pinkerton's *Voyages and Travels,* ix. 581 *sq.*; Mgr.

Agriculture ; all disputes about fields, rice, and so forth, are referred to him. There is moreover another ceremony in which he personates the king. It takes place in the second month (which falls in the cold season) and lasts three days. He is conducted in procession to an open place opposite the Temple of the Brahmans, where there are a number of poles dressed like May-poles, upon which the Brahmans swing. All the while that they swing and dance, the Lord of the Heavenly Hosts has to stand on one foot upon a seat which is made of bricks plastered over, covered with a white cloth, and hung with tapestry. He is supported by a wooden frame with a gilt canopy, and two Brahmans stand one on each side of him. The dancing Brahmans carry buffalo horns with which they draw water from a large copper caldron and sprinkle it on the spectators ; this is supposed to bring good luck, causing the people to dwell in peace and quiet, health and prosperity. The time during which the Lord of the Heavenly Hosts has to stand on one foot is about three hours. This is thought " to prove the dispositions of the Devattas and spirits." If he lets his foot down " he is liable to forfeit his property and have his family enslaved by the king ; as it is believed to be a bad omen, portending destruction to the state, and instability to the throne. But if he stand firm he is believed to have gained a victory over evil spirits, and he has moreover the privilege, ostensibly at least, of seizing any ship which may enter the harbour during these three days, and taking its contents, and also of entering any open shop in the town and carrying away what he chooses." [1]

Brugière, in *Annales de l'Association de la Propagation de la Foi*, v. (1831) pp. 188 sq. ; Pallegoix, *Description du royaume Thai ou Siam* (Paris, 1854), i. 250 ; A. Bastian, *Die Völker des östlichen Asien*, iii. 305-309, 526-528. Bowring (*Siam*, i. 158 sq.) copies, as usual, from Pallegoix. For a description of the ceremony as observed at the present day, see E. Young, *The Kingdom of the Yellow Robe* (Westminster, 1898), pp. 210 sq. The representative of the king no longer enjoys his old privilege of seizing any goods that are exposed for sale along the line of the procession. According to Mr.

Young, the ceremony is generally held about the middle of May, and no one is supposed to plough or sow till it is over. According to Loubère the title of the temporary king was *Oc-ya Kaou*, or Lord of the Rice, and the office was regarded as fatal, or at least calamitous ("*funeste*") to him.

[1] Lieut.-Col. James Low, "On the Laws of Muung Thai or Siam," *Journal of the Indian Archipelago*, i. (Singapore, 1847) p. 339 ; A. Bastian, *Die Völker des östlichen Asien*, iii. 98, 314, 526 sq.

Such were the duties and privileges of the Siamese King Hop down to about the middle of the nineteenth century or later.   Under the reign of the late enlightened monarch this quaint personage was to some extent both shorn of the glories and relieved of the burden of his office.   He still watches, as of old, the Brahmans rushing through the air in a swing suspended between two tall masts, each some ninety feet high ; but he is allowed to sit instead of stand, and, although public opinion still expects him to keep his right foot on his left knee during the whole of the ceremony, he would incur no legal penalty were he, to the great chagrin of the people, to put his weary foot to the ground.   Other signs, too, tell of the invasion of the East by the ideas and civilisation of the West.   The thoroughfares that lead to the scene of the performance are blocked with carriages : lamp-posts and telegraph posts, to which eager spectators cling like monkeys, rise above the dense crowd; and, while a tatter-demalion band of the old style, in gaudy garb of vermilion and yellow, bangs and tootles away on drums and trumpets of an antique pattern, the procession of barefooted soldiers in brilliant uniforms steps briskly along to the lively strains of a modern military band playing " Marching through Georgia." [1]

On the first day of the sixth month, which was regarded as the beginning of the year, the king and people of Samaracand used to put on new clothes and cut their hair and beards.   Then they repaired to a forest near the capital where they shot arrows on horseback for seven days.   On the last day the target was a gold coin, and he who hit it had the right to be king for one day.[2]   In Upper Egypt on the first day of the solar year by Coptic reckoning, that is, on the tenth of September, when the Nile has generally reached its highest point, the regular government is suspended for three days and every town chooses its own ruler.   This

---

[1] E. Young, *The Kingdom of the Yellow Robe*, pp. 212-217. The writer tells us that though the Minister for Agriculture still officiates at the Plough-ing Festival, he no longer presides at the Swinging Festival ; a different nobleman is chosen every year to superintend the latter.

[2] Ed. Chavannes, *Documents sur les Tou-Kiue (Turcs) Occidentaux* (St. Petersburg, 1903), p. 133, note. The documents collected in this volume are translated from the Chinese.

temporary lord wears a sort of tall fool's cap and a long
flaxen beard, and is enveloped in a strange mantle. With
a wand of office in his hand and attended by men disguised
as scribes, executioners, and so forth, he proceeds to the
Governor's house. The latter allows himself to be deposed ;
and the mock king, mounting the throne, holds a tribunal,
to the decisions of which even the governor and his officials
must bow. After three days the mock king is condemned
to death ; the envelope or shell in which he was encased is
committed to the flames, and from its ashes the Fellah
creeps forth.[1] The custom perhaps points to an old practice
of burning a real king in grim earnest. In Uganda the
brothers of the king used to be burned, because it was not
lawful to shed the royal blood.[2]

Temporary
kings in
Morocco. The Mohammedan students of Fez, in Morocco, are
allowed to appoint a sultan of their own, who reigns for a
few weeks, and is known as *Sultan t-tulba,* "the Sultan of
the Scribes." This brief authority is put up for auction and
knocked down to the highest bidder. It brings some substantial privileges with it, for the holder is freed from taxes
thenceforward, and he has the right of asking a favour from
the real sultan. That favour is seldom refused ; it usually
consists in the release of a prisoner. Moreover, the agents
of the student-sultan levy fines on the shopkeepers and
householders, against whom they trump up various humorous
charges. The temporary sultan is surrounded with the
pomp of a real court, and parades the streets in state with
music and shouting, while a royal umbrella is held over his
head. With the so-called fines and free-will offerings, to
which the real sultan adds a liberal supply of provisions, the
students have enough to furnish forth a magnificent banquet ;
and altogether they enjoy themselves thoroughly, indulging
in all kinds of games and amusements. For the first seven
days the mock sultan remains in the college ; then he goes
about a mile out of the town and encamps on the bank of
the river, attended by the students and not a few of the

[1] C. B. Klunzinger, *Bilder aus Ober-
ägypten der Wüste und dem Rothen
Meere* (Stuttgart, 1877), pp. 180 *sq.*
[2] *Taboo and the Perils of the Soul,*
p. 243. For evidence of a practice of
burning divine personages, see *Adonis,
Attis, Osiris,* Second Edition, pp. 84
sqq., 91 *sqq.,* 139 *sqq.*

citizens. On the seventh day of his stay outside the town he is visited by the real sultan, who grants him his request and gives him seven more days to reign, so that the reign of "the Sultan of the Scribes" nominally lasts three weeks. But when six days of the last week have passed the mock sultan runs back to the town by night. This temporary sultanship always falls in spring, about the beginning of April. Its origin is said to have been as follows. When Mulai Rasheed II. was fighting for the throne in 1664 or 1665, a certain Jew usurped the royal authority at Taza. But the rebellion was soon suppressed through the loyalty and devotion of the students. To effect their purpose they resorted to an ingenious stratagem. Forty of them caused themselves to be packed in chests which were sent as a present to the usurper. In the dead of night, while the unsuspecting Jew was slumbering peacefully among the packing-cases, the lids were stealthily raised, the brave forty crept forth, slew the usurper, and took possession of the city in the name of the real sultan, who, to mark his gratitude for the help thus rendered him in time of need, conferred on the students the right of annually appointing a sultan of their own.[1] The narrative has all the air of a fiction devised to explain an old custom, of which the real meaning and origin had been forgotten.

A custom of annually appointing a mock king for a single day was observed at Lostwithiel in Cornwall down to the sixteenth century. On "little Easter Sunday" the freeholders of the town and manor assembled together, either in person or by their deputies, and one among them, as it fell to his lot by turn, gaily attired and gallantly mounted, with a crown on his head, a sceptre in his hand, and a sword borne before him, rode through the principal street to the church, dutifully attended by all the rest on horseback. The clergyman in his best robes received him at the churchyard stile and conducted him to hear divine service. On leaving the church he repaired, with the same pomp, to a

Temporary king in Cornwall.

---

[1] Budgett Meakin, *The Moors* (London, 1902), pp. 312 *sq.* ; E. Aubin, *Le Maroc d'aujourd'hui* (Paris, 1904), pp. 283-287. According to the latter of these writers the flight of the mock sultan takes place the day after his meeting with the real sultan. The account in the text embodies some notes which were kindly furnished me by Dr. E. Westermarck.

house provided for his reception. Here a feast awaited him and his suite, and being set at the head of the table he was served on bended knees, with all the rites due to the estate of a prince. The ceremony ended with the dinner, and every man returned home.[1]

Temporary kings at the beginning of a reign. Sometimes the temporary king occupies the throne, not annually, but once for all at the beginning of each reign. Thus in the kingdom of Jambi, in Sumatra, it is the custom that at the beginning of a new reign a man of the people should occupy the throne and exercise the royal prerogatives for a single day. The origin of the custom is explained by a tradition that there were once five royal brothers, the four elder of whom all declined the throne on the ground of various bodily defects, leaving it to their youngest brother. But the eldest occupied the throne for one day, and reserved for his descendants a similar privilege at the beginning of every reign. Thus the office of temporary king is hereditary in a family akin to the royal house.[2] In Bilaspur it seems to be the custom, after the death of a Rajah, for a Brahman to eat rice out of the dead Rajah's hand, and then to occupy the throne for a year. At the end of the year the Brahman receives presents and is dismissed from the territory, being forbidden apparently to return. " The idea seems to be that the spirit of the Rájá enters into the Bráhman who eats the *khír* (rice and milk) out of his hand when he is dead, as the Brahman is apparently carefully watched during the whole year, and not allowed to go away." The same or a similar custom is believed to obtain among the hill states about Kangra.[3] The custom of banishing the Brahman who represents the king may be a substitute for putting him to death. At the installation of a prince of Carinthia a peasant, in whose family the office

---

[1] R. Carew, *Survey of Cornwall* (London, 1811), p. 322. I do not know what the writer means by "little Easter Sunday." The ceremony has often been described by subsequent writers, but they seem all to copy, directly or indirectly, from Carew, who says that the custom had been yearly observed in past times and was only of late days discontinued. His *Survey of Cornwall* was first printed in 1602. I

have to thank Mr. G. M. Trevelyan, formerly Fellow of Trinity College, Cambridge, for directing my attention to this interesting survival of what was doubtless a very ancient custom.

[2] J. W. Boers, "Oud volksgebruik in het Rijk van Jambi," *Tijdschrift voor Neêrlands Indië*, 1840, dl. i. pp. 372 *sqq.*

[3] *Panjab Notes and Queries*, i. p. 86, § 674 (May 1884).

was hereditary, ascended a marble stone which stood surrounded by meadows in a spacious valley; on his right
stood a black mother-cow, on his left a lean ugly mare. A
rustic crowd gathered about him.   Then the future prince,
dressed as a peasant and carrying a shepherd's staff, drew
near, attended by courtiers and magistrates.   On perceiving
him the peasant called out, "Who is this whom I see
coming so proudly along?"   The people answered, "The
prince of the land."   The peasant was then prevailed on to
surrender the marble seat to the prince on condition of
receiving sixty pence, the cow and mare, and exemption
from taxes.   But before yielding his place he gave the
prince a light blow on the cheek.[1]

Some points about these temporary kings deserve to The
be specially noticed before we pass to the next branch of temporary
the evidence.   In the first place, the Cambodian and charge
Siamese examples shew clearly that it is especially the divine or
divine or magical functions of the king which are trans- functions.
ferred to his temporary substitute.   This appears from the
belief that by keeping up his foot the temporary king of
Siam gained a victory over the evil spirits, whereas by
letting it down he imperilled the existence of the state.
Again, the Cambodian ceremony of trampling down the
"mountain of rice," and the Siamese ceremony of opening
the ploughing and sowing, are charms to produce a plentiful
harvest, as appears from the belief that those who carry
home some of the trampled rice, or of the seed sown, will
thereby secure a good crop.   Moreover, when the Siamese
representative of the king is guiding the plough, the people
watch him anxiously, not to see whether he drives a straight
furrow, but to mark the exact point on his leg to which the
skirt of his silken robe reaches ; for on that is supposed to
hang the state of the weather and the crops during the
ensuing season.   If the Lord of the Heavenly Hosts hitches

---

[1] Aeneas Sylvius, *Opera* (Bâle,
1571), pp. 409 *sq.*; J. Boemus, *Mores,
leges, et ritus omnium gentium* (Lyons,
1541), pp. 241 *sq.*; J. Grimm, *Deutsche
Rechtsalterthümer*, p. 253. According
to Grimm, the cow and mare stood
beside the prince, not the peasant.

The Carinthian ceremony is the subject
of an elaborate German dissertation by
Dr. Emil Goldmann (*Die Einführung
der deutschen Herzogsgeschlechter Kärn-
tens in den Slovenischen Stammesver-
band, ein Beitrag zur Rechts- und
Kulturgeschichte*, Breslau, 1903).

up his garment above his knee, the weather will be wet and heavy rains will spoil the harvest. If he lets it trail to his ankle, a drought will be the consequence. But fine weather and heavy crops will follow if the hem of his robe hangs exactly half-way down the calf of his leg.[1] So closely is the course of nature, and with it the weal or woe of the people, dependent on the minutest act or gesture of the king's representative. But the task of making the crops grow, thus deputed to the temporary kings, is one of the magical functions regularly supposed to be discharged by kings in primitive society. The rule that the mock king must stand on one foot upon a raised seat in the rice-field was perhaps originally meant as a charm to make the crop grow high; at least this was the object of a similar ceremony observed by the old Prussians. The tallest girl, standing on one foot upon a seat, with her lap full of cakes, a cup of brandy in her right hand and a piece of elm-bark or linden-bark in her left, prayed to the god Waizganthos that the flax might grow as high as she was standing. Then, after draining the cup, she had it refilled, and poured the brandy on the ground as an offering to Waizganthos, and threw down the cakes for his attendant sprites. If she remained steady on one foot throughout the ceremony, it was an omen that the flax crop would be good; but if she let her foot down, it was feared that the crop might fail.[2] The same significance perhaps attaches to the swinging of the Brahmans, which the Lord of the Heavenly Hosts had formerly to witness standing on one foot. On the principles of homoeopathic or imitative magic it might

[1] E. Young, *The Kingdom of the Yellow Robe*, p. 211.

[2] Lasicius, "De diis Samagitarum caeterorumque Sarmatarum," in *Respublica sive status regni Poloniae, Lituaniae, Prussiae, Livoniae*, etc. (Elzevir, 1627), pp. 306 *sq.*; *id.*, edited by W. Mannhardt in *Magazin herausgegeben von der Lettisch-Literärischen Gesellschaft*, xiv. 91 *sq.*; J. G. Kohl, *Die deutsch-russischen Ostseeprovinzen* (Dresden and Leipsic, 1841), ii. 27. There, are, however, other occasions when superstition requires a person to stand on one foot. At Toku-toku, in Fiji, the grave-digger who turns the first sod has to stand on one leg, leaning on his digging-stick (Rev. Lorimer Fison, in a letter to the author, dated August 26, 1898). Among the Angoni of British Central Africa, when the corpse of a chief is being burned, his heir stands beside the blazing pyre on one leg with his shield in his hand; and three days later he again stands on one leg before the assembled people when they proclaim him chief. See R. Sutherland Rattray, *Some Folk-lore Stories and Songs in Chinyanja* (London, 1907), pp. 100, 101.

be thought that the higher the priests swing the higher will
grow the rice. For the ceremony is described as a harvest
festival,[1] and swinging is practised by the Letts of Russia
with the avowed intention of influencing the growth of the
crops. In the spring and early summer, between Easter
and St. John's Day (the summer solstice), every Lettish
peasant is said to devote his leisure hours to swinging
diligently; for the higher he rises in the air the higher will
his flax grow that season.[2] The gilded plough with which
the Siamese mock king opens the ploughing may be compared with the bronze ploughs which the Etruscans employed
at the ceremony of founding cities;[3] in both cases the use of
bare iron was probably forbidden on superstitious grounds.[4]

In the foregoing cases the temporary king is appointed
annually in accordance with a regular custom. But in other
cases the appointment is made only to meet a special
emergency, such as to relieve the real king from some actual
or threatened evil by diverting it to a substitute, who takes
his place on the throne for a short time. The history of Persia
furnishes instances of such occasional substitutes for the Shah.
Thus Shah Abbas the Great, the most eminent of all the
kings of Persia, who reigned from 1586 to 1628 A.D., being
warned by his astrologers in the year 1591 that a serious
danger impended over him, attempted to avert the omen
by abdicating the throne and appointing a certain unbeliever
named Yusoofee, probably a Christian, to reign in his stead.
The substitute was accordingly crowned, and for three days,
if we may trust the Persian historians, he enjoyed not only
the name and the state but the power of the king. At the
end of his brief reign he was put to death: the decree of
the stars was fulfilled by this sacrifice; and Abbas, who
reascended his throne in a most propitious hour, was
promised by his astrologers a long and glorious reign.[5]

Temporary kings substituted in certain emergencies for Shahs of Persia.

[1] E. Young, *The Kingdom of the
Yellow Robe*, p. 212.
[2] J. G. Kohl, *Die deutsch-russischen
Ostseeprovinzen*, ii. 25. With regard to
swinging as a magical or religious rite,
see Note B at the end of the volume.
For other charms to make the crops
grow tall by leaping, letting the hair hang
loose, and so forth, see *The Magic Art*

and the *Evolution of Kings*, i. 135 *sqq.*
[3] Macrobius, *Saturn.* v. 19. 13.
[4] See *Taboo and the Perils of the
Soul*, pp. 225 *sqq.*
[5] Sir John Malcolm, *History of
Persia* (London, 1815), i. 527 *sq.* I
am indebted to my friend Mr. W.
Crooke for calling my attention to this
passage.

Again, Shah Sufi II., who reigned from 1668 to 1694 A.D., was crowned a second time and changed his name to Sulaiman or Soliman under the following circumstances: "The King, a few days after, was out of danger, but the matter was to restore him to perfect health. Having been always in a languishing condition, and his physicians never able to discover the cause of his distemper, he suspected that their ignorance retarded his recovery, and two or three of them were therefore ill treated. At length the other physicians, fearing it might be their own turn next, bethought themselves, that Persia being at the same time afflicted with a scarcity of provisions and the King's sickness, the fault must be in the astrologers, who had not chosen a favourable hour when the King was set upon the throne, and therefore persuaded him that the ceremony must be perform'd again, and he change his name in a more lucky minute. The King and his council approving of their notion, the physicians and astrologers together expected the first unfortunate day, which, according to their superstition, was to be followed in the evening by a propitious hour. Among the Gavres, or original Persians, Worshippers of Fire, there are some who boast their descent from the Rustans, who formerly reigned over Persia and Parthia. On the morning of the aforesaid unlucky day, they took one of these Gavres of that Blood-royal, and having plac'd him on the throne, with his back against a figure that represented him to the life, all the great men of the court came to attend him, as if he had been their king, performing all that he commanded. This scene lasted till the favourable hour, which was a little before sun-setting, and then an officer of the court came behind and cut off the head of the wooden statue with his cymiter, the Gaure then starting up and running away. That very moment the King came into the hall, and the Sofy's cap being set on his head, and his sword girt to his side, he sat down on the throne, changing his name for that of Soliman, which was perform'd with the usual ceremonies, the drums beating and trumpets sounding as before. It was requisite to act this farce, in order to satisfy the law, which requires that in order to change his name and take possession of the throne again he must expel a prince that had usurped it upon some pretensions ; and therefore they made choice of a Gaure, who pretended to be descended from the ancient kings of Persia, and was besides of a different religion from that of the government." [1]

[1] Captain John Stevens, *The History of Persia* (London, 1715), pp. 356 *sq*. I have to thank Mr. W. Crooke for his kindness in copying out this passage and sending it to me. I have not seen the original. An Irish legend relates how the abbot Eimine Ban and forty-nine of his monks sacrificed themselves by a voluntary death to save Bran úa Faeláin, King of Leinster, and forty-nine Leinster chiefs, from a pestilence which was then desolating Leinster. They were sacrificed in batches of seven a day for a week, the abbot himself perishing after the last batch on the last day of the week. But it is not said that the abbot enjoyed regal dignity during the seven days. See C. Plummer, " Cáin Eimíne Báin, *Ériu, the Journal of the School of Irish Learning*, Dublin. vol. iv. part i. (1908) pp. 39-46. The legend was pointed out to me by Professor Kuno Meyer.

CHAPTER VI

SACRIFICE OF THE KING'S SON

The temporary kings are sometimes related by blood to the real kings.

A POINT to notice about the temporary kings described in the foregoing chapter is that in two places (Cambodia and Jambi) they come of a stock which is believed to be akin to the royal family. If the view here taken of the origin of these temporary kingships is correct, we can easily understand why the king's substitute should sometimes be of the same race as the king. When the king first succeeded in getting the life of another accepted as a sacrifice instead of his own, he would have to shew that the death of that other would serve the purpose quite as well as his own would have done. Now it was as a god or demigod that the king had to die; therefore the substitute who died for him had to be invested, at least for the occasion, with the divine attributes of the king. This, as we have just seen, was certainly the case with the temporary kings of Siam and Cambodia; they were invested with the supernatural functions, which in an earlier stage of society were the special attributes of the king. But no one could so well represent the king in his divine character as his son, who might be supposed to share the divine afflatus of his father. No one, therefore, could so appropriately die for the king and, through him, for the whole people, as the king's son.

Tradition of On, King of Sweden, and the sacrifice of his nine sons.

According to tradition, Aun or On, King of Sweden, sacrificed nine of his sons to Odin at Upsala in order that his own life might be spared. After he had sacrificed his second son he received from the god an answer that he should live so long as he gave him one of his sons every ninth year. When he had sacrificed his seventh son, he still lived, but was so feeble that he could not walk but had to be carried in a chair.   Then he offered up his eighth son, and lived nine years more, lying in his bed.   After that he sacrificed his ninth son, and lived another nine years, but so that he drank out of a horn like a weaned child.   He now wished to sacrifice his only remaining son to Odin, but the Swedes would not allow him.   So he died and was buried in a mound at Upsala.   The poet Thiodolf told the king's history in verse :—

> " *In Upsal's town the cruel king*
> *Slaughtered his sons at Odin's shrine—*
> *Slaughtered his sons with cruel knife,*
> *To get from Odin length of life.*
> *He lived until he had to turn*
> *His toothless mouth to the deer's horn ;*
> *And he who shed his children's blood*
> *Sucked through the ox's horn his food.*
> *At length fell Death has tracked him down,*
> *Slowly but sure, in Upsal's town.*" [1]

In ancient Greece there seems to have been at least one kingly house of great antiquity of which the eldest sons were always liable to be sacrificed in room of their royal sires.   When Xerxes was marching through Thessaly at the head of his mighty host to attack the Spartans at Thermopylae, he came to the town of Alus.   Here he was shewn the sanctuary of Laphystian Zeus, about which his guides told him a strange tale.   It ran somewhat as follows. Once upon a time the king of the country, by name Athamas, married a wife Nephele, and had by her a son called Phrixus and a daughter named Helle.   Afterwards he took to himself a second wife called Ino, by whom he had two sons, Learchus and Melicertes.   But his second wife was jealous of her step-children, Phrixus and Helle, and plotted their death.   She went about very cunningly to compass her bad end.   First of all she persuaded the women of the country to roast the seed corn secretly before it was committed to the ground.   So next year no crops came

Tradition of King Athamas and his children.

---

[1] " Ynglinga Saga," 29, in *The Heimskringla or Chronicle of the Kings of Norway, translated from the Icelandic of Snorro Sturleson*, by S. Laing (London, 1844), i. 239 *sq.* ; H. M. Chadwick, *The Cult of Othin* (London, 1899), pp. 4, 27.   I have already cited the tradition as evidence of a nine years' tenure of the kingship in Sweden.   See above, p. 57, with note [2].

up and the people died of famine. Then the king sent messengers to the oracle at Delphi to enquire the cause of the dearth. But the wicked step-mother bribed the messenger to give out as the answer of the god that the dearth would never cease till the children of Athamas by his first wife had been sacrificed to Zeus. When Athamas heard that, he sent for the children, who were with the sheep. But a ram with a fleece of gold opened his lips, and speaking with the voice of a man warned the children of their danger. So they mounted the ram and fled with him over land and sea. As they flew over the sea, the girl slipped from the animal's back, and falling into water was drowned. But her brother Phrixus was brought safe to the land of Colchis, where reigned a child of the Sun. Phrixus married the king's daughter, and she bore him a son Cytisorus. And there he sacrificed the ram with the golden fleece to Zeus the God of Flight; but some will have it that he sacrificed the animal to Laphystian Zeus. The golden fleece itself he gave to his wife's father, who nailed it to an oak tree, guarded by a sleepless dragon in a sacred grove of Ares. Meanwhile at home an oracle had commanded that King Athamas himself should be sacrificed as an expiatory offering for the whole country. So the people decked him with garlands like a victim and led him to the altar, where they were just about to sacrifice him when he was rescued either by his grandson Cytisorus, who arrived in the nick of time from Colchis, or by Hercules, who brought tidings that the king's son Phrixus was yet alive. Thus Athamas was saved, but afterwards he went mad, and mistaking his son Learchus for a wild beast shot him dead. Next he attempted the life of his remaining son Melicertes, but the child was rescued by his mother Ino, who ran and threw herself and him from a high rock into the sea. Mother and son were changed into marine divinities, and the son received special homage in the isle of Tenedos, where babes were sacrificed to him. Thus bereft of wife and children the unhappy Athamas quitted his country, and on enquiring of the oracle where he should dwell was told to take up his abode wherever he should be entertained by wild beasts. He fell in with a pack of wolves devouring sheep, and when they saw him they

fled and left him the bleeding remnants of their prey.   In
this way the oracle was fulfilled.   But because King Athamas   Male de-
had not been sacrificed as a sin-offering for the whole country, scendants
it was divinely decreed that the eldest male scion of his Athamas
family in each generation should be sacrificed without fail, liable to be
if ever he set foot in the town-hall, where the offerings were sacrificed.
made to Laphystian Zeus by one of the house of Athamas.
Many of the family, Xerxes was informed, had fled to foreign
lands to escape this doom ; but some of them had returned
long afterwards, and being caught by the sentinels in the
act of entering the town-hall were wreathed as victims, led
forth in procession, and sacrificed.[1]   These instances appear
to have been notorious, if not frequent ; for the writer of a
dialogue attributed to Plato, after speaking of the immolation
of human victims by the Carthaginians, adds that such
practices were not unknown among the Greeks, and he refers
with horror to the sacrifices offered on Mount Lycaeus and
by the descendants of Athamas.[2]

    The suspicion that this barbarous custom by no means Family of
fell into disuse even in later days is strengthened by a case royal
of human sacrifice which occurred in Plutarch's time at descent
Orchomenus, a very ancient city of Boeotia, distant only a sacrificed
few miles across the plain from the historian's birthplace. at Orcho-
Here dwelt a family of which the men went by the name of menus.
Psoloeis or " Sooty," and the women by the name of Oleae
or " Destructive."   Every year at the festival of the Agrionia
the priest of Dionysus pursued these women with a drawn
sword, and if he overtook one of them he had the right
to slay her.   In Plutarch's lifetime the right was actually
exercised by a priest Zoilus.   Now the family thus liable
to furnish at least one human victim every year was of

---

[1] Herodotus, vii. 197 ; Apollodorus,
i. 9. 1 *sq.*; Schol. on Aristophanes, *Clouds*,
257 ; J. Tzetzes, *Schol. on Lycophron*,
21, 229 ; Schol. on Apollonius Rhodius,
Argonautica, ii. 653 ; Eustathius, on
Homer, *Iliad*, vii. 86, p. 667 ; *id.*, on
Odyssey, v. 339, p. 1543 ; Pausanias,
i. 44. 7, ix. 34. 7 ; Zenobius, iv. 38 ;
Plutarch, *De superstitione*, 5 ; Hyginus,
Fab. 1-5 ; *id.*, *Astronomica*, ii. 20 ;
Servius, on Virgil, *Aen.* v. 241.   The
story is told or alluded to by these

writers with some variations of detail.
In piecing their accounts together I
have chosen the features which seemed
to be the most archaic.   According to
Pherecydes, one of the oldest writers
on Greek legendary history, Phrixus
offered himself as a voluntary victim
when the crops were perishing (Schol.
on Pindar, *Pyth.* iv. 288).   On the
whole subject see K. O. Müller, *Orchomenus und die Minyer*,[2] pp. 156, 171.

[2] Plato, *Minos*, p. 315 C.

royal descent, for they traced their lineage to Minyas, the famous old king of Orchomenus, the monarch of fabulous wealth, whose stately treasury, as it is called, still stands in ruins at the point where the long rocky hill of Orchomenus melts into the vast level expanse of the Copaic plain. Tradition ran that the king's three daughters long despised the other women of the country for yielding to the Bacchic frenzy, and sat at home in the king's house scornfully plying the distaff and the loom, while the rest, wreathed with flowers, their dishevelled locks streaming to the wind, roamed in ecstasy the barren mountains that rise above Orchomenus, making the solitude of the hills to echo to the wild music of cymbals and tambourines. But in time the divine fury infected even the royal damsels in their quiet chamber ; they were seized with a fierce longing to partake of human flesh, and cast lots among themselves which should give up her child to furnish a cannibal feast. The lot fell on Leucippe, and she surrendered her son Hippasus, who was torn limb from limb by the three. From these misguided women sprang the Oleae and the Psoloeis, of whom the men were said to be so called because they wore sad-coloured raiment in token of their mourning and grief.[1]

Thessalian and Boeotian kings seem to have sacrificed their sons to Laphystian Zeus instead of themselves.

Now this practice of taking human victims from a family of royal descent at Orchomenus is all the more significant because Athamas himself is said to have reigned in the land of Orchomenus even before the time of Minyas, and because over against the city there rises Mount Laphystius, on which, as at Alus in Thessaly, there was a sanctuary of Laphystian Zeus, where, according to tradition, Athamas purposed to sacrifice his two children Phrixus and Helle.[2] On the whole, comparing the traditions about Athamas with the custom that obtained with regard to his descendants in historical times, we may fairly infer that in Thessaly and probably in Boeotia there reigned of old a dynasty of which the kings were liable

---

[1] Plutarch, *Quaest. Graec.* 38 ; Antoninus Liberalis, *Transform.* 10 ; Ovid, *Metam.* iv. 1 *sqq.*

[2] Pausanias, ix. 34. 5 *sqq.* ; Apollonius Rhodius, *Argonautica*, iii. 265 *sq.* ; Hellanicus, cited by the Scholiast on Apollonius, *l.c.* Apollodorus speaks of Athamas as reigning over Boeotia (*Bibliotheca*, i. 9. 1) ; Tzetzes calls him king of Thebes (*Schol. on Lycophron*, 21).

to be sacrificed for the good of the country to the god called Laphystian Zeus, but that they contrived to shift the fatal responsibility to their offspring, of whom the eldest son was regularly destined to the altar. As time went on, the cruel custom was so far mitigated that a ram was accepted as a vicarious sacrifice in room of the royal victim, provided always that the prince abstained from setting foot in the town-hall where the sacrifices were offered to Laphystian Zeus by one of his kinsmen.[1] But if he were rash enough to enter the place of doom, to thrust himself wilfully, as it were, on the notice of the god who had good-naturedly winked at the substitution of a ram, the ancient obligation which had been suffered to lie in abeyance recovered all its force, and there was no help for it but he must die. The tradition which associated the sacrifice of the king or his children with a great dearth points clearly to the belief, so common among primitive folk, that the king is responsible for the weather and the crops, and that he may justly pay with his life for the inclemency of the one or the failure of the other. Athamas and his line, in short, appear to have united divine or magical with royal functions; and this view is strongly supported by the claims to divinity which Salmoneus, the brother of Athamas, is said to have set up. We have seen that this presumptuous mortal professed to be no other than Zeus himself, and to wield the thunder and lightning, of which he made a trumpery imitation by the help of tinkling kettles and blazing torches.[2] If we may judge from analogy, his mock thunder and lightning were no mere scenic exhibition designed to deceive and impress the beholders; they were

[1] The old Scholiast on Apollonius Rhodius (*Argon.* ii. 653) tells us that down to his time it was customary for one of the descendants of Athamas to enter the town-hall and sacrifice to Laphystian Zeus. K. O. Müller sees in this custom a mitigation of the ancient rule—instead of being themselves sacrificed, the scions of royalty were now permitted to offer sacrifice (*Orchomenus und die Minyer*,[2] p. 158). But this need not have been so. The obligation to serve as victims in certain circumstances lay only on the eldest male of each generation in the direct line; the sacrificers may have been younger brothers or more remote relations of the destined victims. It may be observed that in a dynasty of which the eldest males were regularly sacrificed, the kings, if they were not themselves the victims, must always have been younger sons.

[2] See *The Magic Art and the Evolution of Kings*, vol. i. p. 310.

enchantments practised by the royal magician for the purpose of bringing about the celestial phenomena which they feebly mimicked.[1]

Sacrifice of kings' sons among the Semites. Among the Semites of Western Asia the king, in a time of national danger, sometimes gave his own son to die as a sacrifice for the people. Thus Philo of Byblus, in his work on the Jews, says : " It was an ancient custom in a crisis of great danger that the ruler of a city or nation should give his beloved son to die for the whole people, as a ransom offered to the avenging demons ; and the children thus offered were slain with mystic rites. So Cronus, whom the Phoenicians call Israel, being king of the land and having an only-begotten son called Jeoud (for in the Phoenician tongue Jeoud signifies ' only-begotten '), dressed him in royal robes and sacrificed him upon an altar in a time of war, when the country was in great danger from the enemy." [2] When the king of Moab was besieged by the Israelites and hard beset, he took his eldest son, who should have reigned in his stead, and offered him for a burnt offering on the wall.[3]

But amongst the Semites the practice of sacrificing their children was not confined to kings.[4] In times of great

---

[1] I have followed K. O. Müller (*Orchomenus und die Minyer,*[2] pp. 160, 166 *sq.*) in regarding the ram which saved Phrixus as a mythical expression for the substitution of a ram for a human victim. He points out that a ram was the proper victim to sacrifice to Trophonius (Pausanias, ix. 39. 6), whose very ancient worship was practised at Lebadea not far from Orchomenus. The principle of vicarious sacrifices was familiar enough to the Greeks, as K. O. Müller does not fail to indicate. At Potniae, near Thebes, goats were substituted as victims instead of boys in the sacrifices offered to Dionysus (Pausanias, ix. 8. 2). Once when an oracle commanded that a girl should be sacrificed to Munychian Artemis in order to stay a plague or famine, a goat dressed up as a girl was sacrificed instead (Eustathius on Homer, *Iliad,* ii. 732, p. 331 ; Apostolius, vii. 10 ; *Paroemiogr. Graeci,* ed. Leutsch et Schneidewin, ii. 402; Suidas, *s.v.* Ἔμβαρος). At Salamis in Cyprus a

man was annually sacrificed to Aphrodite and afterwards to Diomede, but in later times an ox was substituted (Porphyry, *De abstinentia,* ii. 54). At Laodicea in Syria a deer took the place of a maiden as the victim yearly offered to Athena (Porphyry, *op. cit.* ii. 56). Since human sacrifices have been forbidden by the Dutch Government in Borneo, the Barito and other Dyak tribes of that island have kept cattle for the sole purpose of sacrificing them instead of human beings at the close of mourning and at other religious ceremonies. See A. W. Nieuwenhuis, *Quer durch Borneo,* ii. (Leyden, 1907), p. 127.

[2] Philo of Byblus, quoted by Eusebius, *Praeparatio Evangelii,* i. 10. 29 *sq.*

[3] 2 Kings iii. 27.

[4] On this subject see Dr. G. F. Moore, *s.v.* " Molech, Moloch," *Encyclopaedia Biblica,* iii. 3183 *sqq.*; C. P. Tiele, *Geschichte der Religion im Altertum,* i. (Gotha, 1896) pp. 240-244.

calamity, such as pestilence, drought, or defeat in war, the Sacrifice of
Phoenicians used to sacrifice one of their dearest to Baal. children to
Baal
" Phoenician history," says an ancient writer, " is full of such among the
sacrifices." [1]   The writer of a dialogue ascribed to Plato Semites.
observes that the Carthaginians immolated human beings as
if it were right and lawful to do so, and some of them, he
adds, even sacrificed their own sons to Baal.[2]   When Gelo,
tyrant of Syracuse, defeated the Carthaginians in the great
battle of Himera he required as a condition of peace that
they should sacrifice their children to Baal no longer.[3]   But
the barbarous custom was too inveterate and too agreeable
to Semitic modes of thought to be so easily eradicated, and
the humane stipulation of the Greek despot probably remained
a dead letter.   At all events the history of this remarkable
people, who combined in so high a degree the spirit of com-
mercial enterprise with a blind attachment to a stern and
gloomy religion, is stained in later times with instances of
the same cruel superstition.   When the Carthaginians were
defeated and besieged by Agathocles, they ascribed their
disasters to the wrath of Baal ; for whereas in former times
they had been wont to sacrifice to him their own offspring,
they had latterly fallen into the habit of buying children and
rearing them to be victims.   So, to appease the angry god,
two hundred children of the noblest families were picked out
for sacrifice, and the tale of victims was swelled by not less
than three hundred more who volunteered to die for the
fatherland.   They were sacrificed by being placed, one by
one, on the sloping hands of the brazen image, from which
they rolled into a pit of fire.[4]   Childless people among
the Carthaginians bought children from poor parents and
slaughtered them, says Plutarch, as if they were lambs or
chickens ; and the mother had to stand by and see it done
without a tear or a groan, for if she wept or moaned she
lost all the credit and the child was sacrificed none the less.
But all the place in front of the image was filled with a
tumultuous music of fifes and drums to drown the shrieks

[1] Porphyry, *De abstinentia*, ii. 56.

[2] Plato, *Minos*, p. 315 C.

[3] Plutarch, *Regum et imperatorum apophthegmata*, *Gelon I.*

[4] Diodorus Siculus, xx. 14. Compare

Clitarchus, cited by Suidas, *s.v.* σαρδάνιος γέλως, and by the Scholiast on Plato, *Republic*, p. 337 A ; J. Selden, *De dis Syris* (Leipsic, 1668), pp. 169 *sq.*

of the victims.[1]   Infants were publicly sacrificed by the Carthaginians down to the proconsulate of Tiberius, who crucified the priests on the trees beside their temples. Yet the practice still went on secretly in the lifetime of Tertullian.[2]

Canaanite and Hebrew custom of burning children in honour of Baal or Moloch.   Among the Canaanites or aboriginal inhabitants of Palestine, whom the invading Israelites conquered but did not exterminate, the grisly custom of burning their children in honour of Baal or Moloch seems to have been regularly practised.[3]   To the best representatives of the Hebrew people, the authors of their noble literature, such rites were abhorrent, and they warned their fellow-countrymen against participating in them.   " When thou art come into the land which the Lord thy God giveth thee, thou shalt not learn to do after the abominations of those nations.   There shall not be found with thee any one that maketh his son or his daughter to pass through the fire, one that useth divination, one that practiseth augury, or an enchanter, or a sorcerer, or a charmer, or a consulter with a familiar spirit, or a wizard, or a necromancer.   For whosoever doeth these things is an abomination unto the Lord : and because of these abominations the Lord thy God doth drive them out from before thee."[4]   Again we read : " And thou shalt not give any of thy seed to pass through the fire to Molech."[5]   Whatever effect these warnings may have had in the earlier days of Israelitish history, there is abundant evidence that in later times the Hebrews lapsed, or rather perhaps relapsed, into that congenial mire of superstition from which the higher spirits of the nation struggled—too often in vain—to rescue them.   The Psalmist laments that his erring countrymen " mingled themselves with the nations, and learned their works : and they served their idols ; which became a snare

---

[1] Plutarch, *De superstitione*, 13. Egyptian mothers were glad and proud when their children were devoured by the holy crocodiles. See Aelian, *De natura animalium*, x. 21 ; Maximus Tyrius, *Dissert.* viii. 5 ; Josephus, *Contra Apion.* ii. 7.

[2] Tertullian, *Apologeticus*, 6. Compare Justin, xviii. 6. 12 ; Ennius, cited by Festus, *s.v.* " Puelli," pp. 248, 249, ed. C. O. Müller ; Augustine, *De civitate Dei*, vii. 19 and 26.

[3] " Every abomination to the Lord, which he hateth, have they done unto their gods ; for even their sons and their daughters do they burn in the fire to their gods," Deuteronomy xii. 31. Here and in what follows I quote the Revised English Version.

[4] Deuteronomy xviii. 9-12.

[5] Leviticus xviii. 21.

unto them : yea, they sacrificed their sons and their daughters unto demons, and shed innocent blood, even the blood of their sons and of their daughters, whom they sacrificed unto the idols of Canaan ; and the land was polluted with blood."[1] When the Hebrew annalist has recorded how Shalmaneser, king of Assyria, besieged Samaria for three years and took it and carried Israel away into captivity, he explains that this was a divine punishment inflicted on his people for having fallen in with the evil ways of the Canaanites. They had built high places in all their cities, and set up pillars and sacred poles (*asherim*) upon every high hill and under every green tree ; and there they burnt incense after the manner of the heathen. " And they forsook all the commandments of the Lord their God, and made them molten images, even two calves, and made an Asherah, and worshipped all the host of heaven, and served Baal. And they caused their sons and their daughters to pass through the fire, and used divination and enchantments."[2] At Jerusalem in these days there was a regularly appointed place where parents burned their children, both boys and girls, in honour of Baal or Moloch. It was in the valley of Hinnom, just outside the walls of the city, and bore the name, infamous ever since, of Tophet. The practice is referred to again and again with sorrowful indignation by the prophets.[3] The kings of Judah set an example to their people by burning their own children at the usual place. Thus of Ahaz, who reigned sixteen years at Jerusalem, we are told that " he burnt incense in the valley of Hinnom, and burnt his children

Sacrifices of children in Tophet.

---

[1] Psalms cvi. 35-38.

[2] 2 Kings xvii. 16, 17.

[3] "And they have built the high places of Topheth, which is in the valley of the son of Hinnom, to burn their sons and their daughters in the fire," Jeremiah vii. 31 ; "And have built the high places of Baal, to burn their sons in the fire for burnt offerings unto Baal," *id.* xix. 5 ; "And they built the high places of Baal, which are in the valley of the son of Hinnom, to cause their sons and their daughters to pass through the fire unto Molech," *id.* xxxii. 35 ; "Moreover thou hast taken thy sons and thy daughters, whom thou hast borne unto me, and these hast thou sacrificed unto them to be devoured. Were thy whoredoms a small matter, that thou hast slain my children, and delivered them up, in causing them to pass through the fire unto them ? " Ezekiel xvi. 20 *sq.* ; compare xx. 26, 31. A comparison of these passages shews that the expression "to cause to pass through the fire," so often employed in this connexion in Scripture, meant to burn the children in the fire. Some have attempted to interpret the words in a milder sense. See J. Spencer, *De legibus Hebraeorum* (The Hague, 1686), i. 288 *sqq.*

in the fire."[1]   Again, King Manasseh, whose long reign covered fifty-five years, "made his children to pass through the fire in the valley of Hinnom."[2]   Afterwards in the reign of the good king Josiah the idolatrous excesses of the people were repressed, at least for a time, and among other measures of reform Tophet was defiled by the King's orders, "that no man might make his son or his daughter to pass through the fire to Molech."[3]   Whether the place was ever used again for the same dark purpose as before does not appear. Long afterwards, under the sway of a milder faith, there was little in the valley to recall the tragic scenes which it had so often witnessed. Jerome describes it as a pleasant and shady spot, watered by the rills of Siloam and laid out in delightful gardens.[4]

Did the Hebrews borrow the custom from the Canaanites?   It would be interesting, though it might be fruitless, to enquire how far the Hebrew prophets and psalmists were right in their opinion that the Israelites learned these and other gloomy superstitions only through contact with the old inhabitants of the land, that the primitive purity of faith and morals which they brought with them from the free air of the desert was tainted and polluted by the grossness and corruption of the heathen in the fat land of Canaan. When we remember, however, that the Israelites were of the same Semitic stock as the population they conquered and professed to despise,[5] and that the practice of human sacrifice is attested for many branches of the Semitic race, we shall, perhaps, incline to surmise that the chosen people may have brought with them into Palestine the seeds which afterwards sprang up and bore such ghastly fruit in Custom of the valley of Hinnom.   It is at least significant of the the Sephar- prevalence of such customs among the Semites that no vites. sooner were the native child-burning Israelites carried off by King Shalmaneser to Assyria than their place was

---

[1] 2 Chronicles xxviii. 3.   In the corresponding passage of 2 Kings (xvi. 3) it is said that Ahaz "made his son to pass through the fire."

[2] 2 Chronicles xxxiii. 6; compare 2 Kings xxi. 6.

[3] 2 Kings xxiii. 10.

[4] Jerome on Jeremiah vii. 31, quoted in Winer's *Biblisches Real-*

wörterbuch,[2] *s.v.* "Thopeth."

[5] The Tel El-Amarna tablets prove that "the prae-Israelitish inhabitants of Canaan were closely akin to the Hebrews, and that they spoke substantially the same language" (S. R. Driver, in *Authority and Archaeology, Sacred and Profane*, edited by D. G. Hogarth (London, 1899), p. 76).

taken by colonists who practised precisely the same rites
in honour of deities who probably differed in little but
name from those revered by the idolatrous Hebrews.
" The Sepharvites," we are told, " burnt their children in
the fire to Adrammelech and Anammelech, the gods of
Sepharvaim." [1] The pious Jewish historian, who saw in
Israel's exile God's punishment for sin, has suggested no
explanation of that mystery in the divine economy which
suffered the Sepharvites to continue on the same spot the
very same abominations for which the erring Hebrews had
just been so signally chastised.

We have still to ask which of their children the Semites
picked out for sacrifice ; for that a choice was made and
some principle of selection followed, may be taken for granted.
A people who burned all their children indiscriminately would
soon extinguish themselves, and such an excess of piety is
probably rare, if not unknown. In point of fact it seems, at
least among the Hebrews, to have been only the firstborn
child that was doomed to the flames. The prophet Micah
asks, in a familiar passage, " Wherewith shall I come before
the Lord, and bow myself before the high God? shall I come
before him with burnt offerings, with calves of a year old?
Will the Lord be pleased with thousands of rams, or with
ten thousands of rivers of oil? shall I give my firstborn for
my transgression, the fruit of my body for the sin of my
soul?" These were the questions which pious and doubting
hearts were putting to themselves in the days of the prophet.
The prophet's own answer is not doubtful. " He hath shewed
thee, O man, what is good ; and what doth the Lord require
of thee, but to do justly and to love mercy, and to walk
humbly with thy God?" [2] It is a noble answer and one
which only elect spirits in that or, perhaps, in any age have
given. In Israel the vulgar answer was given on bloody
altars and in the smoke and flames of Tophet, and the form
in which the prophet's question is cast—" Shall I give my
firstborn for my transgression?"—shews plainly on which
of the children the duty of atoning for the sins of their
father was supposed to fall. A passage in Ezekiel points

Only the firstborn children were burned.

---

[1] 2 Kings xvii. 31. The identification of Sepharvaim is uncertain.

See *Encyclopaedia Biblica*, iv. 4371 *sq.*
[2] Micah vi. 6-8.

no less clearly to the same conclusion. The prophet represents God as saying, " I gave them statutes that were not good, and judgments wherein they should not live ; and I polluted them in their own gifts, in that they caused to pass through the fire all that openeth the womb, that I might make them desolate." That the writer was here thinking specially of the sacrifice of children is proved by his own words a little later on.   " When ye offer your gifts, when ye make your sons to pass through the fire, do ye pollute yourselves with all your idols, unto this day ? " [1]   Further, that by the words " to pass through the fire all that openeth the womb " he referred only to the firstborn can easily be shewn by the language of Scripture in reference to that law of the consecration of firstlings which Ezekiel undoubtedly had in his mind when he wrote this passage.   Thus we find that law enunciated in the following terms : " And the Lord spake unto Moses, saying, Sanctify unto me all the firstborn, whatsoever openeth the womb among the children of Israel, both of man and of beast : it is mine." [2]   Again, it is written : " Thou shalt set apart unto the Lord all that openeth the womb, and every firstling which thou hast that cometh of a beast ; the males shall be the Lord's." [3]   Once more : " All that openeth the womb is mine ; and all thy cattle that is male, the firstlings of ox and sheep." [4]   This ancient Hebrew custom of the consecration to God of all male firstlings, whether of man or beast, was merely the application to the animal kingdom of the law that all first fruits whatsoever belong to the deity and must be made over to him or his representatives.   That general law is thus stated by the Hebrew legislator : " Thou shalt not delay to offer of the abundance of thy fruits, and of thy liquors.   The firstborn of thy sons shalt thou give unto me.   Likewise shalt thou do with thine oxen, and with thy sheep : seven days it shall be with its dam ; and on the eighth day thou shalt give it me." [5]

Thus the god of the Hebrews plainly regarded the first-

---

[1] Ezekiel xx. 25, 26, 31.
[2] Exodus xiii. 1 *sq.*
[3] Exodus xiii. 12
[4] Exodus xxxiv. 19. In the Authorised Version the passage runs thus : " All that openeth the matrix is mine ; and

every firstling among thy cattle, whether ox or sheep, that is male."
[5] Exodus xxii. 29 *sq.*   The Authorised Version has " the first of thy ripe fruits " instead of " the abundance of thy fruits."

born of men and the firstlings of animals as his own, and Hebrew
required that they should be made over to him.   But how? sacrifice of firstlings :
Here a distinction was drawn between sheep, oxen, and redemption
goats on the one hand and men and asses on the other ; the of the first-lings of
firstlings of the former were always sacrificed, the firstlings men and
of the latter were generally redeemed.   "The firstling of an asses.
ox, or the firstling of a sheep, or the firstling of a goat, thou
shalt not redeem ; they are holy : thou shalt sprinkle their
blood upon the altar, and shalt burn their fat for an offering
made by fire for a sweet savour unto the Lord."   The flesh
went to the Levites,[1] who consumed it, no doubt, instead of
the deity whom they represented.   On the other hand, the
ass was not sacrificed by the Israelites, probably because
they did not eat the animal themselves, and hence concluded
that God did not do so either.   In the matter of diet the
taste of gods generally presents a striking resemblance to
that of their worshippers.   Still the firstling ass, like all
other firstlings, was sacred to the deity, and since it was not
sacrificed to him, he had to receive an equivalent for it.   In
other words, the ass had to be redeemed, and the price of
the redemption was a lamb which was burnt as a vicarious
sacrifice instead of the ass, on the hypothesis, apparently,
that roast lamb is likely to be more palatable to the Supreme
Being than roast donkey.   If the ass was not redeemed, it
had to be killed by having its neck broken.[2]   The firstlings
of other unclean animals and of men were redeemed for five
shekels a head, which were paid to the Levites.[3]

We can now readily understand why so many of the Sacrifice of
Hebrews, at least in the later days of their history, sacrificed firstborn children
their firstborn children, and why tender-hearted parents, perhaps

---

[1] Numbers xviii. 17 *sq.*   Elsewhere, however, we read : "All the firstling males that are born of thy herd and of thy flock thou shalt sanctify unto the Lord thy God : thou shalt do no work with the firstling of thine ox, nor shear the firstling of thy flock. Thou shalt eat it before the Lord thy God year by year in the place which the Lord shall choose, thou and thy household," Deuteronomy xv. 19 *sq.*   Compare Deuteronomy xii. 6 *sq.*, 17 *sq.*   To reconcile this ordinance with the other we must suppose that the flesh was divided between the Levite and the owner of the animal.   But perhaps the rule in Deuteronomy may represent the old custom which obtained before the rise of the priestly caste.   Prof. S. R. Driver inclines to the latter view (*Commentary on Deuteronomy*, p. 187).

[2] Exodus xiii. 13, xxxiv. 20.

[3] Numbers xviii. 15 *sq.*   Compare Numbers iii. 46-51 ; Exodus xiii. 13, xxxiv. 20.

regarded as an act of heroic virtue.

whose affection for their offspring exceeded their devotion to the deity, may often have been visited with compunction, and even tormented with feelings of bitter self-reproach and shame at their carnal weakness in suffering the beloved son to live, when they saw others, with an heroic piety which they could not emulate, calmly resigning their dear ones to the fire, through which, as they firmly believed, they passed to God, to reap, perhaps, in endless bliss in heaven the reward of their sharp but transient sufferings on earth. From infancy they had been bred up in the belief that the firstborn was sacred to God, and though they knew that he had waived his right to them in consideration of the receipt of five shekels a head, they could hardly view this as anything but an act of gracious condescension, of generous liberality on the part of the divinity who had stooped to accept so trifling a sum instead of the life which really belonged to him. " Surely," they might argue, " God would be better pleased if we were to give him not the money but the life, not the poor paltry shekels, but what we value most, our first and best-loved child. If we hold that life so dear, will not he also? It is his. Why should we not give him his own?" It was in answer to anxious questions such as these, and to quite truly conscientious scruples of this sort that the prophet Micah declared that what God required of his true worshippers was not sacrifice but justice and mercy and humility. It is the answer of morality to religion—of the growing consciousness that man's duty is not to propitiate with vain oblations those mysterious powers of the universe of which he can know little or nothing, but to be just and merciful in his dealings with his fellows and to humbly trust, though he cannot know, that by acting thus he will best please the higher powers, whatever they may be.

Tradition of the origin of the Passover.

But while morality ranges itself on the side of the prophet, it may be questioned whether history and precedent were not on the side of his adversaries. If the firstborn of men and cattle were alike sacred to God, and the firstborn of cattle were regularly sacrificed, while the firstborn of men were ransomed by a money payment, has not this last provision the appearance of being a later mitigation of an older and harsher custom which

doomed firstborn children, like firstling lambs and calves
and goats, to the altar or the fire? The suspicion is
greatly strengthened by the remarkable tradition told to
account for the sanctity of the firstborn.   When Israel
was in bondage in Egypt, so runs the tradition, God resolved
to deliver them from captivity, and to lead them to the
Promised Land.   But the Egyptians were loth to part with
their bondmen and thwarted the divine purpose by refusing
to let the Israelites go.   Accordingly God afflicted these
cruel taskmasters with one plague after another, but all in
vain, until at last he made up his mind to resort to a strong
measure, which would surely have the desired effect.   At
dead of night he would pass through the land killing all the
firstborn of the Egyptians, both man and beast ; not one of
them would be left alive in the morning.   But the Israelites
were warned of what was about to happen and told to keep
indoors that night, and to put a mark on their houses, so
that when he passed down the street on his errand of
slaughter, God might know them at sight from the houses of
the Egyptians and not turn in and massacre the wrong
children and animals.   The mark was to be the blood of a
lamb smeared on the lintel and side posts of the door.   In
every house the lamb, whose red blood was to be the badge
of Israel that night, as the white scarves were the badge of
the Catholics on the night of St. Bartholomew, was to be
killed at evening and eaten by the household, with very
peculiar rites, during the hours of darkness while the
butchery was proceeding : none of the flesh was to see the
morning light : whatever the family could not eat was to
be burned with fire.   All this was done.   The massacre of
Egyptian children and animals was successfully perpetrated
and had the desired effect ; and to commemorate this great
triumph God ordained that all the firstborn of man and
beast among the Israelites should be sacred to him ever
afterwards in the manner already described, the edible
animals to be sacrificed, and the uneatable, especially men
and asses, to be ransomed by a substitute or by a pecuniary
payment of so much a head.   And a festival was to be
celebrated every spring with rites exactly like those which
were observed on the night of the great slaughter.   The

divine command was obeyed, and the festival thus instituted was the Passover.[1]

The one thing that looms clear through the haze of this weird tradition is the memory of a great massacre of first-born. This was the origin, we are told, both of the sanctity of the firstborn and of the feast of the Passover. But when we are further told that the people whose firstborn were slaughtered on that occasion were not the Hebrews but their enemies, we are at once met by serious difficulties. Why, we may ask, should the Israelites kill the firstlings of their cattle for ever because God once killed those of the Egyptians ? and why should every Hebrew father have to pay God a ransom for his firstborn child because God once slew all the firstborn children of the Egyptians? In this form the tradition offers no intelligible explanation of the custom. But it at once becomes clear and intelligible when we assume that in the original version of the story it was the Hebrew firstborn that were slain ; that in fact the slaughter of the firstborn children was formerly, what the slaughter of

---

[1] Exodus xi. - xiii. 16 ; Numbers iii. 13, viii. 17. While many points in this strange story remain obscure, the reason which moved the Israelites of old to splash the blood of lambs on the doorposts of their houses at the Pass-over may perhaps have been not very different from that which induces the Sea Dyaks of Borneo to do much the same thing at the present day. "When there is any great epidemic in the country—when cholera or smallpox is killing its hundreds on all sides—one often notices little offerings of food hung on the walls and from the ceil-ing, animals killed in sacrifice, and blood splashed on the posts of the houses. When one asks why all this is done, they say they do it in the hope that when the evil spirit, who is thirst-ing for human lives, comes along and sees the offerings they have made and the animals killed in sacrifice, he will be satisfied with these things, and not take the lives of any of the people living in the Dyak village house " (E. H. Gomes, *Seventeen Years among the Sea Dyaks of Borneo*, London, 1911, p. 201). Similarly in Western Africa, when a pestilence or an attack of enemies is expected, it is customary to sacrifice sheep and goats and smear their blood on the gateways of the village (Miss Mary H. Kingsley, *Travels in West Africa*, p. 454, com-pare p. 45). In Peru, when an Indian hut is cleansed and whitewashed, the blood of a llama is always sprinkled on the doorway and internal walls in order to keep out the evil spirit (Col. Church, cited by E. J. Payne, *History of the New World called America*, i. 394, note [2]). For more evidence of the custom of pouring or smearing blood on the threshold, lintel, and side-posts of doors, see Ph. Paulitschke, *Ethno-graphie Nordost-Afrikas, die geistige Cultur der Danâkil, Galla und Somâl* (Berlin, 1896), pp. 38, 48 ; J. Gold-ziher, *Muhamedanische Studien*, ii. 329 ; S. J. Curtiss, *Primitive Semitic Religion To-day*, pp. 181-193, 227 *sq.* ; H. C. Trumbull, *The Threshold Covenant* (New York, 1896), pp. 4 *sq.*, 8 *sq.*, 26-28, 66-68. Perhaps the original intention of the custom was to avert evil influence, especially evil spirits, from the door.

the firstborn cattle always continued to be, not an isolated butchery but a regular custom, which with the growth of more humane sentiments was afterwards softened into the vicarious sacrifice of a lamb and the payment of a ransom for each child.   Here the reader may be reminded of another Hebrew tradition in which the sacrifice of the firstborn child is indicated still more clearly.   Abraham, we are informed, was commanded by God to offer up his firstborn son Isaac as a burnt sacrifice, and was on the point of obeying the divine command, when God, content with this proof of his faith and obedience, substituted for the human victim a ram, which Abraham accordingly sacrificed instead of his son.[1] Putting the two traditions together and observing how exactly they dovetail into each other and into the later Hebrew practice of actually sacrificing the firstborn children by fire to Baal or Moloch, we can hardly resist the conclusion that, before the. practice of redeeming them was introduced, the Hebrews, like the other branches of the Semitic race, regularly sacrificed their firstborn children by the fire or the knife.   The Passover, if this view is right, was the occasion when the awful sacrifice was offered ; and the tradition of its origin has preserved in its main outlines a vivid memory of the horrors of these fearful nights.   They must have been like the nights called Evil on the west coast of Africa, when the people kept indoors, because the executioners were going about the streets and the heads of the human victims were falling in the king's palace.[2]   But seen in the lurid light of superstition or of legend they were no common mortals, no vulgar executioners, who did the dreadful work at the first Passover.   The Angel of Death was abroad that night ; into every house he entered, and a sound of lamentation followed him as he came forth with his dripping sword. The blood that bespattered the lintel and door-posts would at first be the blood of the firstborn child of the house ; and when the blood of a lamb was afterwards substituted, we may suppose that it was intended not so much to appease as to cheat the ghastly visitant.   Seeing the red drops in

[1] Genesis xxii. 1-13.
[2] See for example Father Baudin, in Missions Catholiques, xvi. (1894) p.

333 ; A. B. Ellis, The Yoruba-speaking Peoples of the Slave Coast, pp. 105 sq.

the doorway he would say to himself, "That is the blood of their child. I need not turn in there. I have many yet to slay before the morning breaks grey in the east." And he would pass on in haste. And the trembling parents, as they clasped their little one to their breast, might fancy that they heard his footfalls growing fainter and fainter down the street. In plain words, we may surmise that the slaughter was originally done by masked men, like the Mumbo Jumbos and similar figures of west Africa, who went from house to house and were believed by the uninitiated to be the deity or his divine messengers come in person to carry off the victims. When the leaders had decided to allow the sacrifice of animals instead of children, they would give the people a hint that if they only killed a lamb and smeared its blood on the door-posts, the bloodthirsty but near-sighted deity would never know the difference.

Attempts to outwit a malignant spirit.
The attempt to outwit a malignant and dangerous spirit is common, and might be illustrated by many examples. Some instances will be noticed in a later part of this work. Here a single one may suffice. The Malays believe in a Spectral Huntsman, who ranges the forest with a pack of ghostly dogs, and whose apparition bodes sickness or death. Certain birds which fly in flocks by night uttering a loud and peculiar note are supposed to follow in his train. Hence when Perak peasants hear the weird sound, they run out and make a clatter with a knife on a wooden platter, crying, "Great-grandfather, bring us their hearts!" The Spectral Huntsman, hearing these words, will take the supplicants for followers of his own asking to share his bag. So he will spare the household and pass on, and the tumult of the wild hunt will die away in the darkness and the distance.[1]

The custom of sacrificing all the firstborn, whether of animals or
If this be indeed the origin of the Passover and of the sanctity of the firstborn among the Hebrews, the whole of the Semitic evidence on the subject is seen to fall into line at once. The children whom the Carthaginians, Phoenicians, Canaanites, Moabites, Sepharvites, and probably other

---

[1] W. E. Maxwell, "The Folklore of the Malays," *Journal of the Straits Branch of the Royal Asiatic Society*, No. 7 (June 1881), p. 14; W. W. Skeat, *Malay Magic*, p. 112. The bird in question is thought to be the goat-sucker or night-jar.

branches of the Semitic race burnt in the fire would be men, was
their firstborn only, although in general ancient writers probably
have failed to indicate this limitation of the custom. For ancient
the Moabites, indeed, the limitation is clearly indicated, if Semitic
not expressly stated, when we read that the king of Moab institution.
offered his eldest son, who should have reigned after him,
as a burnt sacrifice on the wall.[1] For the Phoenicians it
comes out less distinctly in the statement of Porphyry that
the Phoenicians used to sacrifice one of their dearest to
Baal, and in the legend recorded by Philo of Byblus that
Cronus sacrificed his only-begotten son.[2] We may suppose
that the custom of sacrificing the firstborn both of men and
animals was a very ancient Semitic institution, which many
branches of the race kept up within historical times ; but
that the Hebrews, while they maintained the custom in
regard to domestic cattle, were led by their loftier morality
to discard it in respect of children, and to replace it by a
merciful law that firstborn children should be ransomed
instead of sacrificed.[3]

The conclusion that the Hebrew custom of redeeming Sacrifice of
the firstborn is a modification of an older custom of sacri- firstborn
ficing them has been mentioned by some very distinguished children
scholars only to be rejected on the ground, apparently, of its various
extreme improbability.[4] To me the converging lines of races.
evidence which point to this conclusion seem too numerous
and too distinct to be thus lightly brushed aside. And the
argument from improbability can easily be rebutted by
pointing to other peoples who are known to have practised
or to be still practising a custom of the same sort. In some
tribes of New South Wales the firstborn child of every
woman was eaten by the tribe as part of a religious cere-

[1] 2 Kings iii. 27.

[2] See above, pp. 166, 167.

[3] As to the redemption of the firstborn among modern Jews, see L. Löw,
*Die Lebensalter in der jüdischen Lite-
ratur* (Szegedin, 1875), pp. 110-118 ;
Budgett Meakin, *The Moors* (London,
1902), pp. 440 *sq.*

[4] J. Wellhausen, *Prolegomena zur
Geschichte Israels,*[3] p. 90 ; W. Robertson Smith, *Religion of the Semites,*[2]

p. 464. On the other hand, when I
published the foregoing discussion in
the second edition of my book, I was
not aware that the conclusion reached
in it had been anticipated by Prof. Th.
Nöldeke, who has drawn the same
inference from the same evidence. See
*Zeitschrift der Deutschen Morgenlän-
dischen Gesellschaft*, xlii. (1888) p.
483. I am happy to find myself in
agreement with so eminent an authority
on Semitic antiquity.

mony.[1] Among the aborigines on the lower portions of the Paroo and Warrego rivers, which join the Darling River in New South Wales, girls used to become wives when they were mere children and to be mothers at fourteen, and the old custom was to kill the firstborn child by strangulation.[2] Again, among the tribes about Maryborough in Queensland a girl's first child was almost always exposed and left to perish.[3] In the tribes about Beltana, in South Australia, girls were married at fourteen, and it was customary to destroy their firstborn.[4] The natives of Rook, an island off the east coast of New Guinea, used to kill all their firstborn children ; they prided themselves on their humanity in burying the murdered infants instead of eating them as their barbarous neighbours did. They spared the second child but killed the third, and so on alternately with the rest of their offspring.[5] Chinese history reports that in a state called Khai-muh, to the east of Yueh, it was customary to devour the firstborn sons,[6] and further, that to the west of Kiao-chi or Tonquin "there was a realm of man-eaters, where the firstborn son was, as a rule, chopped into pieces and eaten, and his younger brothers were nevertheless regarded to have fulfilled their fraternal duties towards him. And if he proved to be appetizing food, they sent some of his flesh to their chieftains, who, exhilarated, gave the father a reward."[7] In India, down to the beginning of the nineteenth century, the custom of

---

[1] R. Brough Smyth, *Aborigines of Victoria*, ii. 311. In the Luritcha tribe of central Australia "young children are sometimes killed and eaten, and it is not an infrequent custom, when a child is in weak health, to kill a younger and healthy one and then to feed the weakling on its flesh, the idea being that this will give the weak child the strength of the stronger one" (Spencer and Gillen, *Native Tribes of Central Australia*, p. 475). The practice seems to have been common among the Australian aborigines. See W. E. Stanbridge, quoted by R. Brough Smyth, *op. cit.* i. 52 ; A. W. Howitt, *Native Tribes of South-East Australia*, pp. 749, 750.

[2] G. Scriviner, in E. Curr's *The Australian Race*, ii. 182.

[3] A. W. Howitt, *Native Tribes of South-East Australia*, p. 750.

[4] S. Gason, in E. Curr's *The Australian Race*, ii. 119.

[5] Father Mazzuconi, in *Annales de la Propagation de la Foi*, xxvii. (1855) pp. 368 *sq.*

[6] J. J. M. de Groot, *Religious System of China*, ii. 679, iv. 364.

[7] J. J. M. de Groot, *op. cit.* iv. 365. On these Chinese reports Prof. de Groot remarks (*op. cit.* iv. 366): "Quite at a loss, however, we are to explain that eating of firstborn sons by their own nearest kinsfolk, absolutely inconsistent as it is with a primary law of tribal life in general, which imperiously demands that the tribe should make itself strong in male cognates, but not indulge in self-destruction by

sacrificing a firstborn child to the Ganges was common.[1]
Again, we are told that among the Hindoos "the firstborn
has always held a peculiarly sacred position, especially if
born in answer to a vow to parents who have long been
without offspring, in which case sacrifice of the child was
common in India. The Mairs used to sacrifice a firstborn
son to Mata, the small-pox goddess." [2]

The Borans, on the southern borders of Abyssinia,
propitiate a sky-spirit called Wak by sacrificing their children
and cattle to him. Among them when a man of any
standing marries, he becomes a Raba, as it is called, and for
a certain period after marriage, probably four to eight years,
he must leave any children that are born to him to die in
the bush. No Boran cares to contemplate the fearful
calamities with which Wak would visit him if he failed to
discharge this duty. After he ceases to be a Raba, a man
is circumcised and becomes a Gudda. The sky-spirit has
no claim on the children born after their father's circumcision,
but they are sent away at a very early age to be reared by
the Wata, a low caste of hunters. They remain with these
people till they are grown up, and then return to their
families.[3] In this remarkable custom it would appear that
the circumcision of the father is regarded as an atoning
sacrifice which redeems the rest of his children from the
spirit to whom they would otherwise belong. The obscure
story told by the Israelites to explain the origin of circumcision seems also to suggest that the custom was supposed
to save the life of the child by giving the deity a substitute
for it.[4] Again, the Kerre, Banna, and Bashada, three tribes
in the valley of the Omo River, to the south of Abyssinia,

Sacrifice of firstborn children among the Borans and other tribes to the south of Abyssinia.

---

killing its natural defenders. We feel,
therefore, strongly inclined to believe
the statement fabulous." Such scepti-
cism implies an opinion of the good
sense and foresight of savages which is
far from being justified by the facts.
Many savage tribes have "indulged in
self-destruction" by killing a large
proportion of their children, both male
and female. See below, pp. 196 *sq.*

[1] W. Crooke, *Popular Religion and Folklore of Northern India*, ii. 169.

[2] H. A. Rose, "Unlucky Children,"
Folklore, xiii. (1902) p. 63; *id.*, in
Indian Antiquary, xxxi. (1902) pp.
162 *sq.* Mr. Rose is Superintendent
of Ethnography in the Punjaub. The
authorities cited by him are Moore's
Hindu Infanticide, pp. 198 *sq.*, and
Sherring's *Hindu Tribes and Castes*,
iii. p. 66.

[3] Captain Philip Maud, "Explora-
tion in the Southern Borderland of
Abyssinia," *The Geographical Journal*,
xxiii. (1904) pp. 567 *sq.*

[4] Exodus iv. 24-26.

are in the habit of strangling their firstborn children and throwing the bodies away. The Kerre cast the bodies into the river Omo, where they are devoured by crocodiles ; the other two tribes leave them in the forest to be eaten by the hyaenas. The only explanation they give of the custom is that it was decreed by their ancestors. Captain C. H. Stigand enquired into the practice very carefully and was told that "for a certain number of years after marriage children would be thrown away, and after that they would be kept. The number of the first children who were strangled, and the period of years during which this was done, appears to be variable, but I could not understand what regulated it. There was one point, however, about which they were certain, and that was that the first-born of all, rich, poor, high and low, had to be strangled and thrown away. The chief of the Kerre said, 'If I had a child now, it would have to be thrown away,' laughing as if it were a great joke. What amused him really was that I should be so interested in their custom." So far as Captain Stigand could ascertain, there is no idea of sacrificing the children to the crocodiles by throwing them into the river. If a Kerre man has a first child born to him while he is on a journey away from the river, he will throw the infant away in the forest.[1] In Uganda if the firstborn child of a chief or any important person is a son, the midwife strangles it and reports that the infant was still-born. "This is done to ensure the life of the father ; if he has a son born first he will soon die, and the child inherit all he has."[2] Amongst the people of Senjero in eastern Africa we are told that many families must offer up their firstborn sons as sacrifices, because once upon a time, when summer and winter were jumbled together in a bad season, and the fruits of the earth would not ripen, the soothsayers enjoined it. At that time a great pillar of iron is said to have stood at the entrance of the capital, which in accordance with the advice of the soothsayers was broken down by order of the king, where-

Firstborn male children put to death in Uganda.

---

[1] Captain C. H. Stigand, *To Abyssinia through an Unknown Land* (London, 1910), pp. 234 *sq.*

[2] J. Roscoe, "Further Notes on the Manners and Customs of the Baganda," *Journal of the Anthropological Institute*, xxxii. (1902) p. 30. Mr. Roscoe informs me that a similar custom prevails also in Koki and Bunyoro.

upon the seasons became regular again. To avert the recurrence of such a calamity the wizards commanded the king to pour human blood once a year on the base of the broken shaft of the pillar, and also upon the throne. Since then certain families have been obliged to deliver up their firstborn sons, who were sacrificed at an appointed time.[1] Among some tribes of south-eastern Africa there is a rule that when a woman's husband has been killed in battle and she marries again, the first child she gives birth to after her second marriage must be put to death, whether she has it by her first or her second husband. Such a child is called "the child of the assegai," and if it were not killed, death or an accident would be sure to befall the second spouse, and the woman herself would be barren. The notion is that the woman must have had some share in the misfortune that overtook her first husband, and that the only way of removing the malign influence is to slay "the child of the assegai." [2]

The heathen Russians often sacrificed their firstborn to the god Perun.[3] It is said that on Mag Slacht or "plain of prostrations," near the present village of Ballymagauran, in the County Cavan, there used to stand a great idol called Cromm Cruach, covered with gold, to which the ancient Irish sacrificed "the firstlings of every issue and the chief scions of every clan" in order to obtain plenty of corn, honey, and milk. Round about the golden image, which was spoken of as the king idol of Erin, stood twelve other idols of stone.[4] The Kutonaqa Indians of British Columbia

Sacrifice of firstborn children in Europe and America.

---

[1] J. L. Krapf, *Travels, Researches, and Missionary Labours during an Eighteen Years' Residence in Eastern Africa* (London, 1860), pp. 69 *sq.* Dr. Krapf, who reports the custom at second hand, thinks that the existence of the pillar may be doubted, but that the rest of the story harmonises well enough with African superstition.

[2] J. Macdonald, *Light in Africa*[2] (London, 1890), p. 156. In the text I have embodied some fuller explanations and particulars which my friend the Rev. Mr. Macdonald was good enough to send me in a letter dated September 16th, 1899. Among the tribes with which Mr. Macdonald is best acquainted the custom is obsolete and lives only in tradition ; formerly it was universally practised.

[3] F. J. Mone, *Geschichte des Heidenthums im nördlichen Europa* (Leipsic and Darmstadt, 1822-1823), i. 119.

[4] Vallancey, *Collectanea de rebus Hibernicis*, vol. iii. (Dublin, 1786) p. 457 ; D. Nutt, *The Voyage of Bran*, ii. 149-151, 304 *sq.* ; P. W. Joyce, *Social History of Ancient Ireland*, i. 275 *sq.*, 281-284. The authority for the tradition is the *Dinnschenchas* or *Dinnsenchus*, a document compiled in the eleventh and twelfth centuries out of older materials. Mr. Joyce discredits the tradition of human sacrifice.

Sacrifice of
firstborn
children to
the sun. worship the sun and sacrifice their firstborn children to him. When a woman is with child she prays to the sun, saying, " I am with child. When it is born I shall offer it to you. Have pity upon us." Thus they expect to secure health and good fortune for their families.[1]   Among the Coast Salish Indians of the same region the first child is often sacrificed to the sun in order to ensure the health and prosperity of the whole family.[2]   The Indians of Florida sacrificed their firstborn male children.[3]   Among the Indians of north Carolina down to the early part of the eighteenth century a remarkable ceremony was performed, which seems to be most naturally interpreted as a modification of an older custom of putting the king's son to death, perhaps as a substitute for his father.   It is thus described by a writer of that period : " They have a strange custom or ceremony amongst them, to call to mind the persecutions and death of the kings their ancestors slain by their enemies at certain seasons, and particularly when the savages have been at war with any nation, and return from their country without bringing home some prisoners of war, or the heads of their enemies.   The king causes as a perpetual remembrance of all his predecessors to beat and wound the best beloved of all his children with the same weapons wherewith they had been kill'd in former times, to the end that by renewing the wound, their death should be lamented afresh. The king and his nation being assembled on these occasions, a feast is prepared, and the Indian who is authorised to wound the king's son, runs about the house like a distracted person crying and making a most hideous noise all the time with the weapon in his hand, wherewith he wounds the king's son ; this he performs three several times, during which interval he presents the king with victuals or *cassena*, and it is very strange to see the Indian that is thus struck never offers to stir till he is wounded the third time, after

---

[1] Fr. Boas, in "Fourth Annual Report on the North-Western Tribes of Canada," *Report of the British Association for 1888*, p. 242 ; *id.*, in *Fifth Report on the North-Western Tribes of Canada*, p. 52 (separate reprint from the *Report of the British Association for 1889*).

[2] Fr. Boas, in *Fifth Report on the North-Western Tribes of Canada*, p. 46 (separate reprint from the *Report of the British Association for 1889*).

[3] W. Strachey, *Historie of travaile into Virginia Britannia* (Hakluyt Society, London, 1849), p. 84

which he falls down backwards stretching out his arms and legs as if he had been ready to expire ; then the rest of the king's sons and daughters, together with the mother and vast numbers of women and girls, fall at his feet and lament and cry most bitterly. During this time the king and his retinue are feasting, yet with such profound silence for some hours, that not one word or even a whisper is to be heard amongst them. After this manner they continue till night, which ends in singing, dancing, and the greatest joy imaginable." [1] In this account the description of the frantic manner assumed by the person whose duty it was to wound the king's son reminds us of the frenzy of King Athamas when he took or attempted the lives of his children.[2] The same feature is said to have characterised the sacrifice of children in Peru. "When any person of note was sick and the priest said he must die, they sacrificed his son, desiring the idol to be satisfied with him and not to take away his father's life. The ceremonies used at these sacrifices were strange, for they behaved themselves like mad men. They believed that all calamities were occasioned by sin, and that sacrifices were the remedy." [3] An early Spanish historian of the conquest of Peru, in describing the Indians of the Peruvian valleys between San-Miguel and Caxamalca, records that "they have disgusting sacrifices and temples of idols which they hold in great veneration ; they offer them their most precious possessions. Every month they sacrifice their own children and smear with the blood of the victims the face of the idols and the doors of the temples." [4] In Puruha, a province of Quito, it used to be customary to sacrifice the firstborn children to the gods. Their remains were dried, enclosed in vessels of metal or stone, and kept in the houses.[5] The Ximanas and Cauxanas, two Indian tribes

Sacrifice of children in Peru.

---

[1] J. Bricknell, *The Natural History of North Carolina* (Dublin, 1737), pp. 342 *sq.* I have taken the liberty of altering slightly the writer's somewhat eccentric punctuation.

[2] See above, p. 162.

[3] A. de Herrera, *The General History of the Vast Continent and Islands of America*, translated by Capt. John Stevens (London, 1725-6), iv. 347 *sq.*

Compare J. de Acosta, *Natural and Moral History of the Indies* (Hakluyt Society, London, 1880), ii. 344.

[4] Fr. Xeres, *Relation véridique de la conquête du Perou et de la Province de Cuzco nommée Nouvelle-Castille* (in H. Ternaux-Compans's *Voyages, relations et mémoires*, etc., Paris, 1837), p. 53.

[5] Juan de Velasco, *Histoire du royaume de Quito*, i. (Paris, 1840)

in the upper valley of the Amazon, kill all their firstborn children.[1] If the firstborn is a girl, the Lengua Indians invariably put it to death.[2]

The "sacred spring" in ancient Italy.

Among the ancient Italian peoples, especially of the Sabine stock, it was customary in seasons of great peril or public calamity, as when the crops had failed or a pestilence was raging, to vow that they would sacrifice to the gods every creature, whether man or beast, that should be born in the following spring. To the creatures thus devoted to sacrifice the name of "the sacred spring" was applied. "But since," says Festus, "it seemed cruel to slay innocent boys and girls, they were kept till they had grown up, then veiled and driven beyond the boundaries."[3] Several Italian peoples, for example the Piceni, Samnites, and Hirpini, traced their origin to a "sacred spring," that is, to the consecrated youth who had swarmed off from the parent stock in consequence of such a vow.[4] When the Romans were engaged in a life-and-death struggle with Hannibal after their great defeat at the Trasimene Lake, they vowed to offer a "sacred spring" if victory should attend their arms and the commonwealth should retrieve its shattered

p. 106 (forming vol. xviii. of H. Ternaux-Compans's *Voyages, relations et mémoires*, etc.).

[1] A. R. Wallace, *Narrative of Travels on the Amazon and Rio Negro* (London, 1889), p. 355.

[2] W. Barbrooke Grubb, *An Unknown People in an Unknown Land* (London, 1911), p. 233.

[3] Festus, *De verborum significatione*, s.vv. "Mamertini," "Sacrani," and "Ver sacrum," pp. 158, 370, 371, 379, ed. C. O. Müller; Servius on Virgil, *Aen.* vii. 796; Nonius Marcellus, s.v. "ver sacrum," p. 522 (p. 610, ed. Quicherat); Varro, *Rerum rusticarum*, iii. 16. 29; Dionysius Halicarnasensis, *Antiquit. Rom.* i. 16 and 23 *sq.*, ii. 1. 2.

[4] Strabo, v. 4. 2 and 12; Pliny, *Nat. hist.* iii. 110; Festus, *De verborum significatione*, s.v. "Irpini," ed. C. O. Müller, p. 106. It is worthy of note that the three swarms which afterwards developed into the Piceni, the Samnites, and the Hirpini were said to have been guided by a woodpecker, a bull, and a wolf

respectively, of which the woodpecker (*picus*) and the wolf (*hirpus*) gave their names to the Piceni and the Hirpini. The tradition may perhaps preserve a trace of totemism, but in the absence of clearer evidence it would be rash to assume that it does so. The woodpecker was sacred among the Latins, and a woodpecker as well as a wolf is said to have fed the twins Romulus and Remus (Plutarch, *Quaest. Rom.* 21; Ovid, *Fasti*, iii. 37 *sq.*). Does this legend point to the existence of a wolf-clan and a woodpecker-clan at Rome? There was perhaps a similar conjunction of wolf and woodpecker at Soracte, for the woodpecker is spoken of as the bird of Feronia ("*picus Feronius*," Festus, s.v. "Oscines," p. 197, ed. C. O. Müller), a goddess in whose sanctuary at Soracte certain men went by the name of Soranian Wolves (Servius, on Virgil, *Aen.* xi. 785; Pliny, *Nat. hist.* vii. 19; Strabo, v. 2. 9). These "Soranian Wolves" will meet us again later on.

fortunes. But the vow extended only to all the offspring of sheep, goats, oxen, and swine that should be brought forth on Italian mountains, plains, and meadows the following spring.[1] On a later occasion, when the Romans pledged themselves again by a similar vow, it was decided that by the "sacred spring" should be meant all the cattle born between the first day of March and the last day of April.[2] Although in later times the Italian peoples appear to have resorted to measures of this sort only in special emergencies, there was a tradition that in former times the consecration of the firstborn to the gods had been an annual custom.[3] Accordingly, it seems not impossible that originally the Italians may, like the Hebrews and perhaps the Semites in general, have been in the habit of dedicating all the firstborn, whether of man or beast, and sacrificing them at a great festival in spring.[4] The custom of the "sacred spring" was not confined to the Italians, but was practised by many other peoples, both Greeks and barbarians, in antiquity.[5]

Thus it would seem that a custom of putting to death all firstborn children has prevailed in many parts of the world. What was the motive which led people to practise a custom which to us seems at once so cruel and so foolish? It cannot have been the purely prudential consideration of adjusting the numbers of the tribe to the amount of the food-supply; for, in the first place, savages do not take such thought for the morrow,[6] and, in the second place, if

Different motives may have led to the practice of killing the firstborn.

---

[1] Livy, xxii. 9 *sq.*; Plutarch, *Fabius Maximus*, 4.

[2] Livy, xxxiv. 44.

[3] Dionysius Halicarnasensis, *Antiquit. Rom.* i. 24.

[4] Schwegler thought it hardly open to question that the "sacred spring" was a substitute for an original custom of human sacrifice (*Römische Geschichte*, i. 240 *sq.*). The inference is denied on insufficient grounds by R. von Ihering (*Vorgeschichte der Indoeuropäer*, pp. 309 *sqq.*).

[5] Dionysius Halicarnasensis, *Antiquit. Rom.* i. 16. 1. Rhegium in Italy was founded by Chalcidian colonists, who in obedience to the Delphic Oracle had been dedicated as a tithe-offering to Apollo on account of a

dearth (Strabo, vi. 1. 6, p. 257). Justin speaks of the Gauls sending out three hundred thousand men, "as it were a sacred spring," to seek a new home (Justin, xxiv. 4. 1).

[6] The Australian aborigines resort to infanticide to keep down the number of a family. But "the number is kept down, not with any idea at all of regulating the food supply, so far as the adults are concerned, but simply from the point of view that, if the mother is suckling one child, she cannot properly provide food for another, quite apart from the question of the trouble of carrying two children about. An Australian native never looks far enough ahead to consider what will be the effect on the food supply in future years if he allows

they did, they would be likely to kill the later born children rather than the firstborn. The foregoing evidence suggests that the custom may have been practised by different peoples from different motives. With the Semites, the Italians, and their near kinsmen the Irish the sacrifice or at least the consecration of the firstborn seems to have been viewed as a tribute paid to the gods, who were thus content to receive a part though they might justly have claimed the whole. In some cases the death of the child appears to be definitely regarded as a substitute for the death of the father, who obtains a new lease of life by the sacrifice of his offspring. This comes out clearly in the tradition of Aun, King of Sweden, who sacrificed one of his sons every nine years to Odin in order to prolong his own life.[1] And in Peru also the son died that the father might live.[2] But in some cases it would seem that the child has been killed, not so much as a substitute for the father, as because it is supposed to endanger his life by absorbing his spiritual essence or vital energy. In fact, a belief in the transmigration or rebirth of souls has operated to produce a regular custom of infanticide, especially infanticide of the firstborn. At Whydah, on the Slave coast of West Africa, where the doctrine of reincarnation is firmly held, it has happened that a child has been put to death because the fetish doctors declared it to be the king's father come to life again. The king naturally could not submit to be pushed from the throne by his predecessor in this fashion ; so he compelled his supposed parent to return to the world of the dead from which he had very inopportunely effected his escape.[3] The Hindoos are of opinion that a man is literally reborn in the person of his son. Thus in the *Laws of Manu* we read that " the husband, after conception by his wife, becomes an embryo and is born again of her ; for that is the wifehood of a wife, that he is born again by her." [4] Hence after the birth

A belief in the rebirth of souls may in some cases have operated to produce infanticide, especially of the firstborn.

The Hindoos believe that a man is reborn in his son, while at the same time he

a particular child to live ; what affects him is simply the question of how it will interfere with the work of his wife so far as their own camp is concerned " (Spencer and Gillen, *Native Tribes of Central Australia*, p. 264).

[1] See above, pp. 57, 160 *sq.*

[2] Above, p. 185.

[3] Father Baudin, "Le Fétichisme," *Missions Catholiques*, xvi. (1884) p. 259.

[4] *The Laws of Manu*, ix. 8, p. 329, G. Bühler's translation (*Sacred Books of the East*, vol. xxv.). On this Hindoo

of a son the father is clearly in a very delicate position. dies in his own person. Since he is his own son, can he himself, apart from his son, be said to exist? Does he not rather die in his own person as soon as he comes to life in the person of his son? This appears to be the opinion of the subtle Hindoo, for in some sections of the Khatris, a mercantile caste of the Punjaub, funeral rites are actually performed for the father in the fifth month of his wife's pregnancy. But apparently he is allowed, by a sort of legal fiction, to come to life again in his own person ; for after the birth of his first son he is formally remarried to his wife, which may be regarded as a tacit admission that in the eye of the law at least he is alive.[1]

Now to people who thus conceive the relation of father and son it is plain that fatherhood must appear a very dubious privilege ; for if you die in begetting a son, can you be quite sure of coming to life again? His existence is at the best a menace to yours, and at the worst it may involve your extinction. The danger seems to lie especially in the birth of your first son ; if only you can tide that over, you are, humanly speaking, safe. In fact, it comes to this, Are you to live? or is he? It is a painful dilemma. Parental affection urges you to die that he may live. Self-love whispers, " Live and let him die. You are in the flower of your age. You adorn the circle in which you move. You are useful, nay, indispensable, to society. He is a mere babe. He never will be missed." Such a train of thought, preposterous as it seems to us, might easily lead to a custom of killing the firstborn.[2]

Painful dilemma of a father.

doctrine of reincarnation, its logical consequences and its analogies in other parts of the world, see J. von Negelein, " Eine Quelle der indischen Seelenwanderungvorstellung," *Archiv für Religionswissenschaft,* vi. (1903) pp. 320-333. Compare E. S. Hartland, *The Legend of Perseus,* i. 218 *sq.* ; *id.,* *Primitive Paternity* (London, 1909-1910), ii. 196 *sqq.*

[1] H. A. [J. A.] Rose, "Unlucky and Lucky Children, and some Birth Superstitions," *Indian Antiquary,* xxxi. (1902) p. 516 ; *id.,* in *Folklore,* xiii. (1902) pp. 278 *sq.* As to the Khatris, see D. C. J. Ibbetson, *Outlines of Panjab Ethnography,* pp. 295

sq. ; H. H. Risley, *The Tribes and Castes of Bengal,* i. 478 *sqq.* ; W. Crooke, *The Tribes and Castes of the North-western Provinces and Oudh,* iii. 264 *sqq.*

[2] The same suggestion has been made by Dr. E. Westermarck (*The Origin and Development of the Moral Ideas,* i. (London, 1906) pp. 460 *sq.*). Some years ago, before the publication of his book and while the present volume was still in proof, Dr. Westermarck and I in conversation discovered that we had independently arrived at the same conjectural explanation of the custom of killing the firstborn.

The same
notion of
the rebirth
of the
father in
the son
would ex-
plain why
in Poly-
nesia in-
fants suc-
ceeded to
the chief-
tainship as
soon as
they were
born, their
fathers
abdicating
in their
favour.

Further, the same notion of the rebirth of the father in his eldest son would explain the remarkable rule of succession which prevailed in Polynesia and particularly in Tahiti, where as soon as the king had a son born to him he was obliged to abdicate the throne in favour of the infant. Whatever might be the king's age, his influence in the state, or the political situation of affairs, no sooner was the child born than the monarch became a subject : the infant was at once proclaimed the sovereign of the people : the royal name was conferred upon him, and his father was the first to do him homage, by saluting his feet and declaring him king. All matters, however, of importance which concerned either the internal welfare or the foreign relations of the country continued to be transacted by the father and his councillors ; but every edict was issued in the name and on the behalf of the youthful monarch, and though the whole of the executive government might remain in the hands of the father, he only acted as regent for his son, and was regarded as such by the nation. The lands and other sources of revenue were appropriated to the maintenance of the infant ruler, his household, and his attendants ; the insignia of royal authority were transferred to him, and his father rendered him all those marks of humble respect which he had hitherto exacted from his subjects. This custom of succession was not confined to the family of the sovereign, it extended also to the nobles and the landed gentry ; they, too, had to resign their rank, honours, and possessions on the birth of a son. A man who but yesterday was a baron, not to be approached by his inferiors till they had ceremoniously bared the whole of the upper part of their bodies, was to-day reduced to the rank of a mere commoner with none to do him reverence, if in the night time his wife had given birth to a son, and the child had been suffered to live. The father indeed still continued to administer the estate, but he did so for the benefit of the infant, to whom it now belonged, and to whom all the marks of respect were at once transferred.[1]

[1] Capt. J. Cook, *Voyages* (London, 1809), i. 225 *sq.* ; Capt. J. Wilson, *Missionary Voyage to the Southern Pacific Ocean* (London, 1799), pp. 327, 330, 333 ; W. Ellis, *Polynesian Researches*,[2] iii. 99-101 ; J. A. Mourenhout, *Voyages aux Îles du Grand Océan*, ii. 13 *sq.* ; Mathias G. * * *, *Lettres sur les Îles Marquises* (Paris, 1843), pp. 103 *sq.* ; H. Hale, *United*

This singular usage becomes intelligible if the spirit of Such a rule of succession might easily lead to a practice of infanticide. the father was supposed to quit him at the birth of his first son and to reappear in the infant. Such a belief and such a practice would, it is obvious, supply a powerful motive to infanticide, since a father could not rear his firstborn son without thereby relinquishing the honours and possessions to which he had been accustomed. The sacrifice was a heavy one, and we need not wonder if many men refused to make it. Certainly infanticide was practised in Polynesia to Prevalence of infanticide in Polynesia. an extraordinary extent. The first missionaries estimated that not less than two-thirds of the children were murdered by their parents, and this estimate has been confirmed by a careful enquirer. It would seem that before the introduction of Christianity there was not a single mother in the islands who was not also a murderess, having imbrued her hands in the blood of her offspring. Three native women, the eldest not more than forty years of age, happened once to be in a room where the conversation turned on infanticide, and they confessed to having destroyed not less than twenty-one infants between them.[1] It would doubtless be a gross mistake to lay the whole blame of these massacres on the doctrine of reincarnation, but we can hardly doubt that it instigated a great many. Once more we perceive the fatal consequences that may flow in practice from a theoretical error.

In some places the abdication of the father does not take In some places the father either abdicates when his son attains to manhood or is forcibly deposed by him. place until the son is grown up. This was the general practice in Fiji.[2] In Raratonga as soon as a son reached manhood, he would fight and wrestle with his father for the mastery, and if he obtained it he would take forcible possession of the farm and drive his parent in destitution from home.[3] Among the Corannas of South Africa the youthful son of a chief is hardly allowed to walk, but has to idle away his time in the hut and to drink much milk in order that he may grow strong. When he has attained to manhood his

States Exploring Expedition, Ethnography and Philology (Philadelphia, 1846), p. 34.

[1] W. Ellis, *Polynesian Researches*,[2] i. 251-253.

[2] J. E. Erskine, *Journal of a Cruise among the Islands of the Western Pacific* (London, 1853), p. 233.

[3] J. Williams, *Narrative of Missionary Enterprises in the South Sea Islands* (London, 1836), pp. 117 *sq.*

father produces two short, bullet-headed sticks and presents one to his son, while he keeps the other for himself. Armed with these weapons the two often fight, and when the son succeeds in knocking his parent down he is acknowledged chief of the kraal.[1] But such customs probably do not imply the theory of rebirth; they may only be applications of the principle that might is right. Still they would equally supply the father with a motive for killing the infant son who, if suffered to live, would one day strip him of his rank and possessions.

The custom of the deposition of the father by his son may perhaps be traced in Greek myth and legend. Cronus and his children.

Perhaps customs of this sort have left traces of themselves in Greek myth and legend. Cronus or Saturn, as the Romans called him, is said to have been the youngest son of the sky-god Uranus, and to have mutilated his father and reigned in his stead as king of gods and men. Afterwards he was warned by an oracle that he himself should be deposed by his son. To prevent that catastrophe Cronus swallowed his children, one after the other, as soon as they were born. Only the youngest of them, Zeus, was saved through a trick of his mother's, and in time he fulfilled the oracle by banishing his father and sitting on his throne. But Zeus in his turn was told that his wife Metis would give birth to a son who would supplant him in the kingdom of heaven. Accordingly, to rid himself of his future rival he resorted to a device like that which his father Cronus had employed for a similar purpose. Only instead of waiting till the child was born and then devouring it, he made assurance doubly sure by swallowing his wife with the unborn babe in her womb.[2] Such barbarous myths become intelligible if we suppose that they took their rise among people who were accustomed to see grown-up sons supplanting their fathers by force, and fathers murdering and perhaps eating their infants in order to secure themselves against their future rivalry. We have met with instances of savage tribes who are said to devour their firstborn children.[3]

[1] J. Campbell, *Travels in South Africa, Second Journey* (London, 1822), ii. 276.

[2] Hesiod, *Theogony*, 137 *sqq.*, 453 *sqq.*, 886 *sqq.*; Apollodorus, *Bibliotheca*, i. 1-3.

[3] Above, pp. 179 *sq.* Traces of a custom of sacrificing the children instead of the father may perhaps be found in the legends that Menoeceus, son of Creon, died to save Thebes, and that one or more of the daughters of Erech-

The legend that Laius, king of Thebes, exposed his infant son Oedipus, who afterwards slew his father and sat on the throne, may well be a reminiscence of a state of things in which father and son regularly plotted against each other. The other feature of the story, to wit the marriage of Oedipus with the widowed queen, his mother, fits in very well with the rule which has prevailed in some countries that a valid title to the throne is conferred by marriage with the late king's widow. That custom probably arose, as I have endeavoured to shew,[1] in an age when the blood-royal ran in the female line, and when the king was a man of another family, often a stranger and foreigner, who reigned only in virtue of being the consort of a native princess, and whose sons never succeeded him on the throne. But in process of time, when fathers had ceased to regard the birth of a son as a menace to their life, or at least to their regal power, kings would naturally scheme to secure the succession for their own male offspring, and this new practice could be reconciled with the old one by marrying the king's son either to his own sister or, after his father's decease, to his stepmother. We have seen marriage with a stepmother actually enjoined for this very purpose by some of the Saxon kings.[2] And on this hypothesis we can understand why the custom of marriage with a full or a half sister has prevailed in so many royal families.[3] It was

Legend of Oedipus, who slew his father and married his mother.

Marriage with a widowed queen sometimes forms a legitimate title to the kingdom.

Marriage with a stepmother or a sister, a mode of securing the succession of the king's own children, and so of transferring the inheritance from the female to the male line.

---

theus perished to save Athens. See Euripides, *Phoenissae*, 889 *sqq.* ; Apollodorus, iii. 6. 7, iii. 15. 4 ; Schol. on Aristides, *Panathen.* p. 113, ed. Dindorf; Cicero, *Tuscul.*, i. 48. 116; *id.*, *De natura deorum*, iii. 19. 50 ; W. H. Roscher, *Lexikon d. griech. und röm. Mythologie*, i. 1298 *sq.*, ii. 2794 *sq.*

[1] See *The Magic Art and the Evolution of Kings*, vol. ii. pp. 269 *sqq.*

[2] See *The Magic Art and the Evolution of Kings*, vol. ii. p. 283. The Oedipus legend would conform still more closely to custom if we could suppose that marriage with a mother was formerly allowed in cases where the king had neither a sister nor a stepmother, by marrying whom he could otherwise legalise his claim to the throne.

[3] Examples of this custom are collected by me in a note on Pausanias,

i. 7. 1 (vol. ii. p. 85). For other instances see V. Noel, " Ile de Madagascar, recherches sur les Sakkalava," *Bulletin de la Société de Géographie* (Paris), Deuxième Série, xx. (Paris, 1843) pp. 63 *sq.* (among the Sakkalavas of Madagascar) ; V. L. Cameron, *Across Africa* (London, 1877), ii. 70, 149 ; J. Roscoe, " Further Notes on the Manners and Customs of the Baganda," *Journal of the Anthropological Institute*, xxxii. (1902) p. 27 (among the Baganda of Central Africa) ; J. G. Frazer, *Totemism and Exogamy*, ii. 523, 538 (among the Banyoro and Bahima) ; J. Dos Santos, " Eastern Ethiopia," in G. McCall Theal's *Records of South-Eastern Africa*, vii. 191 (as to the kings of Sofala in eastern Africa). But Dos Santos's statement is doubted by Dr. McCall Theal (*op. cit.* p. 395).

Brother and sister marriages in royal families.

introduced, we may suppose, for the purpose of giving the king's son the right of succession hitherto enjoyed, under a system of female kinship, either by the son of the king's sister or by the husband of the king's daughter; for under the new rule the heir to the throne united both these characters, being at once the son of the king's sister and, through marriage with his own sister, the husband of the king's daughter. Thus the custom of brother and sister marriage in royal houses marks a transition from female to male descent of the crown.[1] In this connexion it may be significant that Cronus and Zeus themselves married their full sisters Rhea and Hera, a tradition which naturally proved a stone of stumbling to generations who had forgotten the ancient rule of policy which dictated such incestuous unions, and who had so far inverted the true relations of gods and men as to expect their deities to be edifying models of the new virtues instead of warning examples of the old vices.[2] They failed to understand that men create their gods in their own likeness, and that when the creator is a savage, his creatures the gods are savages also.

Kings' sons sacrificed instead of their fathers.

With the preceding evidence before us we may safely infer that a custom of allowing a king to kill his son, as a substitute or vicarious sacrifice for himself, would be in no way exceptional or surprising, at least in Semitic lands, where indeed religion seems at one time to have recommended or enjoined every man, as a duty that he owed to his god, to take the life of his eldest son. And it would be entirely in accordance with analogy if, long after the barbarous custom had been dropped by others, it continued to be observed by kings, who remain in many respects the representatives of a vanished world, solitary pinnacles that topple over the rising waste of waters under which the past lies buried. We have seen that in Greece two families of royal descent

[1] This explanation of the custom was anticipated by McLennan: "Another rule of chiefly succession, which has been mentioned, that which gave the chiefship to a sister's son, appears to have been nullified in some cases by an extraordinary but effective expedient—by the chief, that is, marrying his own sister" (*The Patriarchal Theory, based on the Papers of the late John Ferguson McLennan*, edited and completed by Donald McLennan (London, 1885), p. 95).

[2] Compare Cicero, *De natura deorum*, ii. 26. 66; [Plutarch], *De vita et poesi Homeri*, ii. 96; Lactantius, *Divin. Inst.* i. 10; Firmicus Maternus, *De errore profanarum religionum*, xii. 4.

remained liable to furnish human victims from their number down to a time when the rest of their fellow countrymen and countrywomen ran hardly more risk of being sacrificed than passengers in Cheapside at present run of being hurried into St. Paul's or Bow Church and immolated on the altar. A final mitigation of the custom would be to substitute con- demned criminals for innocent victims. Such a substitution is known to have taken place in the human sacrifices annually offered in Rhodes to Baal,[1] and we have seen good grounds for believing that the criminal, who perished on the cross or the gallows at Babylon, died instead of the king in whose royal robes he had been allowed to masquerade for a few days.

Substitution of condemned criminals.

[1] Porphyry, *De abstinentia*, ii. 54.

CHAPTER VII

SUCCESSION TO THE SOUL

A custom of putting kings to death at short intervals might extinguish the families from which the kings were drawn ; but this tendency would be no bar to the observance of the custom.

Many races have indulged in practices which tend directly to their extinction.

To the view that in early times, and among barbarous races, kings have frequently been put to death at the end of a short reign, it may be objected that such a custom would tend to the extinction of the royal family. The objection might be met by observing, first, that the kingship is often not confined to one family, but may be shared in turn by several ;[1] second, that the office is frequently not hereditary, but is open to men of any family, even to foreigners, who may fulfil the requisite conditions, such as marrying a princess or vanquishing the king in battle ;[2] and, third, that even if the custom did tend to the extinction of a dynasty, that is not a consideration which would prevent its observance among people less provident of the future and less heedful of human life than ourselves. Many races, like many individuals have indulged in practices which must in the end destroy them. Not to mention such customs as collective suicide and the prohibition of marriage,[3] both of which may be set down to religious mania, we have seen that the Polynesians killed two-thirds of their children.[4] In some parts of East Africa the proportion of infants massacred at birth is said to be the same. Only children born in certain presentations are allowed to live.[5] The Jagas, a conquering tribe in Angola, are reported to have put to

---

[1] See *The Magic Art and the Evolution of Kings*, ii. 292 *sqq.*

[2] See *The Magic Art and the Evolution of Kings*, ii. 269 *sqq.*

[3] Men and women of the Khlysti sect in Russia abhor marriage ; and in the sect of the Skoptsi or Eunuchs the devotees mutilate themselves. See

Sir D. Mackenzie Wallace, *Russia.* (London [1877]), p. 302. As to collective suicide, see above, pp. 43 *sqq.*

[4] Above, p. 191.

[5] Father Picarda, "Autour de Mandéra, notes sur l'Ouzigowa, l'Oukwéré et l'Oudoe (Zanguebar)," *Missions Catholiques*, xviii. (1886) p. 284.

death all their children, without exception, in order that the
women might not be cumbered with babies on the march.
They recruited their numbers by adopting boys and girls of
thirteen or fourteen years of age, whose parents they had
killed and eaten.[1]   Among the Mbaya Indians of South
America the women used to murder all their children except
the last, or the one they believed to be the last.   If one of
them had another child afterwards, she killed it.[2]   We need not
wonder that this practice entirely destroyed a branch of the
Mbaya nation, who had been for many years the most formidable enemies of the Spaniards.[3]   Among the Lengua
Indians of the Gran Chaco the missionaries discovered
what they describe as " a carefully planned system of
racial suicide, by the practice of infanticide by abortion,
and other methods."[4]   Nor is infanticide the only mode
in which a savage tribe commits suicide.   A lavish use of
the poison ordeal may be equally effective.   Some time
ago a small tribe named Uwet came down from the hill
country, and settled on the left branch of the Calabar river
in West Africa.   When the missionaries first visited the place,
they found the population considerable, distributed into three
villages.   Since then the constant use of the poison ordeal has
almost extinguished the tribe.   On one occasion the whole
population took poison to prove their innocence.   About
half perished on the spot, and the remnant, we are told,
still continuing their superstitious practice, must soon become
extinct.[5]   With such examples before us we need not
hesitate to believe that many tribes have felt no scruple or
delicacy in observing a custom which tends to wipe out a
single family.   To attribute such scruples to them is to
commit the common, the perpetually repeated mistake of

[1] *The Strange Adventures of Andrew
Battell* (Hakluyt Society, 1901), pp.
32, 84 *sq.*

[2] F. de Azara, *Voyages dans
l'Amérique Méridionale* (Paris, 1809),
ii. 115-117.   The writer affirms that
the custom was universally established
among all the women of the Mbaya
nation, as well as among the women
of other Indian nations.

[3] R. Southey, *History of Brazil*, iii.
(London, 1819) p. 385.

[4] W. Barbrooke Grubb, *An Unknown People in an Unknown Land*
(London, 1911), p. 233.

[5] Hugh Goldie, *Calabar and its
Mission*, new edition with additional
chapters by the Rev. John Taylor
Dean (Edinburgh and London, 1901),
pp. 34 *sq.*, 37 *sq.*   The preface to the
original edition of this work is dated
1890.   By this time the tribal suicide
is probably complete.

judging the savage by the standard of European civilisation. If any of my readers set out with the notion that all races of men think and act much in the same way as educated Englishmen, the evidence of superstitious belief and custom collected in the volumes of this work should suffice to disabuse him of so erroneous a prepossession.

Trans-mission of the soul of the slain king to his successor. The explanation here given of the custom of killing divine persons assumes, or at least is readily combined with, the idea that the soul of the slain divinity is transmitted to his successor. Of this transmission I have no direct proof except in the case of the Shilluk, among whom the practice of killing the divine king prevails in a typical form, and with whom it is a fundamental article of faith that the soul of the divine founder of the dynasty is immanent in every one of his slain successors.[1] But if this is the only actual example of such a belief which I can adduce, analogy seems to render it probable that a similar succession to the soul of the slain god has been supposed to take place in other instances, though direct evidence of it is wanting. For it has been already shewn that the soul of the incarnate deity is often supposed to transmigrate at death into another incarnation;[2] and if this takes place when the death is a natural one, there seems no reason why it should not take place when the death has been brought about by violence. Certainly the idea that the soul of a dying person may be transmitted to his successor is perfectly familiar to primitive peoples. In Nias the eldest son usually succeeds his father in the chieftainship. But if from any bodily or mental defect the eldest son is disqualified for ruling, the father determines in his lifetime which of his sons shall succeed him. In order, however, to establish his right of succession, it is necessary that the son upon whom his father's choice falls shall catch in his mouth or in a bag the last breath, and with it the soul, of the dying chief. For whoever catches his last breath is chief equally with the appointed successor. Hence the other brothers, and sometimes also strangers, crowd round the dying man to catch his soul as it passes. The houses in Nias are raised above the ground on posts, and it has

Trans-mission of the souls of chiefs to their sons in Nias.

[1] See above, pp. 21, 23, 26 *sq.*
[2] See *The Magic Art and the Evolution of Kings*, ii. 410 *sqq.*

happened that when the dying man lay with his face on
the floor, one of the candidates has bored a hole in the floor
and sucked in the chief's last breath through a bamboo
tube. When the chief has no son, his soul is caught in a
bag, which is fastened to an image made to represent the
deceased ; the soul is then believed to pass into the image.[1]

Amongst the Takilis or Carrier Indians of North-West
America, when a corpse was burned the priest pretended to
catch the soul of the deceased in his hands, which he closed
with many gesticulations. He then communicated the
captured soul to the dead man's successor by throwing his
hands towards and blowing upon him. The person to whom
the soul was thus communicated took the name and rank of
the deceased. On the death of a chief the priest thus filled
a responsible and influential position, for he might transmit
the soul to whom he would, though doubtless he generally
followed the regular line of succession.[2] In Guatemala, when
a great man lay at the point of death, they put a precious
stone between his lips to receive the parting soul, and
this was afterwards kept as a memorial by his nearest
kinsman or most intimate friend.[3] Algonquin women who
wished to become mothers flocked to the side of a dying
person in the hope of receiving and being impregnated by
the passing soul. Amongst the Seminoles of Florida when
a woman died in childbed the infant was held over her face
to receive her parting spirit.[4] When infants died within a
month or two of birth, the Huron Indians did not lay them
in bark coffins on poles, as they did with other corpses, but
buried them beside the paths, in order that they might
secretly enter into the wombs of passing women and be born

Succession to the soul among the American Indians and other races.

---

[1] J. T. Nieuwenhuisen en H. C. B. von
Rosenberg, "Verslag omtrent het eiland
Nias," *Verhandelingen van het Batav.
Genootschap van Kunsten en Weten-
schappen*, xxx. (1863) p. 85 ; H. von
Rosenberg, *Der Malayische Archipel*,
p. 160 ; L. N. H. A. Chatelin,
"Godsdienst en bijgeloof der Niassers,"
*Tijdschrift voor Indische Taal- Land- en
Volkenkunde*, xxvi. (1880) pp. 142 *sq.*;
H. Sundermann, "Die Insel Nias und
die Mission daselbst," *Allgemeine Mis-
sions-Zeitschrift*, xi. (1884) p. 445 ;
E. Modigliani, *Un Viaggio a Nias*, pp.

277, 479 *sq.*; *id.*, *L'Isola delle Donne*
(Milan, 1894), p. 195.

[2] Ch. Wilkes, *Narrative of the
United States Exploring Expedition*
(London, 1845), iv. 453; *United States
Exploring Expedition, Ethnography
and Philology*, by H. Hale (Phila-
delphia, 1846), p. 203.

[3] Brasseur de Bourbourg, *Histoire
des nations civilisées du Mexique et de
l'Amérique-Centrale*, ii. 574.

[4] D. G. Brinton, *Myths of the New
World*[2] (New York, 1876), pp. 270
sq.

again.[1] The Tonquinese cover the face of a dying person with a handkerchief, and at the moment when he breathes his last, they fold up the handkerchief carefully, thinking that they have caught the soul in it.[2] The Romans caught the breath of dying friends in their mouths, and so received into themselves the soul of the departed.[3] The same custom is said to be still practised in Lancashire.[4]

Succession to the soul in Africa. On the seventh day after the death of a king of Gingiro the sorcerers bring to his successor, wrapt in a piece of silk, a worm which they say comes from the nose of the dead king ; and they make the new king kill the worm by squeezing its head between his teeth.[5] The ceremony seems to be intended to convey the spirit of the deceased monarch to his successor. The Danakil or Afars of eastern Africa believe that the soul of a magician will be born again in the first male descendant of the man who was most active in attending on the dying magician in his last hours. Hence

Inspired representatives of dead kings in Africa. when a magician is ill he receives many attentions.[6] In Uganda the spirit of the king who had been the last to die manifested itself from time to time in the person of a priest, who was prepared for the discharge of this exalted function by a peculiar ceremony. When the body of the king had been embalmed and had lain for five months in the tomb, which was a house built specially for it, the head was severed from the body and laid in an ant-hill. Having been stript of flesh by the insects, the skull was washed in a particular river (the Ndyabuworu) and filled with native beer. One of the late king's priests then drank the beer out of the skull and thus became himself a vessel meet to receive the spirit of the deceased monarch. The skull was afterwards replaced in the tomb, but the lower jaw was separated from it and deposited in a jar ; and this jar, being swathed in bark-cloth and decorated with beads

---

[1] *Relations des Jésuites*, 1636, p. 130 (Canadian reprint, Quebec, 1858).

[2] A. Bastian, *Die Voelker des oestlichen Asien*, iv. 386.

[3] Servius on Virgil, *Aen.* iv. 685 ; Cicero, *In Verr.* ii. 5. 45 ; K. F. Hermann, *Lehrbuch der griechischen Privatalterthümer*, ed. H. Blümner, p. 362, note [1].

[4] J. Harland and T. T. Wilkinson, *Lancashire Folk-lore* (London, 1882), pp. 7 *sq.*

[5] *The Travels of the Jesuits in Ethiopia*, collected and historically digested by F. Balthazar Tellez (London, 1710), p. 198.

[6] Ph. Paulitschke, *Ethnographie Nordost-Afrikas, die geistige Cultur der Danâkil, Galla und Somâl* (Berlin, 1896), p. 28.

so as to look like a man, henceforth represented the late
king.   A house was built for its reception in the shape of a
beehive and divided into two rooms, an inner and an outer.
Any person might enter the outer room, but in the inner
room the spirit of the dead king was supposed to dwell.   In
front of the partition was set a throne covered with lion and
leopard skins, and fenced off from the rest of the chamber
by a rail of spears, shields, and knives, most of them made of
copper and brass, and beautifully worked.   When the priest,
who had fitted himself to receive the king's spirit, desired to
converse with the people in the king's name, he went to the
throne and addressing the spirit in the inner room informed
him of the business in hand.   Then he smoked one or two
pipes of tobacco, and in a few minutes began to rave, which
was a sign that the spirit had entered into him.   In this
condition he spoke with the voice and made known the
wishes of the late king.   When he had done so, the spirit
left him and returned into the inner room, and he himself
departed a mere man as before.[1]   Every year at the new
moon of September the king of Sofala in eastern Africa used
to perform obsequies for the kings, his predecessors, on the
top of a high mountain, where they were buried.   In the
course of the lamentations for the dead, the soul of the king
who had died last used to enter into a man who imitated
the deceased monarch, both in voice and gesture.   The living
king conversed with this man as with his dead father, con-
sulting him in regard to the affairs of the kingdom and
receiving his oracular replies.[2]   These examples shew that
provision is often made for the ghostly succession of kings
and chiefs.   In the Hausa kingdom of Daura, in Northern
Nigeria, where the kings used regularly to be put to death
on the first symptoms of failing health, the new king had to
step over the corpse of his predecessor and to be bathed in
the blood of a black ox, the skin of which then served as
a shroud for the body of the late king.[3]   The ceremony

[1] This account I received from my
friend the Rev. J. Roscoe in a letter
dated Mengo, Uganda, April 27,
1900. See his " Further Notes on the
Manners and Customs of the Baganda,"
Journal of the Anthropological Institute,
xxxii. (1902) pp. 42, 45 *sq.*, where,
however, the account is in some points
not quite so explicit.

[2] J. Dos Santos, "Eastern Ethiopia,"
in G. McCall Theal's *Records of South-
eastern Africa*, vii. 196 *sq.*

[3] See above, p. 35.

may well have been intended to convey the spirit of the dead king to his successor. Certainly we know that many primitive peoples attribute a magical virtue to the act of stepping over a person.[1]

Right of succession to the kingdom conferred by possession of personal relics of dead kings.

Sometimes it would appear that the spiritual link between a king and the souls of his predecessors is formed by the possession of some part of their persons. In southern Celebes, as we have seen, the regalia often consist of corporeal portions of deceased rajahs, which are treasured as sacred relics and confer the right to the throne.[2] Similarly among the Sakalavas of southern Madagascar a vertebra of the neck, a nail, and a lock of hair of a deceased king are placed in a crocodile's tooth and carefully kept along with the similar relics of his predecessors in a house set apart for the purpose. The possession of these relics constitutes the right to the throne. A legitimate heir who should be deprived of them would lose all his authority over the people, and on the contrary a usurper who should make himself master of the relics would be acknowledged king without dispute. It has sometimes happened that a relation of the reigning monarch has stolen the crocodile teeth with their precious contents, and then had himself proclaimed king. Accordingly, when the Hovas invaded the country, knowing the superstition of the natives, they paid less attention to the living king than to the relics of the dead, which they publicly exhibited under a strong guard on pretext of paying them the honours that were their due.[3] In antiquity, when a king of the Panebian Libyans died, his people buried the body but cut off the head, and having covered it with gold they dedicated it in a sanctuary.[4] Among the Masai of East Africa, when an important chief has been dead and buried for a year, his eldest son or other

---

[1] See *Taboo and the Perils of the Soul*, pp. 423 *sqq.*

[2] See *The Magic Art and the Evolution of Kings*, i. 362 *sqq.*

[3] A. Grandidier, "Madagascar," *Bull. de la Société de Géographie* (Paris), VIème Série, iii. (1872) pp. 402 *sq.*

[4] Nicolaus Damascenus, quoted by Stobaeus, *Florilegium*, cxxiii. 12 (*Fragmenta historicorum Graecorum*, ed. C. Müller, iii. 463). The Issedones of

Scythia used to gild the skulls of their dead fathers and offer great sacrifices to them annually (Herodotus, iv. 26); they also used the skulls as drinking-cups (Mela, ii. 1. 9). The Boii of Cisalpine Gaul cut off the head of a Roman general whom they had defeated, and having gilded the scalp they used it as a sacred vessel for the pouring of libations, and the priests drank out of it (Livy, xxiii. 24. 12).

successor removes the skull of the deceased, while he at the same time offers a sacrifice and a libation with goat's blood, milk, and honey.   He then carefully secrets the skull, the possession of which is understood to confirm him in power and to impart to him some of the wisdom of his predecessor.[1] When the Alake or king of Abeokuta in West Africa dies, the principal men decapitate his body, and placing the head in a large earthen vessel deliver it to the new sovereign ; it becomes his fetish and he is bound to pay it honours.[2] Similarly, when the Jaga or King of Cassange, in Angola, has departed this life, an official extracts a tooth from the deceased monarch and presents it to his successor, who deposits it along with the teeth of former kings in a box, which is the sole property of the crown and without which no Jaga can legitimately exercise the regal power.[3]   Sometimes, in order apparently that the new sovereign may inherit more surely the magical and other virtues of the royal line, he is required to eat a piece of his dead predecessor.   Thus at Abeokuta not only was the head of the late king presented to his successor, but the tongue was cut out and given him to eat.   Hence, when the natives wish to signify that the sovereign reigns, they say, " He has eaten the king."[4]   A custom of the same sort is still practised at Ibadan, a large town in the interior of Lagos, West Africa.   When the king dies his head is cut off and sent to his nominal suzerain, the Alafin of Oyo, the paramount king of Yoruba land ; but his heart is eaten by his successor.   This ceremony was performed a few years ago at the accession of a new king of Ibadan.[5]

Sometimes a king has to eat a portion of his predecessor.

---

[1] Sir H. Johnston, *The Uganda Protectorate* (London, 1902), ii. 828.

[2] Missionary Holley, " Étude sur les Egbas," *Missions Catholiques*, xiii. (1881) p. 353.   The writer speaks of " *le roi d'Alakei*," but this is probably a mistake or a misprint.   As to the Alake or king of Abeokuta, see Sir William Macgregor, " Lagos, Abeokuta, and the Alake," *Journal of the African Society*, No. xii. (July, 1904) pp. 471 *sq*.   Some years ago the Alake visited England and I had the honour of being presented to his Majesty by Sir William Macgregor at Cambridge.

[3] F. T. Valdez, *Six Years of a*

Traveller's Life in Western Africa, ii. 161 *sq*.

[4] Missionary Holley, in *Annales de la Propagation de la Foi*, liv. (1882) p. 87.   The "King of Ake" mentioned by the writer is the Alake or king of Abeokuta ; for Ake is the principal quarter of Abeokuta, and Alake means " Lord of Ake."   See Sir William Macgregor, *l.c.*

[5] Extracted from a letter of Mr. Harold G. Parsons, dated Lagos, September 28th, 1903, and addressed to Mr. Theodore A. Cooke of 54 Oakley Street, Chelsea, London, who was so kind as to send me the letter with leave

Succession
to the soul
of the slain
king or
priest.

Taking the whole of the preceding evidence into account, we may fairly suppose that when the divine king or priest is put to death his spirit is believed to pass into his successor. In point of fact we have seen that among the Shilluk of the White Nile, who regularly kill their divine kings, every king on his accession has to perform a ceremony which appears designed to convey to him the same sacred and worshipful spirit which animated all his predecessors, one after the other, on the throne.[1]

to make use of it. "It is usual for great chiefs to report or announce their succession to the Oni of Ife, or to the Alafin of Oyo, the intimation being accompanied by a present" (Sir W. Macgregor, *l.c.*).

[1] See above, pp. 23, 26 *sq.* Dr. E. Westermarck has suggested as an alternative to the theory in the text, "that the new king is supposed to inherit, not the predecessor's soul, but his divinity or holiness, which is looked upon in the light of a mysterious entity, temporarily seated in the ruling sovereign, but separable from him and transferable to another individual." See his article, "The Killing of the Divine King," *Man*, viii. (1908) pp. 22-24. There is a good deal to be said in favour of Dr. Westermarck's theory, which is supported in particular by the sanctity attributed to the regalia. But on the whole I see no sufficient reason to abandon the view adopted in the text, and I am confirmed in it by the Shilluk evidence, which was unknown to Dr. Westermarck when he propounded his theory.

CHAPTER VIII

THE KILLING OF THE TREE-SPIRIT

§ 1. *The Whitsuntide Mummers*

IT remains to ask what light the custom of killing the divine The single king or priest sheds upon the special subject of our enquiry. In combat of the first part of this work we saw reason to suppose that the the King of the King of the Wood at Nemi was regarded as an incarnation of Wood at a tree-spirit or of the spirit of vegetation, and that as such probably a he would be endowed, in the belief of his worshippers, with a mitigation magical power of making the trees to bear fruit, the crops custom of to grow, and so on.[1]   His life must therefore have been held him to very precious by his worshippers, and was probably hedged death at in by a system of elaborate precautions or taboos like those a fixed by which, in so many places, the life of the man-god has period. been guarded against the malignant influence of demons and sorcerers.   But we have seen that the very value attached to the life of the man-god necessitates his violent death as the only means of preserving it from the inevitable decay of age.   The same reasoning would apply to the King of the Wood ; he, too, had to be killed in order that the divine spirit, incarnate in him, might be transferred in its integrity to his successor.   The rule that he held office till a stronger should slay him might be supposed to secure both the preservation of his divine life in full vigour and its transference to a suitable successor as soon as that vigour began to be impaired.   For so long as he could maintain his position by the strong hand, it might be inferred that his natural force was not abated ; whereas his

---

[1] See *The Magic Art and the Evolution of Kings*, i. 1 *sqq.*, ii. 378 *sqq.*

defeat and death at the hands of another proved that his strength was beginning to fail and that it was time his divine life should be lodged in a less dilapidated tabernacle. This explanation of the rule that the King of the Wood had to be slain by his successor at least renders that rule perfectly intelligible. It is strongly supported by the theory and practice of the Shilluk, who put their divine king to death at the first signs of failing health, lest his decrepitude should entail a corresponding failure of vital energy on the corn, the cattle, and men.[1] Moreover, it is countenanced by the analogy of the Chitomé, upon whose life the existence of the world was supposed to hang, and who was therefore slain by his successor as soon as he shewed signs of breaking up. Again, the terms on which in later times the King of Calicut held office are identical with those attached to the office of King of the Wood, except that whereas the former might be assailed by a candidate at any time, the King of Calicut might only be attacked once every twelve years. But as the leave granted to the King of Calicut to reign so long as he could defend himself against all comers was a mitigation of the old rule which set a fixed term to his life,[2] so we may conjecture that the similar permission granted to the King of the Wood was a mitigation of an older custom of putting him to death at the end of a definite period. In both cases the new rule gave to the god-man at least a chance for his life, which under the old rule was denied him ; and people probably reconciled themselves to the change by reflecting that so long as the god-man could maintain himself by the sword against all assaults, there was no reason to apprehend that the fatal decay had set in.

Custom of killing the human representatives of the tree-spirit. The conjecture that the King of the Wood was formerly put to death at the expiry of a fixed term, without being allowed a chance for his life, will be confirmed if evidence can be adduced of a custom of periodically killing his counterparts, the human representatives of the tree-spirit, in Northern Europe. Now in point of fact such a custom has left unmistakable traces of itself in the rural festivals of the peasantry. To take examples.

At Niederpöring, in Lower Bavaria, the Whitsuntide

---

[1] See above, pp. 21 *sq.*, 27 *sq.*   [2] See above, pp. 47 *sq.*

representative of the tree-spirit—the *Pfingstl* as he was Bavarian customs of beheading the representatives of the tree-spirit at Whitsuntide. called—was clad from top to toe in leaves and flowers. On his head he wore a high pointed cap, the ends of which rested on his shoulders, only two holes being left in it for his eyes. The cap was covered with water-flowers and surmounted with a nosegay of peonies. The sleeves of his coat were also made of water-plants, and the rest of his body was enveloped in alder and hazel leaves. On each side of him marched a boy holding up one of the *Pfingstl's* arms. These two boys carried drawn swords, and so did most of the others who formed the procession. They stopped at every house where they hoped to receive a present; and the people, in hiding, soused the leaf-clad boy with water. All rejoiced when he was well drenched. Finally he waded into the brook up to his middle; whereupon one of the boys, standing on the bridge, pretended to cut off his head.[1] At Wurmlingen, in Swabia, a score of young fellows dress themselves on Whit-Monday in white shirts and white trousers, with red scarves round their waists and swords hanging from the scarves. They ride on horseback into the wood, led by two trumpeters blowing their trumpets. In the wood they cut down leafy oak branches, in which they envelop from head to foot him who was the last of their number to ride out of the village. His legs, however, are encased separately, so that he may be able to mount

---

[1] Fr. Panzer, *Beitrag zur deutschen Mythologie* (Munich, 1848-1855), i. 235 *sq.*; W. Mannhardt, *Baumkultus* (Berlin, 1875), pp. 320 *sq.* In some villages of Lower Bavaria one of the *Pfingstl's* comrades carries "the May," which is a young birch-tree wreathed and decorated. Another name for this Whitsuntide masker, both in Lower and Upper Bavaria, is the Waterbird. Sometimes he carries a straw effigy of a monstrous bird with a long neck and a wooden beak, which is thrown into the water instead of the bearer. The wooden beak is afterwards nailed to the ridge of a barn, which it is supposed to protect against lightning and fire for a whole year, till the next *Pfingstl* makes his appearance. See *Bavaria, Landes- und Volkskunde des Königreichs Bayern*, i. 375 *sq.*, 1003 *sq.*

In Silesia the Whitsuntide mummer, called the *Rauchfiess* or *Raupfiess*, sometimes stands in a leafy arbour, which is mounted on a cart and drawn about the village by four or six lads. They collect gifts at the houses and finally throw the cart and the *Rauchfiess* into a shallow pool outside the village. This is called "driving out the *Rauchfiess*." The custom used to be associated with the driving out of the cattle at Whitsuntide to pasture on the dewy grass, which was thought to make the cows yield plenty of milk. The herdsman who was the last to drive out his beasts on the morning of the day became the *Rauchfiess* in the afternoon. See P. Drechsler, *Sitte, Brauch und Volksglaube in Schlesien*, i. (Leipsic, 1903), pp. 117-123.

his horse again. Further, they give him a long artificial neck, with an artificial head and a false face on the top of it. Then a May-tree is cut, generally an aspen or beech about ten feet high ; and being decked with coloured handkerchiefs and ribbons it is entrusted to a special " Maybearer." The cavalcade then returns with music and song to the village. Amongst the personages who figure in the procession are a Moorish king with a sooty face and a crown on his head, a Dr. Iron-Beard, a corporal, and an executioner. They halt on the village green, and each of the characters makes a speech in rhyme. The executioner announces that the leaf-clad man has been condemned to death, and cuts off his false head. Then the riders race to the May-tree, which has been set up a little way off. The first man who succeeds in wrenching it from the ground as he gallops past keeps it with all its decorations. The ceremony is observed every second or third year.[1]

Killing the Wild Man in Saxony and Bohemia. In Saxony and Thüringen there is a Whitsuntide ceremony called " chasing the Wild Man out of the bush," or " fetching the Wild Man out of the Wood." A young fellow is enveloped in leaves or moss and called the Wild Man. He hides in the wood and the other lads of the village go out to seek him. They find him, lead him captive out of the wood, and fire at him with blank muskets. He falls like dead to the ground, but a lad dressed as a doctor bleeds him, and he comes to life again. At this they rejoice, and, binding him fast on a waggon, take him to the village, where they tell all the people how they have caught the Wild Man. At every house they receive a gift.[2] In the Erzgebirge the following custom was annually observed at Shrovetide about the beginning of the seventeenth century. Two men disguised as Wild Men, the one in brushwood and moss, the other in straw, were led about the streets, and at last taken to the market-place, where they were chased up and down, shot and stabbed. Before falling they reeled about with strange gestures and spirted blood on the people

[1] E. Meier, *Deutsche Sagen, Sitten und Gebräuche aus Schwaben* (Stuttgart, 1852), pp. 409-419 ; W. Mannhardt, *Baumkultus*, pp. 349 *sq.*

[2] E. Sommer, *Sagen, Märchen und Gebräuche aus Sachsen und Thüringen* (Halle, 1846), pp. 154 *sq.*; W. Mannhardt, *Baumkultus*, pp. 335 *sq.*

from bladders which they carried. When they were down, the huntsmen placed them on boards and carried them to the ale-house, the miners marching beside them and winding blasts on their mining tools as if they had taken a noble head of game.[1] A very similar Shrovetide custom is still observed near Schluckenau in Bohemia. A man dressed up as a Wild Man is chased through several streets till he comes to a narrow lane across which a cord is stretched. He stumbles over the cord and, falling to the ground, is overtaken and caught by his pursuers. The executioner runs up and stabs with his sword a bladder filled with blood which the Wild Man wears round his body; so the Wild Man dies, while a stream of blood reddens the ground. Next day a straw-man, made up to look like the Wild Man, is placed on a litter, and, accompanied by a great crowd, is taken to a pool into which it is thrown by the executioner. The ceremony is called " burying the Carnival." [2]

In Semic (Bohemia) the custom of beheading the King is observed on Whit-Monday. A troop of young people disguise themselves; each is girt with a girdle of bark and carries a wooden sword and a trumpet of willow-bark. The King wears a robe of tree-bark adorned with flowers, on his head is a crown of bark decked with flowers and branches, his feet are wound about with ferns, a mask hides his face, and for a sceptre he has a hawthorn switch in his hand. A lad leads him through the village by a rope fastened to his foot, while the rest dance about, blow their trumpets, and whistle. In every farmhouse the King is chased round the room, and one of the troop, amid much noise and outcry, strikes with his sword a blow on the King's robe of bark till it rings again. Then a gratuity is demanded.[3] The ceremony of decapitation, which is here somewhat slurred over, is carried out with a greater semblance of reality in other parts of Bohemia. Thus in some villages of the Königgrätz district on Whit-Monday the girls assemble under one lime-tree and the young men under another, all dressed

Beheading the King on Whit-Monday in Bohemia.

---

[1] W. Mannhardt, *Baumkultus*, p. 336.

[2] Reinsberg-Düringsfeld, *Fest-Kalender aus Böhmen* (Prague, N.D., preface dated 1861), p. 61; W.

Mannhardt, *Baumkultus*, pp. 336 sq.

[3] Reinsberg-Düringsfeld, *Fest-Kalender aus Böhmen*, p. 263; W. Mannhardt, *Baumkultus*, p. 343.

in their best and tricked out with ribbons. The young men twine a garland for the Queen, and the girls another for the King. When they have chosen the King and Queen they all go in procession, two and two, to the ale-house, from the balcony of which the crier proclaims the names of the King and Queen. Both are then invested with the insignia of their office and are crowned with the garlands, while the music plays up. Then some one gets on a bench and accuses the King of various offences, such as ill-treating the cattle. The King appeals to witnesses and a trial ensues, at the close of which the judge, who carries a white wand as his badge of office, pronounces a verdict of "Guilty" or "Not guilty." If the verdict is "Guilty," the judge breaks his wand, the King kneels on a white cloth, all heads are bared, and a soldier sets three or four hats, one above the other, on his Majesty's head. The judge then pronounces the word "Guilty" thrice in a loud voice, and orders the crier to behead the King. The crier obeys by striking off the King's hats with his wooden sword.[1]

Beheading the King on Whit-Monday in Bohemia. But perhaps, for our purpose, the most instructive of these mimic executions is the following Bohemian one, which has been in part described already.[2] In some places of the Pilsen district (Bohemia) on Whit-Monday the King is dressed in bark, ornamented with flowers and ribbons ; he wears a crown of gilt paper and rides a horse, which is also decked with flowers. Attended by a judge, an executioner, and other characters, and followed by a train of soldiers, all mounted, he rides to the village square, where a hut or arbour of green boughs has been erected under the May-trees, which are firs, freshly cut, peeled to the top, and dressed with flowers and ribbons. After the dames and maidens of the village have been criticised and a frog beheaded, in the way already described, the cavalcade rides to a place previously determined upon, in a straight, broad street. Here they draw up in two lines and the King takes to flight. He is given a short start and rides off at full speed, pursued by the whole troop. If they fail to catch him he remains King for another year, and his companions

---

[1] Reinsberg-Düringsfeld, *Fest-Kalender aus Böhmen*, pp. 269 *sq.*

[2] *The Magic Art and the Evolution of Kings*, ii. 86 *sq.*

must pay his score at the ale-house in the evening. But if they overtake and catch him he is scourged with hazel rods or beaten with the wooden swords and compelled to dismount. Then the executioner asks, "Shall I behead this King?" The answer is given, "Behead him"; the executioner brandishes his axe, and with the words, "One, two, three, let the King headless be!" he strikes off the King's crown. Amid the loud cries of the bystanders the King sinks to the ground; then he is laid on a bier and carried to the nearest farmhouse.[1]

In most of the personages who are thus slain in mimicry it is impossible not to recognise representatives of the tree-spirit or spirit of vegetation, as he is supposed to manifest himself in spring. The bark, leaves, and flowers in which the actors are dressed, and the season of the year at which they appear, shew that they belong to the same class as the Grass King, King of the May, Jack-in-the-Green, and other representatives of the vernal spirit of vegetation which we examined in the first part of this work.[2] As if to remove any possible doubt on this head, we find that in two cases[3] these slain men are brought into direct connexion with May-trees, which are the impersonal, as the May King, Grass King, and so forth, are the personal representatives of the tree-spirit. The drenching of the *Pfingstl* with water and his wading up to the middle into the brook are, therefore, no doubt rain-charms like those which have been already described.[4]

The leaf-clad mummers in these customs represent the tree-spirit or spirit of vegetation.

But if these personages represent, as they certainly do, the spirit of vegetation in spring, the question arises, Why kill them? What is the object of slaying the spirit of vegetation at any time and above all in spring, when his services are most wanted? The only probable answer to this question seems to be given in the explanation already proposed of the custom of killing the divine king or priest. The divine life, incarnate in a material and mortal body, is liable to be tainted and corrupted by the weakness of the frail

The tree-spirit is killed in order to prevent its decay and ensure its revival in a vigorous successor.

[1] Reinsberg-Düringsfeld, *Fest-Kalender aus Böhmen*, pp. 264 *sq.* ; W. Mannhardt, *Baumkultus*, pp. 353 *sq.*
[2] See *The Magic Art and the Evolution of Kings*, ii. 73 *sqq.*
[3] See pp. 208, 210.
[4] *The Magic Art and the Evolution of Kings*, i. 247 *sqq.*, 272 *sqq.*

medium in which it is for a time enshrined; and if it is to be saved from the increasing enfeeblement which it must necessarily share with its human incarnation as he advances in years, it must be detached from him before, or at least as soon as, he exhibits signs of decay, in order to be transferred to a vigorous successor. This is done by killing the old representative of the god and conveying the divine spirit from him to a new incarnation. The killing of the god, that is, of his human incarnation, is therefore merely a necessary step to his revival or resurrection in a better form. Far from being an extinction of the divine spirit, it is only the beginning of a purer and stronger manifestation of it. If this explanation holds good of the custom of killing divine kings and priests in general, it is still more obviously applicable to the custom of annually killing the representative of the tree-spirit or spirit of vegetation in spring. For the decay of plant life in winter is readily interpreted by primitive man as an enfeeblement of the spirit of vegetation; the spirit has, he thinks, grown old and weak and must therefore be renovated by being slain and brought to life in a younger and fresher form. Thus the killing of the representative of the tree-spirit in spring is regarded as a means to promote and quicken the growth of vegetation. For the killing of the tree-spirit is associated always (we must suppose) implicitly, and sometimes explicitly also, with a revival or resurrection of him in a more youthful and vigorous form. So in the Saxon and Thüringen custom, after the Wild Man has been shot he is brought to life again by a doctor;[1] and in the Wurmlingen ceremony there figures a Dr. Iron-Beard, who probably once played a similar part; certainly in another spring ceremony, which will be described presently, Dr. Iron-Beard pretends to restore a dead man to life. But of this revival or resurrection of the god we shall have more to say anon.

Resem-
blances
between
these
North
European
customs The points of similarity between these North European personages and the subject of our enquiry—the King of the Wood or priest of Nemi—are sufficiently striking. In these northern maskers we see kings, whose dress of bark and leaves, along with the hut of green boughs and the

---

[1] See above, p. 208.

fir-trees under which they hold their court, proclaim them
unmistakably as, like their Italian counterpart, Kings of
the Wood.   Like him they die a violent death, but like
him they may escape from it for a time by their bodily
strength and agility ; for in several of these northern customs
the flight and pursuit of the king is a prominent part of the
ceremony, and in one case at least if the king can outrun
his pursuers he retains his life and his office for another
year.   In this last case the king in fact holds office on
condition of running for his life once a year, just as the
King of Calicut in later times held office on condition of
defending his life against all comers once every twelve years,
and just as the priest of Nemi held office on condition of
defending himself against any assault at any time.   In every
one of these instances the life of the god-man is prolonged
on condition of his shewing, in a severe physical contest of
fight or flight, that his bodily strength is not decayed, and
that, therefore, the violent death, which sooner or later is inevitable, may for the present be postponed.   With regard
to flight it is noticeable that flight figured conspicuously both
in the legend and in the practice of the King of the Wood.
He had to be a runaway slave in memory of the flight of
Orestes, the traditional founder of the worship ; hence the
Kings of the Wood are described by an ancient writer as
" both strong of hand and fleet of foot." [1]   Perhaps if we
knew the ritual of the Arician grove fully we might find that
the king was allowed a chance for his life by flight, like his
Bohemian brother.   I have already conjectured that the
annual flight of the priestly king at Rome (*regifugium*) was
at first a flight of the same kind ; in other words, that he
was originally one of those divine kings who are either put
to death after a fixed period or allowed to prove by the
strong hand or the fleet foot that their divinity is vigorous
and unimpaired.[2]   One more point of resemblance may be
noted between the Italian King of the Wood and his northern
counterparts.   In Saxony and Thüringen the representative
of the tree-spirit, after being killed, is brought to life again
by a doctor.   This is exactly what legend affirmed to have

[1] Ovid, *Fasti*, iii. 271.
[2] See *The Magic Art and the Evolution of Kings*, ii. 308 *sqq.*

happened to the first King of the Wood at Nemi, Hippolytus or Virbius, who after he had been killed by his horses was restored to life by the physician Aesculapius.[1] Such a legend tallies well with the theory that the slaying of the King of the Wood was only a step to his revival or resurrection in his successor.

§ 2. *Mock Human Sacrifices*

The mock killing of the leaf-clad mummers is probably a substitute for an old custom of killing them in earnest.

In the preceding discussion it has been assumed that the mock killing of the Wild Man and of the King in North European folk-custom is a modern substitute for an ancient custom of killing them in earnest. Those who best know the tenacity of life possessed by folk-custom and its tendency, with the growth of civilisation, to dwindle from solemn ritual into mere pageant and pastime, will be least likely to question the truth of this assumption. That human sacrifices were commonly offered by the ancestors of the civilised races of North Europe, Celts, Teutons, and Slavs, is certain.[2] It is not, therefore, surprising that the modern peasant should do in mimicry what his forefathers did in reality. We know as a matter of fact that in other parts of the world mock human sacrifices have been substituted for real ones. Thus in Minahassa, a district of Celebes, human victims used to be regularly sacrificed at certain festivals, but through Dutch influence the custom was abolished and a sham sacrifice substituted for it. The victim was seated in a chair and all the usual preparations were made for sacrificing him, but at the critical moment, when the chief priest had heaved up his flashing swords (for he wielded two of them) to deal the fatal stroke, his assistants sprang forward, their hands wrapt in cloths, to grasp and arrest the descending blades. The precaution was necessary, for the priest was wound up to such a pitch of excitement that if left alone he might have consummated

Substitution of mock human sacrifices for real ones.

---

[1] See *The Magic Art and the Evolution of Kings*, i. 20.

[2] Caesar, *Bell. Gall.* vi. 16; Adam of Bremen, *Descriptio Insularum Aquilonis*, 27 (Migne's *Patrologia Latina*, cxlvi. col. 644); Olaus Magnus, *De gentium septrionalium variis conditionibus*, iii. 7; J. Grimm, *Deutsche Mythologie*,[4] i. 35 *sqq.*; F. J. Mone, *Geschichte des nordischen Heidenthums*, i. 69, 119, 120, 149, 187 *sq.*

the sacrifice. Afterwards an effigy, made out of the stem of
a banana-tree, was substituted for the human victim ; and
the blood, which might not be wanting, was supplied by
fowls.[1] Near the native town of Luba, in western Busoga,
a district of central Africa, there is a sacred tree of the
species known as *Parinarium*. Its glossy white trunk shoots
up to a height of a hundred feet before it sends out branches.
The tree is surrounded by small fetish huts and curious
arcades. Once when the dry season was drawing to an end
and the new crops were not yet ripe, the Basoga suffered
from hunger. So they came to the sacred tree in canoes, of
which the prows were decked with wreaths of yellow acacia
blossom and other flowers. Landing on the shore they
stripped themselves of their clothing and wrapped ropes
made of green creepers and leaves round their arms and
necks. At the foot of the tree they danced to an accompaniment of song. Then a little girl, about ten years old, was
brought and laid at the base of the tree as if she were to be
sacrificed. Every detail of the sacrifice was gone through in
mimicry. A slight cut was made in the child's neck, and
she was then caught up and thrown into the lake, where a
man stood ready to save her from drowning. By native
custom the girl on whom this ceremony had been performed
was dedicated to a life of perpetual virginity.[2] Captain
Bourke was informed by an old chief that the Indians of
Arizona used to offer human sacrifices at the Feast of Fire
when the days are shortest. The victim had his throat
cut, his breast opened, and his heart taken out by one
of the priests. This custom was abolished by the Mexicans,
but for a long time afterwards a modified form of it was
secretly observed as follows. The victim, generally a young
man, had his throat cut, and blood was allowed to flow
freely ; but the medicine-men sprinkled " medicine " on
the gash, which soon healed up, and the man recovered.[3]
So in the ritual of Artemis at Halae in Attica, a man's

---

[1] H. J. Tendeloo, "Verklaring van
het zoogenaamd Oud-Alfoersch Teeken-
schrift," *Mededeelingen van wege het
Nederlandsche   Zendelinggenootschap*,
xxxvi. (1892) pp. 338 *sq.*

[2] Sir H. Johnston, *The Uganda*

Protectorate (London, 1902), ii. 719 *sq.*
The writer describes the ceremony from
the testimony of an eye-witness.

[3] J. G. Bourke, *Snake Dance of the
Moquis of Arizona*, pp. 196 *sq.*

throat was cut and the blood allowed to gush out, but he
was not killed.[1]   At the funeral of a chief in Nias slaves
are sacrificed ; a little of their hair is cut off, and then they
are beheaded.   The victims are generally purchased for the
purpose, and their number is proportioned to the wealth and
power of the deceased.   But if the number required is
excessively great or cannot be procured, some of the chief's
own slaves undergo a sham sacrifice.   They are told, and
believe, that they are about to be decapitated ; their heads
are placed on a log and their necks struck with the back of
a sword.   The fright drives some of them crazy.[2]   When a
Hindoo has killed or ill-treated an ape, a bird of prey of
a certain kind, or a cobra capella, in the presence of the
worshippers of Vishnu, he must expiate his offence by the
pretended sacrifice and resurrection of a human being.   An
incision is made in the victim's arm, the blood flows, he
grows faint, falls, and feigns to die.   Afterwards he is
brought to life by being sprinkled with blood drawn from
the thigh of a worshipper of Vishnu.   The crowd of spectators is fully convinced of the reality of this simulated
death and resurrection.[3]   The Malayans, a caste of
Southern India, act as devil dancers for the purpose of
exorcising demons who have taken possession of people.
One of their ceremonies, " known as *ucchavēli*, has several
forms, all of which seem to be either survivals, or at least
imitations of human sacrifice.   One of these consists of a
mock living burial of the principal performer, who is placed
in a pit, which is covered with planks, on the top of which
a sacrifice is performed, with a fire kindled with jack wood
(*Artocarpus integrifolia*) and a plant called erinna.   In
another variety, the Malayan cuts his left forearm, and
smears his face with the blood thus drawn." [4]   In Samoa,
where every family had its god incarnate in one or more
species of animals, any disrespect shewn to the worshipful

---

[1] Euripides, *Iphigenia in Taur.* 1458
sqq.

[2] J. T. Nieuwenhuisen en H. C. B.
von Rosenberg, " Verslag omtrent het
eiland Nias," *Verhandelingen van het
Batav. Genootschap van Kunsten en
Wetenschappen*, xxx. (1863) p. 43 ;
E. Modigliani, *Un Viaggio a Nias*

(Milan, 1890), pp. 282 *sq.*

[3] J. A. Dubois, *Mœurs, institutions
et cérémonies des peuples de l'Inde*
(Paris, 1825), i. 151 *sq.*

[4] E. Thurston, *Castes and Tribes
of Southern India* (Madras, 1909),
iv. 437, quoting Mr. A. R. Loftus-
Tottenham.

animal, either by members of the kin or by a stranger in their presence, had to be atoned for by pretending to bake one of the family in a cold oven as a burnt sacrifice to appease the wrath of the offended god. For example, if a stranger staying in a household whose god was incarnate in cuttle-fish were to catch and cook one of these creatures, or if a member of the family had been present where a cuttle-fish was eaten, the family would meet in solemn conclave and choose a man or woman to go and lie down in a cold oven, where he would be covered over with leaves, just as if he were really being baked. While this mock sacrifice was being carried out the family prayed: "O bald-headed Cuttle-fish! forgive what has been done, it was all the work of a stranger." If they had not thus abased themselves before the divine cuttle-fish, he would undoubtedly have come and been the death of somebody by making a cuttle-fish to grow in his inside.[1]

Sometimes, as in Minahassa, the pretended sacrifice is carried out, not on a living person, but on an effigy. At the City of the Sun in ancient Egypt three men used to be sacrificed every day, after the priests had stripped and examined them, like calves, to see whether they were without blemish and fit for the altar. But King Amasis ordered waxen images to be substituted for the human victims.[2] An Indian law-book, the *Calica Puran*, prescribes that when the sacrifice of lions, tigers, or human beings is required, an image of a lion, tiger, or man shall be made with butter, paste, or barley meal, and sacrificed instead.[3] Some of the Gonds of India formerly offered human sacrifices; they now sacrifice straw-men, which are found to answer the purpose just as well.[4] Colonel Dalton was told that in some of their villages the Bhagats "annually make an image of a man in wood, put clothes and ornaments on it, and present it before the altar of a Mahádeo. The person who officiates as priest on the occasion says: 'O Mahádeo, we sacrifice this man to

Mock human sacrifices carried out in effigy.

[1] G. Turner, *Samoa*, pp. 31 *sq.*; compare pp. 38, 58, 59, 69 *sq.*, 72.
[2] Porphyry, *De abstinentia*, ii. 55, citing Manetho as his authority.
[3] "The Rudhirádhyáyă, or sanguinary chapter," translated from the

Calica Puran by W. C. Blaquiere, in *Asiatick Researches*, v. 376 (8vo ed., London, 1807).
[4] E. T. Dalton, *Descriptive Ethnology of Bengal* (Calcutta, 1872), p. 281.

Mock
human
sacrifices
carried
out in
effigy.
you according to ancient customs. Give us rain in due season, and a plentiful harvest.' Then with one stroke of the axe the head of the image is struck off, and the body is removed and buried." [1]   Formerly, when a Siamese army was about to take the field a condemned criminal representing the enemy was put to death, but a humane king caused a puppet to be substituted for the man. The effigy is felled by the blow of an axe, and if it drops at the first stroke, the omen is favourable. [2]   In the East Indian island of Siaoo or Siauw, one of the Sangi group, a child stolen from a neighbouring island used to be sacrificed every year to the spirit of a volcano in order that there might be no eruption. The victim was slowly tortured to death in the temple by a priestess, who cut off the child's ears, nose, fingers, and so on, then consummated the sacrifice by splitting open the breast. The spectacle was witnessed by hundreds of people, and feasting and cock-fighting went on for nine days afterwards. In course of time the annual human victim was replaced by a wooden puppet, which was cut to pieces in the same manner. [3]   The Kayans of Borneo used to kill slaves at the death of a chief and nail them to the tomb, in order that they might accompany the chief on his long journey to the other world and paddle the canoe in which he must travel. This is no longer done, but instead they put up a wooden figure of a man at the head and another of a woman at the foot of the chief's coffin as it lies in state before the funeral. And a small wooden image of a man is usually fixed on the top of the tomb to row the canoe for the dead chief. [4]   In ancient times human sacrifices used to be offered at the graves of Mikados and princes of Japan, the personal attendants of the deceased being buried alive within the precincts of the tomb. But a humane emperor ordered that clay images should thenceforth be substituted for live men and women. One of these images is now in the

[1] E. T. Dalton, *op. cit.* pp. 258 *sq.*

[2] Mgr. Bruguière, in *Annales de l'Association de la Propagation de la Foi*, v. (1831) p. 201.

[3] B. C. A. J. van Dinter, "Eenige geographische en ethnographische aanteekeningen betreffende het eiland Siaoe," *Tijdschrift voor Indische Taal- Land- en Volkenkunde*, xli. (1899) p. 379.

[4] Ch. Hose and W. McDougall, "The Relations between Men and Animals in Sarawak," *Journal of the Anthropological Institute*, xxxi. (1901) p. 208.

British Museum.[1] The Toboongkoos of central Celebes, who are reported still to carry home as trophies the heads of their slain enemies, resort to the following cure for certain kinds of sickness. The heathen priestess cuts the likeness of a human head out of the sheath of a sago-leaf and sets it up on three sticks in the courtyard of the house. The patient, arrayed in his or her best clothes, is then brought down into the court and remains there while women dance and sing round the artificial head, and men perform sham fights with shield, spear, and bow, just as they did, or perhaps still do, when they have brought back a human head from a raid. After that the sick man is taken back to the house, and an improvement in his health is confidently expected.[2] In this ceremony the sham head is doubtless a substitute for a real one.

With these mock sacrifices of human lives we may compare mimic sacrifices of other kinds. In southern India, as in many parts of the world, it used to be customary to sacrifice joints of the fingers on certain occasions. Thus among the Morasas, when a grandchild was born in the family, the wife of the eldest son of the grandfather must have the last two joints of the third and fourth fingers of her right hand amputated at a temple of Bhairava. The amputation was performed by the village carpenter with a chisel. Nowadays, the custom having been forbidden by the English Government, the sacrifice is performed in mimicry. Some people stick gold or silver pieces with flour paste to the ends of their fingers and then cut or pull them off. Others tie flowers round the fingers that used to be amputated, and go through a pantomime of cutting the fingers by putting a chisel on the joint and then taking it away. Others again twist gold wires in the shape of rings round their fingers. These the carpenter removes and appropriates.[3] In Niué or Savage Island, in the South

Mimic sacrifices of various kinds.

Mimic sacrifices of fingers.

---

[1] W. G. Aston, *Shinto* (London, 1905), pp. 56 *sq.*

[2] A. C. Kruijt, "Eenige ethno-grafische aanteekeningen omtrent de Toboengkoe en de Tomori," *Mededeelingen van wege het Nederlandsche Zendelinggenootschap*, xliv. (1900) p. 222.

[3] E. Thurston, "Deformity and Mutilation," *Madras Government Museum, Bulletin*, vol. iv. No. 3 (Madras, 1903), pp. 193-196. As to the custom of sacrificing joints of fingers, see my note on Pausanias, viii. 34. 2, vol. iv. pp. 354 *sqq.* To the evidence there adduced add P. J. de

Pacific, the following custom continued till lately to be observed.   When a boy was a few weeks old the men assembled, and a feast was made.   On the village square an awning was rigged up, and the child was laid on the ground under it.   An old man then approached it, and performed the operation of circumcision on the infant in dumb show with his forefinger.   No child was regarded as a full-born member of the tribe till he had been subjected to this rite. The natives say that real circumcision was never performed in their island ; but as it was commonly practised in Fiji, Tonga, and Samoa, we may assume that its imitation in Niué was a substitute, introduced at some time or other, for the actual operation.[1]   Similarly when an adult Hindoo joins the sect of the Daira or Mahadev Mohammedans in Mysore, a mock rite of circumcision is performed on him instead of the real operation.   A betel leaf is wrapped round the male member of the neophyte and the loose end of the leaf is snipped off instead of the prepuce.[2]

§ 3. *Burying the Carnival*

It has been
customary
to kill
animal
gods and
corn gods
as well as
tree-spirits.
Thus far I have offered an explanation of the rule which required that the priest of Nemi should be slain by his successor.   The explanation claims to be no more than probable ; our scanty knowledge of the custom and of its

Smet, *Western Missions and Missionaries* (New York, 1863), p. 135 ; G. B. Grinnell, *Blackfoot Lodge Tales*, pp. 194, 258 ; A. d'Orbigny, *L'Homme américain*, ii. 24 ; J. Williams, *Narrative of Missionary Enterprises in the South Sea Islands*, pp. 470 *sq.* ; J. Mathew, *Eaglehawk and Crow* (London and Melbourne, 1899), p. 120 ; A. W. Howitt, *Native Tribes of South-East Australia*, pp. 746 *sq.* ; L. Degrandpré, *Voyage à la côte occidentale d'Afrique* (Paris, 1801), ii. 93 *sq.* ; Dudley Kidd, *The Essential Kaffir*, pp. 203, 262 *sq.* ; G. W. Stow, *Native Races of South Africa* (London, 1905), pp. 129, 152 ; *Lettres édifiantes et curieuses*, Nouvelle Édition, ix. 369, xii. 371 ; *Annales de la Propagation de la Foi*, xiii. (1841) p.

20 ; *id.*, xiv. (1842) pp. 68, 192 ; *id.*, xvii. (1845) pp. 12, 13 ; *id.*, xviii. (1846) p. 6 ; *id.*, xxiii. (1851) p. 314 ; *id.*, xxxii. (1860) pp. 95 *sq.* ; *Indian Antiquary*, xxiv. (1895) p. 303 ; *Missions Catholiques*, xxix. (1897) p. 90 ; *Zeitschrift für Ethnologie*, xxxii. (1900) p. 81.   The objects of this mutilation were various.   In ancient Athens it was customary to cut off the hand of a suicide and bury it apart from his body (Aeschines, *Contra Ctesiph.* § 244, p. 193, ed. F. Franke), perhaps to prevent his ghost from attacking the living.

[1] Basil C. Thomson, *Savage Island* (London, 1902), pp. 92 *sq.*

[2] E. Thurston, *Ethnographic Notes in Southern India* (Madras, 1906), p. 390.

history forbids it to be more. But its probability will be augmented in proportion to the extent to which the motives and modes of thought which it assumes can be proved to have operated in primitive society. Hitherto the god with whose death and resurrection we have been chiefly concerned has been the tree-god. But if I can shew that the custom of killing the god and the belief in his resurrection originated, or at least existed, in the hunting and pastoral stage of society, when the slain god was an animal, and that it survived into the agricultural stage, when the slain god was the corn or a human being representing the corn, the probability of my explanation will have been considerably increased. This I shall attempt to do in the sequel, and in the course of the discussion I hope to clear up some obscurities which still remain, and to answer some objections which may have suggested themselves to the reader.

We start from the point at which we left off—the spring customs of European peasantry. Besides the ceremonies already described there are two kindred sets of observances in which the simulated death of a divine or supernatural being is a conspicuous feature. In one of them the being whose death is dramatically represented is a personification of the Carnival ; in the other it is Death himself. The former ceremony falls naturally at the end of the Carnival, either on the last day of that merry season, namely Shrove Tuesday, or on the first day of Lent, namely Ash Wednesday. The date of the other ceremony—the Carrying or Driving out of Death, as it is commonly called —is not so uniformly fixed. Generally it is the fourth Sunday in Lent, which hence goes by the name of Dead Sunday ; but in some places the celebration falls a week earlier, in others, as among the Czechs of Bohemia, a week later, while in certain German villages of Moravia it is held on the first Sunday after Easter. Perhaps, as has been suggested, the date may originally have been variable, depending on the appearance of the first swallow or some other herald of the spring. Some writers regard the ceremony as Slavonic in its origin. Grimm thought it was a festival of the New Year with the old Slavs, who began

Customs of burying the Carnival and carrying out Death.

their year in March.[1]   We shall first take examples of the mimic death of the Carnival, which always falls before the other in the calendar.

Effigy of the Carnival burnt at Frosinone in Latium.

At Frosinone, in Latium, about half-way between Rome and Naples, the dull monotony of life in a provincial Italian town is agreeably broken on the last day of the Carnival by the ancient festival known as the *Radica*.   About four o'clock in the afternoon the town band, playing lively tunes and followed by a great crowd, proceeds to the Piazza del Plebiscito, where is the Sub-Prefecture as well as the rest of the Government buildings.   Here, in the middle of the square, the eyes of the expectant multitude are greeted by the sight of an immense car decked with many-coloured festoons and drawn by four horses.   Mounted on the car is a huge chair, on which sits enthroned the majestic figure of the Carnival, a man of stucco about nine feet high with a rubicund and smiling countenance.   Enormous boots, a tin helmet like those which grace the heads of officers of the Italian marine, and a coat of many colours embellished with strange devices, adorn the outward man of this stately personage.   His left hand rests on the arm of the chair, while with his right he gracefully salutes the crowd, being moved to this act of civility by a string which is pulled by a man who modestly shrinks from publicity under the mercy-seat.   And now the crowd, surging excitedly round the car, gives vent to its feelings in wild cries of joy, gentle and simple being mixed up together and all dancing furiously the *Saltarello*.   A special feature of the festival is that every one must carry in his hand what is called a *radica* (" root "), by which is meant a huge leaf of the aloe or rather the agave.   Any one who ventured into the crowd without

---

[1] J. Grimm, *Deutsche Mythologie*,[4] ii. 645 ; K. Haupt, *Sagenbuch der Lausitz*, ii. 58 ; Reinsberg - Düringsfeld, *Fest-Kalender aus Böhmen*, pp. 86 *sq.* ; *id.*, *Das festliche Jahr*, pp. 77 *sq.*; *Bavaria*, *Landes- und Volkskunde des Königreichs Bayern*, iii. 958 · *sq.* ; Sepp, *Die Religion der alten Deutschen* (Munich, 1890), pp. 67 *sq.*; W. Müller, *Beiträge zur Volkskunde der Deutschen in Mähren* (Vienna and Olmutz, 1893), pp. 258, 353.   The fourth Sunday in Lent is also known as Mid - Lent, because it falls in the middle of Lent, or as *Laetare* from the first word of the liturgy for that day.   In the Roman calendar it is the Sunday of the Rose (*Domenica rosae*), because on that day the Pope consecrates a golden rose, which he presents to some royal lady. In one German village of Transylvania the Carrying out of Death takes place on Ascension Day.   See below, pp. 248 *sq.*

such a leaf would be unceremoniously hustled out of it,
unless indeed he bore as a substitute a large cabbage at the
end of a long stick or a bunch of grass curiously plaited.
When the multitude, after a short turn, has escorted the slow-
moving car to the gate of the Sub-Prefecture, they halt, and
the car, jolting over the uneven ground, rumbles into the
courtyard. A hush now falls on the crowd, their subdued
voices sounding, according to the description of one who has
heard them, like the murmur of a troubled sea. All eyes
are turned anxiously to the door from which the Sub-Prefect
himself and the other representatives of the majesty of the
law are expected to issue and pay their homage to the hero
of the hour. A few moments of suspense and then a storm
of cheers and hand-clapping salutes the appearance of the
dignitaries, as they file out and, descending the staircase,
take their place in the procession. The hymn of the
Carnival is now thundered out, after which, amid a deafening
roar, aloe leaves and cabbages are whirled aloft and descend
impartially on the heads of the just and the unjust, who
lend fresh zest to the proceedings by engaging in a free
fight. When these preliminaries have been concluded to the
satisfaction of all concerned, the procession gets under weigh.
The rear is brought up by a cart laden with barrels of wine
and policemen, the latter engaged in the congenial task of
serving out wine to all who ask for it, while a most inter-
necine struggle, accompanied by a copious discharge of yells,
blows, and blasphemy, goes on among the surging crowd
at the cart's tail in their anxiety not to miss the glorious
opportunity of intoxicating themselves at the public expense.
Finally, after the procession has paraded the principal streets
in this majestic manner, the effigy of Carnival is taken to
the middle of a public square, stripped of his finery, laid
on a pile of wood, and burnt amid the cries of the multitude,
who thundering out once more the song of the Carnival
fling their so-called " roots " on the pyre and give themselves
up without restraint to the pleasures of the dance.[1]

---

[1] G. Targioni - Tozzetti, *Saggio di
novelline, canti ed usanze popolari
della Ciociaria* (Palermo, 1891), pp.
89-95. At Palermo an effigy of the
Carnival (*Nannu*) was burnt at midnight on Shrove Tuesday 1878. See
G. Pitrè, *Usi e costumi, credenze e
pregiudizi del popolo siciliano*, i. 117-
119; G. Trede, *Das Heidentum in
der römischen Kirche*, iii. 11, note *

In the Abruzzi a pasteboard figure of the Carnival is
carried by four grave-diggers with pipes in their mouths and
bottles of wine slung at their shoulder-belts.   In front walks
the wife of the Carnival, dressed in mourning and dissolved
in tears.   From time to time the company halts, and while
the wife addresses the sympathising public, the grave-diggers
refresh the inner man with a pull at the bottle.   In the open
square the mimic corpse is laid on a pyre, and to the roll of
drums, the shrill screams of the women, and the gruffer
cries of the men a light is set to it.   While the figure burns,
chestnuts are thrown about among the crowd.   Sometimes
the Carnival is represented by a straw-man at the top of a
pole which is borne through the town by a troop of
mummers in the course of the afternoon.   When evening
comes on, four of the mummers hold out a quilt or sheet
by the corners, and the figure of the Carnival is made to
tumble into it.   The procession is then resumed, the
performers weeping crocodile tears and emphasising the
poignancy of their grief by the help of saucepans and dinner
bells.   Sometimes, again, in the Abruzzi the dead Carnival
is personified by a living man who lies in a coffin, attended
by another who acts the priest and dispenses holy water in
great profusion from a bathing tub.[1]   In Malta the death of
the Carnival used to be mourned by women on the last day
of the merry festival.   Clad from head to foot in black
mantles, they carried through the streets of the city the linen
effigy of a corpse, stuffed with straw or hay and decked with
leaves and oranges.   As they carried it, they chanted dirges,

[1] A. de Nino, *Usi e costumi abruzzesi*, ii. 198-200.   The writer omits to mention the date of these celebrations. No doubt it is either Shrove Tuesday or Ash Wednesday.   Compare G. Finamore, *Credenze, usi e costumi abruzzesi* (Palermo, 1890), p. 111. In some parts of Piedmont an effigy of Carnival is burnt on the evening of Shrove Tuesday; in others they set fire to tall poplar trees, which, stript of their branches and surmounted by banners, have been set up the day before in public places.   These trees go by the name of *Scarli*.   See G. di Giovanni, *Usi, credenze e pregiudizi del Canavese* (Palermo, 1889), pp. 161, 164 *sq*.   For other accounts of the ceremony of the death of the Carnival, represented either by a puppet or a living person, in Italy and Sicily, see G. Pitrè, *Usi e costumi, credenze e pregiudizi del popolo siciliano*, i. 96-100; G. Amalfi, *Tradizioni ed usi nella Penisola Sorrentina* (Palermo, 1890), pp. 40, 42.   It has been rightly observed by Pitrè (*op. cit.* p. 96), that the personification of the Carnival is doubtless the lineal descendant of some mythical personage of remote Greek and Roman antiquity.

stopping after every verse to howl like professional mourners. The custom came to an end about the year 1737.[1]

At Lerida, in Catalonia, the funeral of the Carnival was witnessed by an English traveller in 1877. On the last Sunday of the Carnival a grand procession of infantry, cavalry, and maskers of many sorts, some on horseback and some in carriages, escorted the grand car of His Grace Pau Pi, as the effigy was called, in triumph through the principal streets. For three days the revelry ran high, and then at midnight on the last day of the Carnival the same procession again wound through the streets, but under a different aspect and for a different end. The triumphal car was exchanged for a hearse, in which reposed the effigy of his dead Grace : a troop of maskers, who in the first procession had played the part of Students of Folly with many a merry quip and jest, now, robed as priests and bishops, paced slowly along holding aloft huge lighted tapers and singing a dirge. All the mummers wore crape, and all the horsemen carried blazing flambeaux. Down the high street, between the lofty, many-storeyed and balconied houses, where every window, every balcony, every housetop was crammed with a dense mass of spectators, all dressed and masked in fantastic gorgeousness, the procession took its melancholy way. Over the scene flashed and played the shifting cross-lights and shadows from the moving torches : red and blue Bengal lights flared up and died out again ; and above the trampling of the horses and the measured tread of the marching multitude rose the voices of the priests chanting the requiem, while the military bands struck in with the solemn roll of the muffled drums. On reaching the principal square the procession halted, a burlesque funeral oration was pronounced over the defunct Pau Pi, and the lights were extinguished. Immediately the devil and his angels darted from the crowd, seized the body and fled away with it, hotly pursued by the whole multitude, yelling, screaming, and cheering. Naturally the fiends were overtaken and dispersed ; and the sham corpse, rescued from their clutches, was laid in a grave that had been made ready for its

Burial of the Carnival at Lerida in Spain.

---

[1] R. Wünsch, *Das Frühlingsfest der Insel Malta* (Leipsic, 1902), pp. 29 *sq.*, quoting Ciantar's supplements to Abelas's *Malta illustrata*.

reception.   Thus the Carnival of 1877 at Lerida died and
was buried.[1]

Funeral
of the
Carnival
in France.

A ceremony of the same sort is observed in Provence on
Ash Wednesday.   An effigy called Caramantran, whimsically
attired, is drawn in a chariot or borne on a litter, accompanied by the populace in grotesque costumes, who carry
gourds full of wine and drain them with all the marks, real
or affected, of intoxication.   At the head of the procession
are some men disguised as judges and barristers, and a tall
gaunt personage who masquerades as Lent; behind them
follow young people mounted on miserable hacks and attired
as mourners who pretend to bewail the fate that is in store
for Caramantran.   In the principal square the procession
halts, the tribunal is constituted, and Caramantran placed
at the bar.   After a formal trial he is sentenced to death
amid the groans of the mob; the barrister who defended
him embraces his client for the last time: the officers of
justice do their duty: the condemned is set with his back to
a wall and hurried into eternity under a shower of stones.
The sea or a river-receives his mangled remains.[2]   At Lussac
in the department of Vienne young people, attired in long
mourning robes and with woebegone countenances, carry an
effigy down to the river on Ash Wednesday and throw it
into the river, crying, " Carnival is dead ! Carnival is dead ! "[3]
Throughout nearly the whole of the Ardennes it was and
still is customary on Ash Wednesday to burn an effigy which
is supposed to represent the Carnival, while appropriate verses
are sung round about the blazing figure.   Very often an
attempt is made to fashion the effigy in the likeness of the
husband who is reputed to be least faithful to his wife of
any in the village.   As might perhaps have been anticipated,
the distinction of being selected for portraiture under these
painful circumstances has a slight tendency to breed domestic
jars, especially when the portrait is burnt in front of the house

---

[1] J. S. Campion, *On Foot in Spain*
(London, 1879), pp. 291-295.

[2] A. de Nore, *Coutumes, mythes et
traditions des provinces de France*
(Paris and Lyons, 1846), pp. 37 *sq.*
The name Caramantran is thought to
be compounded of *carême entrant*,

"Lent entering."   It is said that the
effigy of Caramantran is sometimes
burnt (E. Cortet, *Essai sur les fêtes
religieuses*, Paris, 1867, p. 107).

[3] L. Pineau, *Folk-lore du Poitou*
(Paris, 1892), p. 493.

of the gay deceiver whom it represents, while a powerful
chorus of caterwauls, groans, and other melodious sounds
bears public testimony to the opinion which his friends and
neighbours entertain of his private virtues.   In some villages
of the Ardennes a young man of flesh and blood, dressed up
in hay and straw, used to act the part of Shrove Tuesday
(*Mardi Gras*), as the personification of the Carnival is often
called in France after the last day of the period which he
personates.   He was brought before a mock tribunal, and
being condemned to death was placed with his back to
a wall, like a soldier at a military execution, and fired at
with blank cartridges.   At Vrigne-aux-Bois one of these
harmless buffoons, named Thierry, was accidentally killed
by a wad that had been left in a musket of the firing-party.
When poor Shrove Tuesday dropped under the fire, the
applause was loud and long, he did it so naturally ; but
when he did not get up again, they ran to him and found
him a corpse.   Since then there have been no more of these
mock executions in the Ardennes.[1]   In Franche-Comté
people used to make an effigy of Shrove Tuesday on Ash
Wednesday, and carry it about the streets to the accompaniment of songs.   Then they brought it to the public square,
where the offender was tried in front of the town-hall.
Judges muffled in old red curtains and holding big books in
their hands pronounced sentence of death.   The mode of
execution varied with the place.   Sometimes it was burning,
sometimes drowning, sometimes decapitation.   In the last
case the effigy was provided with tubes of blood, which
spouted gore at the critical moment, making a profound
impression on the minds of children, some of whom wept
bitterly at the sight.   Meantime the onlookers uttered
piercing cries and appeared to be plunged in the deepest
grief.   The proceedings generally wound up in the evening
with a ball, which the young married people were obliged
to provide for the public entertainment ; otherwise their
slumbers were apt to be disturbed by the discordant notes of
a cat's concert chanted under their windows.[2]

(margin note: Execution of Shrove Tuesday in the Ardennes and Franche-Comté.*)*

[1] A. Meyrac, *Traditions, légendes et
contes des Ardennes* (Charleville, 1890),
p. 63.   According to the writer, the
custom of burning an effigy of Shrove
Tuesday or the Carnival is pretty
general in France.

[2] Ch. Beauquier, *Les Mois en
Franche-Comté* (Paris, 1900), p. 30.

Burial of
Shrove
Tuesday in
Normandy. In Normandy on the evening of Ash Wednesday it used
to be the custom to hold a celebration called the Burial of
Shrove Tuesday.   A squalid effigy scantily clothed in rags,
a battered old hat crushed down on his dirty face, his great
round paunch stuffed with straw, represented the disreputable
old rake who after a long course of dissipation was now
about to suffer for his sins.   Hoisted on the shoulders of a
sturdy fellow, who pretended to stagger under the burden,
this popular personification of the Carnival promenaded the
streets for the last time in a manner the reverse of triumphal.
Preceded by a drummer and accompanied by a jeering rabble,
among whom the urchins and all the tag-rag and bobtail of
the town mustered in great force, the figure was carried
about by the flickering light of torches to the discordant din
of shovels and tongs, pots and pans, horns and kettles,
mingled with hootings, groans, and hisses.   From time to
time the procession halted, and a champion of morality
accused the broken-down old sinner of all the excesses he
had committed and for which he was now about to be burned
alive.   The culprit, having nothing to urge in his own
defence, was thrown on a heap of straw, a torch was put to
it, and a great blaze shot up, to the delight of the children
who frisked round it screaming out some old popular verses
about the death of the Carnival.   Sometimes the effigy was
Burning
Shrove
Tuesday at
Saint-Lô. rolled down the slope of a hill before being burnt.[1]   At
Saint-Lô the ragged effigy of Shrove Tuesday was followed
by his widow, a big burly lout dressed as a woman with a
crape veil, who emitted sounds of lamentation and woe in a
stentorian voice.   After being carried about the streets on a
litter attended by a crowd of maskers, the figure was thrown
into the River Vire.   The final scene has been graphically
described by Madame Octave Feuillet as she witnessed it in
her childhood some fifty years ago.   " My parents invited
friends to see, from the top of the tower of Jeanne Couillard,
the funeral procession passing.   It was there that, quaffing
lemonade—the only refreshment allowed because of the fast

In Beauce and Perche the burning
or burial of Shrove Tuesday used
to be represented in effigy, but the
custom has now disappeared.   See
F. Chapiseau, *Le Folk-lore de la Beauce*
et du Perche (Paris, 1902), i. 320
sq.

[1] J. Lecœur, *Esquisses du Bocage
Normand* (Condé-sur-Noireau, 1883-
1887), ii. 148-150.

—we witnessed at nightfall a spectacle of which I shall always preserve a lively recollection.   At our feet flowed the Vire under its old stone bridge.   On the middle of the bridge lay the figure of Shrove Tuesday on a litter of leaves, surrounded by scores of maskers dancing, singing, and carrying torches.   Some of them in their motley costumes ran along the parapet like fiends.   The rest, worn out with their revels, sat on the posts and dozed.   Soon the dancing stopped, and some of the troop, seizing a torch, set fire to the effigy, after which they flung it into the river with redoubled shouts and clamour.   The man of straw, soaked with resin, floated away burning down the stream of the Vire, lighting up with its funeral fires the woods on the bank and the battlements of the old castle in which Louis XI. and Francis I. had slept.   When the last glimmer of the blazing phantom had vanished, like a falling star, at the end of the valley, every one withdrew, crowd and maskers alike, and we quitted the ramparts with our guests.   As we returned home my father sang gaily the old popular song :—

> ' *Shrove Tuesday is dead and his wife has got*
> *His shabby pocket-handkerchief and his cracked old pot.*
> *Sing high, sing low,*
> *Shrove Tuesday will come back no more.*'

' He will come back !   He will come back ! ' we cried warmly, clapping our hands ; and he did come back next year, and I think I should see him still if, after the lapse of half a century, I returned to the land of my birth."[1]

In Upper Brittany the burial of Shrove Tuesday or the Carnival is sometimes performed in a ceremonious manner. Four young fellows carry a straw-man or one of their companions, and are followed by a funeral procession.   A show is made of depositing the pretended corpse in the grave, after which the bystanders make believe to mourn, crying out in melancholy tones, "Ah ! my poor little Shrove Tuesday ! " The boy who played the part of Shrove Tuesday bears the name for the whole year.[2]   At Lesneven in Lower Brittany it was formerly the custom on Ash Wednesday to burn a

Burial of Shrove Tuesday or the Carnival in Brittany.

[1] Madame Octave Feuillet, *Quelques années de ma vie*[5] (Paris, 1895), pp. 59-61.

[2] P. Sébillot, *Coutumes populaires de la Haute-Bretagne* (Paris, 1886), pp. 227 *sq.*

straw-man, covered with rags, after he had been promenaded about the town.   He was followed by a representative of Shrove Tuesday clothed with sardines and cods' tails.[1]   At Pontaven in Finistère an effigy representing the Carnival used to be thrown from the quay into the sea on the morning of Ash Wednesday.[2]   At La Rochelle the porters and sailors carried about a man of straw representing Shrove Tuesday, then burned it on Ash Wednesday and flung the ashes into the sea.[3]   In Saintonge and Aunis, which correspond roughly to the modern departments of Charente, children used to drown or burn a figure of the Carnival on the morning of Ash Wednesday.[4]   The beginning of Lent in England was formerly marked by a custom which has now fallen into disuse.   A figure, made up of straw and cast-off clothes, was drawn or carried through the streets amid much noise and merriment ; after which it was either burnt, shot at, or thrown down a chimney.   This image went by the name of Jack o' Lent, and was by some supposed to represent Judas Iscariot.[5]

Burying the Carnival in Germany and Austria.

A Bohemian form of the custom of " Burying the Carnival " has been already described.[6]   The following Swabian form is obviously similar.   In the neighbourhood of Tübingen on Shrove Tuesday a straw-man, called the Shrovetide Bear, is made up ; he is dressed in a pair of old trousers, and a fresh black-pudding or two squirts filled with blood are inserted in his neck.   After a formal condemnation he is beheaded, laid in a coffin, and on Ash Wednesday is buried in the churchyard.   This is called " Burying the Carnival."[7] Amongst some of the Saxons of Transylvania the Carnival is hanged.   Thus at Braller on Ash Wednesday or Shrove Tuesday two white and two chestnut horses draw a sledge on which is placed a straw-man swathed in a white cloth ;

---

[1] A. de Nore, *Coutumes, mythes et traditions des Provinces de France*, p. 206.

[2] P. Sébillot, *Le Folk-lore de France*, ii. (Paris, 1905) p. 170.

[3] P. Sébillot, *l.c.*

[4] J. L. M. Nogues, *Les Mœurs d'autrefois en Saintonge et en Aunis* (Saintes, 1891), p. 60.   As to the trial and condemnation of the Carnival on Ash Wednesday in France, see further Bérenger-Féraud, *Superstitions et survivances*, iv. 52 *sq.*

[5] T. F. Thiselton Dyer, *British Popular Customs* (London, 1876), p. 93.

[6] See above, p. 209.

[7] E. Meier, *Deutsche Sagen, Sitten und Gebräuche aus Schwaben*, p. 371.

beside him is a cart-wheel which is kept turning round. Two lads disguised as old men follow the sledge lamenting. The rest of the village lads, mounted on horseback and decked with ribbons, accompany the procession, which is headed by two girls crowned with evergreen and drawn in a waggon or sledge. A trial is held under a tree, at which lads disguised as soldiers pronounce sentence of death. The two old men try to rescue the straw-man and to fly with him, but to no purpose; he is caught by the two girls and handed over to the executioner, who hangs him on a tree. In vain the old men try to climb up the tree and take him down; they always tumble down, and at last in despair they throw themselves on the ground and weep and howl for the hanged man. An official then makes a speech in which he declares that the Carnival was condemned to death because he had done them harm, by wearing out their shoes and making them tired and sleepy.[1] At the " Burial of Carnival " in Lechrain, a man dressed as a woman in black clothes is carried on a litter or bier by four men; he is lamented over by men disguised as women in black clothes, then thrown down before the village dung-heap, drenched with water, buried in the dung-heap, and covered with straw.[2] Similarly in Schörzingen, near Schömberg, the " Carnival (Shrovetide) Fool " was carried all about the village on a bier, preceded by a man dressed in white, and followed by a devil who was dressed in black and carried chains, which he clanked. One of the train collected gifts. After the procession the Fool was buried under straw and dung.[3] In Rottweil the " Carnival Fool " is made drunk on Ash Wednesday and buried under straw amid loud lamentation.[4] In Wurmlingen the Fool is represented by a young fellow enveloped in straw, who is led about the village by a rope as a " Bear " on Shrove Tuesday and the preceding day. He dances to the flute. Then on Ash Wednesday a straw-man is made, placed on a trough, carried out of the village to the sound of drums and

[1] J. Haltrich, *Zur Volkskunde der Siebenbürger Sachsen* (Vienna, 1885), pp. 284 *sq*.

[2] K. von Leoprechting, *Aus dem Lechrain*, pp. 162 *sqq.*; W. Mannhardt, *Baumkultus*, p. 411.

[3] E. Meier, *Deutsche Sagen, Sitten und Gebräuche aus Schwaben*, p. 374; compare A. Birlinger, *Volksthümliches aus Schwaben* (Freiburg im Breisgau, 1861-1862), ii. pp. 54 *sq.*, § 71.

[4] E. Meier, *op. cit.* p. 372.

mournful music, and buried in a field.[1]   In Altdorf and
Weingarten on Ash Wednesday the Fool, represented by a
straw-man, is carried about and then thrown into the water
to the accompaniment of melancholy music.   In other
villages of Swabia the part of fool is played by a live person,
who is thrown into the water after being carried about in
procession.[2]   At Balwe, in Westphalia, a straw-man is made
on Shrove Tuesday and thrown into the river amid rejoicings.
This is called, as usual, " Burying the Carnival." [3]   At Burge-
brach, in Bavaria, it used to be customary, as a public pastime,
to hold a sort of court of justice on Ash Wednesday.   The
accused was a straw-man, on whom was laid the burden of
all the notorious transgressions that had been committed in
the course of the year.   Twelve chosen maidens sat in
judgment and pronounced sentence, and a single advocate
pleaded the cause of the public scapegoat.   Finally the
effigy was burnt, and thus all the offences that had created a
scandal in the community during the year were symbolically
atoned for.   We can hardly doubt that this custom of
burning a straw-man on Ash Wednesday for the sins of a
whole year is only another form of the custom, observed on
the same day in so many other places, of burning an effigy
which is supposed to embody and to be responsible for all
the excesses committed during the licence of the Carnival.

Burning the
Carnival
in Greece.   In Greece a ceremony of the same sort was witnessed at
Pylos by Mr. E. L. Tilton in 1895. On the evening of the first
day of the Greek Lent, which fell that year on the twenty-fifth
of February, an effigy with a grotesque mask for a face was
borne about the streets on a bier, preceded by a mock priest
with long white beard.   Other functionaries surrounded the
bier and two torch-bearers walked in advance.   The procession moved slowly to melancholy music played by a pipe
and drum.   A final halt was made in the public square,
where a circular space was kept clear of the surging crowd.
Here a bonfire was kindled, and round it the priest led a wild
dance to the same droning music.   When the frenzy was at

[1] E. Meier, *op. cit.* p. 373.
[2] E. Meier, *op. cit.* pp. 373, 374.
[3] A. Kuhn, *Sagen, Gebräuche und
Märchen aus Westfalen* (Leipsic, 1859),

ii. p. 130, § 393.
[4] *Bavaria, Landes- und Volkskunde
des Königreichs Bayern,* iii. 958,
note.

its height, the chief performer put tow on the effigy and set fire to it, and while it blazed he resumed his mad career, brandishing torches and tearing off his venerable beard to add fuel to the flames.[1]   On the evening of Shrove Tuesday the Esthonians make a straw figure called *metsik* or "wood-spirit"; one year it is dressed with a man's coat and hat, next year with a hood and a petticoat.   This figure is stuck on a long pole, carried across the boundary of the village with loud cries of joy, and fastened to the top of a tree in the wood. The ceremony is believed to be a protection against all kinds of misfortune.[2]

Esthonian custom on Shrove Tuesday.

Sometimes at these Shrovetide or Lenten ceremonies the resurrection of the pretended dead person is enacted.   Thus, in some parts of Swabia on Shrove Tuesday Dr. Iron-Beard professes to bleed a sick man, who thereupon falls as dead to the ground; but the doctor at last restores him to life by blowing air into him through a tube.[3]   In the Harz Mountains, when Carnival is over, a man is laid on a baking-trough and carried with dirges to a grave; but in the grave a glass of brandy is buried instead of the man.   A speech is delivered and then the people return to the village-green or meeting-place, where they smoke the long clay pipes which are distributed at funerals.   On the morning of Shrove Tuesday in the following year the brandy is dug up and the festival begins by every one tasting the spirit which, as the phrase goes, has come to life again.[4]

Resurrection enacted in these ceremonies.

§ 4. *Carrying out Death*

The ceremony of "Carrying out Death" presents much the same features as "Burying the Carnival"; except that the carrying out of Death is generally followed by a ceremony, or at least accompanied by a profession, of bringing in Summer, Spring, or Life.   Thus in Middle Franken, a province of Bavaria, on the fourth Sunday in Lent, the village urchins used to make a straw effigy of Death, which

Carrying out Death in Bavaria.

---

[1] *Folk-lore*, vi. (1895) p. 206.

[2] F. J. Wiedemann, *Aus dem inneren und äusseren Leben der Ehsten* (St. Petersburg, 1876), p. 353.

[3] E. Meier, *op. cit.* p. 374.

[4] H. Pröhle, *Harzbilder* (Leipsic, 1855), p. 54.

they carried about with burlesque pomp through the streets, and afterwards burned with loud cries beyond the bounds.[1] The Frankish custom is thus described by a writer of the sixteenth century : " At Mid-Lent, the season when the church bids us rejoice, the young people of my native country make a straw image of Death, and fastening it to a pole carry it with shouts to the neighbouring villages. By some they are kindly received, and after being refreshed with milk, peas, and dried pears, the usual food of that season, are sent home again.   Others, however, treat them with anything but hospitality ; for, looking on them as harbingers of misfortune, to wit of death, they drive them from their boundaries with weapons and insults." [2]   In the villages near Erlangen, when the fourth Sunday in Lent came round, the peasant girls used to dress themselves in all their finery with flowers in their hair.   Thus attired they repaired to the neighbouring town, carrying puppets which were adorned with leaves and covered with white cloths.   These they took from house to house in pairs, stopping at every door where they expected to receive something, and singing a few lines in which they announced that it was Mid-Lent and that they were about to throw Death into the water.   When they had collected some trifling gratuities they went to the river Regnitz and flung the puppets representing Death into the stream.   This was done to ensure a fruitful and prosperous year; further, it was considered a safeguard against pestilence and sudden death.[3] At Nuremberg girls of seven to eighteen years of age go through the streets bearing a little open coffin, in which is a doll hidden under a shroud.   Others carry a beech branch, with an apple fastened to it for a head, in an open box. They sing, " We carry Death into the water, it is well," or " We carry Death into the water, carry him in and out again." [4]   In other parts of Bavaria the ceremony took place on the Saturday before the fifth Sunday in Lent, and the performers were boys or girls, according to the sex of

[1] *Bavaria, Landes- und Volkskunde des Königreichs Bayern*, iii. 958.

[2] J. Boemus, *Omnium gentium mores, leges, et ritus* (Paris, 1538), p. 83.

[3] *Bavaria, Landes- und Volkskunde des Königreichs Bayern*, iii. 958.

[4] J. Grimm, *Deutsche Mythologie*,[4] ii. 639 *sq.*; W. Mannhardt, *Baumkultus*, p. 412.

the last person who died in the village. The figure was thrown into water or buried in a secret place, for example under moss in the forest, that no one might find Death again. Then early on Sunday morning the children went from house to house singing a song in which they announced the glad tidings that Death was gone.[1] In some parts of Bavaria down to 1780 it was believed that a fatal epidemic would ensue if the custom of " Carrying out Death " were not observed.[2]

In some villages of Thüringen, on the fourth Sunday of Lent, the children used to carry a puppet of birchen twigs through the village, and then threw it into a pool, while they sang, " We carry the old Death out behind the herdsman's old house ; we have got Summer, and Kroden's (?) power is destroyed." [3] At Debschwitz or Dobschwitz, near Gera, the ceremony of " Driving out Death " is or was annually observed on the first of March. The young people make up a figure of straw or the like materials, dress it in old clothes, which they have begged from houses in the village, and carry it out and throw it into the river. On returning to the village they break the good news to the people, and receive eggs and other victuals as a reward. The ceremony is or was supposed to purify the village and to protect the inhabitants from sickness and plague. In other villages of Thüringen, in which the population was originally Slavonic, the carrying out of the puppet is accompanied with the singing of a song, which begins, " Now we carry Death out of the village and Spring into the village." [4] At the end of the seventeenth and beginning of the eighteenth century the custom was observed in Thüringen as follows. The boys and girls made an effigy of straw or the like materials, but the shape of the figure varied from year to year. In one year it would represent an old man, in the next an old woman, in the third a young man, and in the fourth a maiden, and the dress of the figure varied with the character

Carrying out Death in Thüringen.

---

[1] Sepp, *Die Religion der alten Deutschen* (Munich, 1876), p. 67.

[2] Fr. Kauffmann, *Balder* (Strasburg, 1902), p. 283.

[3] Aug. Witzschel, *Sagen, Sitten und Gebräuche aus Thüringen* (Vienna, 1878), p. 193.

[4] A. Witzschel, *op. cit.* p. 199 ; J. A. E. Köhler, *Volksbrauch, Aberglauben, Sagen und andre alte Überlieferungen im Voigtlande* (Leipsic, 1867), pp. 171 *sq.*

it personated. There used to be a sharp contest as to where the effigy was to be made, for the people thought that the house from which it was carried forth would not be visited with death that year. Having been made, the puppet was fastened to a pole and carried by a girl if it represented an old man, but by a boy if it represented an old woman. Thus it was borne in procession, the young people holding sticks in their hands and singing that they were driving out Death. When they came to water they threw the effigy into it and ran hastily back, fearing that it might jump on their shoulders and wring their necks. They also took care not to touch it, lest it should dry them up. On their return they beat the cattle with the sticks, believing that this would make the animals fat or fruitful. Afterwards they visited the house or houses from which they had carried the image of Death, where they received a dole of half-boiled peas.[1] The custom of " Carrying out Death " was practised also in Saxony. At Leipsic the bastards and public women used to make a straw effigy of Death every year at Mid-Lent. This they carried through all the streets with songs and shewed it to the young married women. Finally they threw it into the river Parthe. By this ceremony they professed to make the young wives fruitful, to purify the city, and to protect the inhabitants for that year from plague and other epidemics.[2]

Carrying out Death in Silesia. Ceremonies of the same sort are observed at Mid-Lent in Silesia. Thus in many places the grown girls with the help of the young men dress up a straw figure with women's clothes and carry it out of the village towards the setting sun. At the boundary they strip it of its clothes, tear it in pieces, and scatter the fragments about the fields. This is called " Burying Death." As they carry the image out, they sing that they are about to bury death under an oak, that

[1] Fr. Kauffmann, *Balder* (Strasburg, 1902), p. 283 note, quoting J. K. Zeumer, *Laetare vulgo Todten Sonntag* (Jena, 1701), pp. 20 *sqq.* ; J. Grimm, *Deutsche Mythologie*,[4] ii. 640 *sq.* The words of the song are given as " *So treiben wir den todten auss,*" but this must be a mistake for " *So treiben wir den Tod hinaus,*" as the line is given

by P. Drechsler (*Sitte, Brauch und Volksglaube in Schlesien*, i. 66). In the passage quoted the effigy is spoken of as " *mortis larva.*"

[2] Zacharias Schneider, *Leipziger Chronik*, iv. 143, cited by K. Schwenk, *Die Mythologie der Slaven* (Frankfort, 1853), pp. 217 *sq.*, and Fr. Kauff- mann, *Balder*, pp. 284 *sq.*

he may depart from the people. Sometimes the song runs
that they are bearing death over hill and dale to return no
more. In the Polish neighbourhood of Gross-Strehlitz the
puppet is called Goik. It is carried on horseback and
thrown into the nearest water. The people think that the
ceremony protects them from sickness of every sort in the
coming year. In the districts of Wohlau and Guhrau the
image of Death used to be thrown over the boundary of the
next village. But as the neighbours feared to receive the
ill-omened figure, they were on the look-out to repel it, and
hard knocks were often exchanged between the two parties.
In some Polish parts of Upper Silesia the effigy, representing
an old woman, goes by the name of Marzana, the goddess
of death. It is made in the house where the last death
occurred, and is carried on a pole to the boundary of the
village, where it is thrown into a pond or burnt. At Polk-
witz the custom of " Carrying out Death " fell into abeyance ;
but an outbreak of fatal sickness which followed the intermission of the ceremony induced the people to resume it.[1]
Some of the Moravians of Silesia make three puppets on
this occasion : one represents a man, another a bride, and
the third a bridesmaid. The first is carried by the boys, the
two last by the girls. Formerly these effigies were torn to
pieces at a brook ; now they are brought home again.[2] In
this last custom two of the figures are clearly conceived as
bride and bridegroom.

In Bohemia the children go out with a straw-man, re- *Carrying
presenting Death, to the end of the village, where they burn *out
Death in*
it, singing— *Bohemia.*

> " *Now carry we Death out of the village,*
> *The new Summer into the village,*
> *Welcome, dear Summer,*
> *Green little corn.*" [3]

At Tabor in Bohemia the figure of Death is carried out
of the town and flung from a high rock into the water, while
they sing—

[1] P. Drechsler, *Sitte, Brauch und
Volksglaube in Schlesien*, i. 65 - 71.
Compare A. Peter, *Volksthümliches aus
Österreichisch - Schlesien* (Troppau,
1865-1867), ii. 281 *sq.*

[2] F. Tetzner, "Die Tschechen und
Mährer in Schlesien," *Globus*, lxxviii.
(1900) p. 340.

[3] J. Grimm, *Deutsche Mythologie*,[4]
ii. 642.

> "*Death swims on the water,*
> *Summer will soon be here,*
> *We carried Death away for you,*
> *We brought the Summer.*
> *And do thou, O holy Marketa,*
> *Give us a good year*
> *For wheat and for rye.*" [1]

In other parts of Bohemia they carry Death to the end of the village, singing—

> "*We carry Death out of the village,*
> *And the New Year into the village.*
> *Dear Spring, we bid you welcome,*
> *Green grass, we bid you welcome.*"

Behind the village they erect a pyre, on which they burn the straw figure, reviling and scoffing at it the while.   Then they return, singing—

> "*We have carried away Death,*
> *And brought Life back.*
> *He has taken up his quarters in the village,*
> *Therefore sing joyous songs.*" [2]

Carrying out Death in Moravia.   In some German villages of Moravia, as in Jassnitz and Seitendorf, the young folk assemble on the third Sunday in Lent and fashion a straw-man, who is generally adorned with a fur cap and a pair of old leathern hose, if such are to be had.   The effigy is then hoisted on a pole and carried by the lads and lasses out into the open fields.   On the way they sing a song, in which it is said that they are carrying Death away and bringing dear Summer into the house, and with Summer the May and the flowers.   On reaching an appointed place they dance in a circle round the effigy with loud shouts and screams, then suddenly rush at it and tear it to pieces with their hands.   Lastly, the pieces are thrown together in a heap, the pole is broken, and fire is set to the whole.   While it burns the troop dances merrily round it, rejoicing at the victory won by Spring; and when the fire has nearly died out they go to the house-holders to beg for a present of eggs wherewith to hold a

---

[1] Reinsberg-Düringsfeld, *Fest-Kalender aus Böhmen*, pp. 90 *sq.*
[2] *Ibid.* p. 91.

feast, taking care to give as a reason for the request that
they have carried Death out and away.[1]

The preceding evidence shews that the effigy of Death is   The effigy
often regarded with fear and treated with marks of hatred   of Death
feared and
and abhorrence.   Thus the anxiety of the villagers to transfer   abhorred.
the figure from their own to their neighbours' land, and the
reluctance of the latter to receive the ominous guest, are
proof enough of the dread which it inspires.   Further, in
Lusatia and Silesia the puppet is sometimes made to look
in at the window of a house, and it is believed that some
one in the house will die within the year unless his life is
redeemed by the payment of money.[2]   Again, after throwing
the effigy away, the bearers sometimes run home lest Death
should follow them, and if one of them falls in running, it is
believed that he will die within the year.[3]   At Chrudim, in
Bohemia, the figure of Death is made out of a cross, with a
head and mask stuck at the top, and a shirt stretched out
on it.   On the fifth Sunday in Lent the boys take this
effigy to the nearest brook or pool, and standing in a line
throw it into the water.   Then they all plunge in after it ; but
as soon as it is caught no one more may enter the water.   The
boy who did not enter the water or entered it last will die
within the year, and he is obliged to carry the Death back
to the village.   The effigy is then burned.[4]   On the other
hand, it is believed that no one will die within the year in
the house out of which the figure of Death has been
carried ;[5] and the village out of which Death has been
driven is sometimes supposed to be protected against sickness
and plague.[6]   In some villages of Austrian Silesia on the
Saturday before Dead Sunday an effigy is made of old
clothes, hay, and straw, for the purpose of driving Death out
of the village.   On Sunday the people, armed with sticks

---

[1] W. Müller, *Beiträge zur Volkskunde der Deutschen in Mähren*
(Vienna and Olmütz, 1893), pp. 353-
355.

[2] J. Grimm, *Deutsche Mythologie*,[4]
ii. 644 ; K. Haupt, *Sagenbuch der
Lausitz* (Leipsic, 1862-1863), ii. 55 ;
P. Drechsler, *Sitte, Brauch und Volksglaube in Schlesien*, i. 70 *sq.*

[3] J. Grimm, *op. cit.* ii. 640, 643 ;

P. Drechsler, *op. cit.* i. 70.   See also
above, p. 236.

[4] Th. Vernaleken, *Mythen und
Bräuche des Volkes in Österreich*
(Vienna, 1859), pp. 294 *sq.*; Reins-
berg-Düringsfeld, *Fest-Kalender aus
Böhmen*, p. 90.

[5] See above, p. 236.

[6] See above, pp. 234, 235, 236,
237.

and straps, assemble before the house where the figure is lodged. Four lads then draw the effigy by cords through the village amid exultant shouts, while all the others beat it with their sticks and straps. On reaching a field which belongs to a neighbouring village they lay down the figure, cudgel it soundly, and scatter the fragments over the field. The people believe that the village from which Death has been thus carried out will be safe from any infectious disease for the whole year.[1] In Slavonia the figure of Death is cudgelled and then rent in two.[2] In Poland the effigy, made of hemp and straw, is flung into a pool or swamp with the words " The devil take thee." [3]

§ 5. *Sawing the Old Woman*

Sawing the Old Woman at Mid-Lent in Italy.

The custom of " Sawing the Old Woman," which is or used to be observed in Italy, France, and Spain on the fourth Sunday in Lent, is doubtless, as Grimm supposes, merely another form of the custom of " Carrying out Death." A great hideous figure representing the oldest woman of the village was dragged out and sawn in two, amid a prodigious noise made with cow-bells, pots and pans, and so forth.[4] In Palermo the representation used to be still more lifelike. At Mid-Lent an old woman was drawn through the streets on a cart, attended by two men dressed in the costume of the *Compagnia de' Bianchi*, a society or religious order whose function it was to attend and console prisoners condemned to death. A scaffold was erected in a public square ; the old woman mounted it, and two mock executioners proceeded, amid a storm of huzzas and hand-clapping, to saw through her neck, or rather through a bladder of blood which had been previously fitted to it. The blood gushed out and the old woman pretended to swoon and die. The last of these mock executions took place in 1737.[5] In Florence, during

[1] Reinsberg-Düringsfeld, *Das fest- liche Jahr* (Leipsic, 1863), p. 80.

[2] W. R. S. Ralston, *Songs of the Russian People* (London, 1872), p. 211.

[3] *Ibid.* p. 210.

[4] J. Grimm, *Deutsche Mythologie,*[4] ii. 652 ; H. Usener, " Italische Mythen," *Rheinisches Museum*, N.F., xxx. (1875) pp. 191 *sq.*

[5] G. Pitrè, *Spettacoli e feste popolari siciliane* (Palermo, 1881), pp. 207 *sq.*, *id., Usi e costumi, credenze e pregiu- dizi del popolo siciliano*, i. 107 *sq.*

the fifteenth and sixteenth centuries, the Old Woman was represented by a figure stuffed with walnuts and dried figs and fastened to the top of a ladder. At Mid-Lent this effigy was sawn through the middle under the *Loggie* of the Mercato Nuovo, and as the dried fruits tumbled out they were scrambled for by the crowd. A trace of the custom is still to be seen in the practice, observed by urchins, of secretly pinning paper ladders to the shoulders of women of the lower classes who happen to shew themselves in the streets on the morning of Mid-Lent.[1] A similar custom is observed by urchins in Rome ; and at Naples on the first of April boys cut strips of cloth into the shape of saws, smear them with gypsum, and strike passers-by with their " saws " on the back, thus imprinting the figure of a saw upon their clothes.[2] At Montalto, in Calabria, boys go about at Mid-Lent with little saws made of cane and jeer at old people, who therefore generally stay indoors on that day. The Calabrian women meet together at this time and feast on figs, chestnuts, honey, and so forth ; this they call " Sawing the Old Woman "—a reminiscence probably of a custom like the old Florentine one.[3] In Lombardy the Thursday of Mid-Lent is known as the Day of the Old Wives (*il giorno delle vecchie*). The children run about crying out for the oldest woman, whom they wish to burn ; and failing to possess themselves of the original, they make a puppet representing her, which in the evening is consumed on a bonfire. On the Lake of Garda the blaze of light flaring at different points on the hills produces a picturesque effect.[4]

In Berry, a region of central France, the custom of " Sawing the Old Woman " at Mid-Lent used to be popular, and has probably not wholly died out even now. Here the name of " Fairs of the old Wives " was given to certain fairs held in Lent, at which children were made to believe that they would see the Old Woman of Mid-Lent split or sawn asunder. At Argenton and Cluis-Dessus, when Mid-Lent has come, children of ten or twelve years of age scour the streets with

Sawing the Old Woman at Mid-Lent in France.

---

[1] *Archivio per lo studio delle tradizioni popolari*, iv. (1885) pp. 294 *sq.*

[2] H. Usener, *op. cit.* p. 193.

[3] Vincenzo Dorsa, *La Tradizione greco-latina negli usi e nelle credenze*

popolari della Calabria citeriore (Cosenza, 1884), pp. 43 *sq.*

[4] E. Martinengo-Cesaresco, in *The Academy*, No. 671, March 14, 1885, p. 188.

wooden swords, pursue the old crones whom they meet, and even try to break into the houses where ancient dames are known to live. Passers-by, who see the children thus engaged, say, "They are going to cut or sabre the Old Woman." Meantime the old wives take care to keep out of sight as much as possible. When the children of Cluis-Dessus have gone their rounds, and the day draws towards evening, they repair to Cluis-Dessous, where they mould a rude figure of an old woman out of clay, hew it in pieces with their wooden swords, and throw the bits into the river. At Bourges on the same day, an effigy representing an old woman was formerly sawn in two on the crier's stone in a public square. About the middle of the nineteenth century, in the same town and on the same day, hundreds of children assembled at the Hospital "to see the old woman split or divided in two." A religious service was held in the building on this occasion, which attracted many idlers. In the streets it was not uncommon to hear cries of " Let us cleave the Old Wife! let us cleave the oldest woman of the ward!" At Tulle, on the day of Mid-Lent, the people used to enquire after the oldest woman in the town, and to tell the children that at mid-day punctually she was to be sawn in two at Puy-Saint-Clair.[1]

In Barcelona on the fourth Sunday in Lent boys run about the streets, some with saws, others with billets of wood, others again with cloths in which they collect gratuities. They sing a song in which it is said that they are looking for the oldest woman of the city for the purpose of sawing her in two in honour of Mid-Lent; at last, pretending to have found her, they saw something in two and burn it. A like custom is found amongst the South Slavs. In Lent the Croats tell their children that at noon an old woman is being sawn in two outside the gates; and in Carniola also the saying is current that at Mid-Lent an old woman is taken out of the village and sawn in two. The North Slavonian expression for keeping Mid-Lent is *bábu rezati*, that is, "sawing the Old Wife." [2] In the Graubünden Canton of Switzerland,

[1] Laisnel de la Salle, *Croyances et légendes du centre de la France* (Paris, 1875), i. 43 *sq.*

[2] J. Grimm, *Deutsche Mythologie*,[4]

ii. 652; H. Usener, "Italische Mythen," *Rheinisches Museum*, N.F., xxx. (1875) pp. 191 *sq.*

on *Invocavit* Sunday, grown people used to assemble in the ale-house and there saw in two a straw puppet which they called Mrs. Winter or the Ugly Woman (*bagorda*), while the children in the streets teased each other with wooden saws.[1]

Among the gypsies of south-eastern Europe the custom of "sawing the Old Woman in two" is observed in a very graphic form, not at Mid-Lent, but on the afternoon of Palm Sunday. The Old Woman, represented by a puppet of straw dressed in women's clothes, is laid across a beam in some open place and beaten with clubs by the assembled gypsies, after which it is sawn in two by a young man and a maiden, both of whom wear a disguise. While the effigy is being sawn through, the rest of the company dance round it singing songs of various sorts. The remains of the figure are finally burnt, and the ashes thrown into a stream. The ceremony is supposed by the gypsies themselves to be observed in honour of a certain Shadow Queen ; hence Palm Sunday goes by the name Shadow Day among all the strolling gypsies of eastern and southern Europe. According to the popular belief, this Shadow Queen, of whom the gypsies of to-day have only a very vague and confused conception, vanishes underground at the appearance of spring, but comes forth again at the beginning of winter to plague mankind during that inclement season with sickness, hunger, and death. Among the vagrant gypsies of southern Hungary the effigy is regarded as an expiatory and thank offering made to the Shadow Queen for having spared the people during the winter. In Transylvania the gypsies who live in tents clothe the puppet in the cast-off garments of the woman who has last become a widow. The widow herself gives the clothes gladly for this purpose, because she thinks that being burnt they will pass into the possession of her departed husband, who will thus have no excuse for returning from the spirit-land to visit her. The ashes are thrown by the Transylvanian gypsies on the first graveyard that they pass on their journey.[2]

Sawing the Old Woman on Palm Sunday among the gypsies.

[1] E. Hoffmann-Krayer, "Fruchtbarkeitsriten im schweizerischen Volksbrauch," *Schweizerisches Archiv für Volkskunde*, xi. (1903) p. 239.

[2] H. von Wlislocki, *Volksglaube und religiöser Brauch der Zigeuner* (Münster i. W., 1891), pp. 145 *sq.*

In this gypsy custom the equivalence of the effigy of the Old Woman to the effigy of Death in the customs we have just been considering comes out very clearly, thus strongly confirming the opinion of Grimm that the practice of "sawing the Old Woman" is only another form of the practice of "carrying out Death."

Seven-
legged
effigies of
Lent in
Spain.The same perhaps may be said of a somewhat different form which the custom assumes in parts of Spain and Italy. In Spain it is sometimes usual on Ash Wednesday to fashion an effigy of stucco or pasteboard representing a hideous old woman with seven legs, wearing a crown of sorrel and spinach, and holding a sceptre in her hand. The seven skinny legs stand for the seven weeks of the Lenten fast which begins on Ash Wednesday. This monster, proclaimed Queen of Lent amid the chanting of lugubrious songs, is carried in triumph through the crowded streets and public places. On reaching the principal square the people put out their torches, cease shouting, and disperse. Their revels are now ended, and they take a vow to hold no more merry meetings until all the legs of the old woman have fallen one by one and she has been beheaded. The effigy is then deposited in some place appointed for the purpose, where the public is admitted to see it during the whole of Lent. Every week, on Saturday evening, one of the Queen's legs is pulled off; and on Holy Saturday, when from every church tower the joyous clangour of the bells proclaims the glad tidings that Christ is risen, the mutilated body of the fallen Queen is carried with great solemnity to the principal square and publicly beheaded.[1]

Seven-
legged
effigies of
Lent in
Italy.A custom of the same sort prevails in various parts of Italy. Thus in the Abruzzi they hang a puppet of tow, representing Lent, to a cord, which stretches across the street from one window to another. Seven feathers are attached to the figure, and in its hand it grasps a distaff and spindle. Every Saturday in Lent one of the seven feathers is plucked out, and on Holy Saturday, while the bells are ringing, a

---

[1] E. Cortet, *Essai sur les fêtes religieuses* (Paris, 1867), pp. 107 *sq.*; Laisnel de la Salle, *Croyances et légendes du centre de la France*, i. 45 *sq.* A similar custom appears to be observed in Minorca. See *Globus*, lix. (1891) pp. 279, 280.

string of chestnuts is burnt for the purpose of sending Lent
and its meagre fare to the devil. In houses, too, it is usual to
amuse children by cutting the figure of an old woman with
seven legs out of pasteboard and sticking it beside the
chimney. The old woman represents Lent, and her seven legs
are the seven weeks of the fast; every Saturday one of the
legs is amputated. At Mid-Lent the effigy is cut through
the middle, and the part of which the feet have been already
amputated is removed. Sometimes the figure is stuffed
with sweets, dried fruits, and halfpence, for which the street
urchins scramble when the puppet is bisected.[1] In the
Sorrentine peninsula Lent is similarly represented by the
effigy of a wrinkled old hag with a spindle and distaff,
which is fastened to a balcony or a window. Attached to
the figure is an orange with as many feathers stuck into it
as there are weeks in Lent, and at the end of each week one
of the feathers is plucked out. At Mid-Lent the puppet is
sawn in two, an operation which is sometimes attended by a
gush of blood from a bladder concealed in the interior of the
figure. Any old women who shew themselves in the streets
on that day are exposed to jibes and jests, and may be
warned that they ought to remain at home.[2] At Castel-
lamare, to the south of Naples, an English lady observed a
rude puppet dangling from a string which spanned one of
the narrow streets of the old town, being fastened at either
end, high overhead, to the upper part of the many-storied
houses. The puppet, about a foot long, was dressed all
in black, rather like a nun, and from the skirts projected
five or six feathers which bore a certain resemblance to legs.
A peasant being asked what these things meant, replied
with Italian vagueness, " It is only Lent." Further enquiries,
however, elicited the information that at the end of every
week in Lent one of the feather legs was pulled off the
puppet, and that the puppet was finally destroyed on the last
day of Lent.[3]

[1] A. de Nino, *Usi e costumi abruz-*
zesi, ii. 203-205 (Florence, 1881); G.
Finamore, *Credenze, usi e costumi*
abruzzesi (Palermo, 1890), pp. 112,
114.

[2] G. Amalfi, *Tradizioni ed usi nella*
Penisola Sorrentina (Palermo, 1890),
p. 41.

[3] Lucy E. Broadwood, in *Folk-lore,*
iv. (1893) p. 390.

§ 6. *Bringing in Summer*

The custom of carrying out Death is often followed by the ceremony of bringing in Summer, in which the Summer is represented by a tree or branches.

In the preceding ceremonies the return of Spring, Summer, or Life, as a sequel to the expulsion of Death, is only implied or at most announced. In the following ceremonies it is plainly enacted. Thus in some parts of Bohemia the effigy of Death is drowned by being thrown into the water at sunset; then the girls go out into the wood and cut down a young tree with a green crown, hang a doll dressed as a woman on it, deck the whole with green, red, and white ribbons, and march in procession with their *Líto* (Summer) into the village, collecting gifts and singing—

> " *Death swims in the water,*
> *Spring comes to visit us,*
> *With eggs that are red,*
> *With yellow pancakes.*
> *We carried Death out of the village,*
> *We are carrying Summer into the village.*" [1]

In many Silesian villages the figure of Death, after being treated with respect, is stript of its clothes and flung with curses into the water, or torn to pieces in a field. Then the young folk repair to a wood, cut down a small fir-tree, peel the trunk, and deck it with festoons of evergreens, paper roses, painted egg-shells, motley bits of cloth, and so forth. The tree thus adorned is called Summer or May. Boys carry it from house to house singing appropriate songs and begging for presents. Among their songs is the following:—

> " *We have carried Death out,*
> *We are bringing the dear Summer back,*
> *The Summer and the May*
> *And all the flowers gay.*"

Sometimes they also bring back from the wood a prettily adorned figure, which goes by the name of Summer, May, or the Bride; in the Polish districts it is called Dziewanna, the goddess of spring.[2]

---

[1] Reinsberg-Düringsfeld, *Fest-Kalender aus Böhmen*, pp. 89 *sq.*; W. Mannhardt, *Baumkultus*, p. 156. This custom has been already referred to. See *The Magic Art and the Evolution of Kings*, ii. 73 *sq.*

[2] P. Drechsler, *Sitte, Brauch und Volksglaube in Schlesien*, i. 71 *sqq.*; Reinsberg-Düringsfeld, *Das festliche Jahr*, p. 82; Philo vom Walde, *Schlesien in Sage und Brauch* (Berlin, N.D., preface dated 1883), p. 122.

At Eisenach on the fourth Sunday in Lent young people used to fasten a straw-man, representing Death, to a wheel, which they trundled to the top of a hill. Then setting fire to the figure they allowed it and the wheel to roll down the slope. Next they cut a tall fir-tree, tricked it out with ribbons, and set it up in the plain. The men then climbed the tree to fetch down the ribbons.[1] In Upper Lusatia the figure of Death, made of straw and rags, is dressed in a veil furnished by the last bride and a shirt provided by the house in which the last death took place. Thus arrayed the figure is stuck on the end of a long pole and carried at full speed by the tallest and strongest girl, while the rest pelt the effigy with sticks and stones. Whoever hits it will be sure to live through the year. In this way Death is carried out of the village and thrown into the water or over the boundary of the next village. On their way home each one breaks a green branch and carries it gaily with him till he reaches the village, when he throws it away. Sometimes the young people of the next village, upon whose land the figure has been thrown, run after them and hurl it back, not wishing to have Death among them. Hence the two parties occasionally come to blows.[2]

In these cases Death is represented by the puppet which is thrown away, Summer or Life by the branches or trees which are brought back. But sometimes a new potency of life seems to be attributed to the image of Death itself, and by a kind of resurrection it becomes the instrument of the general revival. Thus in some parts of Lusatia women alone are concerned in carrying out Death, and suffer no male to meddle with it. Attired in mourning, which they wear the whole day, they make a puppet of straw, clothe it in a white shirt, and give it a broom in one hand and a scythe in the other. Singing songs and pursued by urchins throwing stones, they carry the puppet to the village boundary, where they tear it in pieces. Then they cut down a fine tree, hang the shirt on it, and carry it home singing.[3] On

New potency of life ascribed to the image of Death.

---

[1] A. Witzschel, *Sagen, Sitten und Gebräuche aus Thüringen*, pp. 192 *sq.*; compare pp. 297 *sqq.*

[2] J. Grimm, *Deutsche Mythologie*,[4] ii. 643 *sq.*; K. Haupt, *Sagenbuch der Lausitz*, ii. 54 *sq.*; W. Mannhardt, *Baumkultus*, pp. 412 *sq.*; W. R. S. Ralston, *Songs of the Russian People*, p. 211.

[3] J. Grimm, *op. cit.* ii. 644 ; K. Haupt, *op. cit.* ii. 55.

the Feast of Ascension the Saxons of Braller, a village
of Transylvania, not far from Hermannstadt, observe the
ceremony of "Carrying out Death" in the following
manner. After morning service all the school-girls repair
to the house of one of their number, and there dress up the
Death. This is done by tying a threshed-out sheaf of corn
into a rough semblance of a head and body, while the arms
are simulated by a broomstick thrust through it horizontally.
The figure is dressed in the holiday attire of a young
peasant woman, with a red hood, silver brooches, and a
profusion of ribbons at the arms and breast. The girls
bustle at their work, for soon the bells will be ringing to
vespers, and the Death must be ready in time to be placed
at the open window, that all the people may see it on their
way to church. When vespers are over, the longed-for
moment has come for the first procession with the Death to
begin ; it is a privilege that belongs to the school-girls
alone. Two of the older girls seize the figure by the arms
and walk in front : all the rest follow two and two. Boys
may take no part in the procession, but they troop after it
gazing with open-mouthed admiration at the "beautiful
Death." So the procession goes through all the streets of
the village, the girls singing the old hymn that begins—

> "*Gott mein Vater, deine Liebe*
> *Reicht so weit der Himmel ist,*"

to a tune that differs from the ordinary one. When the
procession has wound its way through every street, the girls
go to another house, and having shut the door against the
eager prying crowd of boys who follow at their heels, they
strip the Death and pass the naked truss of straw out of
the window to the boys, who pounce on it, run out of the
village with it without singing, and fling the dilapidated
effigy into the neighbouring brook. This done, the second
scene of the little drama begins. While the boys were
carrying away the Death out of the village, the girls
remained in the house, and one of them is now dressed in all
the finery which had been worn by the effigy. Thus arrayed
she is led in procession through all the streets to the singing
of the same hymn as before. When the procession is over

they all betake themselves to the house of the girl who
played the leading part. Here a feast awaits them from
which also the boys are excluded. It is a popular belief
that the children may safely begin to eat gooseberries and
other fruit after the day on which Death has thus been
carried out ; for Death, which up to that time lurked especially in gooseberries, is now destroyed. Further, they may
now bathe with impunity out of doors.[1] Very similar is the
ceremony which, down to recent years, was observed in some
of the German villages of Moravia. Boys and girls met on
the afternoon of the first Sunday after Easter, and together
fashioned a puppet of straw to represent Death. Decked
with bright-coloured ribbons and cloths, and fastened to the
top of a long pole, the effigy was then borne with singing
and clamour to the nearest height, where it was stript of its
gay attire and thrown or rolled down the slope. One of
the girls was next dressed in the gauds taken from the
effigy of Death, and with her at its head the procession
moved back to the village. In some villages the practice
is to bury the effigy in the place that has the most evil
reputation of all the country-side : others throw it into
running water.[2]

In the Lusatian ceremony described above,[3] the tree Life-giving
which is brought home after the destruction of the figure of virtue
ascribed to
Death is plainly equivalent to the trees or branches which, the effigy
in the preceding customs, were brought back as representa- of Death.
tives of Summer or Life, after Death had been thrown away
or destroyed. But the transference of the shirt worn by the
effigy of Death to the tree clearly indicates that the tree is
a kind of revivification, in a new form, of the destroyed effigy.[4]
This comes out also in the Transylvanian and Moravian
customs : the dressing of a girl in the clothes worn by the
Death, and the leading her about the village to the same
song which had been sung when the Death was being

---

[1] J. K. Schuller, *Das Todaustragen
und der Muorlef, ein Beitrag zur Kunde
sächsischer Sitte und Sage in Sieben-
bürgen* (Hermannstadt, 1861), pp. 4
sq. The description of this ceremony
by Miss E. Gerard (*The Land beyond
the Forest*, ii. 47-49) is plainly borrowed
from Mr. Schuller's little work.

[2] W. Müller, *Beiträge zur Volkskunde
der Deutschen in Mähren* (Vienna and
Olmütz, 1893), pp. 258 *sq.*

[3] P. 247.

[4] This is also the view taken of the
custom by W. Mannhardt, *Baumkultus*,
p. 419.

carried about, shew that she is intended to be a kind of
resuscitation of the being whose effigy has just been destroyed.
These examples therefore suggest that the Death whose
demolition is represented in these ceremonies cannot be
regarded as the purely destructive agent which we understand by Death. If the tree which is brought back as an
embodiment of the reviving vegetation of spring is clothed
in the shirt worn by the Death which has just been destroyed,
the object certainly cannot be to check and counteract the
revival of vegetation : it can only be to foster and promote
it. Therefore the being which has just been destroyed—the
so-called Death—must be supposed to be endowed with a
vivifying and quickening influence, which it can communicate to the vegetable and even the animal world. This
ascription of a life-giving virtue to the figure of Death is put
beyond a doubt by the custom, observed in some places, of
taking pieces of the straw effigy of Death and placing them
in the fields to make the crops grow, or in the manger to
make the cattle thrive. Thus in Spachendorf, a village of
Austrian Silesia, the figure of Death, made of straw, brushwood, and rags, is carried with wild songs to an open place
outside the village and there burned, and while it is burning
a general struggle takes place for the pieces, which are pulled
out of the flames with bare hands. Each one who secures
a fragment of the effigy ties it to a branch of the largest
tree in his garden, or buries it in his field, in the belief that
this causes the crops to grow better.[1] In the Troppau
district of Austrian Silesia the straw figure which the boys
make on the fourth Sunday in Lent is dressed by the girls
in woman's clothes and hung with ribbons, necklace, and
garlands. Attached to a long pole it is carried out of the
village, followed by a troop of young people of both sexes,
who alternately frolic, lament, and sing songs. Arrived at
its destination—a field outside the village—the figure is
stripped of its clothes and ornaments ; then the crowd
rushes at it and tears it to bits, scuffling for the fragments.
Every one tries to get a wisp of the straw of which the
effigy was made, because such a wisp, placed in the manger,

[1] Th. Vernaleken, *Mythen und Bräuche des Volkes in Österreich*, pp.
293 *sq.*

is believed to make the cattle thrive.[1]   Or the straw is put
in the hens' nest, it being supposed that this prevents the
hens from carrying away their eggs, and makes them brood
much better.[2]   The same attribution of a fertilising power
to the figure of Death appears in the belief that if the
bearers of the figure, after throwing it away, beat cattle
with their sticks, this will render the beasts fat or prolific.[3]
Perhaps the sticks had been previously used to beat the
Death,[4] and so had acquired the fertilising power ascribed
to the effigy.   We have seen, too, that at Leipsic a straw
effigy of Death was shewn to young wives to make them
fruitful.[5]

It seems hardly possible to separate from the May-trees *The*
the trees or branches which are brought into the village *Summer-*
after the destruction of the Death.   The bearers who *tree*
bring them in profess to be bringing in the Summer,[6] *equivalent*
therefore the trees obviously represent the Summer ; *to the May-tree.*
indeed in Silesia they are commonly called the Summer
or the May,[7] and the doll which is sometimes attached
to the Summer-tree is a duplicate representative of
the Summer, just as the May is sometimes represented at the same time by a May-tree and a May
Lady.[8]   Further, the Summer-trees are adorned like May-
trees with ribbons and so on ; like May-trees, when large,
they are planted in the ground and climbed up ; and like
May-trees, when small, they are carried from door to door
by boys or girls singing songs and collecting money.[9]   And
as if to demonstrate the identity of the two sets of customs
the bearers of the Summer-tree sometimes announce that
they are bringing in the Summer and the May.[10]   The
customs, therefore, of bringing in the May and bringing in
the Summer are essentially the same ; and the Summer-tree
is merely another form of the May-tree, the only distinction

[1] Reinsberg-Düringsfeld, *Das festliche Jahr*, p. 82.

[2] Philo vom Walde, *Schlesien in
Sage und Brauch*, p. 122 ; P. Drechs-
ler, *Sitte, Brauch und Volksglaube in
Schlesien*, i. 74.

[3] See above, p. 236.

[4] See above, pp. 239 *sq.*

[5] See above, p. 236.

[6] Above, p. 246.

[7] Above, p. 246.

[8] See *The Magic Art and the Evolution of Kings*, ii. 73 *sqq.*

[9] Above, p. 246, and J. Grimm,
Deutsche Mythologie,[4] ii. 644 ; Reins-
berg-Düringsfeld, *Fest-Kalender aus
Böhmen*, pp. 87 *sq.*

[10] Above, p. 246.

(besides that of name) being in the time at which they are respectively brought in ; for while the May-tree is usually fetched in on the first of May or at Whitsuntide, the Summer-tree is fetched in on the fourth Sunday in Lent.   Therefore, if the May-tree is an embodiment of the tree-spirit or spirit of vegetation, the Summer-tree must likewise be an em-

But the
Summer-
tree is a
revival of
the image
of Death ;
hence the
image of
Death
must be an
embodi-
ment of the
spirit of
vegetation.

bodiment of the tree-spirit or spirit of vegetation.   But we have seen that the Summer-tree is in some cases a revivifica-tion of the effigy of Death.   It follows, therefore, that in these cases the effigy called Death must be an embodiment of the tree-spirit or spirit of vegetation.   This inference is confirmed, first, by the vivifying and fertilising influence which the frag-ments of the effigy of Death are believed to exercise both on vegetable and on animal life ;[1] for this influence, as we saw in the first part of this work,[2] is supposed to be a special attribute of the tree-spirit.   It is confirmed, secondly, by observing that the effigy of Death is sometimes decked with leaves or made of twigs, branches, hemp, or a threshed-out sheaf of corn ;[3] and that sometimes it is hung on a little tree and so carried about by girls collecting money,[4] just as is done with the May-tree and the May Lady, and with the Summer-tree and the doll attached to it.   In short we are driven to regard the expulsion of Death and the bringing in of Summer as, in some cases at least, merely another form of that death and revival of the spirit of vegetation in spring which we saw enacted in the killing and resurrection of the Wild Man.[5]   The burial and resurrection of the Carnival is prob-ably another way of expressing the same idea.   The inter-ment of the representative of the Carnival under a dung-heap[6] is natural, if he is supposed to possess a quickening and fertilising influence like that ascribed to the effigy of Death.   The Esthonians, indeed, who carry the straw figure out of the village in the usual way on Shrove Tuesday, do not call it the Carnival, but the Wood-spirit (*Metsik*), and they clearly

---

[1] See above, pp. 250 *sq.*

[2] See *The Magic Art and the Evolution of Kings*, ii. 45 *sqq.*

[3] Above, pp. 234, 235, 240, 248, 250 ; and J. Grimm, *Deutsche Mythologie*,[4] ii. 643.

[4] Reinsberg-Düringsfeld, *Fest-Kalen-der aus Böhmen*, p. 88.   Sometimes the effigy of Death (without a tree) is carried round by boys who collect gratuities (J. Grimm, *Deutsche Mythologie*,[4] ii. 644).

[5] Above, p. 208.

[6] Above, p. 231.

indicate the identity of the effigy with the wood-spirit by
fixing it to the top of a tree in the wood, where it remains
for a year, and is besought almost daily with prayers and
offerings to protect the herds ; for like a true wood-spirit the
Metsik is a patron of cattle.   Sometimes the *Metsik* is made
of sheaves of corn.[1]

Thus we may fairly conjecture that the names Carnival, The names
Death, and Summer are comparatively late and inadequate of Carnival, Death, and
expressions for the beings personified or embodied in the Summer
customs with which we have been dealing.   The very ab- in the preceding
stractness of the names bespeaks a modern origin ; for the customs
personification of times and seasons like the Carnival and seem to cover an
Summer, or of an abstract notion like death, is hardly ancient
primitive.   But the ceremonies themselves bear the stamp tree-spirit or spirit of
of a dateless antiquity ; therefore we can hardly help sup- vegetation.
posing that in their origin the ideas which they embodied
were of a more simple and concrete order.   The notion of a
tree, perhaps of a particular kind of tree (for some savages
have no word for tree in general), or even of an individual
tree, is sufficiently concrete to supply a basis from which by
a gradual process of generalisation the wider idea of a spirit
of vegetation might be reached.   But this general idea of
vegetation would readily be confounded with the season in
which it manifests itself ; hence the substitution of Spring,
Summer, or May for the tree-spirit or spirit of vegetation
would be easy and natural.   Again, the concrete notion of
the dying tree or dying vegetation would by a similar process
of generalisation glide into a notion of death in general ; so
that the practice of carrying out the dying or dead vegetation in spring, as a preliminary to its revival, would in time
widen out into an attempt to banish Death in general from
the village or district.   The view that in these spring ceremonies Death meant originally the dying or dead vegetation
of winter has the high support of W. Mannhardt ; and he
confirms it by the analogy of the name Death as applied to
the spirit of the ripe corn.   Commonly the spirit of the ripe

---

[1] F. J. Wiedemann, *Aus dem inneren und äusseren Leben der Ehsten*, p. 353 ; Holzmayer, "Osiliana," in *Verhandlungen der gelehrten Estnischen Gesell-* *schaft zu Dorpat*, vii. Heft 2, pp. 10 *sq.* ; W. Mannhardt, *Baumkultus*, pp. 407 *sq.*

corn is conceived, not as dead, but as old, and hence it goes by the name of the Old Man or the Old Woman. But in some places the last sheaf cut at harvest, which is generally believed to be the seat of the corn spirit, is called "the Dead One": children are warned against entering the corn-fields because Death sits in the corn; and, in a game played by Saxon children in Transylvania at the maize harvest, Death is represented by a child completely covered with maize leaves.[1]

§ 7. *Battle of Summer and Winter*

Dramatic contests between representatives of Summer and Winter.

Sometimes in the popular customs of the peasantry the contrast between the dormant powers of vegetation in winter and their awakening vitality in spring takes the form of a dramatic contest between actors who play the parts respectively of Winter and Summer. Thus in the towns of Sweden on May Day two troops of young men on horseback used to meet as if for mortal combat. One of them was led by a representative of Winter clad in furs, who threw snowballs and ice in order to prolong the cold weather. The other troop was commanded by a representative of Summer covered with fresh leaves and flowers. In the sham fight which followed the party of Summer came off victorious, and the ceremony ended with a feast.[2] Again, in the region of the middle Rhine, a representative of Summer clad in ivy combats a representative of Winter clad in straw or moss and finally gains a victory over him. The vanquished foe is thrown to the ground and stripped of his casing of straw, which is torn to pieces and scattered about, while the youthful comrades of the two champions sing a song to commemorate the defeat of Winter by Summer. Afterwards they carry about a summer garland or branch and collect gifts of eggs and bacon from house to house. Sometimes the champion who acts the part of Summer is dressed in leaves and flowers and wears a chaplet of flowers on his head. In the Palatinate this mimic

[1] W. Mannhardt, *Baumkultus*, pp. 417-421.

[2] Olaus Magnus, *De gentium septentrionalium variis conditionibus*, xv. 8 sq. In *Le Temps*, No. 15,669, May 11, 1902, p. 2, there is a description of this ceremony as it used to be performed in Stockholm. The description seems to be borrowed from Olaus Magnus.

conflict takes place on the fourth Sunday in Lent.[1]   All over
Bavaria the same drama used to be acted on the same day,
and it was still kept up in some places down to the middle
of the nineteenth century or later.   While Summer appeared
clad all in green, decked with fluttering ribbons, and carrying
a branch in blossom or a little tree hung with apples and
pears, Winter was muffled up in cap and mantle of fur and
bore in his hand a snow-shovel or a flail.   Accompanied by
their respective retinues dressed in corresponding attire, they
went through all the streets of the village, halting before the
houses and singing staves of old songs, for which they
received presents of bread, eggs, and fruit.   Finally, after a
short struggle, Winter was beaten by Summer and ducked in
the village well or driven out of the village with shouts and
laughter into the forest.[2]   In some parts of Bavaria the boys
who play the parts of Winter and Summer act their little
drama in every house that they visit, and engage in a war
of words before they come to blows, each of them vaunting
the pleasures and benefits of the season he represents and
disparaging those of the other.   The dialogue is in verse.   A
few couplets may serve as specimens :—

SUMMER

" *Green, green are meadows wherever I pass*
And the mowers are busy among the grass."

WINTER

" *White, white are the meadows wherever I go,*
And the sledges glide hissing across the snow."

SUMMER

" *I'll climb up the tree where the red cherries glow,*
And Winter can stand by himself down below."

WINTER

" *With you I will climb the cherry-tree tall,*
Its branches will kindle the fire in the hall."

---

[1] J. Grimm, *Deutsche Mythologie,*[4] ii. 637-639 ; *Bavaria, Landes- und Volkskunde des Königreichs Bayern,* iv. 2, pp. 357 *sq.* See also E. Krause, "Das Sommertags-Fest in Heidelberg," *Verhandlungen der Berliner Gesellschaft für Anthropologie,* 1895, p. (145) ; A. Dieterich, "Sommertag," *Archiv für Religionswissenschaft,* viii. (1905) Beiheft, pp. 82 *sqq.*

[2] *Bavaria, Landes- und Volkskunde des Königreichs Bayern,* i. 369 *sq.*

SUMMER

" O Winter, you are most uncivil
To send old women to the devil."

WINTER

" By that I make them warm and mellow,
So let them bawl and let them bellow."

SUMMER

" I am the Summer in white array,
I'm chasing the Winter far, far away."

WINTER

" I am the Winter in mantle of furs,
I'm chasing the Summer o'er bushes and burs."

SUMMER

" Just say a word more, and I'll have you bann'd
At once and for ever from Summer land."

WINTER

" O Summer, for all your bluster and brag,
You'd not dare to carry a hen in a bag."

SUMMER

" O Winter, your chatter no more can I stay,
I'll kick and I'll cuff you without delay."

Here ensues a scuffle between the two little boys, in which Summer gets the best of it, and turns Winter out of the house. But soon the beaten champion of Winter peeps in at the door and says with a humbled and crestfallen air :—

" O Summer, dear Summer, I'm under your ban,
For you are the master and I am the man."

To which Summer replies :—

" 'Tis a capital notion, an excellent plan,
If I am the master and you are the man.
So come, my dear Winter, and give me your hand,
We'll travel together to Summer Land." [1]

---

[1] *Bavaria, Landes- und Volkskunde des Königreichs Bayern,* ii. 259 *sq.* ; F. Panzer, *Beitrag zur deutschen Mythologie,* i. pp. 253-256 ; K. von Leoprechting, *Aus dem Lechrain,* pp. 167 *sq.* A dialogue in verse between representatives of Winter and Summer is spoken at Hartlieb in Silesia, near Breslau. See *Zeitschrift des Vereins für Volkskunde,* iii. (1893) pp. 226-228.

At Goepfritz in Lower Austria, two men personating Summer and Winter used to go from house to house on Shrove Tuesday, and were everywhere welcomed by the children with great delight. The representative of Summer was clad in white and bore a sickle ; his comrade, who played the part of Winter, had a fur-cap on his head, his arms and legs were swathed in straw, and he carried a flail. In every house they sang verses alternately.[1] At Drömling in Brunswick, down to the present time, the contest between Summer and Winter is acted every year at Whitsuntide by a troop of boys and a troop of girls. The boys rush singing, shouting, and ringing bells from house to house to drive Winter away ; after them come the girls singing softly and led by a May Bride, all in bright dresses and decked with flowers and garlands to represent the genial advent of spring. Formerly the part of Winter was played by a straw-man which the boys carried with them ; now it is acted by a real man in disguise.[2] In Wachtl and Brodek, a German village and a little German town of Moravia, encompassed by Slavonic people on every side, the great change that comes over the earth in spring is still annually mimicked. The long village of Wachtl, with its trim houses and farmyards, nestles in a valley surrounded by pretty pine-woods. Here, on a day in spring, about the time of the vernal equinox, an elderly man with a long flaxen beard may be seen going from door to door. He is muffled in furs, with warm gloves on his hands and a bearskin cap on his head, and he carries a threshing flail. This is the personification of Winter. With him goes a younger beardless man dressed in white, wearing a straw hat trimmed with gay ribbons on his head, and carrying a decorated May-tree in his hands. This is Summer. At every house they receive a friendly greeting and recite a long dialogue in verse, Winter punctuating his discourse with his flail, which he brings down with rude vigour on the backs of all within reach.[3] Amongst the Slavonic population near Ungarisch Brod, in Moravia, the ceremony took a somewhat different form.

[1] Th. Vernaleken, *Mythen und Bräuche des Völkes in Österreich*, pp. 297 *sq.*

[2] R. Andree, *Braunschweiger Volks-kunde* (Brunswick, 1896), p. 250.

[3] W. Müller, *Beiträge zur Volks-kunde der Deutschen in Mähren*, pp. 430-436.

Girls dressed in green marched in procession round a May-tree. Then two others, one in white and one in green, stepped up to the tree and engaged in a dialogue. Finally, the girl in white was driven away, but returned afterwards clothed in green, and the festival ended with a dance.[1]

Queen of Winter and Queen of May in the Isle of Man.

On May Day it used to be customary in almost all the large parishes of the Isle of Man to choose from among the daughters of the wealthiest farmers a young maiden to be Queen of May. She was dressed in the gayest attire and attended by about twenty others, who were called maids of honour. She had also a young man for her captain with a number of inferior officers under him. In opposition to her was the Queen of Winter, a man attired as a woman, with woollen hoods, fur tippets, and loaded with the warmest and heaviest clothes, one upon another. Her attendants were habited in like manner, and she too had a captain and troop for her defence. Thus representing respectively the beauty of spring and the deformity of winter they set forth from their different quarters, the one preceded by the dulcet music of flutes and violins, the other by the harsh clatter of cleavers and tongs. In this array they marched till they met on a common, where the trains of the two mimic sovereigns engaged in a mock battle. If the Queen of Winter's forces got the better of their adversaries and took her rival prisoner, the captive Queen of Summer was ransomed for as much as would pay the expenses of the festival. After this ceremony, Winter and her company retired and diverted themselves in a barn, while the partisans of Summer danced on the green, concluding the evening with a feast, at which the Queen and her maids sat at one table and the captain and his troop at another. In later times the person of the Queen of May was exempt from capture, but one of her slippers was substituted and, if captured, had to be ransomed to defray the expenses of the pageant. The procession of the Summer, which was subsequently composed of little girls and called the Maceboard, outlived that of its rival the Winter for some years; but both have now long been things of the past.[2]

[1] W. Müller, *op. cit.* p. 259.

[2] J. Train, *Historical and Statistical*   *Account of the Isle of Man* (Douglas, Isle of Man, 1845), ii. 118-120. It

Among the central Esquimaux of North America the contest between representatives of summer and winter, which in Europe has long degenerated into a mere dramatic performance, is still kept up as a magical ceremony of which the avowed intention is to influence the weather. In autumn, when storms announce the approach of the dismal Arctic winter, the Esquimaux divide themselves into two parties called respectively the ptarmigans and the ducks, the ptarmigans comprising all persons born in winter, and the ducks all persons born in summer. A long rope of sealskin is then stretched out, and each party laying hold of one end of it seeks by tugging with might and main to drag the other party over to its side. If the ptarmigans get the worst of it, then summer has won the game and fine weather may be expected to prevail through the winter.[1] In this ceremony it is clearly assumed that persons born in summer have a natural affinity with warm weather, and therefore possess a power of mitigating the rigour of winter, whereas persons born in winter are, so to say, of a cold and frosty disposition and can thereby exert a refrigerating influence on the temperature of the air. In spite of this natural antipathy between the representatives of summer and winter, we may be allowed to conjecture that in the grand tug of war the ptarmigans do not pull at the rope with the same hearty goodwill as the ducks, and that thus the genial influence of summer commonly prevails over the harsh austerity of winter. The Indians of Canada seem also to have imagined that

---

has been suggested that the name Maceboard may be a corruption of May-sports.

[1] Fr. Boas, "The Central Eskimo," *Sixth Annual Report of the Bureau of Ethnology* (Washington, 1888), p. 605. The account of this custom given by Captain J. S. Mutch is as follows : "The people take a long rope, the ends of which are tied together. They arrange themselves so that those born during the summer stand close to the water, and those born in the winter stand inland ; and then they pull at the rope to see whether summer or winter is the stronger. If winter should win, there will be plenty of food ; if summer should win, there will be a bad winter." See Fr. Boas, "The Eskimo of Baffin Land and Hudson Bay," *Bulletin of the American Museum of Natural History*, xv. (1901) pp. 140 *sq.* At Memphis in Egypt there were two statues in front of the temple of Hephaestus (Ptah), of which the more northern was popularly called Summer and the more southern Winter. The people worshipped the image of Summer and execrated the image of Winter. It has been suggested that the two statues represented Osiris and Typhon, the good and the bad god. See Herodotus, ii. 121, with the notes of Bähr and Wiedemann.

Canadian
Indians
drove away
Winter
with burn-
ing brands.

persons are endowed with distinct natural capacities according as they are born in summer or winter, and they turned
the distinction to account in much the same fashion as the
Esquimaux. When they wearied of the long frosts and the
deep snow which kept them prisoners in their huts and pre-
vented them from hunting, all of them who were born in
summer rushed out of their houses armed with burning
brands and torches which they hurled against the One who
makes Winter ; and this was supposed to produce the desired
effect of mitigating the cold. But those Indians who were
born in winter abstained from taking part in the ceremony,
for they believed that if they meddled with it the cold would
increase instead of diminishing.[1] We may surmise that in
the corresponding European ceremonies, which have just been
described, it was formerly deemed necessary that the actors,
who played the parts of Winter and Summer, should have
been born in the seasons which they personated.

The burn-
ing of
Winter at
Zurich.

Every year on the Monday after the spring equinox
boys and girls attired in gay costume flock at a very early
hour into Zurich from the country. The girls, generally
clad in white, are called *Mareielis* and carry two and two a
small May tree or a wreath decked with flowers and ribbons.
Thus they go in bands from house to house, jingling the
bells which are attached to the wreath and singing a song,
in which it is said that the *Mareielis* dance because the
leaves and the grass are green and everything is bursting
into blossom. In this way they are supposed to celebrate
the triumph of Summer and to proclaim his coming. The
boys are called *Böggen*. They generally wear over their
ordinary clothes a shirt decked with many-coloured ribbons,
tall pointed paper caps on their heads, and masks before
their faces. In this quaint costume they cart about through
the streets effigies made of straw and other combustible
materials which are supposed to represent Winter. At
evening these effigies are burned in various parts of the
city.[2] The ceremony was witnessed at Zurich on Monday, April 20th, 1903, by my friend Dr. J. Sutherland

---

[1] *Relations des Jésuites*, 1636, p. 38
(Canadian reprint, Quebec, 1858).

[2] H. Herzog, *Schweizerische Volks-*
feste, Sitten und Gebräuche (Aarau,
1884), pp. 164-166 ; W. Mannhardt,
Baumkultus, pp. 498 *sq.*

Black, who has kindly furnished me with some notes on the subject. The effigy of Winter was a gigantic figure composed in great part, as it seemed, of cotton-wool. This was laid on a huge pyre, about thirty feet high, which had been erected on the Stadthausplatz close to the lake. In presence of a vast concourse of people fire was set to the pyre and all was soon in a blaze, while the town bells rang a joyous peal. As the figure gradually consumed in the flames, the mechanism enclosed in its interior produced a variety of grotesque effects, such as the gushing forth of bowels. At last nothing remained of the effigy but the iron backbone ; the crowd slowly dispersed, and the fire brigade set to work to quench the smouldering embers.[1] In this ceremony the contest between Summer and Winter is rather implied than expressed, but the significance of the rite is unmistakable.

§ 8. *Death and Resurrection of Kostrubonko*

In Russia funeral ceremonies like those of " Burying the Carnival " and " Carrying out Death " are celebrated under the names, not of Death or the Carnival, but of certain mythic figures, Kostrubonko, Kostroma, Kupalo, Lada, and Yarilo. These Russian ceremonies are observed both in spring and at midsummer. Thus "in Little Russia it used to be the custom at Eastertide to celebrate the funeral of a being called Kostrubonko, the deity of the spring. A circle was formed of singers who moved slowly around a girl who lay on the ground as if dead, and as they went they sang,—

‘ Dead, dead is our Kostrubonko !
Dead, dead is our dear one !’

until the girl suddenly sprang up, on which the chorus joyfully exclaimed,—

‘ Come to life, come to life has our Kostrubonko !
Come to life, come to life has our dear one !’ "[2]

[marginal note: Funeral of Kostrubonko, Kostroma, Kupalo, and Yarilo in Russia.]

---

[1] Letter to me of Dr. J. S. Black, dated Lauriston Cottage, Wimbledon Common, 28th May, 1903. In a subsequent letter (dated 9th June, 1903) Dr. Black enclosed some bibliographical references to the custom which were kindly furnished to him by Professor P. Schmiedel of Zurich, who speaks of the effigy as a representative of Winter. It is not expressly so called by H. Herzog and W. Mannhardt. See the preceding note.

[2] W. R. S. Ralston, *Songs of the Russian People*, p. 221.

Funeral
of Kos-
trubonko,
Kostroma,
Kupalo,
and Yarilo
in Russia.
On the Eve of St. John (Midsummer Eve) a figure of Kupalo
is made of straw and " is dressed in woman's clothes, with a
necklace and a floral crown. Then a tree is felled, and, after
being decked with ribbons, is set up on some chosen spot.
Near this tree, to which they give the name of Marena
[Winter or Death], the straw figure is placed, together with a
table, on which stand spirits and viands. Afterwards a bonfire is lit, and the young men and maidens jump over it in
couples, carrying the figure with them. On the next day
they strip the tree and the figure of their ornaments, and
throw them both into a stream." [1] On St. Peter's Day, the
twenty-ninth of June, or on the following Sunday, "the
Funeral of Kostroma" or of Lada or of Yarilo is celebrated
in Russia. In the Governments of Penza and Simbirsk the
funeral used to be represented as follows. A bonfire was
kindled on the twenty-eighth of June, and on the next day
the maidens chose one of their number to play the part of
Kostroma. Her companions saluted her with deep obei-
sances, placed her on a board, and carried her to the bank of
a stream. There they bathed her in the water, while the
oldest girl made a basket of lime-tree bark and beat it like
a drum. Then they returned to the village and ended the
day with processions, games, and dances.[2] In the Murom
district Kostroma was represented by a straw figure dressed
in woman's clothes and flowers. This was laid in a trough
and carried with songs to the bank of a lake or river. Here
the crowd divided into two sides, of which the one attacked
and the other defended the figure. At last the assailants
gained the day, stripped the figure of its dress and ornaments,
tore it in pieces, trod the straw of which it was made under
foot, and flung it into the stream ; while the defenders of the
figure hid their faces in their hands and pretended to bewail
the death of Kostroma.[3] In the district of Kostroma the
burial of Yarilo was celebrated on the twenty-ninth or
thirtieth of June. The people chose an old man and gave
him a small coffin containing a Priapus-like figure represent-

[1] W. R. S. Ralston, *Songs of the
Russian People*, p. 241.
[2] W. R. S. Ralston, *op. cit.* pp.
243 *sq.* ; W. Mannhardt, *Baumkultus*,

p. 414.
[3] W. Mannhardt, *Baumkultus*, pp.
414 *sq.* ; W. R. S. Ralston, *op. cit.* p.
244.

ing Yarilo. This he carried out of the town, followed by women chanting dirges and expressing by their gestures grief and despair. In the open fields a grave was dug, and into it the figure was lowered amid weeping and wailing, after which games and dances were begun, " calling to mind the funeral games celebrated in old times by the pagan Slavonians." [1] In Little Russia the figure of Yarilo was laid in a coffin and carried through the streets after sunset surrounded by drunken women, who kept repeating mournfully, " He is dead ! he is dead ! " The men lifted and shook the figure as if they were trying to recall the dead man to life. Then they said to the women, " Women, weep not. I know what is sweeter than honey." But the women continued to lament and chant, as they do at funerals. " Of what was he guilty ? He was so good. He will arise no more. O how shall we part from thee ? What is life without thee ? Arise, if only for a brief hour. But he rises not, he rises not." At last the Yarilo was buried in a grave.[2]

§ 9. *Death and Revival of Vegetation*

These Russian customs are plainly of the same nature as those which in Austria and Germany are known as " Carrying out Death." Therefore if the interpretation here adopted of the latter is right, the Russian Kostrubonko, Yarilo, and the rest must also have been originally embodiments of the spirit of vegetation, and their death must have been regarded as a necessary preliminary to their revival. The revival as a sequel to the death is enacted in the first of the ceremonies described, the death and resurrection of Kostrubonko. The reason why in some of these Russian ceremonies the death of the spirit of vegetation is celebrated at midsummer may be that the decline of summer is dated from Midsummer Day, after which the days begin to shorten, and the sun sets out on his downward journey—

The Russian Kostrubonko, Yarilo, and so on, were probably at first spirits of vegetation dying and coming to life again.

" *To the darksome hollows*
Where the frosts of winter lie."

[1] W. R. S. Ralston, *op. cit.* p. 245; W. Mannhardt, *Baumkultus*, p. 416.   [2] W. Mannhardt, *l.c.* ; W. R. S. Ralston, *l.c.*

Such a turning-point of the year, when vegetation might be thought to share the incipient though still almost imperceptible decay of summer, might very well be chosen by primitive man as a fit moment for resorting to those magic rites by which he hopes to stay the decline, or at least to ensure the revival, of plant life.

In these ceremonies grief and gladness, love and hatred appear to be curiously combined. But while the death of vegetation appears to have been represented in all, and its revival in some, of these spring and midsummer ceremonies, there are features in some of them which can hardly be explained on this hypothesis alone. The solemn funeral, the lamentations, and the mourning attire, which often characterise these rites, are indeed appropriate at the death of the beneficent spirit of vegetation. But what shall we say of the glee with which the effigy is often carried out, of the sticks and stones with which it is assailed, and the taunts and curses which are hurled at it? What shall we say of the dread of the effigy evinced by the haste with which the bearers scamper home as soon as they have thrown it away, and by the belief that some one must soon die in any house into which it has looked? This dread might perhaps be explained by a belief that there is a certain infectiousness in the dead spirit of vegetation which renders its approach dangerous. But this explanation, besides being rather strained, does not cover the rejoicings which often attend the carrying out of Death. We must therefore recognise two distinct and seemingly opposite features in these ceremonies: on the one hand, sorrow for the death, and affection and respect for the dead; on the other hand, fear and hatred of the dead, and rejoicings at his death. How the former of these features is to be explained I have attempted to shew: how the latter came to be so closely associated with the former is a question which I shall try to answer in the sequel.

Expulsion of Death sometimes enacted without an effigy. Before we quit these European customs to go farther afield, it will be well to notice that occasionally the expulsion of Death or of a mythic being is conducted without any visible representative of the personage expelled. Thus at Königshain, near Görlitz in Silesia, all the villagers, young and old, used to go out with straw torches to the top of a neighbouring hill, called *Todtenstein* (Death-stone), where

they lit their torches, and so returned home singing, " We
have driven out Death, we are bringing back Summer." [1]
In Albania young people light torches of resinous wood on
Easter Eve, and march in procession through the village
brandishing them.   At last they throw the torches into the
river, saying, " Ha, Kore, we fling you into the river, like
these torches, that you may return no more."   Some say
that the intention of the ceremony is to drive out winter ;
but Kore is conceived as a malignant being who devours
children.[2]

§ 10. *Analogous Rites in India*

In the Kanagra district of India there is a custom Images of
observed by young girls in spring which closely resembles Siva and
Pârvatî
some of the European spring ceremonies just described.   It married,
is called the *Ralî Ka melâ*, or fair of Ralî, the *Ralî* being a drowned,
and
small painted earthen image of Siva or Pârvatî.   The custom mourned
is in vogue all over the Kanagra district, and its celebration, for in
India.
which is entirely confined to young girls, lasts through most
of Chet (March-April) up to the Sankrânt of Baisâkh (April).
On a morning in March all the young girls of the village
take small baskets of *dûb* grass and flowers to an appointed
place, where they throw them in a heap.   Round this
heap they stand in a circle and sing.   This goes on every
day for ten days, till the heap of grass and flowers has
reached a fair height.   Then they cut in the jungle two
branches, each with three prongs at one end, and place them,
prongs downwards, over the heap of flowers, so as to make
two tripods or pyramids.   On the single uppermost points
of these branches they get an image-maker to construct two
clay images, one to represent Siva, and the other Pârvatî.
The girls then divide themselves into two parties, one for
Siva and one for Pârvatî, and marry the images in the usual
way, leaving out no part of the ceremony.   After the marriage they have a feast, the cost of which is defrayed by
contributions solicited from their parents.   Then at the next
Sankrânt (Baisâkh) they all go together to the river-side,
throw the images into a deep pool, and weep over the place,

---

[1] J. Grimm, *Deutsche Mythologie,*[4]
ii. 644.

[2] J. G. von Hahn, *Albanesische
Studien* (Jena, 1854), i. 160.

as though they were performing funeral obsequies. The boys of the neighbourhood often tease them by diving after the images, bringing them up, and waving them about while the girls are crying over them. The object of the fair is said to be to secure a good husband.[1]

In this Indian custom Siva and Pârvatî seem to be the equivalents of the King and Queen of May.

That in this Indian ceremony the deities Siva and Pârvatî are conceived as spirits of vegetation seems to be proved by the placing of their images on branches over a heap of grass and flowers. Here, as often in European folk-custom, the divinities of vegetation are represented in duplicate, by plants and by puppets. The marriage of these Indian deities in spring corresponds to the European ceremonies in which the marriage of the vernal spirits of vegetation is represented by the King and Queen of May, the May Bride, Bridegroom of the May, and so forth.[2] The throwing of the images into the water, and the mourning for them, are the equivalents of the European customs of throwing the dead spirit of vegetation under the name of Death, Yarilo, Kostroma, and the rest, into the water and lamenting over it. Again, in India, as often in Europe, the rite is performed exclusively by females. The notion that the ceremony helps to procure husbands for the girls can be explained by the quickening and fertilising influence which the spirit of vegetation is believed to exert upon the life of man as well as of plants.[3]

§ 11. *The Magic Spring*

The foregoing customs were originally rites intended to ensure the revival of nature in spring by means of imitative magic.

The general explanation which we have been led to adopt of these and many similar ceremonies is that they are, or were in their origin, magical rites intended to ensure the revival of nature in spring. The means by which they were supposed to effect this end were imitation and sympathy. Led astray by his ignorance of the true causes of things, primitive man believed that in order to produce the great phenomena of nature on which his life depended he had only to imitate them, and that immediately by a secret

---

[1] R. C. Temple, in *Indian Antiquary*, xi. (1882) pp. 297 *sq.*

[2] See *The Magic Art and the Evolu-*tion *of Kings*, ii. 45 *sqq.*

[3] See *The Magic Art and the Evolution of Kings*, ii. 84 *sqq.*

sympathy or mystic influence the little drama which he acted in forest glade or mountain dell, on desert plain or wind-swept shore, would be taken up and repeated by mightier actors on a vaster stage. He fancied that by masquerading in leaves and flowers he helped the bare earth to clothe herself with verdure, and that by playing the death and burial of winter he drove that gloomy season away, and made smooth the path for the footsteps of returning spring. If we find it hard to throw ourselves even in fancy into a mental condition in which such things seem possible, we can more easily picture to ourselves the anxiety which the savage, when he first began to lift his thoughts above the satisfaction of his merely animal wants, and to meditate on the causes of things, may have felt as to the continued operation of what we now call the laws of nature. To us, familiar as we are with the conception of the uniformity and regularity with which the great cosmic phenomena succeed each other, there seems little ground for apprehension that the causes which produce these effects will cease to operate, at least within the near future. But this confidence in the stability of nature is bred only by the experience which comes of wide observation and long tradition ; and the savage, with his narrow sphere of observation and his short-lived tradition, lacks the very elements of that experience which alone could set his mind at rest in face of the ever-changing and often menacing aspects of nature. No wonder, therefore, that he is thrown into a panic by an eclipse, and thinks that the sun or the moon would surely perish, if he did not raise a clamour and shoot his puny shafts into the air to defend the luminaries from the monster who threatens to devour them. No wonder he is terrified when in the darkness of night a streak of sky is suddenly illumined by the flash of a meteor, or the whole expanse of the celestial arch glows with the fitful light of the Northern Streamers.[1] Even phenomena which recur at

---

[1] When the Kurnai of Victoria saw the Aurora Australis, which corresponds to the Northern Streamers of Europe, they exchanged wives for the day and swung the severed hand of a dead man towards it, shouting, " Send it away ! do not let it burn us up ! " See A. W. Howitt, " On some Australian Beliefs," *Journal of the Anthropological Institute*, xiii. (1884) p. 189 ; *id.*, *Native Tribes of South-East Australia*, pp. 276 *sq.*, 430.

fixed and uniform intervals may be viewed by him with apprehension, before he has come to recognise the orderliness of their recurrence. The speed or slowness of his recognition of such periodic or cyclic changes in nature will depend largely on the length of the particular cycle. The cycle, for example, of day and night is everywhere, except in the polar regions, so short and hence so frequent that men probably soon ceased to discompose themselves seriously as to the chance of its failing to recur, though the ancient Egyptians, as we have seen, daily wrought enchantments to bring back to the east in the morning the fiery orb which had sunk at evening in the crimson west. But it was far otherwise with the annual cycle of the seasons. To any man a year is a considerable period, seeing that the number of our years is but few at the best. To the primitive savage, with his short memory and imperfect means of marking the flight of time, a year may well have been so long that he failed to recognise it as a cycle at all, and watched the changing aspects of earth and heaven with a perpetual wonder, alternately delighted and alarmed, elated and cast down, according as the vicissitudes of light and heat, of plant and animal life, ministered to his comfort or threatened his existence. In autumn when the withered leaves were whirled about the forest by the nipping blast, and he looked up at the bare boughs, could he feel sure that they would ever be green again? As day by day the sun sank lower and lower in the sky, could he be certain that the luminary would ever retrace his heavenly road? Even the waning moon, whose pale sickle rose thinner and thinner every night over the rim of the eastern horizon, may have excited in his mind a fear lest, when it had wholly vanished, there should be moons no more.

Feelings with which the primitive savage may have regarded the changes of the seasons.

These and a thousand such misgivings may have thronged the fancy and troubled the peace of the man who first began to reflect on the mysteries of the world he lived in, and to take thought for a more distant future than the morrow. It was natural, therefore, that with such thoughts and fears he should have done all that in him lay to bring back the faded blossom to the bough, to swing the low sun of winter up to his old place in the summer sky, and to restore its orbed fulness to

In modern Europe the old magical rites for the revival of nature in spring have degenerated into mere pageants and pastimes.

the silver lamp of the waning moon.   We may smile at his vain endeavours if we please, but it was only by making a long series of experiments, of which some were almost inevitably doomed to failure, that man learned from experience the futility of some of his attempted methods and the fruitfulness of others.   After all, magical ceremonies are nothing but experiments which have failed and which continue to be repeated merely because, for reasons which have already been indicated,[1] the operator is unaware of their failure.   With the advance of knowledge these ceremonies either cease to be performed altogether or are kept up from force of habit long after the intention with which they were instituted has been forgotten.   Thus fallen from their high estate, no longer regarded as solemn rites on the punctual performance of which the welfare and even the life of the community depend, they sink gradually to the level of simple pageants, mummeries, and pastimes, till in the final stage of degeneration they are wholly abandoned by older people, and, from having once been the most serious occupation of the sage, become at last the idle sport of children. It is in this final stage of decay that most of the old magical rites of our European forefathers linger on at the present day, and even from this their last retreat they are fast being swept away by the rising tide of those multitudinous forces, moral, intellectual, and social, which are bearing mankind onward to a new and unknown goal.   We may feel some natural regret at the disappearance of quaint customs and picturesque ceremonies, which have preserved to an age often deemed dull and prosaic something of the flavour and freshness of the olden time, some breath of the springtime of the world ; yet our regret will be lessened when we remember that these pretty pageants, these now innocent diversions, had their origin in ignorance and superstition ; that if they are a record of human endeavour, they are also a monument of fruitless ingenuity, of wasted labour, and of blighted hopes ; and that for all their gay trappings—their flowers, their ribbons, and their music—they partake far more of tragedy than of farce.

The interpretation which, following in the footsteps of

[1] See *The Magic Art and the Evolution of Kings*, i. 242 *sq.*

Parallel to
the spring
customs of
Europe in
the magical
rites of the
Central
Australian
aborigines. W. Mannhardt, I have attempted to give of these ceremonies has been not a little confirmed by the discovery, made since this book was first written, that the natives of Central Australia regularly practise magical ceremonies for the purpose of awakening the dormant energies of nature at the approach of what may be called the Australian spring. Nowhere apparently are the alternations of the seasons more sudden and the contrasts between them more striking than in the deserts of Central Australia, where at the end of a long period of drought the sandy and stony wilderness, over which the silence and desolation of death appear to brood, is suddenly, after a few days of torrential rain, transformed into a landscape smiling with verdure and peopled with teeming multitudes of insects and lizards, of frogs and birds. The marvellous change which passes over the face of nature at such times has been compared even by European observers to the effect of magic;[1] no wonder, then, that the savage should regard it as such in very deed. Now it is just when there is promise of the approach of a good season that the natives of Central Australia are wont especially to perform those magical ceremonies of which the avowed intention is to multiply the plants and animals they use as food.[2] These ceremonies, therefore, present a close analogy to the spring customs of our European peasantry not only in the time of their celebration, but also in their aim ; for we can hardly doubt that in instituting rites designed to assist the revival of plant life in spring our primitive forefathers were moved, not by any sentimental wish to smell at early violets, or pluck the rathe primrose, or watch yellow daffodils dancing in the breeze, but by the very practical consideration, certainly not formulated in abstract terms, that the life of man is inextricably bound up with that of plants, and that if they were to perish he could not survive. And as the faith of the Australian savage in the efficacy of his magic rites is confirmed by observing that their performance is invariably followed, sooner or later, by that increase of vegetable and animal life which it is their

---

[1] Spencer and Gillen, *Native Tribes of Central Australia*, pp. 4 *sq.*, 170.

[2] Spencer and Gillen, *op. cit.* p. 170. For a description of some of these ceremonies see *The Magic Art and the Evolution of Kings*, i. 85 *sqq.*

object to produce, so, we may suppose, it was with European savages in the olden time. The sight of the fresh green in brake and thicket, of vernal flowers blowing on mossy banks, of swallows arriving from the south, and of the sun mounting daily higher in the sky, would be welcomed by them as so many visible signs that their enchantments were indeed taking effect, and would inspire them with a cheerful confidence that all was well with a world which they could thus mould to suit their wishes. Only in autumn days, as summer slowly faded, would their confidence again be dashed by doubts and misgivings at symptoms of decay, which told how vain were all their efforts to stave off for ever the approach of winter and of death.

NOTE A

CHINESE INDIFFERENCE TO DEATH

LORD AVEBURY kindly allows me to print the letter of Mr. M. W. Lampson, referred to above (p. 146, note [1]). It runs as follows:— Letter of Mr. M. W. Lampson.

FOREIGN OFFICE, *August* 7, 1903.

DEAR LORD AVEBURY—As the result of enquiries I hear from a Mr. Eames, a lawyer who practised for some years at Shanghai and has considerable knowledge of Chinese matters, that for a small sum a substitute can be found for execution. This is recognised by the Chinese authorities, with certain exceptions, as for instance parricide. It is even asserted that the local Taotai gains pecuniarily by this arrangement, as he is as a rule not above obtaining a substitute for the condemned man for a less sum than was paid him by the latter.

It is, I believe, part of the doctrine of Confucius that it is one of the highest virtues to increase the family prosperity at the expense of personal suffering. According to Eames, the Chinamen [*sic*] looks upon execution in another man's stead in this light, and consequently there is quite a competition for such a "substitution."

Should you wish to get more definite information, the address is: W. Eames, Esq., c/o Norman Craig, Inner Temple, E.C.

The only man in this department who has actually been out to China is at present away. But on his return I will ask him about it.— Yours sincerely,   MILES W. LAMPSON.

On this subject Lord Avebury had stated: "It is said that in China, if a rich man is condemned to death, he can sometimes purchase a willing substitute at a very small expense."[1] In regard to his authority for this statement Lord Avebury wrote to me (August 10, 1903): "I believe my previous information came from Sir T. Wade, but I have been unable to lay my hand on his letter, and do not therefore like to state it as a fact." Sir Thomas Wade Lord Avebury's statement.

[1] Lord Avebury, *Origin of Civilisation*,[5] pp. 378 *sq.*; compare *id.*, *Prehistoric Times*,[5] p. 561.

was English Ambassador at Peking, and afterwards Professor of Chinese at Cambridge.

On the same subject Mr. Valentine Chirol, editor of the foreign department of *The Times*, wrote to me as follows :—

QUEEN ANNE'S MANSIONS, WESTMINSTER, S.W.,
August 21st, 1905.

DEAR SIR—I shall be very glad to do what I can to obtain for you the information you require. It was a surprise to me to hear that the accuracy of the statement was called in question. It is certainly a matter of common report in China that the practice exists. The difficulty, I conceive, will be to obtain evidence enabling one to quote concrete cases. My own impression is that the practice is quite justifiable according to Chinese ethics when life is given up from motives of filial piety, that is to say in order to relieve the wants of indigent parents, or to defray the costs of ancestral rights [*sic*]. Your general thesis that life is less valued and more readily sacrificed by some races than by modern Europeans seems to be beyond dispute. Surely the Japanese practice of *sepuku*, or *harikari*, as it is vulgarly called, is a case in point. Life is risked, as in duelling, by Europeans, for the mere point of honour, but it is never deliberately laid down in satisfaction of the exigencies of the social code. I will send you whatever information I can obtain when it reaches me, but that will not of course be for some months.—Yours truly,   VALENTINE CHIROL.

P.S.—A friend of mine who has just been here entirely confirms my own belief as to the accuracy of your statement, and tells me he has himself seen several Imperial Decrees in the *Peking Gazette*, calling provincial authorities to order for having allowed specific cases of substitution to occur, and ordering the death penalty to be carried out in a more severe form on the original culprits as an extra punishment for obtaining substitutes. He has promised to look up some of these Impe. Decrees on his return to China, and send me translations. I am satisfied personally that his statement is conclusive.   V. C.

On the same subject I have received the following letter from Mr. J. O. P. Bland, for fourteen years correspondent of *The Times* in China :—

THE CLOCK HOUSE, SHEPPERTON,
March 22nd, 1911.

DEAR PROFESSOR FRAZER—My friend Mr. Valentine Chirol, writing the other day from Crete on his way East, asked me to communicate with you on the subject of your letter of the 3rd ulto., namely, the custom, alleged to exist in China, of procuring substitutes for persons condemned to death, the substitutes' families or relatives receiving compensation in cash.

To speak of this as a custom is to exaggerate the frequency of a class of incident which has undoubtedly been recorded in China and of which there has been mention in Imperial Decrees. I am sorry to say that I have not my file of the *Peking Gazette* here, for immediate reference, but I am writing to my friend Mr. Backhouse in Peking, and have no doubt but that he will be able to give chapter and verse of instances thus recorded. I had expected to find cases of the kind recorded in Mr. Werner's recently-published "Descriptive Sociology" of the Chinese (Spencerian publications), but have not been able to do so in the absence of an index to that voluminous work. More than one of the authors whom he quotes have certainly referred to cases of substitution for death-sentence prisoners. Parker, for instance ("China Past and Present," page 378), asserts that substitutes were to be had in Canton at the reasonable price of fifty taels (say £10). Dr. Matignon (in "Superstition, Crime et Misère en Chine," page 113) says that filial piety is a frequent motive. The negative opinion of Professors Giles and de Groot is entitled to consideration, but cannot be regarded as any more conclusive than the views expressed by Professor Giles on the question of infanticide which are outweighed by a mass of direct proof of eye-witnesses.

In a country where men submit voluntarily to mutilation and grave risk of death for a comparatively small gain to themselves and their relatives, where women commit suicide in hundreds to escape capture by invaders or strangers, where men and women alike habitually sacrifice their life for the most trivial motives of revenge or distress, it need not greatly surprise us that some should be found, especially among the wretchedly poor class, willing to give up their life in order to relieve their families of want or otherwise to "acquire merit."

The most important thing, I think, in expressing any opinion about the Chinese, is to remember the great extent and heterogeneous elements of the country, and to abstain from any sweeping generalisations based on isolated acts or events.—Yours very truly,   J. O. P. BLAND.

As the practice in question involves a grave miscarriage of justice, the discovery of which might entail serious consequences on the magistrate who connived at it, we need not wonder that it is generally hushed up, and that no instances of it should come to the ears of many Europeans resident in China. My friend Professor H. A. Giles of Cambridge in conversation expressed himself quite incredulous on the subject, and Professor J. J. M. de Groot of Leyden wrote to me (January 31, 1902) to the same effect. The Rev. Dr. W. T. A. Barber, Headmaster of the Leys School, Cambridge, and formerly a missionary in China, wrote to me (January 30, 1902): "As to the possibility that a man condemned to death may secure a substitute on payment of a moderate sum of money, we used to hear that this was the case; but I have no proof that would justify you in using the fact." Another experienced missionary, the Rev. W. A. Cornaby, wrote to Dr. Barber: "I have heard of no such custom in capital crimes. The man in whose house a fire starts may, and often does, pay another to receive the blows and three days in a cangue.   But unless where 'foreign riots' were the case, and a previously condemned criminal handy, I should hardly think it possible.   Every precaution is taken that no one is beheaded but the man who cannot possibly be let off.   The expense on the county mandarin is over £100 in 'stationery expenses' with higher courts."   On this I would observe that if every execution costs the local mandarin so dear, he must be under a strong temptation to get the expenses out of the prisoner whenever he can do so without being detected.

Substitutes for corporal punishment in China.   With regard to the custom, mentioned by Mr. Cornaby, of procuring substitutes for corporal punishment, we are told that in China there are men who earn a livelihood by being thrashed instead of the real culprits.   But they bribe the executioner to lay on lightly ; otherwise their constitution could not long resist the tear and wear of so exhausting a profession.[1]   Thus the theory and practice of vicarious suffering are well understood in China.

---

[1] De Guignes, *Voyages à Peking, Manille et l'Île de France*, iii. (Paris, 1808) pp. 114 *sq.*

NOTE B

THE custom of swinging has been practised as a religious or rather magical rite in various parts of the world, but it does not seem possible to explain all the instances of it in the same way.   People appear to have resorted to the practice from different motives and with different ideas of the benefit to be derived from it.   In the text we have seen that the Letts, and perhaps the Siamese, swing to make the crops grow tall.[1]   The same may be the intention of the ceremony whenever it is specially observed at harvest festivals. Among the Buginese and Macassars of Celebes, for example, it used to be the custom for young girls to swing one after the other on these occasions.[2]   At the great Dassera festival of Nepaul, which immediately precedes the cutting of the rice, swings and kites come into fashion among the young people of both sexes.   The swings are sometimes hung from boughs of trees, but generally from a cross-beam supported on a framework of tall bamboos.[3]   Among the Dyaks of Sarawak a feast is held at the end of harvest, when the soul of the rice is secured to prevent the crops from rotting away. On this occasion a number of old women rock to and fro on a rude swing suspended from the rafters.[4]   A traveller in Sarawak has described how he saw many tall swings erected and Dyaks swinging to and fro on them, sometimes ten or twelve men together on one swing, while they chanted in monotonous, dirge-like tones an invocation to the spirits that they would be pleased to grant a plentiful harvest of sago and fruit and a good fishing season.[5]

In the East Indian island of Bengkali elaborate and costly cere-

The custom of swinging practised for various reasons.

Swinging at harvest.

---

[1] Above, pp. 156 sq.

[2] B. F. Matthes, *Einige Eigenthumlichkeiten in den Festen und Gewohnheiten der Makassaren und Buginesen* (Leyden, 1884), p. 1 ; *id.*, " Over de âdá's of gewoonten der Makassaren en Boegineezen," *Verslagen en Mededeelingen der koninklijke Akademie van Wetenschappen*, Afdeeling Letterkunde, Derde Reeks, Tweede Deel (Amsterdam, 1885), pp. 169 sq.

[3] H. A. Oldfield, *Sketches from Nipal* (London, 1880), ii. 351.

[4] Spenser St. John, *Life in the Forests of the Far East*,[2] i. 194 sq.

[5] Ch. Brooke, *Ten Years in Sarawak*, ii. 226 sq.

Swinging for fish and game. monies are performed to ensure a good catch of fish. Among the rest an hereditary priestess, who bears the royal title of Djindjang Rajah, works herself up by means of the fumes of incense and so forth into that state of mental disorder which with many people passes for a symptom of divine inspiration. In this pious frame of mind she is led by her four handmaids to a swing all covered with yellow and hung with golden bells, on which she takes her seat amid the jingle of the bells. As she rocks gently to and fro in the swing, she speaks in an unknown tongue to each of the sixteen spirits who have to do with the fishing.[1] In order to procure a plentiful supply of game the Tinneh Indians of North-West America perform a magical ceremony which they call "the young man bounding or tied." They pinion a man tightly, and having hung him by the head and heels from the roof of the hut, rock him backwards and forwards.[2]

Thus we see that people swing in order to procure a plentiful supply of fish and game as well as good crops. In such cases the notion seems to be that the ceremony promotes fertility, whether in the vegetable or the animal kingdom; though why it should be Indian custom of swinging on hooks. supposed to do so, I confess myself unable to explain. There seem to be some reasons for thinking that the Indian rite of swinging on hooks run through the flesh of the performer is also resorted to, at least in some cases, from a belief in its fertilising virtue. Thus Hamilton tells us that at Karwar, on the west coast of India, a feast is held at the end of May or beginning of June in honour of the infernal gods, "with a divination or conjuration to know the fate of the ensuing crop of corn." Men were hung from a pole by means of tenter-hooks inserted in the flesh of their backs; and the pole with the men dangling from it was then dragged for more than a mile over ploughed ground from one sacred grove to another, preceded by a young girl who carried a pot of fire on her head. When the second grove was reached, the men were let down and taken off the hooks, and the girl fell into the usual prophetic frenzy, after which she unfolded to the priests the revelation with which she had just been favoured by the terrestrial gods. In each of the groves a shapeless black stone, daubed with red lead to stand for a mouth, eyes, and ears, appears to have represented the indwelling divinity.[3] Sometimes this custom of swinging on hooks, which is known among the Hindoos as *Churuk Puja*, seems to be intended

---

[1] J. S. G. Gramberg, "De Troeboek-visscherij," *Tijdschrift voor Indische Taal- Land- en Volkenkunde*, xxiv. (1887) pp. 314 *sq.*

[2] E. Petitot, *Monographie des Dènè-Dindjiè* (Paris, 1876), p. 38. The same ceremony is performed, oddly enough, to procure the death of an enemy.

[3] Hamilton's "Account of the East Indies," in Pinkerton's *Voyages and Travels*, viii. 360 *sq.* In general we are merely told that these Indian devotees swing on hooks in fulfilment of a vow or to obtain some favour of a deity. See Duarte Barbosa, *Description of the Coasts of East Africa and Malabar in the beginning of the Six-*

to propitiate demons.   Some Santals asked Mr. V. Ball to be allowed
to perform it because their women and children were dying of sickness, and their cattle were being killed by wild beasts; they believed
that these misfortunes befell them because the evil spirits had not
been appeased.[1]   These same Santals celebrate a swinging festival
of a less barbarous sort about the month of February.   Eight men
sit in chairs and rotate round posts in a sort of revolving swing, like
the merry-go-rounds which are so dear to children at English fairs.[2]
At the Nauroz and Eed festivals in Dardistan the women swing on
ropes suspended from trees.[3]   During the rainy season in Behar *Swinging*
young women swing in their houses, while they sing songs appro- *in the rainy*
priate to the season.   The period during which they indulge in this *season.*
pastime, if a mere pastime it be, is strictly limited; it begins with a
festival which usually falls on the twenty-fifth of the month Jeyt and
ends with another festival which commonly takes place on the twenty-
fifth of the month Asin.   No one would think of swinging at any
other time of the year.[4]   It is possible that this last custom may
be nothing more than a pastime meant to while away some of the
tedious hours of the inclement season; but its limitation to a certain
clearly-defined portion of the year seems rather to point to a religious
or magical origin.   Possibly the intention may once have been to
drive away the rain.   We shall see immediately that swinging is sometimes resorted to for the purpose of expelling the powers of evil.
About the middle of March the Hindoos observe a swinging festival *Swinging*
of a different sort in honour of the god Krishna, whose image is *in honour*
placed in the seat or cradle of a swing and then, just when the dawn *of Krishna.*
is breaking, rocked gently to and fro several times.   The same ceremony is repeated at noon and at sunset.[5]   In the Rigveda the sun
is called, by a natural metaphor, "the golden swing in the sky," and
the expression helps us to understand a ceremony of Vedic India.
A priest sat in a swing and touched with the span of his right hand at
once the seat of the swing and the ground.   In doing so he said, "The

teenth Century, translated by the Hon.
H. E. J. Stanley (Hakluyt Society,
London, 1866), pp. 95 *sq.*; Gaspar
Balbi's " Voyage to Pegu," in Pinker-
ton's *Voyages and Travels*, ix. 398 ;
Sonnerat, *Voyage aux Indes orientales
et à la Chine*, i. 244 ; S. Mateer, *The
Land of Charity*, p. 220 ; W. W.
Hunter, *Annals of Rural Bengal*,[5] p.
463 ; *North Indian Notes and Queries*,
i. p. 76, § 511.

[1] V. Ball, *Jungle Life in India*
(London, 1880), p. 232.

[2] W. W. Hunter, *Annals of Rural
Bengal*[5] (London, 1872), p. 463.

[3] G. W. Leitner, *The Languages and*

Races of Dardistan (Lahore, 1878),
p. 12.

[4] Sarat Chandra Mitra, " Notes on
two Behari Pastimes," *Journal of the
Anthropological Society of Bombay*, iii.
95 *sq.*

[5] H. H. Wilson, " The Religious
Festivals of the Hindus," *Journal of
the Royal Asiatic Society*, ix. (1848)
p. 98.   Compare E. T. Dalton, *Descriptive Ethnology of Bengal*, p. 314 ;
Monier Williams, *Religious Life and
Thought in India*, p. 137 ; W. Crooke,
" The Legends of Krishna," *Folk-lore*,
xi. (1900) pp. 21 *sqq.*

great lord has united himself with the great lady, the god has united himself with the goddess." Perhaps he meant to indicate in a graphic way that the sun had reached that lowest point of its course where it was nearest to the earth.[1] In this connexion it is of interest to note that in the Esthonian celebration of St. John's Day or the summer solstice swings play, along with bonfires, the most prominent part. Girls sit and swing the whole night through, singing old songs to explain why they do so. For legend tells of an Esthonian prince who wooed and won an Islandic princess. But a wicked enchanter spirited away the lover to a desert island, where he languished in captivity, till his lady-love contrived to break the magic spell that bound him. Together they sailed home to Esthonia, which they reached on St. John's Day, and burnt their ship, resolved to stray no longer in far foreign lands. The swings in which the Esthonian maidens still rock themselves on St. John's Day are said to recall the ship in which the lovers tossed upon the stormy sea, and the bonfires commemorate the burning of it. When the fires have died out, the swings are laid aside and never used again either in the village or at the solitary alehouse until spring comes round once more.[2] Here it is natural to connect both swings and bonfires with the apparent course of the sun, who reaches the highest and turning point of his orbit on St. John's Day. Bonfires and swings perhaps were originally charms intended to kindle and speed afresh on its heavenly road "the golden swing in the sky." Among the Letts of South Livonia and Curland the summer solstice is the occasion of a great festival of flowers, at which the people sing songs with the constant refrain of *lihgo, lihgo*. It has been proposed to derive the word *lihgo* from the Lettish verb *ligot*, "to swing," with reference to the sun swinging in the sky at this turning-point of his course.[3]

At Tengaroeng, in Eastern Borneo, the priests and priestesses receive the inspiration of the spirits seated in swings and rocking themselves to and fro. Thus suspended in the air they appear to be in a peculiarly favourable position for catching the divine afflatus. One end of the plank which forms the seat of the priest's swing is carved in the rude likeness of a crocodile's head; the swing of the priestess is similarly ornamented with a serpent's head.[4]

Again, swings are used for the cure of sickness, but it is the doctor who rocks himself in them, not the patient. In North Borneo the Dyak medicine man will sometimes erect a swing in

Marginal notes: Esthonian custom of swinging at the summer solstice. Swinging for inspiration. Swinging as a cure for sickness.

[1] *The Hymns of the Rigveda*, vii. 87. 5 (vol. iii. p. 108 of R. T. H. Griffith's translation, Benares, 1891); H. Oldenberg, *Die Religion des Veda*, pp. 444 *sq.*

[2] J. G. Kohl, *Die deutsch-russischen Ostseeprovinzen* (Dresden and Leipsic, 1841), ii. 268 *sqq.*

[3] L. v. Schroeder, "Lihgo (Refrain der lettischen Sonnwendlieder)," *Mitteilungen der Anthropologischen Gesellschaft in Wien*, xxxii. (1902) pp. 1-11.

[4] S. W. Tromp, "Uit de Salasila van Koetei," *Bijdragen tot de Taal- Land- en Volkenkunde van Nederlandsch-Indië*, xxxvii. (1888) pp. 87-89.

front of the sick man's house and sway backwards and forwards on it for the purpose of kicking away the disease, frightening away evil spirits, and catching the stray soul of the sufferer.[1] Clearly in his passage through the air the physician is likely to collide with the disease and the evil spirits, both of which are sure to be loitering about in the neighbourhood of the patient, and the rude shock thus given to the malady and the demons may reasonably be expected to push or hustle them away. At Tengaroeng, in Eastern Borneo, a traveller witnessed a ceremony for the expulsion of an evil spirit in which swinging played a part. After four men in blue shirts bespangled with stars, and wearing coronets of red cloth decorated with beads and bells, had sought diligently for the devil, grabbling about on the floor and grunting withal, three hideous hags dressed in faded red petticoats were brought in with great pomp, carried on the shoulders of Malays, and took their seats, amid solemn silence, on the cradle of a swing, the ends of which were carved to represent the head and tail of a crocodile. Not a sound escaped from the crowd of spectators during this awe-inspiring ceremony; they regarded the business as most serious. The venerable dames then rocked to and fro on the swing, fanning themselves languidly with Chinese paper fans. At a later stage of the performance they and three girls discharged burning arrows at a sort of altar of banana leaves, maize, and grass. This completed the discomfiture of the devil.[2]

The Athenians in antiquity celebrated an annual festival of swinging. Boards were hung from trees by ropes, and people sitting on them swung to and fro, while they sang songs of a loose or voluptuous character. The swinging went on both in public and private. Various explanations were given of the custom; the most generally received was as follows. When Bacchus came among men to make known to them the pleasures of wine, he lodged with a certain Icarus or Icarius, to whom he revealed the precious secret and bade him go forth and carry the glad tidings to all the world. So Icarus loaded a waggon with wine-skins, and set out on his travels, the dog Maera running beside him. He came to Attica, and there fell in with shepherds tending their sheep, to whom he gave of the wine. They drank greedily, but when some of them fell down dead drunk, their companions thought the stranger had poisoned them with intent to steal the sheep; so they knocked him on the head. The faithful dog ran home and guided his master's daughter Erigone to the body. At sight of it she was smitten with

Athenian festival of swinging.

[1] J. Perham, "Manangism in Borneo," *Journal of the Straits Branch of the Royal Asiatic Society*, No. 19 (Singapore, 1887), pp. 97 *sq.*; E. H. Gomes, *Seventeen Years among the Sea Dyaks of Borneo* (London, 1911), pp. 169, 170, 171 ; H. Ling Roth, *The Natives of Sarawak and British North Borneo*, i. 279.

[2] C. Bock, *The Head-hunters of Borneo* (London, 1881), pp. 110-112.

despair and hanged herself on a tree beside her dead father, but not until she had prayed that, unless the Athenians should avenge her sire's murder, their daughters might die the same death as she. Her curse was fulfilled, for soon many Athenian damsels hanged themselves for no obvious reason. An oracle informed the Athenians of the true cause of this epidemic of suicide; so they sought out the bodies of the unhappy pair and instituted the swinging festival to appease Erigone; and at the vintage they offered the first of the grapes to her and her father.[1]

Swinging as a mode of expiation and purification.
Thus the swinging festival at Athens was regarded by the ancients as an expiation for a suicide or suicides by hanging. This opinion is strongly confirmed by a statement of Varro, that it was unlawful to perform funeral rites in honour of persons who had died by hanging, but that in their case such rites were replaced by a custom of swinging images, as if in imitation of the death they had died.[2] Servius says that the Athenians, failing to find the bodies of Icarius and Erigone on earth, made a pretence of seeking them in the air by swinging on ropes hung from trees; and he seems to have regarded the custom of swinging as a purification by means of air.[3] This explanation probably comes very near the truth; indeed if we substitute "souls" for "bodies" in the wording of it we may almost accept it as exact. It might be thought that the souls of persons who had died by hanging were, more than the souls of the other dead, hovering in the air, since their bodies were suspended in air at the moment of death. Hence it would be considered needful to purge the air of these vagrant spirits, and this might be done by swinging persons or things to and fro, in order that by their impact they might disperse and drive away the baleful ghosts. Thus the custom would be exactly analogous, on the one hand, to the practice of the Malay medicine-man, who swings to and fro in front of the patient's house in order to chase away the disease, or to frighten away evil spirits, or to catch the stray soul of the sick man, and, on the other hand, to the practice of the Central Australian

---

[1] Hyginus, *Astronomica*, ii. 4, pp. 34 *sqq.*, ed. Bunte; *id.*, *Fabulae*, 130; Servius and Probus on Virgil, *Georg.* ii. 389; Festus, *s.v.* "Oscillantes," p. 194, ed. C. O. Müller; Athenaeus, xiv. 10, p. 618 E F; Pollux, iv. 55; Hesychius, *s.vv.* 'Αλῆτις and Αἰώρα; *Etymologicum magnum*, *s.v.* Αἰώρα, p. 42. 3; Schol. on Homer, *Iliad*, xxii. 29. The story of the murder of Icarius is told by a scholiast on Lucian (*Dial. meretr.* vii. 4) to explain the origin of a different festival (*Rheinisches Museum*, N.F., xxv. (1870) pp. 557 *sqq.*; *Scholia in Lucianum*, ed. H. Rabe,

p. 280). As to the swinging festival at Athens see O. Jahn, *Archäologische Beiträge*, pp. 324 *sq.*; Daremberg et Saglio, *Dictionnaire des antiquités grecques et romaines*, *s.v.* "Aiora"; Miss J. E. Harrison, in *Mythology and Monuments of Ancient Athens*, by Mrs. Verrall and Miss J. E. Harrison, pp. xxxix *sqq.*

[2] Servius on Virgil, *Aen.* xii. 603: "*Et Varro ait: Suspendiosis quibus iusta fieri ius non sit, suspensis oscillis veluti per imitationem mortis parentari.*"

[3] Servius on Virgil, *Georg.* ii. 389; *id.*, on *Aen.* vi. 741.

aborigines who beat the air with their weapons and hands in order to drive the lingering ghost away to the grave.[1]   At Rome swinging seems to have formed part of the great Latin festival (*Feriae Latinae*), and its origin was traced to a search in the air for the body or even the soul of King Latinus, who had disappeared from earth after the battle with Mezentius, King of Caere.[2]

Yet on the other hand there are circumstances which point to an intimate association, both at Athens and Rome, of these swinging festivals with an intention of promoting the growth of cultivated plants.   Such circumstances are the legendary connexion of the Athenian festival with Bacchus, the custom of offering the first-fruits of the vintage to Erigone and Icarius,[3] and at Rome the practice of hanging masks on trees at the time of sowing[4] and in order to make the grapes grow better.[5]   Perhaps we can reconcile the two apparently discrepant effects attributed to swinging as a means of expiation on the one side and of fertilisation on the other, by supposing that in both cases the intention is to clear the air of dangerous influences, whether these are ghosts of the unburied dead or spiritual powers inimical to the growth of plants.   Independent of both appears to be the notion that the higher you swing the higher will grow the crops.[6]   This last is homoeopathic or imitative magic pure and simple, without any admixture of the ideas of purification or expiation.

Swinging to promote the growth of plants.

In modern Greece and Italy the custom of swinging as a festal rite, whatever its origin may be, is still observed in some places. At the small village of Koukoura in Elis an English traveller observed peasants swinging from a tree in honour of St. George, whose festival it was.[7]   On the Tuesday after Easter the maidens of Seriphos play their favourite game of the swing.   They hang a rope from one wall to another of the steep, narrow, filthy street, and putting some clothes on it swing one after the other, singing as they swing.   Young men who try to pass are called upon to pay toll in the shape of a penny, a song, and a swing.   The words which the youth sings are generally these : "The gold is swung, the silver is swung, and swung too is my love with the golden hair"; to

Swinging as a festal rite in modern Greece and Italy.

[1] Spencer and Gillen, *Native Tribes of Central Australia*, pp. 505 *sq*.

[2] Festus, *s.v.* "Oscillantes," p. 194, ed. C. O. Müller. This festival and its origin are also alluded to in a passage of one of the manuscripts of Servius (on Virgil, *Georg*. ii. 389), which is printed by Lion in his edition of Servius (vol. ii. 254, note), but not by Thilo and Hagen in their large critical edition of the old Virgilian commentator.   "In *Schol. Bob.* p. 256 we are told that there was a reminis-

cence of the fact that, the bodies of Latinus and Aeneas being undiscoverable, their *animae* were sought in the air" (G. E. M. Marindin, *s.v.* "Oscilla," W. Smith's *Dictionary of Greek and Roman Antiquities*,³ ii. 304).

[3] Hyginus, *Fab.* 130.

[4] Probus on Virgil, *Georg*. ii. 385.

[5] Virgil, *Georg*. ii. 388 *sqq*.

[6] See above, p. 157.

[7] W. G. Clark, *Peloponnesus* (London, 1858), p. 274.

which the girl replies, "Who is it that swings me that I may gild him with my favour, that I may work him a fez all covered with pearls?"[1]   In the Greek island of Karpathos the villagers assemble at a given place on each of the four Sundays before Easter, a swing is erected, and the women swing one after the other, singing death wails such as they chant round the mimic tombs in church on the night of Good Friday.[2]   On Christmas Day peasant girls in some villages of Calabria fasten ropes to iron rings in the ceiling and swing on them, while they sing certain songs prescribed by custom for the occasion.   The practice is regarded not merely as an amusement but also as an act of devotion.[3]   "It is a custom in Cadiz, when Christmas comes, to fasten swings in the courtyards of houses, and even in the houses themselves when there is no room for them outside.   In the evenings lads and lasses assemble round the swings and pass the time happily in swinging amid joyous songs and cries. The swings are taken down when Carnival is come."[4]   The observance of the custom at Christmas, that is, at the winter solstice, suggests that in Calabria and Spain, as in Esthonia, the pastime may originally have been a magical rite designed to assist the sun in climbing the steep ascent to the top of the summer sky.   If this were so, we might surmise that the gold and the golden hair mentioned by youths and maidens of Seriphos as they swing refer to "the golden swing in the sky," in other words to the sun whose golden lamp swings daily across the blue vault of heaven.

Swinging at festivals in spring.

However that may be, it would seem that festivals of swinging are especially held in spring.   This is true, for example, of North Africa, where such festivals are common.   At some places in that part of the world the date of the swinging is the time of the apricots; at others it is said to be the spring equinox.   In some places the festival lasts three days, and fathers who have had children born to them within the year bring them and swing them in the swings.[5]   In Corea "the fifth day of the fifth moon is called *Tano-nal.*   Ancestors are then worshipped, and swings are put up in the yards of most houses for the amusement of the people.   The women on this day may go about the streets; during the rest of the year they may go out only after dark.   Dressed in their prettiest clothes, they visit the various houses and amuse themselves swinging.   The swing is said to convey the idea of keeping cool in the approaching summer.   It is one of

[1] J. T. Bent, *The Cyclades* (London, 1885), p. 5.

[2] J. T. Bent, quoted by Miss J. E. Harrison, *Mythology and Monuments of Ancient Athens*, p. xliii.

[3] Vincenzo Dorsa, *La Tradizione greco-latina negli usi e nelle credenze popolari della Calabria Citeriore* (Cosenza, 1884), p. 36.   In one village the custom is observed on Ascension Day instead of at Christmas.

[4] Valdés, *Los Majos de Cadiz*, extract sent to me in the original Spanish by Mr. W. Moss, of 21 Abbey Grove, Bolton, March 23rd, 1907.

[5] E. Doutté, *Magie et religion dans l'Afrique du nord* (Algiers, 1908), pp. 580 *sq.*

the most popular feasts of the year." [1]   Perhaps the reason here assigned for swinging may explain other instances of the custom ; on the principles of homoeopathic magic the swinging may be regarded as a means of ensuring a succession of cool refreshing breezes during the oppressive heat of the ensuing summer.

[1] W. W. Rockhill, " Notes on some of the Laws, Customs, and Super- stitions of Korea," *American Anthropologist*, iv. (1891) pp. 185 *sq.*

ADDENDA

P. 104. **The sacred precinct of Pelops at Olympia.**—It deserves to be noted that just as Pelops, whose legend reflects the origin of the chariot-race, had his sacred precinct and probably his tomb at Olympia, in like manner Endymion, whose legend reflects the origin of the foot-race,[1] had his tomb at the end of the Olympic stadium, at the point where the runners started in the race.[2] This presence at Olympia of the graves of the two early kings, whose names are associated with the origin of the foot-race and of the chariot-race respectively, can hardly be without significance; it indicates the important part played by the dead in the foundation of the Olympic games.

P. 188. **A man is literally reborn in the person of his son.**— This belief in the possible rebirth of the parent in the child may sometimes explain the seemingly widespread dislike of people to have children like themselves. Examples of such a dislike have met us in a former part of this work.[3] A similar superstition prevails among the Papuans of Doreh Bay in Dutch New Guinea. When a son resembles his father or a daughter resembles her mother closely in features, these savages fear that the father or mother will soon die.[4] Again, in the island of Savou, to the south-west of Timor, if a child at birth is thought to be like its father or mother, it may not remain under the parental roof, else the person whom it resembles would soon die.[5] Such superstitions, it is obvious, might readily suggest the expedient of killing the child in order to save the life of the parent.

[1] Pausanias, v. 1. 4.
[2] Pausanias, vi. 20. 9.
[3] *Taboo and the Perils of the Soul,* pp. 88 *sq.*
[4] J. L. van Hasselt, "Aanteekeningen aangaande de gewoonten der Papoeas in de Dorebaai, ten opzichte van zwangerschap en geboorte," *Tijd-schrift voor Indische Taal- Land- en Volkenkunde,* xliii. (1901) p. 566.
[5] J. H. Letteboer, "Eenige aanteekeningen omtrent de gebruiken bij zwangerschap en geboorte onder de Savuneezen," *Mededeelingen van wege het Nederlandsche Zendelinggenootschap,* xlvi. (1902) p. 45.

INDEX

Printed by R. & R. CLARK, LIMITED, *Edinburgh.*

Works by J. G. FRAZER, D.C.L., LL.D., Litt.D.

THE GOLDEN BOUGH

A STUDY IN MAGIC AND RELIGION

Third Edition, revised and enlarged. 8vo.

Part I. THE MAGIC ART AND THE EVOLUTION OF KINGS. Two volumes. 20s. net.

   II. TABOO AND THE PERILS OF THE SOUL. One volume. 10s. net.

   III. THE DYING GOD. One volume. 10s. net.

   IV. ADONIS, ATTIS, OSIRIS. One volume. Second Edition. 10s. net.

   V. THE MAN OF SORROWS. [*In preparation.*

   VI. BALDER THE BEAUTIFUL. [*In preparation.*

TIMES.—"The verdict of posterity will probably be that *The Golden Bough* has influenced the attitude of the human mind towards supernatural beliefs and symbolical rituals more profoundly than any other books published in the nineteenth century except those of Darwin and Herbert Spencer."

LECTURES ON THE EARLY HISTORY OF THE KINGSHIP. 8vo. 8s. 6d. net.

ATHENÆUM.—"It is the effect of a good book not only to teach, but also to stimulate and to suggest, and we think this the best and highest quality, and one that will recommend these lectures to all intelligent readers, as well as to the learned."

PSYCHE'S TASK. A Discourse concerning the Influence of Superstition on the Growth of Institutions. 8vo. 2s. 6d. net.

TIMES.—"Dr. Frazer has answered the question of how the moral law has been safeguarded, especially in its infancy, with a wealth of learning and a clearness of utterance that leave nothing to be desired. Perhaps the uses of superstition is not quite such a new theme as he seems to fancy. Even the most ignorant of us were aware that many false beliefs of a religious or superstitious character had had very useful moral or physical, or especially sanitary, results. But if the theme is fairly familiar, the curious facts which are adduced in support of it will be new to most people, and will make the book as interesting to read as the lectures must have been to hear."

MACMILLAN AND CO., LTD., LONDON.

Works by J. G. FRAZER, D.C.L., LL.D., Litt.D.

TOTEMISM AND EXOGAMY. A Treatise on Certain Early Forms of Superstition and Society. With Maps. Four vols. 8vo. 50s. net.

MR. A. E. CRAWLEY in *NATURE*.—"Prof. Frazer is a great artist as well as a great anthropologist. He works on a big scale; no one in any department of research, not even Darwin, has employed a wider induction of facts. No one, again, has dealt more conscientiously with each fact; however seemingly trivial, it is prepared with minute pains and cautious tests for its destiny as a slip to be placed under the anthropological microscope. He combines, so to speak, the merits of Tintoretto and Meissonier. . . . That portion of the book which is concerned with totemism (if we may express our own belief at the risk of offending Prof. Frazer's characteristic modesty), is actually 'The Complete History of Totemism, its Practice and its Theory, its Origin and its End.' . . . Nearly two thousand pages are occupied with an ethnographical survey of totemism, an invaluable compilation. The maps, including that of the distribution of totemic peoples, are a new and useful feature."

THE SCOPE OF SOCIAL ANTHROPOLOGY. 8vo. Sewed. 6d. net.

OXFORD MAGAZINE.—"In his inaugural lecture the new Professor of Social Anthropology in the University of Liverpool defines his Science, states its aims, and puts in a spirited plea for the scientific study of primitive man while there is still time, before the savage in his natural state becomes as extinct as the dodo."

PAUSANIAS'S DESCRIPTION OF GREECE. Translated with a Commentary, Illustrations, and Maps. Six vols. 8vo. 126s. net.

ATHENÆUM.—"All these writings in many languages Mr. Frazer has read and digested with extraordinary care, so that his book will be for years *the* book of reference on such matters, not only in England, but in France and Germany. It is a perfect thesaurus of Greek topography, archæology, and art. It is, moreover, far more interesting than any dictionary of the subject; for it follows the natural guidance of the Greek traveller, examining every town or village which he describes; analysing and comparing with foreign parallels every myth or fairy tale which he records; citing every information which can throw light on the works of art he admires."

PAUSANIAS AND OTHER GREEK SKETCHES. Globe 8vo. 4s. net.

GUARDIAN.—"Here we have material which every one who has visited Greece, or purposes to visit it, most certainly should read and enjoy. . . . We cannot imagine a more excellent book for the educated visitor to Greece."

MACMILLAN AND CO., LTD., LONDON.

9 781108 047333